CLASSIC
AUSTRIAN
COOKING

CLASSIC AUSTRIAN COOKING

GRETEL BEER

With illustrations by Sandra Oakins

ANDRE DEUTSCH

First published in 1993 by
Andre Deutsch Ltd
105–106 Great Russell Street
London WC1B 3LJ

ISBN 0 233 98827 0

CIP Data available from the British Library

Printed in Great Britain by
St Edmundsbury Press, Bury St Edmunds, Suffolk

TO
DIANA ATHILL

GRATEFUL ACKNOWLEDGEMENTS

— to Werner von Alvensleben (Peter Pirbright), co-author of numerous articles, who started me on my culinary career and who set standards which I have been trying to live up to ever since

— to Diana Athill for editing *Austrian Cooking* – probably not fully appreciated by me at the time, but I am sure that the book would not have stood the test of time and stayed in print for forty years if it had not been for her master touch

— to Austrian chefs, believers in the glory of Austrian cooking who create new dishes and improve on old favourites – notably Ewald Plachutta at the 3 Husaren in Vienna, the Obauer brothers at Werfen, Lisl Wagner-Bacher at Mautern, Karl Eschlböck at Plomberg, Guastav Lugerbauer at Mondsee (the list could go on forever), who generously allowed me to share their findings and quote their recipes

— to Evelyn Forbes who had the courage to publish an 'unknown' in *Vogue*

— to the great Olga Hess, author of *Viennese Cooking* who knew it all and more than generously shared her knowledge

— to Frieda and Victor Juza in Graz, centre of my culinary world (and that of countless other food writers and gastronomes), who not only helped me with perfecting a number of recipes, but encouraged me and pointed my nose in the right culinary direction

— to Gisela Köstler (Dagobert of the Kleine Zeitung in Graz), indefatigable finder of old favourites (I defy anyone in the world to locate the recipe for the special almond pastries they served at the fourth gallery buffet of the Vienna Opera House before the war asked for by a reader – Gisela did and you will find the recipe on page 292). Gisela would think nothing of calling me long-distance in England to clarify a point, whether the recipe be one which I had begged from her or to dispute the extra pinch of sage I had advocated in a recipe for her readers . . .

— to Lia Miklau, author of *Kärntner Kochbüchl*, who taught me the finer aspects of Carinthian cooking and, aged nearly eighty, stood at a Klagenfurt crossroads at seven in the morning because she knew I would be passing at this hour, to press an oven-fresh *Reinkale* into my hand ('that's what it should taste like – thought you should know!') and for allowing me to quote from her book

— to Hanna Perwanger, author of *Südtiroler Leibgerichte*, who did the same for Tyrolean cooking and whose family hotel Zirmer Hof at Radein in the South Tyrol is a shining example of Tyrolean hospitality and fine food

— to Zoë Ross for editing this book with infinite care and patience for my faults and omissions

— to Oberschulrat Ludwig Scheibenpflug at Salzburg, late mentor of famous chefs (Eckart Witzigmann was one of his pupils and never ceased to call him 'Meister'), who placed years of his own research at my disposal with a mere 'there you are – help yourself.'
— to Ferdinand Schreiber at Hof near Salzburg who took the cover photograph and greatly improved a number of my recipes
— to all members of my family, indefatigable collectors, creators and improvers of fine recipes and above all to my late husband for his encouragement, help and criticism (no one in their right mind would argue with his palate).

INTRODUCTION

It is now nearly forty years since the original *Austrian Cooking* was first published. Rationing was still with us when I wrote it, but I was not prepared to make concessions when it came to ingredients. Substitutes were definitely 'out'; I advocated making your own cream cheese, gave instructions on how to syphon the cream off the milk, frequently added 'if you can spare another egg' and relentlessly halved quantities for rich *Torten* – better a small cake and the real thing than the aftertaste and mockery of synthetic flavourings. My mother-in-law would send me small packets of real vanilla sugar from Vienna, slipping them into my husband's pockets whenever he visited – much to the bewilderment of British customs officials, who were deeply suspicious of the white powder until the packet was opened and the scent of vanilla permeated the air . . .

Austrian Cooking has never been out of print since it was first published, but although there have been numerous editions, no changes were made to the contents. I have wanted to add to it ever since – improvements on existing recipes and new and long forgotten ones which I had discovered over the years. I wanted to add all the regional dishes I had left out – rich soups from Carinthia, stews from Styria, the highly spiced dishes of the Burgenland and gentle ones from the shores of the Austrian lakes. I also wanted puddings, cakes and biscuits to appear in their full glory with no holds barred and all eggs present and correct. 'Gretel Beer's *Austrian Cooking* devotes 111 pages to desserts, pastries and biscuits and 94 pages to everything else, which shows us where Viennese tastes lie,' Joseph Wechsberg wrote. The 'sweet side' still takes up more than half of this new book – unashamedly so, for this is the pride and glory of Austrian cooking.

The new book is nearly twice as long as envisaged; some recipes may seem similar and in several cases there is more than one recipe for the same dish, because I could not decide between two or even three versions, each and every one worthy of inclusion and being saved from oblivion.

Austrian cooking has not changed much in these forty years; it is gloriously rich but never stodgy and relies entirely on the method of preparation and the true flavour of the ingredients. Spices and fresh herbs are used with discretion, never too many conflicting ones which cancel each other out. Cakes and puddings (and even dumplings which bear no relation to their English cousins) are featherlight and although puddings are called *Mehlspeisen* (dishes made with flour) most of them contain barely any flour at all – walnuts, toasted hazelnuts and almonds being used instead. Best of all, Austrian cooking does not rely on ingredients which are difficult to find – they are all available in this country.

Austrian cooks rarely admit to using a cookery book, always referring to family recipes handed down from mother to daughter. There is one great exception: Olga Hess' *Wiener Küche* – in its 48th edition at the last count – a giant tome which despite its name covers the cooking of all Austria. Olga Hess had always been a legendary figure to me (even my grandmother admitted to occasional references to her book) and I was slightly overawed when I first met her in 1955 – an enchanting woman, white-haired with fierce blue eyes which missed absolutely nothing. How old was she when she wrote *Wiener Küche*? Twenty-six, she said. The same age as Isabella Beeton, I commented and this took a little explaining. Suddenly Olga Hess leant forward and gently tapped me on the shoulder: '*Grundlegende Werke* (definitive – or classic – works) one can only write when one is very young. Later on one knows too much.'

Remembering this, you will understand why I had reservations about my publisher calling this book *Classic Austrian Cooking*. Olga Hess might not have approved and I feel I don't know enough – yet.

Gretel Beer

CONTENTS

I'D LIKE TO EXPLAIN

Preferences, prejudices and other useful comments.

About breadcrumbs: called *Semmelbrösel* (crumbs made from a roll) in Austria, though they are of course often made from bread, also known as *Paniermehl* ('flour' used for coating food). Both names are relevant: *semmelblond* (as blonde as a roll) is a definite shade which means that the crumbs should be light in colour and 'flour' is an allusion to the fineness. Most breadcrumbs sold in this country are too coarse and dark, are often made from different kinds of bread and contain too much crust which makes them unsuitable for coating food which is to be fried. Austrian breadcrumbs are occasionally available at good delicatessen – otherwise make your own in a food processor, using white crustless bread.

About vanilla sugar: keep a vanilla pod in a jar of icing sugar to be sure of the real flavour of vanilla and use this whenever a recipe calls for vanilla sugar. If you buy vanilla sugar sold in small packets, make sure it contains real vanilla and not vanilla flavouring (study the list of ingredients on the packet).

About Topfen: curd cheese containing about 20% fat. Consistency is all important – *Topfen*, as used in many Austrian recipes, should be smooth and fairly dry. If necessary put it in a sieve to drain and then sieve it for smoothness. Quark (which is 'proper' German for *Topfen*) sold in this country under that name can vary considerably in consistency and fat content.

About butter: unsalted butter is used throughout the recipes.

About anchovies: you will find them used quite lavishly throughout the book as indeed they are in Austrian cooking, for meat as well as for fish and other dishes. In the old days – and often nowadays – anchovies sold in Austria are those preserved whole in salt. They are much larger than the fillets of anchovies in oil sold here and the salt has to be rinsed or soaked off before filleting and use. Recipes in this book give quantities for fillets of anchovies preserved in oil as sold here.

About Speck: smoked or lightly smoked pork in varying degrees of fatness (some *Speck* is all fat). Smoked streaky bacon in one piece can be used instead.

About mustard: there are various typically Austrian mustards such as the slightly sweet *Kremser Senf* or *Krensenf* which contains horseradish, but the one used the most in Austrian cooking is *Estragon Senf* (tarragon). Straightforward French or Dijon mustard can be used instead, but use Tarragon Vinegar to make up for the flavour.

About Grammeln: the crispy bits of crackling left after rendering down fat, mostly pork, but also goose and duck (both a delicacy). Used

extensively throughout Austrian cooking and also for special recipes
such as *Grammelpogatscherln.*

About pepper: if there is one phrase which I genuinely hate it is 'freshly
milled black pepper' which I consider a culinary pretence as well as a
nonsense. In some recipes white pepper is preferable to black pepper
and I have indicated this where appropriate (and perhaps in time we
shall have fewer delicate sauces scattered with what appears at first sight
to be ashes). There are, however, worse culinary sins committed every
hour of the day than using ground black or white pepper if you are in
a hurry!

About paprika: good paprika is bright deep red and not the colour
of faded brick walls. It is a wonderful spice which brings out the
full flavour of ingredients in a dish (and is full of Vitamin C for
good measure!). Paprika comes in six degrees of fieriness, but most
Austrian recipes call for 'noble-sweet' (known as *edelsüss* in Austria).
Unless otherwise stated, all recipes in this book are for 'noble-sweet'
paprika which is usually marked as such on the packet. (Rose paprika
is second from the top for fieriness and not the sweet and gentle 'rose'
you might expect.)

About Kipfler: special waxy potatoes about the thickness of a thumb and
essential for every good potato salad as well as a number of other dishes
in the book. Small waxy 'salad' potatoes will do – but only just!

About garlic: used extensively but not wildly in Austrian cooking, usually
crushed with salt under the blade of a knife. A trick culled from my
favourite Austrian chef: take a small screw-top jar and half fill it with
crushed garlic cloves. Top up with olive oil and keep in a dark, cool
place. Shake or stir gently from time to time. Use (with discretion as it
is very potent) in casseroles, stews etc. or added to the oil when making
salads and frying croutons.

About pickled cucumbers: there is a vast difference between *Essiggurken*
(cucumbers pickled in wine vinegar) and *Salzgurken* (cucumbers pickled
in brine), herbs such as dill, bayleaf etc. being added to either.
Salzgurken are much milder and are often added to sauces and various
other dishes. Cucumbers pickled in wine vinegar can be used instead of
those pickled in brine, but be careful and use with discretion. Pickled
gherkins will not do however as they are much too sharp and often
pickled in malt vinegar.

About Powidl: very thick dark plum jam made with blue plums (*Zwetschken*)
cooked with cloves, cinnamon and lemon rind – but without sugar –
until the right consistency has been reached, i.e. a wooden spoon will
stand up in it unaided. *Powidl* is then put into warmed jars with a round
of greaseproof paper dipped in rum set on top before sealing. Sold at
some delicatessen in this country.

About Sterz: often called *Steirischer Sterz*, possibly more for the alliteration
than for its Styrian origin since most Austrian provinces can lay claim
to their own version (called *Riebel* in Vorarlberg). Basically it is made
by pouring flour into boiling water which then forms a large lump. It

is cooked gently, thrown into a large pan with fat, torn into shreds with a special fork called *Sterzgabel* and left to dry out in the oven until crisp. The procedure may sound rather revolting, but the result is delicious, particularly if served with clear mushroom soup and crispy bits of crackling (*Grammeln*). *Sterz* varies according to the flour used – *Türkensterz* is made with cornmeal, *Heidensterz* with buckwheat flour and if made with dried beans, a speciality of the Burgenland, it is called *Bohnensterz* and a dish in its own right.

About mushrooms: dried boletus mushrooms are an absolute joy – albeit an expensive one – when used in cooking. Sold as ceps, *porcini* or *Steinpilze* depending on their country of origin and a little goes a long way. Soak them in warm water, but do not waste the liquid in which they are soaked, and strain it before use.

About Himbeersaft: raspberry syrup. Not only a popular drink for children of all ages when mixed with soda water (a sort of non-alcoholic *G'spritzter*), but also used with puddings.

About parsley root: used frequently in soups and stews in Austria where it is easily available as part of *Suppengrün*. If you cannot get parsley root, use a small piece of parsnip instead.

About stock: Austrian cooks have never heard of a stockpot which is kept simmering for days and to which bits of this and that are added. Flavours are well defined: it may be the smokey flavour of the liquid in which a ham has been cooked or stock made from the residue left in the roasting tin; stock made from veal or beef bones; rich game or good vegetable stock, or an honest stock cube, although in Austria these days the latter is more likely to be replaced by stock granules because it is easier to gauge quantities.

About temperatures: times and temperatures given apply to my oven and you may find that they have to be varied slightly in accordance with your own.

About Zwetschkenröster: the almost obligatory accompaniment to dishes like *Kaiserschmarrn, Topfenknödel* and all manners of light and delicious puddings – in fact wherever I have said 'served with stewed fruit' this would be *Zwetschkenröster* in Austria. A typically Austrian misnomer for it translates as 'roasted' plums when in fact blue plums (*Zwetschken*) are halved and then stewed with sugar, cloves, cinnamon, some lemon juice and rind and very little water until the skins curl slightly. There is also *Marillenröster* made with apricots and *Ribislröster* made with redcurrants – in theory, that is, for I have encountered them mostly in books and only very rarely on menus!

SOUPS
AND THEIR
GARNISHES

SOUPS AND THEIR GARNISHES

'You can tell a good cook by her beef broth' they say in Austria and there is something infinitely comforting about the scent of good strong beef broth wafting over from a kitchen. Soups in Austria certainly start with beef broth and its wide variety of additions, but they do not end there. There is rich *Fischbeuschelsuppe* made with carps roe for Christmas, tomato soup with the scent of summer and green peppers, and there are the soups which are a heritage of the former Austro-Hungarian Empire, like *Gulaschsuppe* and *Prager Erdäpfelsuppe* based on ham stock.

Some of the soups are light and frothy, like Georg Lugerbauer's cucumber soup – a fairly recent invention for which he deserves a medal – whilst others are rich and satisfying and practically a meal in themselves. In fact in the country a meal may well consist of soup followed by pudding. And the pudding will not be elaborate at all, but good homely *Kaiserschmarrn* apricot dumplings sprinkled with fried breadcrumbs and dusted with vanilla sugar, or little pasta envelopes filled with curd cheese and covered with melted butter, sugar and cinnamon.

KLARE RINDSUPPE

Clear Beef Broth

Olga Hess's *Wiener Küche* lists over a hundred soups based on Clear Beef Broth. There is Clear Beef Broth with dumplings large and small, there are additions light and luxurious like *Kaisergerstl*, and some, such as *Lungenstrudelsuppe* which almost constitute a main course. The soup is always named after the addition. All this should give some measure of the importance of clear beef broth and its preparation. Most of the broth consumed in Austria is a by-product of *gekochtes Rindfleisch*, the Viennese beef dish so beloved throughout the country.

Strictly speaking the method of preparation differs: for *gekochtes Rindfleisch* the meat is put into boiling water, whilst for soup it is started off in cold water and ox liver or melts are often added for extra flavour. When cooking beef for soup, the meat should be used only for meat salads, *Fleischstrudel* and the like, since most of its goodness will have gone into the soup. Lesser cuts of beef, such as shin, can therefore be used.

There is a strict distinction made between *weisse Rindsuppe* (White Beef Broth – though its colour is really golden yellow) and *braune Rindsuppe* (Brown Beef Broth). For the latter, vegetables and bones should be browned first. (I also brown them – very lightly – for *weisse Rindsuppe*, since I find that it greatly improves the flavour.)

Serves 6 – 8

2¼ lb (1 kg) beef in one piece	1 leek
about ¾ lb (300 g) marrow bones	parsley and parsley root
	a few peppercorns
1 large onion	salt
2 – 3 carrots	a sprig of marjoram
1 celery top or ½ celeriac	2 oz (50 g) ox liver or melts (optional)
1 green or red pepper	a few lovage leaves (not traditional but I find that it greatly intensifies the beef flavour)
½ parsnip	
½ turnip	
1 tomato	

Wipe the meat with a cloth wrung out in hot water. Scald the marrow bones and rinse in cold water – you may also have to remove a few jagged edges. Put the bones in a large saucepan and simmer them, covered, over very low heat, shaking the pan from time to time, until the fat on them begins to melt. Halve, but do not peel, the onion. Wash and clean the vegetables and cut into pieces of a convenient size – halve the carrots if very large, quarter the red or green pepper etc. Put the onion into the saucepan, cut side down and leave to brown, then add the other vegetables.

At this point it may be necessary to add a little more fat – do this only if absolutely necessary and if so use butter or a few drops of olive oil. Leave vegetables and bones to brown lightly (or more if aiming for *Braune Rindsuppe*) and also brown liver or melts, if used.

Add meat and about 5 pints (3 litres) cold water, salt, peppercorns, marjoram and lovage. Bring water to the boil, then lower the heat immediately and simmer very slowly for 2½ – 3 hours. Do not allow the liquid to boil and do not remove any scum which may rise to the top.

Remove the meat. Line a sieve with a tea towel previously wrung out in cold water (for an extra touch sprinkle the cloth lightly with grated nutmeg or powdered mace) and strain the soup through the cloth. Leave to cool a little, remove excess fat and adjust seasoning if necessary. Reheat gently.

Straining in this way is usually sufficient. Perfectionists can clear the soup as follows. Reheat strained soup and bring to just below boiling point. Whisk together 1 egg white and the crushed egg shells. Whisk in half a cup of white wine (or half a cup of cold water with a few drops of lemon juice) and a cup of the soup, then stir carefully into the strained soup which should be just on the point of boiling. Leave over lowest possible heat for another ten or fifteen minutes. You will find that all impurities have sunk to the bottom of the saucepan. Strain off soup.

Some of the additions to Clear Beef Broth are so simple that they do not need a recipe – like a little rice sprinkled into the soup. But one

Viennese speciality is little known outside Austria – *Bouillon mit Ei*. For this you slip an egg yolk (or whole egg) into each soup bowl and then pour hot Beef Broth over it. The heat from the soup just sets the outer 'layer' of the egg and you stir it into the soup as you eat it.

Additions to Clear Beef Broth are listed on pages 33 to 40. Some – like *Markknöderl, Bröselknödel* or *Butternockerl*, are also used for cream soups and stews. *Fleckerl* form the basis of *Schinkenfleckerl* (see page 143) and *Farferl* and *Reibgerstl* can also be cooked to accompany meat dishes.

BAUMWOLLSUPPE

'Cotton Wool' Soup

A number of old Austrian cookery books feature this soup, the origin of which is believed to be Upper Austria.

Serves 4 – 6
2 eggs   salt
2 teaspoons plain flour   chopped chives
1¾ pints (1 litre) Clear
  Beef Broth

Whisk together eggs and flour. Heat soup to just below boiling point and pour onto egg mixture, whisking all the time. Return soup to saucepan and whisk over medium heat until soup starts to rise. Add salt and serve sprinkled with chopped chives.

GULASCHSUPPE

Goulash Soup

Some of the best Goulash Soup is made from left-over Goulash – one of the reasons why it always tastes best in a restaurant (and probably why I am invariably asked for my recipe for 'that delicious Goulash soup' whenever I've used left-over Goulash to make it). The procedure is simple: for four servings take roughly one portion of Goulash and reheat it very gently, preferably in the saucepan in which it was cooked, and add about 1¾ pints (about 1 litre) clear beef broth. Bring to the boil slowly, scraping up all the bits from the bottom of the saucepan. When the liquid boils, add two large potatoes cut into cubes and leave to cook until the potatoes are just done. Adjust seasoning. If the portion of left-over Goulash was very small, slice up a pair of Frankfurter sausages, add to the Goulash and heat gently before serving.

To make *Gulaschsuppe* from scratch:

Serves 4 – 6

1 lb (450 g) beef, shin for
   preference
½ lb (225 g) onions
1 clove garlic
2 tablespoons lard or oil
1 tablespoon paprika
salt
marjoram
caraway seeds

1 tablespoon tomato purée
3 large potatoes
dash of wine vinegar
about 2¾ pints (1½ litres)
   water or clear beef
   broth

Cut the beef into small cubes. Slice onions finely. Crush garlic with salt under the blade of a knife. Melt the lard or oil and fry onions and garlic until golden brown. Add paprika, stir, and then add about a cupful of the water or the beef broth. Bring to boil and cook until liquid is reduced by half, then add meat, salt, marjoram, caraway seeds, wine vinegar and tomato purée. Cover and simmer until meat is nearly cooked, adding water or broth only if necessary. Peel and dice the potatoes, add to meat, together with remaining water or broth, and simmer until meat and potatoes are cooked.

I do not use flour to thicken Goulash Soup, but if you want a slightly thicker soup, add a tablespoon of flour before adding the potatoes, stir and brown it in the fat which will have separated from the meat, then add water (or beef broth) and potatoes and proceed as before.

BIERSUPPE

Beer Soup

Serves 4

1¾ pints (1 litre) dark
   beer
salt and pepper
sugar
nutmeg

1 egg yolk
2 – 3 tablespoons double
   cream
small nut of butter

Heat the beer with salt, pepper, pinch of sugar and a grating of nutmeg. Whisk the yolk with the cream, pour the heated beer onto the yolk mixture. Return liquid to saucepan, stir in a small lump of butter. Whisk until frothy and serve at once.

BROTSUPPE

Bread Soup

Almost every Austrian region has its own version of this soup, which is a country cousin of Vienna's more elegant *Panadlsuppe*. Unlike *Panadlsuppe*, *Brotsuppe* is based on dark country bread. Additions such as caraway seeds and fennel vary according to the region, as does the type of bread, so the flavour of the soup can vary quite a lot. The simplest way of preparing it is to cover the bottom of each warmed soup plate with thin slices of bread sprinkled with salt and pepper. Cover with thinly sliced onions fried in clarified butter, then ladle boiling hot Beef Broth over bread and onions, leave to stand for a minute – preferably on a warming plate – then add a dollop of sour cream and sprinkle with chopped chives.

A slightly more sophisticated version runs thus:

Serves 4 – 5

11 oz (300 g) dark country bread, thinly sliced	1 crushed clove garlic
3 tablespoons lard	salt and pepper
5 oz (140 g) onions, thinly sliced	paprika
	3 eggs
	chopped chives

Spread the bread on a baking sheet and dry it in the oven. Heat the fat in a saucepan, add onions and garlic and soften over low heat. Add the bread and brown everything together. Add 2¾ pints (1½ litres) water, salt, pepper and a pinch of paprika. Bring to boil, then simmer gently for about twenty minutes. Whisk the eggs and add to soup away from heat, stirring constantly. Serve sprinkled with chopped chives.

PANADLSUPPE

The name sounds truly Viennese, but it stems from the French *pain*. Rolls rather than bread are used for this soup more often than not.

Serves 4 – 6

4 day-old bread rolls	nutmeg
2¼ pints (1¼ litres) clear veal or beef stock	2 eggs
salt and pepper	1 teaspoon butter
	chopped chives

Grate the crust off the rolls and slice the crumb thinly or cut into small cubes. Cook the rolls in the stock until they have completely dissolved, whisking to speed up the process. Season with salt, pepper and a little grated nutmeg or mace. Whisk the eggs lightly, then whisk into the soup (off the heat) and reheat gently. Stir in the butter and serve sprinkled with chopped chives.

A slightly richer version of this recipe uses egg yolks only, whisked with about 5 fluid oz (140 ml) single cream and added to the soup as before.

KÄSESUPPE

Cheese Soup

The cheese varies according to region: at the famous Steirerhof in Graz they used Gorgonzola, which gives a particularly good flavour – though not particularly Styrian! Alas, the Steirerhof is no more – all the more reason to make sure that the recipe survives.

Serves 4

1 heaped tablespoon
  butter
1 small, finely chopped
  onion or shallot
2 – 3 fluid oz (60 – 85 ml)
  medium-dry white wine
1 heaped tablespoon plain
  flour
1 heaped tablespoon finely
  chopped parsley
1¾ pints (1 litre) beef
  stock
4½ oz (125 g) chopped or
  crumbled Gorgonzola
  cheese

salt
white pepper
chopped chives
fried croutons

Melt the butter in a saucepan. Add chopped onion or shallot and simmer gently until transparent. Pour in the white wine and cook until the liquid is reduced to about half. Remove from heat, stir in the flour and the chopped parsley. Return saucepan to heat and gradually pour in the stock. Blend well over low heat – a balloon whisk is best for this – and leave to simmer for ten minutes. Add the cheese and allow to simmer for another five minutes. Season with white pepper and add a little salt if necessary. Sprinkle with chopped chives and serve with fried croutons.

BOHNENSUPPE MIT RAHM

Dried Bean Soup with Sour Cream

Serves 4 – 5

9 oz (250 g) dried white
  beans
2¼ pints (1¼ litre) ham
  stock
parsley
1 teaspoon caraway seeds
1½ oz (40 g) lard
1 medium-sized onion,
  finely chopped

1 crushed clove garlic
1½ oz (40 g) plain flour
chopped marjoram
dash of wine vinegar
9 fluid oz (250 ml) sour
  cream

Soak the beans overnight in cold water. Pour away the water, put beans
into a large saucepan, add ham stock, parsley, marjoram and caraway
seeds and bring to the boil, then allow to simmer gently until the beans
are cooked. Sieve the beans if you want a smooth soup, leave whole for
the sturdier version. Melt the fat, add onion and garlic and soften over
low heat. Stir in flour and brown lightly together. Add to soup, swilling
out the pan with liquid from the soup. Simmer until well blended, then
stir in sour cream and a dash of vinegar. Adjust seasoning if necessary
– usually the ham stock contains sufficient salt.

This is a good, hearty soup: to turn it into almost a complete meal,
add some sliced, spicy sausage.

BOHNENSUPPE MIT SPECK

Dried Bean Soup with Bacon

Serves 4 – 6

11 oz (300 g) dried white
  beans
9 oz (250 g) smoked
  streaky bacon in one
  piece
parsley root
1 onion
1 – 2 carrots
1 bayleaf

a sprig of thyme
1 tablespoon oil
1 tablespoon plain flour
salt and pepper
paprika

Soak the beans overnight in cold water. Cook the bacon in about
2¾ pints (1½ litres) water. Lift bacon from the liquid, leave liquid to
get cold, then skim off the fat. Pour off the water in which the beans
were soaked. Put beans into a large saucepan, add parsley root, onion,
carrots, bayleaf and thyme and liquid in which bacon was cooked. Bring
to boil, then simmer until beans are cooked.

Discard bayleaf and thyme. Set aside half the cooked beans. Sieve remainder with all the liquid and the vegetables. Dice the bacon. Heat oil in a frying pan and fry the bacon until crisp. Drain on kitchen paper. Stir flour into fat in frying pan and brown lightly, then add to sieved beans and simmer gently for twenty minutes. Add beans previously set aside, reheat gently and season with salt, pepper and paprika.

Serve the soup sprinkled with crispy bacon.

LINSENPUREESUPPE

Cream of Lentil Soup

Serves 4 – 5

½ lb (225 g) brown lentils	1 large onion
2 pints (1⅛ litre) ham stock	2 tablespoons butter
3 large potatoes, peeled and cut into chunks	1 scant tablespoon plain flour
1 chopped carrot	lemon juice
small piece celeriac or a few celery tops	2 egg yolks
1 bayleaf	4 fluid oz (110 ml) single cream
sprig of thyme	croutons or crispy bacon
few slivers lemon rind	

Soak the lentils in cold water overnight or at least for a few hours. Strain off the water. Put the lentils into a large saucepan, add the stock, potatoes, carrot, celeriac (or celery tops), bayleaf, thyme and lemon rind. Bring to boil, then simmer until the lentils are soft.

Chop the onion finely. Melt butter in a pan, add the chopped onion and allow it to soften gently. Dust with flour, stir and cook until faintly tinged with colour. Add to the lentils – be sure to add all the scrapings from the pan, swilling it out with a little liquid from the lentils. Leave to cook for another five minutes, then sieve. (You can use a blender or food processor, but remove bayleaf, thyme and lemon rind first.)

Return purée to the saucepan, adding a little more stock if necessary. Taste and adjust seasoning if necessary and add a dash of lemon juice. Whisk together egg yolks and cream and add to soup gradually. Reheat very gently – do not allow the mixture to boil.

Serve with fried croutons or crispy bits of bacon sprinkled over the top.

ABERSEER FISCHSUPPE

Lake Wolfgang Fish Soup

Abersee was the old name for Lake Wolfgang in the Salzkammergut and this particular recipe comes from the famous White Horse Inn at St Wolfgang.

Serves 6 – 8

3½ oz (100 g) butter	sliced parsley root
3½ oz (100 g) onions, chopped	salt and pepper
3½ oz (100 g) yellow, red and green peppers, chopped	1¾ pints (1 litre) dry white wine
3 crushed garlic cloves	4 fluid oz (110 ml) Noilly Prat
chopped fresh dill and parsley	2¼ lbs (1 kg) freshwater fish such as trout, pike, perch etc, filleted and cut into chunks
a few chopped celery tops	1¾ pints (1 litre) clear fish stock

Melt the butter and gently soften onion, garlic and peppers. Add dill, parsley, celery tops and parsley root and stir over low heat for a minute or two. Season with salt and pepper, add Noilly Prat and wine and leave to simmer for fifteen minutes. Add fish stock, bring to boil and then gently poach the fish in the liquid for eight minutes. Adjust seasoning if necessary.

FISCHBEUSCHELSUPPE

Carp-roe Soup

The traditional soup for Christmas. *Beuschel* is typically Viennese for lights (or lung, in the case of humans), but in this case it means roe. It is generally accepted that the roe should be that of carp and that it should be hard roe – though there are those who think that soft roe might be preferable. (You could always adopt a good old Austrian compromise and use some of each.) Since fried carp is usually part of the Christmas Eve menu, the best pieces of the fish are naturally used for that; the tail, head and some of the carcass go to make the soup. This particular recipe – using hard roes only – comes from Vienna's famous Zu den 3 Husaren restaurant.

Serves 4

head, tailpiece and carcass of a carp	4½ oz (120 g) grated carrot, celeriac and turnip (joint weight)
2½ pints (1¼ l) water	1 teaspoon sugar
1 small onion	2½ fluid oz (65 ml) red wine
1 bayleaf	
few peppercorns	1 carp roe (hard)
salt	dash of wine vinegar
thyme	about 2 tablespoons sour cream (optional)
2 oz (50 g) plain flour	
2½ oz (70 g) butter or olive oil	croutons fried in butter

Wash the fish pieces and put into a large saucepan. Add water, onion, bayleaf, peppercorns, thyme and salt. Cook gently for about twenty minutes, then strain, retaining liquid. Remove and flake any flesh from head and tailpiece and set aside. Heat the butter or oil, add flour and sugar and brown lightly. Add the grated vegetables, stir and allow to brown as well. Add the red wine and all but a cupful of the fish stock. Simmer gently for fifteen minutes. Poach the roe in the remaining fish stock to which a dash of wine vinegar has been added, first breaking up the roe with a fork, then whisking it into the liquid until well blended. Add to the soup, together with the flaked fish. Stir and taste for seasoning – the soup should have a slightly sweet and sour flavour – then stir in the sour cream and reheat gently. Serve with croutons.

SARDELLENSUPPE

Anchovy Soup

Serves 4

1½ oz (40 g) butter	1¾ pints (1 litre) water
1½ oz (40 g) plain flour	6 – 8 anchovy fillets
2 tablespoons chopped parsley	4 fluid oz (100 ml) sour cream
2 tablespoons grated celeriac	salt and pepper
4 fluid oz (100 ml) dry white wine	fried croutons

Melt the butter in a saucepan. Add the flour, stir and add the celeriac and half the chopped parsley. Allow to colour slightly, then pour in the wine and stir until well blended. Add the water and simmer gently for twenty to thirty minutes. Finely chop the anchovies, mix with the remaining chopped parsley and the sour cream. Stir into the hot soup. Leave to simmer very gently for another ten to fifteen minutes. Season with salt and pepper if necessary. Serve with croutons fried in butter.

WILDPUREESUPPE

Cream of Game Soup

Serves 4 – 5

8 oz (225 g) chestnuts	1 bayleaf
³/₄ lb (330 g) game, weighed	salt and pepper
without bones	nutmeg
1 tablespoon butter	1 tablespoon plain flour
1 sliced carrot	2¹/₂ pints (1.4 l) water
1 small onion	small knob of butter
¹/₄ celeriac	large dash of brandy
parsley and parsley root	

Make an incision across top of chestnuts, cook in water until soft. Drain, remove skins and pass chestnuts through a sieve while still hot. Cut meat into convenient pieces. Melt butter in a large saucepan, add sliced carrot, onion, celeriac, parsley and parsley root and toss until very lightly browned. Add meat, stir and season with salt, pepper and nutmeg. Add bayleaf and chestnuts and sufficient water to prevent burning. Cover with a lid and simmer until meat is tender. Remove onion and bayleaf, pass everything through a sieve or purée in the blender. Return mixture to saucepan, add remaining water and cook gently for another twenty minutes. Slake flour with a little water and add to hot soup. Cook for five more minutes, adjust seasoning and stir in a knob of butter and the brandy just before serving.

Another version of Game Soup is made by using the carcasses of roast pheasant or partridges with – hopefully – quite a bit of meat still clinging to the bones. Start the soup by cooking the chestnuts and browning the vegetables as above, then brown the carcass, cover with water and proceed as before, not adding any more water. A spoonful of cranberry preserve and a dash of Madeira instead of brandy are good alternative flavourings.

GEGENDTALER GELBE SUPPE

Carinthian Mutton Soup

Kärntner Reinling (see page 317) is the traditional accompaniment to this unusually spiced soup. The meat is served as a second course in a thick horseradish sauce.

Serves 10

2 lbs (900 g) mutton	mace
1 carrot	fennel
¹/₄ celeriac	aniseed
parsley root	10 peppercorns

2 pinches of saffron

1 egg yolk

1 tablespoon butter

dash of red wine

powdered allspice or
    cinnamon

1 teaspoon salt

5½ pints (3 litres) water

9 fluid oz (¼ litre) sour
    cream

4½ fluid oz (125 ml)
    double cream

1 tablespoon plain flour

Put the meat into a large saucepan, add coarsely chopped root vegetables, mace, fennel, aniseed, peppercorns and salt. Cover with the water and bring to the boil, then simmer until the meat is tender. Strain the soup and skim off all fat. Mix together sour cream, cream, saffron and flour, add to the hot soup and leave to simmer for fifteen to twenty minutes. Whisk the egg yolk lightly, add to the soup (off the boil), together with the butter cut into small flakes. Season with a dash of red wine and allspice or cinnamon.

KLACHLSUPPE

Knuckle of Pork Soup

A very robust soup – I'd go as far as to call it an acquired taste . . . but there *was* this very high-ranking, retired Civil Servant who travelled from Vienna to Graz every week, just to eat *Klachlsuppe* at the famous Steirerhof. This is their recipe.

Serves 4 – 6

1 unsmoked knuckle of
    pork weighing about
    2 lbs (1 kg)

1 carrot

1 medium-sized onion

½ leek

¼ celeriac

1 bayleaf

pinch of marjoram

3 – 4 juniper berries

a few peppercorns

salt

good dash of wine vinegar

1 generous oz (30 g) plain
    flour

freshly grated horseradish

2¾ pints (1½ litres) water

Get the butcher to cut the knuckle of pork into slices about ½" (1 cm) thick. Put the meat into a saucepan, add the vegetables, bayleaf, marjoram, juniper berries, peppercorns and salt and cover with the water. Bring to the boil, then allow to simmer gently until the meat is very tender, removing any scum rising to the top. Strain the liquid into a bowl and leave to cool a little, then remove any fat from the top. Slake the flour with a little of the cooled soup, add the vinegar. Reheat soup to just below boiling point, stir in the flour mixture, then leave to simmer until well blended. Add the cooked meat – if you want to be elegant you can remove the bones (it should be falling off them in any case). Adjust seasoning – the soup should have a sharp tang. Serve with plain boiled potatoes and plenty of freshly grated horseradish.

As with all traditional recipes, there are endless variations: one of the best Styrian cooks I know uses breast of pork rather than knuckle (although *Klachl* means knuckle or trotter), adds a little crushed garlic and a generous amount of cream or sour cream.

GERÖSTETE GRIESS SUPPE

Semolina Soup

In old cookery books this soup is sometimes called *Himmelthau* (heavenly dew) soup, *Himmelthau* being one of the ancient terms for semolina.

Serves 4

1 heaped tablespoon butter or dripping	salt and pepper
2 oz (50 g) coarse semolina	nutmeg
2¼ pints (1¼ litres) veal, beef or vegetable stock	saffron
	chopped chives

Melt butter or dripping, add semolina and brown very lightly. Gradually add stock, bring to the boil and then simmer gently for half an hour. Season with salt, pepper, nutmeg and saffron. Serve sprinkled with chopped chives.

Sliced mushrooms or peas and chopped carrots may be added to the stock and the soup can be thickened with an egg yolk whisked in just before serving.

STOSS SUPPE (STO SUPPE)

Sour Cream Soup

The traditional 'Friday' (meatless day) soup of my childhood, often followed by a light pasta dish and a green salad; or – on a 'soup and pudding' occasion – by a particularly delectable dessert: *Reisauflauf* perhaps, into which strawberries would find their way in summer and soft, fragrant apples in winter. Or *Kaiserschmarrn*, with lots of cinnamon and clove-scented *Zwetschkenröster*. It is not strictly traditional to sprinkle this soup with chopped chives or parsley, but it is often done. My own favourite departure from tradition is a generous sprinkling of chopped fresh dill.

Serves 4

1½ pints (generous ¾ litre) water	2 medium-sized potatoes
1 heaped teaspoon caraway seeds	1 scant dessertspoon plain flour
salt	¼ pint (140 ml) sour milk
	¼ pint (140 ml) sour cream

Bring water to the boil, add salt and caraway seeds, then lower the heat and allow to simmer for ten minutes. Peel and dice the potatoes and boil in a separate pan of salted water until just tender, then drain. Slake flour with the sour milk, add the boiling caraway water gradually, stirring or whisking all the time. Return mixture to saucepan over medium heat, bring to boil once. Put sour cream into a large bowl, strain hot mixture into this. Add potatoes, return soup to saucepan and reheat gently.

A dash of lemon juice or vinegar may be added to increase sharpness of flavour.

KALBSEINMACHSUPPE

Cream of Veal Soup

Serves 4

2¼ pints (1¼ litre) veal stock	nutmeg
½ lb (225 g) stewing veal	4½ fluid oz (120 ml) double cream
2 oz (50 g) butter	1 – 2 egg yolks
1½ oz (40 g) plain flour	1 teaspoon butter
salt	dash of white wine
white pepper	

Cook the veal in the stock until tender. Melt butter, add flour and stir over low heat until barely coloured. Gradually strain in the liquid in which the veal was cooked and simmer for about half an hour. Season with salt, white pepper and nutmeg. Chop the veal very finely. Mix cream with egg yolk(s), add a ladleful of the soup, stir and add a dash of white wine. Stir into soup, reheat very gently without letting it come to the boil. Add the finely chopped veal and a teaspoon of butter. Adjust seasoning if necessary.

Markknöderl (see page 38) are a good addition – and you may care to add a handful of cooked peas and sliced carrots to the soup as well.

ERBSENSCHOTENSUPPE

Fresh Pea-pod Soup

Fresh pea-pods encasing small young peas – not the leathery, mottled flaps covering marrowfat peas – are much too good to waste and can be turned into the most delicious of soups.

Serves 4 – 5

1 large saucepanful of
  pea-pods
1 heaped tablespoon
  butter
6 spring onions
a handful of lettuce leaves
  (outer leaves will do)

5 fluid oz (140 ml) double
  cream
salt and pepper
water or stock

The pea-pods must be absolutely fresh – use them as soon as you have
shelled the peas. Rinse the pods well under running cold water and put
them into a large saucepan, together with the butter, spring onions and
washed lettuce leaves. Cover with a lid and simmer gently, shaking the
pan from time to time, until the pods have softened. Cover with water
or stock, bring to the boil and then simmer until the pods are tender.
Put pods, lettuce leaves and spring onions through a blender or food
processor, adding a little of the liquid, and then sieve. Return purée to
the remaining liquid, add cream and seasoning and reheat gently.

Fried croutons go well with this soup and it tastes equally good
served chilled with a sprinkling of chopped parsley or chives. But if
it is to be served cold, remove all traces of fat from the soup and swirl
in the cream at the last moment.

ERDÄPFELSUPPE

Potato Soup

Serves 4 – 6

6 large potatoes
1 clove garlic
salt
1 medium-sized onion
1 heaped tablespoon
  butter
1 sliced carrot
1/4 celeriac or a few celery
  tops
1 tomato

1 tablespoon chopped
  parsley
1/2 tablespoon chopped
  marjoram
2 1/2 pints (1.4 litres) beef
  or veal stock
5 fluid oz (140 ml) sour
  cream
a little paprika

Peel and dice the potatoes. Crush garlic under the blade of a knife with
salt. Peel and thinly slice the onion. Heat butter in a saucepan, add
onion and garlic and simmer gently until softened and just tinged with
colour. Add the potatoes, carrot, celeriac, roughly chopped tomato and
herbs. Cover with the stock and simmer until the potatoes are soft, then
push everything through a sieve. Reheat gently and adjust the seasoning
if necessary. Stir in the sour cream just before serving or put a large
dollop of it to float on top of each soup bowl. Sprinkle with paprika.

Fried croutons and grated cheese go well with this soup, or pour it
into a large ovenproof bowl – or small individual soup bowls – and
sprinkle with fried croutons and grated cheese. Put the large bowl into

a hot oven or, in the case of individual soup bowls, under a hot grill until the cheese has melted and browned a little on top.

FISOLENSUPPE

French Bean Soup

Serves 3 – 4

1 lb (450 g) French beans	5 fluid oz (140 ml) sour
sprig of winter savory	cream
1 pint (½ litre) veal stock	salt and pepper
1 large potato	chopped parsley

String the French beans and slice them fairly thinly. Cover with veal stock, add a sprig of winter savory and cook until the beans are almost tender, then cover with thin slivers of peeled potato. Simmer until the potato slices are cooked. Add sour cream, reheat gently and season with salt and pepper. Serve sprinkled with chopped parsley.

FRÜHLINGSKRÄUTERSUPPE

Soup of Spring Herbs

'Herb' in this case, often includes young strawberry and violet leaves as well as watercress, sorrel, wild garlic, thyme, dill and chives – so pick a bouquet according to your taste.

Serves 4 – 5

2 oz (50 g) butter	a little lemon juice
2 tablespoons plain flour	4 fluid oz (⅛ l) double
2¼ pints (1¼ l) veal stock	cream
salt	croutons fried in butter
white pepper	
7 oz (200 g) fresh herbs	
(see above)	

Finely chop the herbs, melt the butter, add two thirds of the chopped herbs and soften over low heat. Sprinkle in the flour, stir and gradually add the stock. Simmer for ten minutes. Purée in a blender, or sieve. Reheat gently, adding lemon juice, salt, pepper and finally the cream. Sprinkle with remaining chopped herbs and serve with croutons.

GRAUPENSUPPE MIT SCHWAMMERLN

Pearl Barley Soup with Mushrooms

Serves 4 – 6

4½ oz (120 g) pearl barley	1 egg yolk
½ oz (15 g) dried boletus mushrooms	5 fluid oz (140 ml) double cream
2½ pints (1400 ml) ham stock	2 tablespoons finely chopped ham
salt and pepper	chopped chives
nutmeg	

Soak the pearl barley in cold water for about an hour, and drain. Put the mushrooms into a cup and cover with warm water.

Put the pearl barley into a large saucepan, add the stock and the mushrooms, then strain in the liquid in which they were soaked (there is usually a bit of sand, hence the straining). Simmer gently until the pearl barley is cooked – stir from time to time to prevent it from sticking to the pan and if necessary, add a little more stock during cooking. Season with pepper and nutmeg and, if necessary, with salt, though the ham stock may contain enough salt.

Take soup off heat. Whisk together egg yolk and cream and gradually add to the soup. Reheat gently, add the chopped ham and serve sprinkled with chopped chives.

GRÜNE ERBSENSUPPE MIT NOCKERL

Green Pea Soup with Small Dumplings

My grandmother used to bottle large quantities of green peas as soon as they were harvested. The peas would go into a large vat at first, to be covered with water, and any peas floating to the top would be skimmed off as being unsuitable for bottling. This soup was one of the ways in which the skimmed-off peas were used – and very delicious it is, too. I have never found the recipe in any cookery book, but a similar soup made with sliced French beans is popular throughout Lower Austria.

Serves 4 – 5

2¼ pints (1¼ litre) good clear beef or veal stock	*Butternockerl* (see page 33)
8 oz (250 g) shelled fresh peas	salt and pepper

Bring stock to the boil, add peas and simmer until the peas are tender. Prepare paste for *Butternockerl*, drop the small dumplings into the soup and cook as described on page 33. Adjust seasoning.

A pinch of mace or nutmeg added to either dumplings or soup adds extra flavour, but is not strictly necessary. When cooking larger quantities my grandmother would sometimes make a light roux and add it to the soup to thicken it, but this is a matter of personal preference.

GURKENSCHAUMSUPPE

Frothy Cucumber Soup

Gustav Lugerbauer at the Weisses Kreuz in Mondsee is the creator of many fine dishes, of which this soup is my favourite. It is a rather extravagant dish, using a whole cucumber for each portion, but well worthwhile.

Serves 4

4 cucumbers	6 fluid oz (¹/₆ l) double
1 tablespoon butter	cream
1 scant tablespoon plain	salt
flour	white pepper

Do not cut the rind off the cucumbers but cut into chunks, put into a blender and reduce to a purée, then push through a hair sieve. Melt butter, stir in the flour and blend to a very light roux. Add cucumber juice and purée, bring to boil and simmer for one minute. Add cream, bring to the boil, season with salt and pepper and serve at once.

JÄGERSUPPE

Hunters' Soup

Serves 4 – 6

3 onions	¹/₂ bayleaf
2 leeks, finely sliced	1 crushed clove garlic
¹/₂ stick of celery, sliced	1 tablespoon potato flour
¹/₂ lb (¹/₄ kg) chanterelles	3 eggs
thyme	4 – 6 thin slices bread
parsley	3 oz (85 g) butter
2 cloves	2¹/₂ pints (1.4 litres) water
salt and pepper	

Finely slice the onions and sweat them gently in about a third of the butter. Add sliced leeks and celery, chanterelles, herbs, spices and seasoning. Stir over low heat for a few minutes, then add water and simmer until the vegetables are cooked.

Slake potato flour with a little water, add eggs and whisk. Beat egg mixture into hot soup, allow to simmer gently for a little while until well blended and thickened. Cut bread slices into halves and fry in remaining butter. Put into warmed soup tureen (or if using individual soup bowls, put two slices into each bowl). Pour soup over bread slices and serve.

KARFIOLSUPPE

Cauliflower Soup

> *Serves 4 – 6*
>
> | | |
> |---|---|
> | 1 medium-sized cauliflower | salt and pepper |
> | 2¼ pints (1¼ litres) veal stock | nutmeg |
> | 2 oz (50 g) butter | 2 egg yolks |
> | 2 flat tablespoons plain flour | 5 fluid oz (140 ml) milk or single cream |
> | | chopped parsley |

Cook cauliflower in the veal stock until just tender. Lift out carefully and separate into small sprigs. Keep back a handful of the sprigs, pass remainder, and stalk, through a sieve, or purée in a food processor. Make a white roux with butter and flour, add stock in which cauliflower was cooked, cauliflower purée, salt, pepper and nutmeg. Simmer for ten to fifteen minutes.

Whisk together egg yolks and milk or cream, whisk into the soup and reheat gently. Add cauliflower sprigs, adjust seasoning if necessary and serve sprinkled with chopped parsley.

KNOBLAUCHSUPPE

Garlic Soup

Particularly good, though rather rich if made with rendered goose fat. Traditionally the soup is poured into soup plates lined with a slice or two of lightly toasted bread, but I find it even better if served with croutons fried in butter or the above-mentioned goose fat.

> *Serves 4 – 5*
>
> | | |
> |---|---|
> | ¼ celeriac | 2 oz (50 g) goose dripping or olive oil |
> | 1 carrot | a few dried mushrooms |
> | a few leek tops | 3 grains allspice |
> | 1 – 2 parsley roots | a pinch of ginger |
> | salt | 2 tablespoons plain flour |
> | 1 teaspoon caraway seeds | 2¼ pints (1¼ litres) veal stock |
> | 1 small onion, finely grated | croutons or slices of bread |
> | 3 – 5 crushed garlic cloves | |
> | 1 medium-sized onion, finely sliced | |

Chop celeriac, carrot, leek tops and parsley root. Soak the dried mushrooms in warm water for about ten minutes. Cook the chopped vegetables in the stock for ten minutes, then add salt, caraway seeds, grated onion and drained mushrooms. Strain in the water in which mushrooms were soaked. Cook for another twenty minutes, then strain. Melt goose dripping or oil in a thick saucepan, soften sliced onion and crushed garlic in the fat, then brown lightly. Dust with flour, stir and add crushed allspice and ginger. Gradually pour on the strained stock and leave to simmer for five minutes. Adjust seasoning if necessary. Pour over slices of lightly toasted bread in soup plates or serve with croutons.

KOHLMINESTRASUPPE

Savoy Cabbage Soup

A Viennese version of Minestrone.

Serves 4 – 6

1 Savoy cabbage weighing about 1½ lbs (¾ kg)
1 small onion
5 oz (140 g) fat bacon
generous 2½ pints (1½ litres) beef or veal stock
1 crushed garlic clove
chopped fresh marjoram

4 oz (110 g) rice
salt and pepper
Parmesan cheese

Remove and discard coarse outer leaves of cabbage. Quarter the cabbage and shred roughly. Pour boiling water over the cabbage, leave for one minute, then drain. Peel and finely chop the onion. De-rind and dice the bacon.

Put bacon into a thick saucepan and render down the fat over low heat. Remove any bacon bits which have not melted and set aside. Add onion and garlic to the fat and soften over low heat. Add marjoram and rice and stir until rice turns transparent, then add cabbage and reserved bacon bits. Pour in about ½ pint (250 ml) of the meat stock and simmer gently until rice is cooked.

Add remaining meat stock, simmer for another five minutes, adjust seasoning and serve with plenty of grated Parmesan cheese.

KRENSUPPE

Horseradish Soup

Serves 4 – 6

2 oz (60 g) plain flour
6 tablespoons cold milk
2¾ pints (1½ litres) good
  beef broth
2 – 3 tablespoons freshly
  grated horseradish

1 tablespoon butter
2 tablespoons double
  cream

Slake the flour with the cold milk and whisk into boiling beef broth. Simmer for two to three minutes, whisking constantly. Melt the butter and gently fry the grated horseradish. Remove soup from stove, add the horseradish and swill out the pan in which it was fried with a little of the soup. Put cream into soup tureen, add the hot soup and stir gently so that there are swirls of cream on top – or put a little cream into each individual soup bowl before pouring on the soup.

KÜMMELSUPPE

Caraway Soup

As far back as I can remember, this soup was known for its soothing and restorative qualities. Made with water for 'poor people's soup' (or with beef broth for a richer version), in all fairness it must be said that an egg was more often than not whisked into the first and the bread for the croutons rubbed with garlic for extra flavour – additions which can of course also be applied to the soup when it is made with beef broth.

Serves 4

2 tablespoons dripping or
  butter
1 dessertspoon caraway
  seeds
2 flat tablespoons plain
  flour

2¼ pints (1¼ litre) water
  or clear beef broth
salt and pepper
fried croutons

Melt dripping or butter and add the caraway seeds. Fry gently for thirty seconds or so, then stir in the flour. (If you use powdered caraway seeds, use only a scant teaspoonful and stir as you add it to the fat – it will froth up and brown almost immediately.) Stir over low heat until golden brown, then add water or beef broth. Stir until blended, then bring to the boil, add salt and pepper and simmer for twenty to twenty-five minutes.

If using an egg, whisk it and pour the hot soup onto it, whisking all the time. Return soup to the saucepan and reheat gently. Serve croutons separately.

PARADEISSUPPE MIT PAPRIKA

Tomato Soup with Green Peppers

Not quite traditional – in Austria tomato soup is usually served with rice, but in my native Lower Austria green peppers were always grown between rows of tomatoes to give extra flavour to the tomatoes, and it was only a short step to transferring that extra flavour to tomato soup as well . . .

Serves 4

2 tablespoons butter
1 small onion, finely
  chopped
1½ lb (¾ kg) very ripe
  tomatoes
3 green peppers,
  de-seeded and cut into
  strips

parsley root
salt and pepper
½ bayleaf
generous pinch of sugar
clear broth if necessary
4 dessertspoons double or
  sour cream

Melt the butter, add the finely chopped onion and soften it over low heat. Add the tomatoes – no need to slice them, just break them up – and the green peppers. Add parsley root, salt, pepper, bayleaf and a generous pinch of sugar. Simmer gently until tomatoes and peppers are cooked. Sieve and, if necessary, add a little clear broth (though most tomatoes sold here contain too much water as it is). Reheat gently, adjust seasoning if necessary and just before serving swirl in the cream or sour cream.

Equally good hot or cold – serve the former with croutons, the latter sprinkled with chopped chives.

PRAGER ERDÄPFELSUPPE

Prague Potato Soup

A slightly 'smokey' flavour is an essential part of this soup: liquid in which not-too-salted ham or bacon has been cooked is ideal as stock.

Serves 4 – 5

6 large potatoes
1 large carrot
¼ lb (100 g) celeriac
2 pints (a generous litre)
  ham stock
few sprigs parsley and 1
  parsley root
1 teaspoon chopped fresh
  marjoram

few peppercorns
1 medium-sized onion
1 oz (25 g) butter
¾ oz (20 g) plain flour
5 – 6 oz (150 – 175 g)
  cooked ham or bacon
little double or sour cream
chopped parsley
croutons fried in butter

Peel potatoes and cut into convenient chunks. Peel and slice the carrot and celeriac. Remove any fat from the stock and add vegetables, parsley, parsley root, marjoram and peppercorns. Do not add salt at this stage as the stock will probably be sufficiently salty. Cook until potatoes are soft.

Chop the onion very finely. Melt butter and gently fry the onion until golden brown. Stir in flour. Press vegetables and soup through a sieve and add gradually to the onion. Stir and add a little more stock if necessary. Leave to simmer for ten minutes. Adjust seasoning if necessary. Chop ham and add to soup to heat through. Stir in cream just before serving. Sprinkle with chopped parsley and serve croutons separately.

SCHWAMMERLSUPPE

Mushroom Soup

Mushroom soup in Austria is not thick and creamy – unless it is called *Champignoncremesuppe*, which is a different thing altogether. *Schwammerlsuppe* is usually made with wood mushrooms – chanterelles perhaps, or a mixture of several varieties – and there are numerous regional variations. Some cooks prefer stock to water, others insist that garlic forms an essential part of the soup's flavour, and one of my favourite cooks in Styria swears that mushroom soup must have a definite acid tang which means a dash of vinegar or lemon juice, or using sour cream instead of fresh cream. In Styria *Heidensterz* (see page 2) and *Grammeln* (crispy bits of pork crackling) are the obligatory accompaniments. These are served separately: you take up a little of each with your soup spoon before dipping it into your plate to scoop up some soup. The combination of flavour and textures is superb: the crispness of the pork crackling, the mellow flavour of the buckwheat and the rich tang of mushrooms are irresistible even to non-Styrian palates. And the soup is still commendable even if served 'only' with croutons fried in butter or rendered bacon fat.

Serves 4 – 6

7 oz (200 g) mushrooms	2½ pints (1400 ml) water
1 small onion	or good stock
2 oz (50 g) butter	salt and pepper
1 tablespoon chopped	1 bayleaf
parsley	3½ fluid oz (100 ml)
a little chopped marjoram	double or sour cream
1 scant oz (20 g) plain	
flour	

Clean – but do not peel – and slice the mushrooms. Chop the onion. Melt the butter, add the onion and cook very gently until it is tender and lightly coloured. Add the mushrooms, parsley and marjoram. Stir and cover with a lid. Leave to simmer for about eight minutes. Dust with flour, stir and then gradually add water or stock, salt, pepper and bayleaf. Leave to simmer for twenty minutes. Remove the bayleaf. Mix a little of the soup with the cream and stir into the soup. Reheat gently and serve.

Dried mushrooms can be used instead of fresh ones. Use about 1 oz (25 g) dried mushrooms, soak them for about ten minutes in tepid water and then proceed as above. The water in which the mushrooms were soaked should be added to the soup, but strain it to get rid of any sand which may have adhered to the mushrooms.

TIROLER SUPPE

Tyrolean Soup

Serves 4

5 oz (150 g) split yellow peas	1 scant tablespoon plain flour
1 small celeriac	a sprig of thyme
2 – 3 potatoes	about 2¼ pints (1¼ l) ham stock
1 onion	
1 tablespoon butter or good pork dripping	

Soak the peas overnight in cold water. Pour away the water, cover peas with ham stock from which all fat has been removed, add a sprig of thyme and cook until the peas are soft.

Chop the onion very finely, peel and dice the potatoes and the celeriac. Melt butter or dripping in a thick saucepan, add onions and leave them to soften without browning, then add cubed celeriac and potatoes and simmer gently until vegetables are cooked but still firm. Dust with flour and brown everything together lightly.

Sieve the peas and add purée and liquid to the vegetables. Blend well, gently reheat, adjust seasoning and serve.

There are various embellishments which may be added to this soup – a little cream or sour cream floated in the centre of each soup bowl, perhaps with a sprinkling of finely diced ham or crisply fried bacon, or simply some chopped chives. To turn the soup into almost a main course add some sliced Frankfurter sausages.

BURGENLÄNDISCHE WEINSUPPE

Burgenland Wine Soup

Take a Viennese chef, a good measure of local wine and a touch of Hungarian spicing, and you've got a true Burgenland speciality. Aloïs

Schmidl ran the restaurant adjacent to the Esterhazy wine cellars at
Eisenstadt for many years and the following recipe is his creation.

Serves 5

4 oz (110 g) onions	2 – 3 crushed garlic cloves
1½ oz (40 g) butter	2 fluid oz (60 ml) double
1½ oz (40 g) smoked	cream
bacon, chopped	2 fluid oz (60 ml) sour
chopped fresh parsley	cream
1½ oz (40 g) plain flour	4 fluid oz (110 ml)
1¾ pints (1 litre) Clear	Riesling
Beef Broth	1 egg yolk
salt and pepper	

Slice the onions finely. Melt butter in a saucepan, add the onions and
soften, then brown them very lightly. Add the chopped bacon, sauté
until onions and bacon are golden brown, then sprinkle in the chopped
parsley. Dust with flour and stir to blend. Add beef broth, season with
salt and pepper and add the crushed garlic. Bring to boil, then simmer
for twenty minutes.

Mix together cream, sour cream, Riesling and egg yolk. Add to the
soup and reheat gently – do not allow to boil. Adjust seasoning if
necessary.

TERLANER WEINSUPPE

Terlaner Wine Soup

A favourite mid-morning refresher for those engaged in strenuous
work, be it felling trees, repairing roads or taking a long walk up a
mountain. Incidentally, I am fully aware that Terlan is in the South
Tyrol and, according to the map, in Italy. Culinarily speaking – and in
every other sense as well – it is in Austria.

Serves 4

18 fluid oz (½ litre) beef	salt
broth	powdered cinnamon
4 – 5 egg yolks	croutons fried in butter
9 fluid oz (¼ litre) white	
wine (Terlaner if	
possible, of course!)	
9 fluid oz (¼ litre) double	
cream	

The great Hanna Perwanger, author of *Südtiroler Leibgerichte*, whose
recipe this is, maintains that the best and indeed the only way to cook
Terlaner Weinsuppe is to put all the ingredients, except the croutons,
into a large enamelled saucepan and whisk over low heat until the soup
is smooth and creamy. So far I have lacked the courage to do this –

I heat the beef broth to just below boiling point, whisk together egg yolks, wine, cream, salt and a pinch of cinnamon and pour the heated broth onto this mixture. The soup is then whisked to the right creamy consistency in a double boiler or in a large bowl set over a pan of simmering water.

Whichever way you choose – a glass or two of Terlaner may give you the necessary courage to follow Hanna Perwanger's advice – serve the soup with croutons sprinkled liberally with cinnamon.

SOUP GARNISHES

BACKERBSEN

'Fried Peas'

Crisp little mounds, the size of large peas – hence the name – to serve with Clear Beef Broth. A thrifty way of preparing them is to keep the trimmings from *Strudel* pastry and cut out small rounds (using a thimble) which are dropped into smoking hot fat and fried until golden brown. The 'proper' recipe for *Backerbsen* however is as follows:

1 egg	salt
2 tablespoons milk	deep fat or oil for frying
1½ oz (45 g) plain flour	

Prepare a batter with the above ingredients – the mixture should be of a thick running consistency. Have ready a pan of smoking hot fat or oil, about three-quarters of an inch deep. Holding a ladle with batter in one hand, pour the batter through a sieve with large holes (or a perforated spoon) into the hot fat. Fish out as soon as the little 'peas' are golden brown, drain on kitchen paper and keep hot. Use only a small quantity of batter at a time, allowing the 'peas' to spread in the hot fat and to fry crisply. Serve separately.

BUTTERNOCKERL

2 oz (50 g) butter	salt
1 egg	3 oz (75 g) plain flour

Cream butter, beat in the egg, then fold in the flour. Salt to taste. Cover bowl and leave to stand for about half an hour. Cut small balls with the help of a teaspoon and drop into boiling soup. As soon as the mixture has been used up, lower heat and leave to simmer for about fifteen minutes.

EINGETROPFTES

In old cookery books *Eingetropftes* is sometimes called *eingegossene Nudeln* (poured-in noodles), because the batter sets into long strands like noodles.

2 eggs
about 2 tablespoons plain
   flour
salt

Mix flour, salt and egg to a smooth batter. Leave to stand for half an hour, then mix again to blend. Pour batter through a funnel into boiling Clear Beef Broth. Leave to rise once, then remove soup from heat and serve.

FARFERL

5 – 6 oz (140 g – 160 g)
   plain flour
salt
1 egg

Sift flour and salt into a bowl. Lightly beat the egg with a tablespoon of water and gradually add to the flour. Using a two-pronged fork if possible, work the mixture until it forms small lumps about the size of barleycorns. Dry in the oven, sprinkled on baking sheets. Sprinkle into boiling soup and cook for a few minutes.

FLECKERLN

Small Pasta Squares

Fleckerl means 'little patch', and these small squares are used not only in soup (*Fleckerlsuppe*) but to make *Schinkenfleckerl* (see page 143) and *Krautfleckerl* (see page 142). Any left-over paste can be used to make *Reibgerstl* (see page 39), thus using the last scrap!

9 oz (250 g) plain flour   1 – 2 eggs
pinch salt   water

Sift flour and salt onto a wooden pastry board. Make a well in the centre and drop in the egg(s). Draw in the flour with a knife, then knead to a soft, smooth dough, adding a minimum of water. Divide dough into several portions and roll out each portion as thinly as possible. Cut into strips about the width of a finger. Pile the strips on top of each other and cut into squares. Spread out to dry, then use as required.

FRITTATEN

Crisp pancakes cut into strips are a favourite Viennese addition to Clear Beef Broth. Sometimes finely chopped herbs are added to the basic batter, turning plain *Frittaten* into *Kräuterfrittaten*.

5 fluid oz (125 ml) milk	salt
1 egg	butter for frying
2 oz (50 g) plain flour	

Mix together milk, egg, flour and salt to make a batter which just about covers the back of a spoon. Melt a little butter in an omelette pan and pour in just enough batter to cover the bottom of the pan. Fry pancake on both sides, then use up remaining batter in the same way. Roll up each pancake and cut into thin strips. Put strips into soup bowl (or individual bowls) and pour hot Clear Beef Broth over them.

GRIESSNOCKERL

Small Semolina Gnocchi

1 heaped tablespoon butter	11 heaped teaspoons coarse semolina
salt	1 egg

Cream butter with a pinch of salt, beat in half the semolina, then the egg and finally remaining semolina. Cover and leave to stand for one hour. Scoop out small bits of the mixture with a spoon and throw into boiling broth. Lower heat and simmer *Nockerl* for eight to ten minutes, until they rise to the top. Or you can cook the *Nockerl* in a large pan of slightly salted water, fish them out with a slotted spoon when they rise to the top, and add them to the soup.

KAISERGERSTL

Ordinary people have *Gerstl*, or *Reibgerstl* (see page 39) in their Clear Beef Broth. Emperors, of course, have 'Emperor's *Gerstl*', the ultimate in soup additions.

3 eggs	salt
3½ fluid oz (100 ml) Clear Beef Broth	pinch of nutmeg
	a little butter for the dish

Butter a dish which will sit comfortably in a bain-marie or in a pan with hot water to come half-way up the dish. Beat eggs lightly, then add the cold Beef Broth, salt and a pinch of nutmeg. Stand the dish in the bain-marie over low heat until the mixture is firm. Scoop out small portions with a dessertspoon and serve in hot Beef Broth.

KAISERSCHÖBERL

Kaiserschöberl are a simple but particularly delicious version of *Schöberl* (see page 40), well deserving the Imperial seal of approval.

1½ oz (40 g) butter	2 oz (55 g) plain flour
2 eggs	salt
2 tablespoons single cream	nutmeg
2 tablespoons finely grated	butter and flour for the
Parmesan cheese	baking dish

Cream butter until light and fluffy. Separate eggs. Beat yolks into creamed butter, alternately with the cream. Add Parmesan cheese, flour and seasoning. Whisk whites until stiff and fold into the mixture. Spread on a buttered and floured baking tin. Bake at Gas Mark 4, 350°F, 180°C until golden brown – about fifteen minutes. Remove from the tin and set to cool on a rack, then cut into squares or diamonds when cold. Gently reheat in the oven just before serving.

LEBERKNÖDERL

Small Liver Dumplings

2 day-old rolls	1 tablespoon plain flour
1 small onion or shallot	2 oz (50 g) fine fresh
6 oz (170 g) pig's or calves'	breadcrumbs
liver	1 egg
1 oz (30 g) butter or lard	salt and pepper
chopped parsley and	
marjoram	

Grate the crust off the rolls, then break or cut the rolls into quarters and soak in water to soften. Chop the onion or shallot finely. Mince the liver, then squeeze out all moisture from the rolls and mince them as well. Melt butter or lard, fry onion very lightly. Add minced rolls, stir once, then remove pan from heat. Add parsley and marjoram, liver, flour, breadcrumbs and egg. Season with salt and pepper. Mix everything well, then set aside for about fifteen to twenty minutes.

Form a small dumpling – about 1 inch (2½ cm) – and drop into boiling Beef Broth, lower heat and leave to simmer – lid slightly tilted – for about fifteen minutes. Test the dumpling: if the mixture is too soft, add a little extra flour or breadcrumbs, if too dry add a little milk to the remaining mixture. Shape remaining mixture into dumplings and cook as described.

LEBERNOCKERL

Small Liver Gnocchi

3 rolls (crumb only)	1 tablespoon chopped
5 oz (140 g) ox liver	parsley
1 small onion, finely	salt and pepper
chopped	1 egg
1 oz (25 g) butter or	4 tablespoons plain flour
dripping	

Soak the rolls in milk or water, squeeze out all moisture. Mince the liver and rolls finely – if you use a food processor, do this in sharp 'bursts'. Melt dripping or butter, lightly fry onion and parsley. Remove pan from heat, stir in liver, minced rolls, egg and flour. Season with salt and pepper. Leave to stand for twenty minutes. Scoop out small portions with a teaspoon and drop into boiling soup or salted water. Lower heat and simmer very gently for ten to fifteen minutes.

LEBERREIS

Prepare mixture as for *Lebernockerl*. Holding a large-holed grater or perforated spoon in one hand, force mixture through the holes with the help of a spoon or palette knife, so that the mixture drops into the boiling soup in the shape of rice kernels. Leave to simmer for a few minutes only.

LUNGENSTRUDEL

Savoury Strudel

6 portions

Strudel pastry (see	caraway seeds
page 275), using 6 oz	a little fresh marjoram
(170 g) plain flour and	1 – 2 tablespoons clear
accordingly less liquid	beef broth
½ lb (225 g) calves' or	1 egg yolk
pig's lights	1 tablespoon breadcrumbs
1 small onion	1 egg
1 oz (25 g) butter or lard	
chopped parsley	
salt and pepper	

Clean lights and cook in lightly salted water. Drain, then chop, or push them through the mincer. Chop the onion. Melt butter or lard, fry onion lightly, then add lights, parsley, seasonings and herbs. Simmer over low heat for a few minutes, adding Beef Broth to moisten, then stir in egg yolk and breadcrumbs away from heat. Set aside.

Pull out *Strudel* pastry as described on page 276, but do not brush with melted butter. Brush instead with lightly beaten egg. Spread filling over two-thirds of the pastry, roll up as for Swiss Roll, starting at the filled end. Secure ends, then make indentations about two inches apart with the handle of a wooden cooking spoon. Cut into slices where marked, press down again. Drop into boiling Beef Broth, lower heat and leave to simmer for ten to twelve minutes. Alternatively, wrap *Strudel* in a buttered tea towel previously wrung out in cold water. Twist ends of tea towel to secure and tie well, then suspend in a large pan of boiling water for fifteen minutes and cut into convenient portions. Serve in Clear Beef Broth or serve separately on a warmed plate.

MARKKNÖDERL

Small Bone Marrow Dumplings

These are particularly good with *Eingemachtes Kalbfleisch* (see page 83) as well as in thick and clear soups. They are rather delicate and a test dumpling should always be cooked before shaping and cooking the remainder.

3½ oz (100 g) fine breadcrumbs	1 egg
scant ¼ pint (⅛ litre) milk	salt and pepper
3½ oz (100 g) beef bone marrow	grated nutmeg

Moisten breadcrumbs with the milk. Crush the bone marrow lightly, put it into a bowl and set it over steam or just in a warm place to soften. It should just melt, but not get really hot (in the Viennese vernacular this is called *zerschleichen*, meaning that it 'slinks away', which I have always found a most apt description). Strain through a sieve in case of small bone splinters, and allow to cool a little, then cream the bone marrow rather like creaming butter when preparing a cake. Beat egg and breadcrumbs into the mixture, season with salt, pepper and nutmeg. Work together well, then leave in a cool place for thirty minutes.

Form a small test dumpling, drop into boiling hot broth – or salted water – and simmer gently for about ten minutes (the dumpling will rise to the top when cooked). Fish out the dumpling with a slotted spoon and check texture. If the mixture is too soft, add more breadcrumbs. Shape remaining mixture into small dumplings and cook as for test dumpling.

MILZSCHNITTEN

Melts Croutons

2 oz (50 g) melts	salt and pepper
1 shallot	chopped marjoram
1 tablespoon butter	slices of bread
1 egg	fat or oil for frying

Mince the melts finely. Chop the shallot. Melt the butter and soften chopped shallot. Mix together melts, shallot and egg, season with salt, pepper and chopped marjoram. Spread on crustless bread, cut into squares. Fry in deep fat or oil, spread side down first, then turn and fry other side. Drain on kitchen paper. Serve with Clear Beef Broth.

REIBGERSTL

Very similar to *Farferl*, but the method of preparation is slightly different. 'Grated barley' is the literal translation since the pasta is grated to the size of barleycorns. You can use left-over *Strudel* pastry or noodle paste or – if starting from scratch – make a very firm paste with one egg, salt and about 3½ oz (100 g) flour. Pat into a round and leave to dry, then grate on a coarse grater. Spread on a baking sheet and dry in the oven, then sprinkle into boiling soup and cook for a few minutes.

Reibgerstl is also served with meat, instead of potatoes, in which case it is cooked like rice (see page 165) and a finely chopped shallot is softened in the fat before browning the *Reibgerstl*.

SCHINKENKNÖDERL

Small Ham Dumplings

Excellent in Clear Beef Broth, these can also be fried and served on their own with a crisp green salad.

5 oz (140 g) butter	10 oz (280 g) finely
3 egg yolks	chopped ham
2 eggs	2 - 3 oz (55 g – 85 g) fine
salt and pepper	breadcrumbs
mace	plain flour

Cream butter, gradually beat in the yolks and then the whole eggs. Add chopped ham and season with salt, pepper and mace. Add enough breadcrumbs to form a fairly loose mixture and leave to stand for half an hour. With floured hands form a small dumpling and drop it into boiling salted water, or directly into hot Beef Broth, lower heat and leave to simmer until dumpling rises to the top. If necessary add more breadcrumbs to the mixture. Form small dumplings with the remaining mixture and cook as before.

SCHÖBERL

Schöberl are a typically Viennese addition to Clear Beef Broth – a light savoury sponge mixture often baked in a special tin (*Schöberlpfanne*), cut into squares or diamonds when cold and gently reheated in the oven just before serving. Any square or oblong baking dish can be used, but the mixture should not be spread higher than the thickness of a finger. In restaurants *Schöberl* are served in the soup; at home they are usually handed separately on a dish. There are numerous variations on the theme of *Schöberl*, ranging from the addition of finely chopped parsley or ham, or both, to quite elaborate versions incorporating lightly cooked and chopped calves brains. The basic mixture – sometimes also called *Biskuitschöberl* – is as follows:

2 eggs	butter and flour for the
salt	baking tin
2 oz (60 g) plain flour	

Separate eggs. Whisk whites with a pinch of salt until stiff, then fold into lightly beaten yolks. Fold in the sifted flour. Spread on a buttered and floured baking tin. Bake at Gas Mark 4, 350°F, 180°C until golden brown – about fifteen minutes. Remove from the tin and set to cool on a rack, then cut into squares or diamonds when cold. Gently reheat in the oven just before serving. (See also page 36 for *Kaiserschöberl*, a typically Viennese luxurious understatement.)

SUPPENNUDELN

Noodles for Soup

For working all dough mixtures such as *Nudeln* and *Fleckerln*, as well as for *Strudel* paste, a wooden pastry board or wooden table top is best.

4 oz (110 g) plain flour	1 egg
salt	1 tablespoon water

Sift together flour and salt. Make a small well in the centre, drop in egg and water. Draw in flour with a knife, then knead well. Pat dough into a round, then roll out very thinly. Leave to dry for about half an hour. Cut into strips about three inches wide. Place strips on top of each other, cut into thin noodles. Leave to dry on the pastry board, then cook as required.

FISH

FISH

Lakes and rivers in Austria yield a large variety of superb fish, the preparation of which is kept very simple. A respectable carp or trout is cooked *au bleu* – not really an Austrian recipe but a way of cooking fish widely adopted throughout Austria. Or it is baked in the oven with lots of butter and possibly cream, often larded with anchovies or bacon.

In the case of larger fish, such as pike and carp, it is quite often sliced, floured, dipped in egg and breadcrumbs then fried and there is also fish in aspic with some regional variations.

Some of the richer fish dishes hail from Bohemia, Moravia and Hungary, but *Hechtnockerln* (pike dumplings) are truly Viennese, better known throughout the culinary world as *quenelles de brochet*.

BÖHMISCHER KARPFEN

Bohemian Carp

An early nineteenth century recipe still in use, almost unchanged. Since in Austria practically all carp is bought alive, collecting the blood – as stipulated in the recipe – presents no problem; but even if your fish comes from a fishmonger's slab rather than a tank, there should be enough blood from along the backbone.

Serves 6

1 carp, weighing about 3½ lbs (about 1.6 kg)	grated rind of 1 lemon
2 tablespoons wine vinegar	2 cloves
salt	a few peppercorns
1 large onion	good pinch of ground allspice
1 large carrot	a sprig of thyme
parsley root	1 bayleaf
¼ celeriac	good dash of wine vinegar
3½ oz (85 g) butter	3 oz (80 g) dark honeycake
1¾ pints (1 litre) dark beer (brown ale or Guinness)	2 tablespoons sugar
1 tablespoon honey	2 oz (50 g) chopped walnuts

Scale and gut the fish, cut off the head and reserve. Collect the blood from the fish and stir the two tablespoons of wine vinegar into it. Wash the fish, cut into slices and rub the slices with salt. Leave for a few hours in a cool place. Peel onion and celeriac, scrape carrot and parsley root. Cut vegetables into strips, or grate on a coarse grater. Melt the butter in a large flameproof casserole, add vegetables and brown gently in the butter. Add the beer, carp's head, honey, lemon rind, seasonings, spices and the honeycake, as well as a dash of vinegar. Bring to the boil and gently poach the fish slices in this. Lift out as soon as they are cooked and put them onto a large and fairly deep serving dish. Leave the carp's head and the vegetables to simmer until liquid is reduced to about half the original quantity. Meanwhile put the sugar into a small thick saucepan and cook over a low heat until the sugar starts to colour. Throw in the chopped nuts, stir and remove from heat. Strain the fish stock from the casserole into this, bring to boil again, then lower the heat and thicken with the blood. Strain over fish and leave to set in a cool place. This dish is also served hot accompanied by – what else in a dish that hails from Bohemia? – dumplings.

GEBACKENER KARPFEN

Fried Carp

On Christmas Eve there is always a large platter of fried carp, accompanied by various salads of which a good potato mayonnaise made with waxy *Kipfler* potatoes is the most traditional. The carp is usually bought live and head and tail pieces are used for *Fischbeuschelsuppe* (see page 15). Carp is not the easiest fish to fry, but this is the time-honoured way it was always done in my family and it does work.

Serves 4

4 carp steaks, weighing about 6 oz (170 g) each
1 egg
few drops olive oil
salt and pepper

2 teaspoons water
plain flour and fine fresh breadcrumbs for coating
olive oil or lard for frying

Rinse the fish under cold running water and dry with paper towels. Make a few incisions in the skin, sprinkle fish with salt and leave in a cool place for about half an hour, then pat dry once more with paper towels.

Break the egg into a soup plate, add a few drops olive oil, salt, pepper and two teaspoons water. Whisk lightly with a fork. Dip the steaks first into flour, then into the beaten egg and finally into the bread crumbs.

Heat olive oil or lard to the depth of about 1½ inches in a deep frying pan and when really hot put in the carp steaks – do not put in all the steaks at the same time – and fry them very gently on both sides. This usually takes about twenty minutes. Stand away from the pan – carp has a nasty habit of 'jumping' in the frying pan. ('It's still alive' my grandmother was once heard to say with displeasure, as if the carp had done her a personal injury.) To test if sufficiently cooked, remove the fish from the frying pan and pierce with a needle or fine skewer – if the liquid which runs out is completely clear, the fish is cooked. (Do not make this test while the fish is in the frying pan – it will spit straight in your eye.) Arrange fish on a hot serving dish and garnish with parsley and wedges of lemon.

GEFÜLLTER KARPFEN

Stuffed Carp

Serves 6 – 8

1 large carp weighing about 4 lbs (1.8 kg)	salt and pepper 1 tablespoon chopped parsley
2 eggs	
3 rolls	5 oz (140 g) grated Parmesan cheese
4 oz (100 g) beef suet, finely chopped	milk
5 oz (140 g) chopped mushrooms	breadcrumbs 5 anchovy fillets
1 – 2 rashers bacon	5 oz (140 g) butter
1 shallot, finely chopped	

Scale the carp, cut open along the backbone, remove backbone and guts. Wash the fish and pat dry, then sprinkle lightly with salt, inside and out.

Soak two of the rolls in a little milk, then squeeze out all moisture. Mix with finely chopped shallot, suet, parsley, Parmesan, eggs, chopped mushrooms and salt and pepper. Cut the bacon into thin strips, sprinkle with pepper and lard the fish with them. Fill the fish with the stuffing and sew up carefully.

Cut remaining roll into thin slices. Pound anchovies with butter. Melt the anchovy butter in a large roasting tin and turn the roll slices in the butter so that they are covered with it.

Arrange the roll slices in the roasting tin and place fish on top. Roast at Gas Mark 5, 375°F, 190°C, basting frequently (add a little white wine for basting if necessary).

Usually the fish is served sprinkled with breadcrumbs fried in butter, but I prefer it with just the juices from the pan poured over it. Don't forget to remove the sewing thread before serving.

GESULZTER KARPFEN

Carp in Aspic

Serves 6 – 8
This is the way my grandmother cooked carp in Lower Austria – the fish came from the nearby March (Morava) river which forms the border between Austria and Slovakia. Wash, clean and scale a carp (weighing about $1^1/_2$ – 2kg) and cut it into steaks about 1 inch thick.

Finely slice a small onion. Cut two carrots and a small celeriac into strips. Cook the vegetables in salted water until tender. Strain, reserving the vegetables and the liquid in which they were cooked.

Make up the liquid to 2 pints (900 ml), add a few peppercorns, a bayleaf, salt, a little lemon juice, thyme and two tablespoons good wine vinegar, and simmer for twenty minutes. Add the sliced carp, including the head – having removed the gills etc – and simmer until fish is cooked, about twelve to fifteen minutes. Leave to cool in the liquid for about ten minutes, then lift out the slices and carefully arrange them in a deep dish, in such a way that the fish is re-assembled from head to tail, but leaving a little space between each slice. Sprinkle the cooked vegetables round the fish and between the slices.

Reduce stock in which the fish was cooked to half by cooking it briskly in an uncovered saucepan, adjust seasoning, adding a little more vinegar if necessary, then strain it over the fish and leave to set.

My grandmother always cooked some potatoes in the fish stock which she would then slice and arrange around the fish together with the other vegetables and she would also stir a handful of ground walnuts into the strained stock before pouring it over the fish. I do not remember that she ever used powdered gelatine – the mere idea was probably anathema to her ('a decent carp sets all on its own' I can almost hear her say); but I always dissolve a heaped teaspoon of powdered gelatine in hot water and then stir it into the hot fish stock – just for luck!

Gesulzter Karpfen II

As cooked at the famous Zu den 3 Husaren restaurant in Vienna.

Serves 4

4 carp steaks weighing about 9 oz (250 g) each	2 hardboiled eggs
3 oz (80 g) carrots	1 small bayleaf and peppercorns in a muslin bag
3 oz (80 g) turnips	
3 oz (80 g) celeriac	salt
½ onion	wine vinegar
½ oz (15 g) powdered gelatine	chopped parsley

Put into a saucepan enough water just to cover the fish – the fish is added later – with onion, a dash of vinegar, salt and the peppercorns and bayleaf. Cut the root vegetables into fine strips and add to the water. Bring liquid to the boil, then add the carp steaks and poach them very gently for about ten minutes. Switch off the heat and leave the fish in the hot liquid for another fifteen minutes. Remove muslin bag and onion.

Dilute gelatine in a few teaspoons of hot water. Strain fish stock and mix with the gelatine whilst still warm. Pour fish stock into a suitable mould and leave until sides have set. Pour out the liquid into a bowl, decorate mould with sliced hardboiled egg and sprinkle with chopped parsley. Put carp steaks into the aspic, add the root vegetables having patted them dry with kitchen paper. Cover fish with the liquid. Leave to set in the refrigerator.

Before turning out onto a platter, dip the mould into hot water for a second or two. Divide into four portions before serving.

PAPRIKAKARPFEN

Carp with Paprika and Sour Cream

Serves 4

1 carp weighing about 2 lbs (900 g)	5 fluid oz (140 ml) sour cream
salt	4 tomatoes, peeled and quartered
paprika	grated rind of 1 lemon
2 medium-sized onions	1 crushed garlic clove
1 tablespoon lard	
1 glass white wine	

Scale, clean and fillet the fish. Sprinkle fillets with salt and paprika and set aside. Chop onion and soften in the lard over low heat, together with the crushed garlic, then add tomatoes and pour in the wine. Reduce liquid a little, then add sour cream, grated lemon rind, salt and paprika. Stir to blend, then add the fish and simmer gently until the fillets are cooked. Do not stir, simply shake the pan gently from time to time.

PFEFFERKARPFEN

Poached Carp

Serves 6 – 8

1 carp weighing about 3½ lbs (1½ kg)	7 oz (200 g) onions, finely sliced
1 teaspoon crushed peppercorns	3½ oz (100 g) celeriac cut into strips
1 bayleaf	3½ oz (100 g) carrots cut into strips
sprig of thyme	5 fluid oz (140 ml) red wine
1 crushed garlic clove	salt
2 tablespoons tarragon vinegar	
27 fluid oz (¾ litre) water	

Scale and clean the carp and cut into 6 – 8 steaks. Put the head into a large saucepan, add peppercorns, bayleaf, thyme, garlic, vinegar and water. Bring to boil and simmer for forty minutes. Strain and add carrots, celeriac, onions and red wine and simmer for ten minutes.

Add salt and then the carp steaks and poach the fish very gently in the liquid for about fifteen minutes.

Serve in a large terrine, accompanied by boiled potatoes.

RAHMKARPFEN

Carp in Cream

Like so many really delicious things, this is simple – and extravagant. Carp is used for the original recipe, but any firm-fleshed fish is suitable and I have found it particularly successful with halibut.

Serves 5 – 6

1 carp weighing
  about 3 – 4 lbs
  (1kg 350 g – 1 kg 800 g)
salt
white pepper
1 lb (450 g) new potatoes
4 oz (100 g) butter
½ pint (300 ml) double or
  sour cream

3 oz (80 g) fine fresh
  breadcrumbs

Clean, wash and scale the carp, but leave it whole. Make three or four incisions down the back of the fish, sprinkle with salt and pepper.

Butter a deep flameproof dish well and cover bottom with scraped and sliced new potatoes. Dot with flakes of butter and sprinkle with salt and pepper. Pour about half the cream or sour cream over the potatoes and place the fish on top. Pour remaining cream over the fish and dot with butter. Bake at Gas Mark 4, 350°F, 180°C for about forty-five minutes, basting frequently, then increase the heat to Gas Mark 7, 425°F, 220°C, sprinkle breadcrumbs over the fish, dot with butter and return to the oven to brown for about ten minutes.

The whole secret of this dish, which is far more delicious than many more complicated recipes, lies in prejudging the length of time the fish and potatoes will take so that they are both ready at the same time, and gauging the thickness of the potato slices accordingly. New potatoes take surprisingly long when cooked in this way, so when using fish off the bone cut the potatoes as thinly as possible.

SERBISCHER KARPFEN

Serbian Carp

Serves 6

1 lb (450 g) potatoes
butter for the dish
2½ lbs (1¼ kg) carp fillets
¼ lb (110 g) streaky bacon
salt
2 oz (50 g) melted butter
1 tablespoon paprika
1 medium-sized onion,
   thinly sliced

½ lb (¼ kg) tomatoes
2 large green peppers
8 fluid oz (225 ml) sour
   cream
1 scant dessertspoon plain
   flour

Boil potatoes in their skins until only just done, then peel and slice
them. Butter a large gratin dish thickly and cover bottom with sliced
potatoes.

Dust fish with salt and paprika and lard with bacon cut into strips.
Put fish on top of sliced potatoes, cover with sliced onion, then with
slices of green pepper and finally with sliced tomatoes. Season with salt
and pour the melted butter over it. Bake at Gas Mark 5, 375°F, 190°C
for about twenty-five minutes. Slake sour cream with flour, pour over
fish etc. and bake for another twenty minutes.

Alternatively, soften the onion in lard or dripping, stir in a dessertspoon
of paprika and about 3 – 4 tablespoons water and cook until thickened.
Add sliced or quartered tomatoes and sliced green peppers. Arrange
potatoes in a buttered dish as before, put fish fillets larded with bacon
on top and pour the onion, green pepper and tomato mixture over it.
Top with sour cream and bake for about forty minutes.

FOGOSCH MIT SAUCE

Pike/Perch with a Light Sauce

Serves 4

1 pike/perch weighing
   about 2 lbs (900 g)
salt
paprika
4 oz (100 g) streaky bacon
2 tablespoons melted
   butter

2 – 3 fish heads
1 bayleaf
a few peppercorns
juice of 2 lemons
dash of tarragon vinegar
4 eggs
1 dessertspoon butter

Clean and gut the fish, cut off head and set aside. Rub inside and out
of fish with salt and paprika. Cut the bacon into strips and lard the fish
with it. Turn the fish in melted butter so that it is well covered and set
it on a rack in a baking dish. Brush any remaining butter over the fish.

Bake the fish at Gas Mark 5, 375°F, 190°C for about twenty-five to thirty-five minutes.

Meanwhile put the fish heads into a saucepan, add bayleaf, peppercorns, a dash of vinegar, and salt and cover with water. Bring to the boil, then simmer for about fifteen to twenty minutes. Strain and measure out 11 fluid oz (300 ml). Put liquid into a bowl or saucepan set over a saucepan of simmering water, add four eggs, lemon juice and the butter cut into small pieces. Whisk over steam until frothy and thickened (if you are brave you can do this over direct heat, but you have to be very careful or the mixture will curdle). Set the fish in a deep serving dish, pour the sauce over it and serve at once.

GEBRATENER HECHT

Roast Pike

Serves 4

1 pike weighing about	3 anchovy fillets
2¼ – 2½ lbs (1 – 1¼ kg)	breadcrumbs
3 oz (90 g) butter	

Wash, clean and scale the fish. Cream butter with finely chopped anchovies and spread thickly over the fish. Set the fish in a buttered roasting tin and sprinkle with breadcrumbs. Roast the fish at Gas Mark 5, 375°F, 190°C, basting frequently.

Peeled and sliced potatoes can be put around the fish and baked at the same time, but they must be dotted with extra butter before the dish is put into the oven.

GESPICKTER HECHT I

Pike Larded with Bacon

Serves 6 – 8

1 pike weighing about	3 – 4 anchovy fillets
4½ lbs (2 kg)	1 glass white wine
3½ oz (100 g) fat bacon	8 fluid oz (225 ml) clear
salt	stock
5 oz (140 g) butter	5 fluid oz (140 ml) double
1 onion	or sour cream

Clean the pike, then remove the skin. Cut bacon into thin strips and use them to lard the pike. Sprinkle very lightly with salt. Heat the butter in roasting tin, add onion and chopped anchovies, then add the fish and bake it at Gas Mark 5, 375°F, 190°C, basting frequently, with wine and stock. Arrange fish on platter. Add cream to liquid in pan, reduce then strain over fish.

GESPICKTER HECHT II

Pike Larded with Anchovies

Serves 4
1 pike weighing about   juice of 1 lemon
   2½ lbs (1.2 kg)   2 – 3 tablespoons butter
salt   grated lemon rind
anchovy fillets
5 tablespoons sour cream

Clean the pike and rub inside with salt. Lard the pike with anchovies.
Melt about two tablespoons butter in a large flameproof baking dish,
add the fish and turn it over in the butter so that it is evenly covered.
Add three tablespoons sour cream and the lemon juice and bake the
fish at Gas Mark 5, 375°F, 190°C, basting frequently. Carefully remove
fish to a warmed serving dish. Add remaining sour cream to the juices
in the pan, place baking dish over direct heat and add remaining butter
cut into small pieces. Bring to boil quickly, stir to blend and pour over
the fish. Sprinkle with finely grated lemon rind.

HECHT MIT KREN UND WURZELWERK

Pike with Horseradish and Root Vegetables

Equally good with carp or – for that matter – any firm-fleshed white
fish.

Serves 4
4 pike steaks
salt   3 – 4 allspice
½ lb (250 g) root   4 tablespoons wine vinegar
   vegetables – carrots,   6 tablespoons water
   celeriac, parsley root etc   freshly grated horseradish
a few peppercorns

Wash the pike steaks, pat dry with kitchen paper and sprinkle with salt.
Set aside in a cool place. Cut the root vegetables into fine strips. Mix
together water and vinegar and put into a saucepan or fish kettle. Add
the root vegetables, peppercorns and allspice and put the fish on top.
Simmer gently until the fish is cooked. Serve sprinkled with freshly
grated horseradish.

HECHT MIT SARDELLENBUTTER

Pike with Anchovy Butter

Serves 4 – 5
1 pike weighing 2¼ – 2½   4 anchovy fillets
    lbs (1 – 1¼ kg)   4 oz (110 g) butter

Wash, clean and scale the pike. Make a few incisions down the back
of the fish and stuff the slits with thin slivers of two of the anchovies.
Melt a tablespoon of butter in a roasting tin, add the pike and turn it
carefully so that it is completely covered with the melted butter. Bake
the pike at Gas Mark 6, 400°F, 200°C, basting frequently. Pound the
remaining two anchovies to a paste. Melt remaining butter in a pan,
add the pounded anchovies, stir and let the butter froth up. Pour over
pike arranged on a serving dish.

HECHTNOCKERLN

'Pike dumplings' sounds much too stodgy for these delicate concoctions.
Give them their French name – *quenelles de brochet* – and it is something
else again, though *Hechtnockerln* is in fact a very old Viennese dish.

Serves 6 – 8   *Sauce*
18 oz (550 g) filleted pike   2 oz (50g) butter
    (without skin or bones)   1 shallot, finely chopped
11 fluid oz (300 ml) milk   1 tablespoon plain flour
5½ oz (160 g) plain flour   7 fluid oz (200 ml) clear
4½ oz (125 g) butter   fish stock
4 egg yolks   7 fluid oz (200 ml) double
3½ oz (100 g) butter,   cream
    softened   3 fluid oz (90 ml) sour
4½ fluid oz (125 ml)   cream
    double cream   salt
2 eggs   chopped fresh dill
4 egg whites   a little lemon juice
salt and pepper
nutmeg
dash of sherry
clear fish stock for
    poaching

Mince the pike very finely or use a food processor. Put the milk into
a saucepan, add the 4½ oz butter and bring slowly to the boil, then
tip in the flour. Stir over low heat until mixture leaves sides of the
saucepan clean. Remove from heat, beat in the egg yolks gradually.
Set aside to cool.

Mix together pike, flour mixture, softened butter and whole eggs. Season with salt, pepper, nutmeg and a dash of sherry. (This is best done in a food processor.) Whisk egg whites until stiff and fold into the mixture. Shape quenelles with a tablespoon and poach them very gently in fish stock for about eight to ten minutes. Lift out with a slotted spoon, arrange on a heated serving dish and mask with the sauce.

To prepare the sauce melt the butter, add the chopped shallot and soften. Sprinkle with flour, stir, then add fish stock and cream and blend well over low heat. Gradually add sour cream and dill. Season with salt and a little lemon juice.

FISCHGULYAS

Fish Goulash

Serves 4

2 lbs (1 kg) mixed freshwater fish such as carp, pike or perch etc	1 tablespoon paprika
	8 fluid oz (225 ml) fish stock or water
salt and pepper	1 large green pepper
2 oz (60 g) lard or olive oil	1 tablespoon tomato purée
2 medium-sized onions	5 fluid oz (140 ml) sour cream
1 tablespoon plain flour	

Cut the cleaned fish into fairly large pieces. Sprinkle with salt and pepper. Heat the fat and fry the fish briefly on all sides and set aside.

Chop the onions finely and fry in the same fat until golden brown, sprinkle with flour and stir, then add de-seeded green pepper cut into strips, and the paprika. Gradually add stock or water, sour cream and tomato purée. Season with a little salt and leave to simmer until well blended and thickened, then add the fish pieces. Simmer very gently for about eight to ten minutes in a covered saucepan – do not stir, merely shake the pan very gently.

Adjust seasoning if necessary – a little lemon juice may be added – and serve with rice, boiled potatoes or *Nockerl*.

KRENFISCH

Fish in Horseradish Cream

The best fish for this is pike, but any firm-fleshed white fish can be used.

Serves 4 – 5

1 pike weighing about 2¼ – 2½ lbs (1 kg – 1.2 kg)	2 – 3 tablespoons finely grated horseradish
2 generous oz (60 g) butter	7 fluid oz (200 ml) sour cream
salt	

Clean and gut the pike, rub inside and out with salt. Heat the butter in a deep, thick pan or fish kettle, add the fish and turn it over carefully so that the fish is covered. Sprinkle with finely grated horseradish and pour over the sour cream. Cover pan with a lid and leave the fish to simmer very gently for about three quarters of an hour, turning it over carefully after fifteen minutes. Baste frequently. Plain boiled potatoes are the best accompaniment.

The fish can also be baked in the oven in the same way – cover it with melted butter first, then sprinkle it with horseradish and cover with sour cream. Bake at Gas Mark 5, 375°F, 190°C. Cover the dish with foil at the beginning. Baste frequently and remove foil towards the end of baking time.

PAPRIKAFISCH

Fish with Paprika Sauce

Carp or pike are best for this dish, but any firm-fleshed white fish can be used. Good hot or cold, but if you plan to serve this as a cold dish, remember that the flavouring should be intensified a little. In the old days it was an unwritten rule that the weight of onions should equal that of the fish, but this is a matter of taste.

Serves 5 – 6

1 carp or pike weighing about 2½ lb (1 kg)	1 heaped tablespoon paprika
salt	18 fluid oz (½ litre) double or sour cream
1 large onion	
5 oz (140 g) butter	2 egg yolks
sprig of parsley	lemon juice

Scale, clean and fillet the fish, removing as many bones as possible. Cut the fish into pieces about 1 inch by 2 inches (2½ cm × 5 cm), sprinkle with salt and set aside. Slice the onion very finely. Melt the butter in a thick saucepan, add the onion and parsley and soften the onion over low heat without browning, then add the fish.

Cover pan with a lid and leave to simmer for about ten minutes. Add the cream, or sour cream, and the paprika and simmer for a further ten minutes. Lift out the fish carefully and keep warm. Beat together egg yolks and a good dash of lemon juice. Sieve the sauce from the pan into a double saucepan. Add a little of the sauce to the egg yolks before adding them to the sauce. Cook carefully in a double boiler until thickened, adjust seasoning and pour sauce over the fish. Sometimes chopped capers are added to the sauce for a little extra piquancy.

MEAT

MEAT

GEKOCHTES RINDFLEISCH

Boiled Beef

What Roast Beef is to England, Boiled Beef is to Vienna. Its importance is famously demonstrated in Josef Roth's *Radetzky Marsch*, in which a character beset by family worries eats the sacred dish 'without uttering a word, as if it had been an ordinary *Schnitzel*', while on a previous occasion he has held forth about it with such eloquence and critical finesse that his words never fail to be quoted whenever *gekochtes Rindfleisch* is discussed in Austrian culinary circles – which happens only too frequently.

Gekochtes Rindfleisch is no ordinary boiled beef (and certainly never pickled or salted). Infinite care is taken over selecting the cut to be boiled. Indeed, you will not see the words *gekochtes Rindfleisch* on menus in restaurants, or hear it in private households: the dish will always carry the name of the cut. *Tafelspitz*, a cut from the upper leg, is probably the best known, but there are many others with typically Viennese names such as *Hieferschwanzl, Beinscherzl* and *Schulterscherzl* (all classified as *Gustostückln* – especially delectable cuts), and the more robust *Kruspelspitz* and *Beinfleisch*. Each has a different quality, appreciated by true connoisseurs of boiled beef. The Hietzinger Bräu – celebrated as the place where these subtle differences are best appreciated (and suitably near Schönbrunn Palace, where the Emperor Franz Josef was said to have lunched on boiled beef every day of his life), lists no less than ten different cuts on its menu, giving a detailed description of each – except for *Tafelspitz*, which is simply described as 'a Viennese legend'.

The beef should always be served with a little of the broth poured over it, to prevent dryness, and should be cut across the grain. *Erdäpfelschmarrn* (see page 160) is the traditional accompaniment, as are at least two sauces (usually chive, as well as apple and horseradish), and a vegetable *nach Wiener Art*, which means in a creamy sauce.

To prepare this famous dish for 4 people:

2¼ lbs (1 kg) beef in one piece	parsley root
	1 leek
1 lb (450g) marrow bones	½ celeriac
1 onion	a few peppercorns
2 carrots	salt
celery tops	chopped chives
parsley	

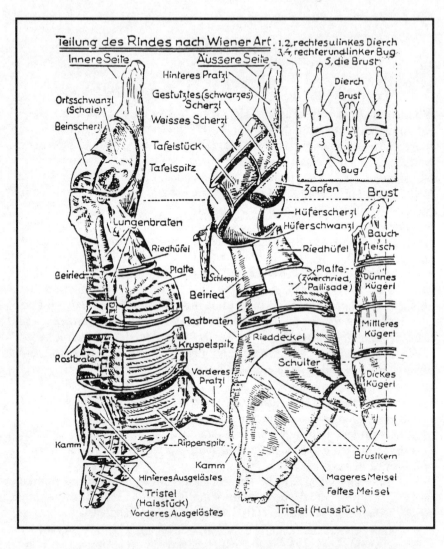

A Guide to Austrian Cuts of Beef

MEAT

Scald the marrow bones with boiling water, then rinse in cold water. Put them into a large saucepan, add about 3½ pints (2 litres) cold water, salt and peppercorns. Bring to the boil and cook for about half an hour, then add meat and vegetables to hot liquid. Cook very gently until the meat is tender – depending on the cut and quality of the meat this will take between two and three hours.

Lift out the meat carefully, place on a warmed dish and cut into thick slices across the fibre. Moisten meat with a little of the broth in which it was cooked and sprinkle with chopped chives. Garnish with slices of cooked bone marrow.

ESTERHAZY ROSTBRATEN

Sirloin Steak à la Esterhazy

Recipes for *Esterhazy Rostbraten* are as many and as varied as the stories concerning its origin. According to George Lang (*The Cuisine of Hungary*), *Esterhazy rostelyos* – to give it its proper Hungarian name – was created by the chef of Miklos Esterhazy in the eighteenth century, but Count Peter Esterhazy is confident that 'it is a dish created by one, possibly several, chefs in honour of the Esterhazy family and not one particular member of the family'. Personally, I'd always fancied that it was created in honour of Prince Nicholas Esterhazy, known as 'the Magnificent', who had refused the crown of Hungary when it was offered to him by Napoleon and who appeared at the Congress of Vienna in a truly magnificent uniform, resplendent with diamonds and pearls – there were even strings of pearls dangling from the top of his boots!

Since there are so many versions of the recipe, I have given my two favourites.

Esterhazy Rostbraten I

Serves 4

4 sirloin steaks weighing about 6 oz (160 g) each	1 medium-sized carrot cut into strips
salt and pepper	¼ celeriac cut into strips
2 oz (50 g) lard or dripping	1 parsley root cut into strips
½ onion	1 heaped teaspoon plain flour
about ¼ pint clear beef broth	4 fluid oz (⅛ l) sour cream
1 tablespoon butter	a little grated lemon rind
1 teaspoon French mustard	1 teaspoon chopped capers

Trim the steaks neatly, flatten with a mallet and make a few incisions around the edges. Melt the lard or dripping in a frying pan, brown steaks on both sides, and transfer to a casserole or thick saucepan.

Gently brown the onion in the same fat, add beef broth, stir to take up all the scrapings from the frying pan and pour over steaks. Season with salt and pepper and simmer over very low heat until the steaks are nearly cooked. Meanwhile melt the butter, add vegetables cut into strips and add to meat. If necessary add a little more beef broth.

Simmer until meat is tender, then add chopped capers, grated lemon rind, mustard and sour cream and the flour slaked with a little cold water. Stir well to blend, then lift out steaks and arrange them on a warmed serving dish. Cook sauce until thickened and well blended. Adjust seasoning if necessary – some cooks add a small pinch of sugar at this point – and pour over and around the steaks.

Esterhazy Rostbraten II

Serves 4

4 sirloin steaks weighing about 6 oz (160 g) each	about ¼ pint (⅛ l) clear beef broth
salt	1 teaspoon grated lemon rind
strips of unsmoked (green) fat bacon	4 fluid oz (120 ml) sour cream
1 onion	1 tablespoon butter
1 carrot	1 carrot cut into matchstick strips
¼ celeriac	1 parsley root cut into matchstick strips
sprig of thyme	
1 bayleaf	¼ celeriac cut into matchstick strips
3 – 4 peppercorns	
allspice	1 heaped teaspoon plain flour
a few lovage leaves	

Trim the steaks, make a few incisions round the edges. Cover the bottom of a thick pan with strips of de-rinded bacon. Chop onion, carrot and celeriac and put on top of bacon. Add seasonings and herbs and heat slowly at first and then, as the fat from the bacon begins to melt, increase the heat. Cover with a lid and simmer gently without stirring until the vegetables have softened a little, adding just enough of the beef broth from time to time to prevent burning. Remove lid and brown the vegetables. The temptation to 'give a good stir' is great at this point, but you must not do this; just shake the pan from time to time. When the vegetables are nicely browned, add the steaks and brown on both sides.

Cover with a lid and simmer very gently until meat and vegetables are tender, adding a little more stock if necessary. Meanwhile melt the butter, add the vegetables cut into matchstick strips, stir and simmer gently until just tender, adding a little of the beef broth if necessary.

When the meat is cooked, remove it from the pan and sieve contents of the pan or purée in a blender. Add lemon rind and sour cream slaked with the flour. Return steaks to the pan and simmer gently for a few minutes. Arrange meat and sauce on a warmed serving dish and top with the matchstick vegetables.

FLEDERMAUS

Named not after the operetta by Johann Strauss, but after the cut of beef used, which is rather like a bat (*Fledermaus*) in shape (though with some imagination one could also say 'like a butterfly'). You will not find this particular cut on an English meat chart – it is the small piece of meat, usually not weighing more than 11 – 13 oz (300 g – 350 g) lying near the hip bone, enough for two portions. Failing this particular cut, use any of the cuts suitable for *gekochtes Rindfleisch*. The recipe comes from the Hietzinger Bräu restaurant in Vienna, the best restaurant for *gekochtes Rindfleisch* and all its subtle variations.

Serves 4
1½ lbs (about 700 g) beef
  suitable for boiling
½ onion
½ leek
1 carrot
parsley root
¼ celeriac
salt
few peppercorns

For the sauce:
1 generous oz (30 g) butter
1 oz (25 g) plain flour
9 fluid oz (250 ml) clear
  beef broth
4½ fluid oz (125 ml)
  double cream
1 heaped tablespoon
  freshly grated
  horseradish
2 egg yolks
salt and pepper

Bring about 4½ pints (2½ litres) water to the boil. Add the meat and bring to boil again, then simmer slowly for half an hour. Add vegetables, salt and peppercorns. Simmer slowly until the meat is tender, removing any scum rising to the top, then leave the meat in the broth. Melt the butter, add flour and stir over low heat – do not brown the flour. Gradually add the 9 fluid oz (250 ml) strained beef broth and the cream. Blend until smooth over low heat, season and quickly stir in the lightly beaten egg yolks and the horseradish. Remove from heat. Slice the meat and arrange it in a gratin dish. Cover with the sauce and put under hot grill until nicely browned on top.

MAJORANFLEISCH

Beef Cooked with Marjoram

Serves 4
1 lb 9 oz (700 g) lean beef
  suitable for frying or
  braising
1 large onion
2 – 3 tablespoons olive oil
4 fluid oz (100 ml) wine
  vinegar diluted with the
  same quantity of water

salt and pepper
1 tablespoon finely
  chopped fresh marjoram
1 teaspoon plain flour
4 fluid oz (100 ml) sour
  cream

Cut the meat into small cubes or thin slivers. Chop the onion finely. Heat the oil and soften the onion in it, then turn up the heat to brown the onion lightly. Add the meat and stir to seal it. Pour just enough of the vinegar/water mixture to stop the meat from burning, and add salt, pepper and marjoram. Cover and leave the meat to simmer over a low heat – or in a low oven (Gas Mark 3, 325°F, 160°C) – until the meat is tender, adding the remaining vinegar solution as and when necessary. Stir in the flour slaked with the sour cream and simmer for another five minutes before serving.

MATROSENFLEISCH

Serves 4

1 shallot	1 teaspoon plain flour
5 – 6 mushrooms	4 tablespoons clear beef
1 tablespoon finely	broth
chopped parsley	2 tablespoons red wine
3 tablespoons butter	dash of wine vinegar
1 lb 9 oz (700 g) beef	small pinch of sugar
(end of fillet is best,	1 tablespoon tomato purée
but frying steak may	
be used)	
salt and pepper	
finely chopped basil or	
marjoram	

Finely chop the shallot and slice the mushrooms. Gently sauté shallot, mushrooms and parsley in one tablespoon of the butter. Cut meat into strips, flattening each strip with the blade of the knife. Fry the meat in small portions in the remaining butter, then return all the meat to the frying pan, dust with flour, add salt, pepper and herbs. Stir and then add clear beef broth, red wine, a dash of wine vinegar and a small pinch of sugar. Add tomato purée and sautéed mushrooms. Let it bubble up once and serve immediately.

RINDSBRATEN

Braised Beef

Braten means 'roast', but is a misnomer in this particular case since the meat is braised in one piece (in Austria roast beef is invariably described as such, and never as *Braten*). The cuts of beef used for *Rindsbraten* are almost identical to those used for *gekochtes Rindfleisch*, but failing such typically Viennese cuts as *Kavalierspitz, Hieferschwanzl* or *Tafelspitz*, Chuck or Bladebone will do. My own preference is a good old-fashioned 'leg of mutton' cut – if you can get it. Silverside and topside are also suitable, but on no account allow the meat to be wrapped in fat. If it is a lean cut, lard it with strips of bacon – a thick layer of fat wrapped round it would ruin the dish.

Serves 6

joint of beef weighing
about 2½ lbs (1 ¼ kg)
2 – 3 tablespoons oil
3 oz (80 g) streaky bacon
(depending on the cut of
beef)
7 oz (200 g) chopped
carrots, celeriac, parsnip
1 medium-sized onion,
finely chopped
some chopped veal and
beef bones
salt and pepper
peppercorns
1 bayleaf
3 – 4 juniper berries

few sprigs parsley
some celery tops
1 crushed garlic clove
small sprig of thyme
1 tablespoon plain flour
1 scant dessertspoon
cornflour
1 – 2 tomatoes
9 fluid oz (¼ l) white wine
about 1 pint (560 ml) beef
stock or water

Trim the meat and rub with salt and pepper. Depending on the cut, lard the meat with strips of bacon. Heat the oil in a large pan, brown bones and meat. Lift out meat and bones and keep warm. Brown chopped vegetables including onion in the same fat, adding a little more if necessary. Sprinkle with flour and brown everything together. Add tomatoes broken in half, stir and then add half the white wine.

Transfer everything to a casserole, being sure to take up all the scrapings from the pan. Add peppercorns, salt, bayleaf, juniper berries, parsley, celery tops, garlic, thyme and stock or water. Cover casserole and put in the oven at Gas Mark 3, 325°F, 160°C until the meat is tender – which varies considerably according to the cut of meat and may well take up to two hours. Baste the meat frequently with the liquid in the casserole, adding a little more stock or water if necessary and turning the meat over once or twice.

When the meat is tender, take it out of the casserole, set it on a warmed serving dish and moisten with a little of the liquid to prevent drying. Keep the meat warm. Take the bones out of the casserole. Remove grease from liquid in casserole. Slake the cornflour with the remaining wine and add to liquid in the casserole. Cook to thicken, then strain into a small saucepan. Simmer gently to blend and if necessary add a little more stock. Slice the meat and pour the sauce over it.

RINDSROULADEN I

Beef Olives

Serves 4

4 frying steaks	2 large or 4 small
salt and pepper	cucumbers pickled in
paprika	brine
1 onion	1/2 red or green pepper
2 tablespoons olive oil or	French mustard
lard	4 anchovy fillets
	about 1/4 pint (140 ml) red
	wine

Flatten the steaks with a mallet and season one side with salt, pepper and paprika. Spread other side of steaks with mustard and put an anchovy down the centre of each steak. Chop the pickled cucumber finely and sprinkle over the steaks. Roll up the steaks and fasten with wooden cocktail sticks, or tie securely. Chop the onion and soften it in the fat, together with chopped green or red pepper. Add the steaks, turn up the heat and brown steaks and onions. Pour in a little of the wine, cover with a lid and cook over low heat or in the oven at Gas Mark 3, 325°F, 160°C for about an hour, adding more wine only if necessary. Arrange the meat roulades in a heated dish, remove fastening and sieve the hot contents of the pan over them.

Rindsrouladen II

Serves 4

4 frying steaks	1 egg
salt and pepper	1 oz (25 g) butter
1/2 lb (225 g) veal	1 1/2 oz (40 g) bacon,
1 roll (crumb only)	chopped
1 anchovy fillet	a few bread crusts
1/2 onion, finely chopped	1 carrot
chopped parsley	parsley root
nutmeg	a little celeriac
	9 fluid oz (1/4 l) red wine

Flatten steaks with a mallet, sprinkle with salt and pepper. Soak the roll in a little water to soften, then squeeze out all moisture. Mince veal, roll and anchovy, or put everything into a food processor or blender. Add onion, parsley, salt, nutmeg and mix in the egg.

Spread this mixture over the steaks, roll them up, and fasten with wooden cocktail sticks or tie with thread. Melt the butter, add the bacon and fry until bacon is transparent. Add the steaks and fry on all sides until nicely browned. Grate carrot, parsley root and celeriac and add to the steaks, together with bread crusts. Pour in the wine and simmer gently for about an hour. Arrange the steaks in a warmed dish, remove fastening and sieve the hot contents of the saucepan over them.

SAUERBRATEN

Marinaded Beef

Serves 6

joint of beef as for
  Rindsbraten, weighing
  about 3 lbs (1.35 kg)
¼ pint (⅛ l) red wine
  vinegar
¼ pint (⅛ l) water
1 bayleaf
2 cloves
thyme

2 onions
1 teaspoon sugar
1 chopped carrot
about 2 fluid oz (50 ml)
  sour cream
salt and pepper
2 fluid oz (50 g) olive oil

Chop one of the onions and put it into a saucepan with vinegar, water, bayleaf, cloves and thyme. Bring to boil and then simmer very gently for fifteen minutes. Remove from heat and allow to cool. Put the meat into an earthenware or porcelain bowl, pour the cold marinade over it, taking care that the meat is completely covered. Cover bowl and put it in a cool place or the refrigerator for at least four days, turning the meat over from time to time.

When required, take out the meat and wipe dry. Chop the remaining onion and soften it in the oil in a large pan. Sprinkle with sugar and brown onion and sugar together with the chopped carrot. Fry meat on all sides with onion and carrot.

Transfer everything to a casserole. Swill out frying pan with the strained marinade and add a little of it to the beef. Season with salt and pepper. Gently simmer the meat either on top of the stove or at Gas Mark 4, 350°F, 180°C, adding marinade gradually until the beef is tender. Turn meat onto a warmed serving dish and slice. Add sour cream to contents of casserole, bring to boil to thicken and strain over meat.

WIENER ROSTBRATEN (ZWIEBELROSTBRATEN)

Sirloin Steaks

Serves 4

4 sirloin steaks weighing
  about 6 oz (170 g) each
salt and pepper
plain flour
2 tablespoons lard
1 tablespoon butter

1 teaspoon plain flour
¾ cup good beef or veal
  stock (or water)
1 large onion, finely sliced
oil for frying

Trim the steaks neatly, make a few incisions round the edges and flatten with a mallet. Rub both sides of the meat with salt and pepper and dust one side of the meat very lightly with flour. Heat the lard in a large frying pan, put in the steaks, floured side down to start with, and fry briskly on both sides – they should still be pink inside. Lift out steaks and keep hot.

Pour off surplus fat from the frying pan, add butter and let it froth up. Sprinkle with the teaspoon of flour, stir and then pour in the stock or water. Take up all the scrapings from the pan, stir and cook until thickened. Fry onion separately in hot oil, fish out with a slotted spoon and drain on kitchen paper. Sprinkle with salt. Pour sauce over steaks and sprinkle with fried onions.

WIENER SAFTGULASCH

Viennese Beef Goulash

Gulasch derives from *Gulyas*, which is the Hungarian name for shepherd. The dish is what shepherds cooked in their iron kettles, except that Hungarian *Gulyas* is more like Austrian Goulash Soup. What the Austrians call *Gulasch* (sometimes – wrongly – spelled *Gollasch*) is more like Hungarian *Pörkölt*. *Gulasch* – spelled thus – is very Viennese. They've even invented a few variations completely unheard of in Hungary, such as embellishing a typically Viennese *Gulasch* with a special pickled cucumber from Znojmo in Czechoslovakia and calling it *Znaimer Gulasch*. There's even a *Gulasch auf Pester Art* (Goulash Budapest style), duly recorded by the great Rokitansky as being a Goulash without paprika (!) but with *Farferl* (*Tarhonya* in Hungary). Rokitansky was first published in 1897 – but I'll bet the Hungarians never got to know about this one!

Serves 6

2½ lbs (1 kg) beef, preferably shin or 'leg of mutton' cut	1½ – 1¾ oz (40g – 50g) edelsüss (noble sweet) paprika
1½ lbs (700 g) onions, finely sliced	1 scant teaspoon crushed caraway seeds
4 oz (120 g) lard	1 scant teaspoon chopped marjoram
dash of wine vinegar	salt
1 crushed garlic clove	

Cut the beef into strips, about the thickness of a finger and about 1½ – 2 inches long.

In a thick saucepan fry the onions in the fat until deep golden brown – slowly at first, then stepping up the heat. Add the paprika, stir and immediately add a dash of vinegar and about 2 fluid oz (60 ml) water.

On no account must the paprika be allowed to brown as this would alter the colour and also give a bitter taste. Blend together garlic, caraway seeds and marjoram and also add salt. Cover saucepan with a lid and simmer for about five minutes, then add the meat, stir and leave the meat to simmer over a very low heat until the meat is just tender – about one and a half hours. Add more water during this time only if it is absolutely necessary to prevent burning.

When the meat is just tender and the resulting gravy almost transparent ('like a mirror' they say in Vienna) add enough cold water to come to the top of the meat and simmer for another ten minutes.

Wiener Saftgulasch is not thickened with flour, but for ordinary *Rindsgulasch* dust a scant tablespoon flour over the meat when it is just tender, stir and then add the water. Cook uncovered for another ten minutes (if you are nervous about lumps forming, slake the flour first with a little cold water, but this is not really necessary).

Goulash can of course be cooked in the oven (Gas Mark 3, 325°F, 160°C), though they are remarkably silent about this in Vienna.

The recipe for *Wiener Saftgulasch* was given to me by the great Karl Duch, chef extra-ordinary and author of several cookery books, during a long argument we had about the proper way of cooking Goulash, over thirty years ago – too late to be included in my original *Austrian Cooking*, but I have not used any other recipe since that day!

There are numerous variations on the theme of Beef Goulash, such as:

ZNAIMER GULASCH: Znojmo is a small town in Czechoslovakia, just across the Austrian border, known for its excellent cucumber. *Znaimer Gulasch* is topped with strips of pickled cucumber; lots of it.

FILLET GULASCH: sometimes called *Rostbratengulasch*, and made with more expensive cuts of meat such as the thin end of the fillet. This takes a shorter time to cook as the meat is more tender.

HERRENGULASCH (Gentlemen's Goulash): which can vary, though it is always Goulash made with beef. Sometimes sausage of some kind is added – usually Frankfurter – and occasionally a fried or poached egg is placed on top of the Goulash.

FIAKERGULASCH: similar to *Herrengulasch*, but a pickled cucumber is also added.

WÜRSTELBRATEN

Pot Roast Beef

I have never found this in any cookery book or seen it on a restaurant menu, and can only assume that it must be a family recipe. It was certainly part of my favourite birthday menu for as long as I can remember ...

Serves 4 – 6

piece of beef weighing
  about 3 lbs (topside or
  any cut suitable for pot
  roasting)
5 – 6 Frankfurter sausages
salt and pepper
paprika

1 large onion
lard or oil for frying
1 tablespoon plain flour
scant 1/2 pint (250 ml) beef
  broth or water
3 – 4 tablespoons double
  or sour cream

Choose a piece of meat suitable for pot roasting – not too fatty and certainly with no additional fat tied around the outside of the joint. (You could, of course, use a more expensive cut, but this is not necessary.) If at all possible, the meat should be the same length as a Frankfurter sausage.

Make five or six holes through the meat, *along* the fibres, using a skewer or a knife-sharpening steel (I use my fingers after the skewer has done the initial work). Push a Frankfurter sausage through each hole and, if the sausages are longer than the joint, chop off the ends. Dust the meat with salt, pepper and paprika.

Peel and chop the onion. Heat oil or lard in a frying pan and fry the onion over low heat, very slowly, until it is light golden brown. Add the meat and fry quickly to seal on all sides.

Sprinkle with flour, stir and fry for another minute.

Transfer contents of frying pan to a casserole, pour a cup of the beef broth (or water) into the frying pan and scrape up all the bits from the pan, then pour over the meat. If there are any chopped off ends of the Frankfurter sausages, add these as well. Cover casserole with a lid and cook gently in the oven – Gas Mark 3, 325°F, 160°C – for 1 1/2 – 2 hours until tender, adding a little more stock or water if necessary. Baste the meat from time to time and turn it over once or twice to prevent drying.

Lift out the meat and set it on a warmed serving dish. If some of the Frankfurters are protruding, slice them off and put them with the meat. Sieve the gravy, stir in the cream or sour cream and reheat gently. Slice the meat across the grain so that each slice contains small rounds of sausage, and arrange on the serving dish. Serve with the gravy.

GEDÄMPFTE KALBSLEBER

Casseroled Calves Liver

Serves 6 – 7

2 lbs (900 g) calves liver in
  one piece
6 – 8 oz (170 g – 240 g)
  unsmoked streaky
  bacon, de-rinded
salt and pepper
finely chopped parsley

1 bayleaf
1 medium-sized onion
2 – 3 carrots
1 glass dry white wine
1 cup clear beef broth
2 – 3 tablespoons double
  cream

Rinse the liver under cold running water, pat dry with kitchen paper. Cut the fat part of the bacon into strips suitable for larding. Line an ovenproof casserole with the remaining bacon. Mix together chopped parsley, salt and pepper. Roll the larding strips in the parsley, then roll them between the palms of your hands to make the parsley adhere. Using a larding needle, lard the liver all over with the strips of bacon fat. Slice the onion very finely. Scrape and slice the carrots. Set the liver in the casserole on top of the bacon, surround with sliced onion and carrots. Add bayleaf and a little pepper and pour over the wine (no salt at this stage as there is probably enough salt in the bacon). Cover well and cook at Gas Mark 2, 300°F, 150°C for about two hours. Carefully lift out the liver and keep warm. Pour beef broth into the casserole, bring to boil and strain into a saucepan. Leave to stand for a little while so that the fat rises to the top. Skim off fat. Add cream and cook gently until thickened. Adjust seasoning if necessary. Slice the liver, and if you want to give that extra touch, toss each slice briefly in a little melted butter to glaze. Arrange liver in a circle on a warmed dish and either serve the sauce separately or pour it over the liver.

TIROLER LEBER

Calves Liver Tyrolean Style

Serves 4

1¼ – 1½ lbs (about 600 g) calves liver	1 dessertspoon wine vinegar
2 scant tablespoons plain flour	1 dessertspoon chopped capers
1 small onion, finely chopped	scant teaspoon grated lemon rind
2 oz (60 g) lard or pork dripping	about 2 tablespoons good stock
salt and pepper	
¼ pint (125 ml) sour cream	

Slice the liver and dust one side of each slice lightly with about half the flour. Melt the fat and fry the liver for two or three minutes, turning it over once, then remove and keep hot. Fry the chopped onion in the same fat – add a little more if necessary – until softened and just tinged with colour. Add remaining flour, stir and continue frying until the onions are deep golden brown. Add salt, pepper, capers, lemon rind, vinegar and stock. Stir to blend well, then add the cream. Stir over low heat until well blended and thickened, then add the liver. Leave to simmer for another three to four minutes, then serve.

Rice is a good accompaniment, as are dumplings or *Nockerln* (see page 136).

TIROLER OFENLEBER

Tyrolean 'Oven' Liver

In the Tyrol this is eaten as an accompaniment to roast pork, but I think
it makes a good dish in its own right, eaten hot or cold. It is a traditional
Tyrolean dish and was a speciality of the Hotel Europa at Innsbruck,
whose recipe I am quoting. The combination of ox liver and pig's lights
is an essential part of the dish, though proportions may be varied, using
less lights and more liver according to taste and availability.

Serves 4 – 6

3 day-old rolls	chopped parsley and
milk or milk and water	marjoram
1 lb (500 g) ox liver	salt and pepper
1 lb (500 g) pig's lights	3 eggs
1 small onion	1 pig's caul
1 clove garlic	

Grate the crust off the rolls and soak the rolls in milk or milk and
water. Mince the liver, onion, lights and finally the rolls from which
all moisture has been squeezed. Crush the garlic under the blade of
a knife with a little salt or use a garlic press. Mix everything – except
the caul, of course – together, working in the eggs and adding salt and
pepper. (You can put everything through a food processor, adding the
crushed garlic and the eggs last, but the mixture should not be too fine
– be careful not to over-process.)

Line a baking dish with the caul so that the surplus caul overhangs
the edges of the dish. Spread the mixture over the caul and fold the
surplus over the top. Bake for about half an hour at Gas Mark 4,
350°F, 180°C. Serve hot with roast pork and potato salad, or as a
separate dish.

BAUERNSCHÖPSERNES

Tyrolean Mutton

This is very similar to *Steirisches Schöpsernes* (see page 72) the main
difference being the red wine, which is typical of the Tyrol.

Serves 6 – 8

4 ½ lbs (2 kg) mutton, cut	2 medium-sized onions
from the shoulder	sprig of rosemary
1 – 2 tablespoons plain	1 bayleaf
flour	few fresh sage leaves
salt and pepper	generous ¾ pint (½ litre)
¼ pint (140 ml) oil	red wine
1 garlic clove	clear meat stock

Cut the meat into six or eight large pieces. Sprinkle with flour, salt and pepper. Heat about a third of the oil in a large frying pan, brown the meat very lightly and then transfer it to a large flameproof casserole.

Chop the onions and fry in the same oil, adding a little more if necessary. Crush garlic with a little salt and add to the onions. Stir well, then transfer onions and garlic to the casserole. Add the herbs and a little more salt and pepper. Swill out the frying pan with the wine, taking up all the scrapings from the pan and pour over the meat in the casserole. Cover and simmer very gently for about one hour, adding a little stock if necessary.

Meanwhile peel and slice the potatoes. Heat remaining oil in a frying pan and fry potatoes until golden brown on both sides. Add potatoes to the meat and continue cooking over low heat until meat and potatoes are tender – about another half hour, adding more stock if necessary. Serve straight from the casserole.

LAMMKEULE AUF BAUERN–ART

Stuffed Leg of Lamb

Serves 6 – 8
1 leg of lamb weighing
   about 3½ lbs (1½ kg)
   after boning
1 garlic clove
salt and pepper
pinch of curry powder
powdered rosemary
pig's caul

Stuffing
1 large onion, finely
   chopped
2 garlic cloves
2 oz (60 g) streaky bacon
fresh marjoram, thyme
   and coriander
11 oz (300 g) lean minced
   pork and veal
salt and pepper

Remove and discard any surplus fat from the lamb. Carefully remove the bone so that there is a hollow centre in the meat. Rub meat with salt, pepper, curry powder, rosemary and the crushed garlic clove (you can also make little slits in the meat and insert small slivers of garlic).

For the stuffing crush the garlic with salt under the blade of a knife. Chop or mince the bacon. Finely chop the herbs. Mix together all the ingredients for the stuffing and work them well to blend, then fill the leg of lamb with the stuffing. Sew up the opening and wrap the meat in the pig's caul. Tie with string so that it will keep its shape. Roast at Gas Mark 5, 375°F, 190°C for approximately 1¾ hours, basting frequently.

MURTALER LAMMRAGOUT

Ragout of Lamb from the Mur Valley

Serves 4

1¼ lb (500 – 600 g) lean
  lamb
crushed bayleaf and
  rosemary
marjoram
thyme
curry powder
1 large onion
1 garlic clove
lard or oil for frying

1 bayleaf
salt and pepper
¼ lb (100 g) carrots
¼ lb (100 g) celeriac
1 tablespoon plain flour
about 8 fluid oz (¼ l) clear
  broth
½ cup red wine

Cut the meat into cubes, sprinkle with rosemary, bayleaf, marjoram, thyme, curry powder and pepper. Put the meat into a bowl and mix so that the herbs and spices are well distributed. Cover and leave in a cool place overnight.

Chop the onion and crush the garlic. Heat oil or lard and gently fry onion until pale golden brown, then add the meat, bayleaf, crushed garlic and a little pepper and salt. Continue to sauté the meat very gently. Dice carrots and celeriac and add to the meat and continue sautéing, stirring all the time, but do not add any liquid. After about fifteen to twenty minutes, dust with the flour, stir and add a little clear stock and simmer for another twenty minutes.

Take out the meat and keep hot. Sieve contents of pan into another saucepan, add the wine and reheat to reduce and thicken. Pour the sauce over the meat.

It is customary to surround the meat with freshly cooked sliced carrots, French beans and sometimes mushrooms. Dumplings or plain boiled potatoes go particularly well with this dish.

STEIRISCHES SCHÖPSERNES

Styrian Mutton Stew

A dish found in all the best Austrian cookery books, though I have had my doubts as to its Austrian ancestry ever since I found this recipe for a mutton stew in a nineteenth-century cookery book of the old monarchy. 'Irish Stew' it said, for all the world to see, adding: 'a kind of English goulash'. Did 'Irish Stew' with a little misspelling here and there finally become 'Steirisches Stew' – mutton being a speciality of Styria? We'll probably never know, but it is an excellent recipe, whatever its origin.

Serves 4

2½ lb (1 kg) boned shoulder of mutton	few peppercorns
1 carrot	sprig of thyme
1 parsley root	1 bayleaf
¼ celeriac	salt
1 small onion	dash of wine vinegar
1 oz (30 g) lard or good dripping	1 lb (500 g) potatoes

Remove skin and surplus fat from the meat. Place meat in a bowl, cover with boiling water and leave for four to five minutes. Drain off water, rinse meat under cold running water and drain well. Cut meat into convenient pieces. Scrape or peel the vegetables and cut all except the potatoes into matchstick strips.

Heat the fat in a frying pan and fry the vegetables, then transfer them to a large saucepan. Add the meat, enough boiling water to cover, a dash of vinegar, salt, peppercorns, thyme and bayleaf. Simmer until meat is almost tender – about one hour – then add quartered potatoes and continue simmering until meat and potatoes are tender.

Arrange meat, vegetables and potatoes on a large heated serving dish and pour a little of the liquid over meat and vegetables. Breadcrumbs fried crisply in butter and/or freshly grated horseradish are often sprinkled over the dish and it is usually served with more potatoes cooked separately.

BIERFLEISCH

Pork Cooked with Beer

Serves 2 – 3

2 medium-sized onions	coarsely crushed black peppercorns
1 generous lb (500 g) pork, shoulder for preference	2 teaspoons caraway seeds
1 heaped tablespoon butter or 2 tablespoons oil	1¼ pints (700 ml) lager
salt	about 3 heaped tablespoons soft wholemeal breadcrumbs

The darker the bread for the breadcrumbs, the better the dish will taste.

Chop the onions finely. Cut the meat into convenient pieces. Heat the butter or oil and lightly brown the chopped onion. Add salt, peppercorns (I use coarsely crushed peppercorns rather than milled pepper) and the caraway seeds and stir. Add the meat, stir until the meat is sealed, but not browned, then pour in the beer. Cover with a lid and simmer gently on top of the stove for half an hour.

Sprinkle with the breadcrumbs, cover again and put the dish into the oven at Gas Mark 3, 325°F, 160°C, for about an hour, until the meat is tender.

DEBREZINER GULASCH

Debreziner sausages, which are used for this dish, are more coarsely cut and more highly spiced than Frankfurter sausages, which they resemble. Like Frankfurters, they are sold in pairs and are available all over Austria (and often in this country as well), though probably not in their native town of Debrecen in Hungary – any more than this particular dish which is a purely Viennese invention. If you cannot get Debreziner sausages, Spanish Chorizo make a good substitute; and so do Frankfurters, of course, but in the latter case increase the quantity of paprika.

Serves 4

1 teaspoon lard	salt
2 oz (50 g) diced bacon	1 teaspoon caraway seeds
5 oz (140 g) onions, finely sliced	1 heaped teaspoon paprika
2 crushed cloves garlic	1 pair Debreziner sausages
1 tablespoon tomato purée	2 pickled cucumbers
1 lb 6 oz (600 g) pork (shoulder)	

For this dish the hotter *Rosenpaprika* might be preferred. More often than not, cucumbers pickled in vinegar are used – cucumbers pickled in brine are considered too mild – but on no account use pickled gherkins, which are much too acidic.

Melt the lard in a thick saucepan or flameproof casserole, add the diced bacon and fry until the fat from the bacon has melted. Add the onion and garlic, cover with a lid and allow them to soften. Increase the heat, remove the lid and fry gently until the onion is golden brown. Add the tomato purée and the finely sliced meat. Stir, then add salt, caraway seeds, paprika and just enough water to prevent burning. Simmer very gently in a covered saucepan or casserole until the meat is tender, adding liquid only if necessary. Slice the sausages fairly thinly and chop the pickled cucumber, and add both to the meat. Simmer for another five minutes and serve. The gravy is sometimes thickened with a teaspoon of flour slaked with a little water towards the end of the cooking time and before adding sausages and cucumber, but I much prefer it in its 'natural' state.

FLEISCH RAUGGN MIT KRÄUTER RAHMSAUCE

Meat Balls with Herb Sauce

A Carinthian speciality. To be really authentic the top and sides of the meat balls should be flattened a little during the frying.

Serves 4
5 oz (150 g) rye bread
  (without crusts)
1 lb (500 g) lean minced
  smoked pork
1 – 2 eggs
salt
chopped basil and
  chopped savory
lard or oil for frying

For the sauce
1 heaped teaspoon each of
  chopped tarragon, basil,
  chervil and lovage
$\frac{1}{2}$ teaspoon chopped mint
salt
1 tablespoon plain flour
scant $\frac{1}{4}$ pint (125 ml) sour
  cream
8 fluid oz (225 ml) water

Soak the bread in water, then squeeze out all moisture. Mix together meat, eggs, bread, salt and herbs. Shape into small dumplings with a spoon and fry them crisply on all sides in hot oil or lard. Set them aside as soon as they are fried.

Pour off all superfluous fat from the pan and add the chopped herbs, a pinch of salt and about 2 tablespoons water. Scrape bottom and sides of the pan so that all the bits adhering are incorporated. Stir, then add the meat balls. Cover with a lid and leave to simmer for about ten minutes. Do not add any more liquid unless absolutely necessary. Mix the flour with the water, add to the meat, bring to boil and leave to simmer until well thickened. Add sour cream, leave to cook for a little to blend. Adjust seasoning if necessary.

GEFÜLLTE SCHWEINSSCHNITZEL

Stuffed Pork Escalopes

Serves 4
1 small onion
a sprig of thyme
a little parsley
6 oz (160 g) lean minced
  pork
2 eggs
fine fresh breadcrumbs
salt and pepper
8 small pork escalopes

1 tablespoon butter, lard
  or oil
a little clear stock
2 – 3 tablespoons finely
  chopped capers
salt and pepper
5 fluid oz (140 ml) double
  or sour cream

Chop onion very finely, together with thyme and parsley, and add to the minced pork. Work in the eggs and just enough fine breadcrumbs to give a fairly loose mixture. Season with salt and pepper. Set aside for about fifteen minutes, by which time the mixture will have thickened a little.

Flatten the pork escalopes with a rolling pin or cleaver and spread each escalope with a little of the minced pork. Roll up the escalopes and fasten each roll with a small wooden cocktail stick or a toothpick. Heat the fat and brown the little meat rolls on all sides in a thick frying pan, then add just enough stock to prevent them from burning. Cover with a lid and leave to simmer very gently until the meat is tender. Arrange the meat rolls on a warmed dish and keep hot.

Stir capers into the residue in the pan, add cream or sour cream and cook until thickened. Season with salt and pepper and pour over the meat before serving.

SCHWAMMERLFLEISCH

Pork and Mushroom Casserole

Serves 4

1 medium-sized onion	chopped marjoram
2 tablespoons olive oil	2 – 3 juniper berries
½ lb (225 g) mushrooms	coriander
1 lb (450 g) small potatoes	salt
1½ – 2 lbs (670 g – 900 g) lean pork	peppercorns
2 chopped tomatoes	

Finely slice the onion and soften in the oil over low heat in a flameproof casserole dish. Clean the mushrooms, leave whole if small; otherwise halve or quarter them. Add mushrooms to softened onion, turn up the heat and fry onion and mushrooms together, then add scrubbed but not peeled potatoes and stir over heat until browned. Add sliced meat, stir, then add tomatoes, marjoram, crushed juniper berries, coriander, salt and a few peppercorns. Put into the oven at Gas Mark 3, 325°F, 160°C for about 1½ hours – there is practically no added liquid needed, but check from time to time.

SCHWEINSBRATEN

Roast Pork

Braten means 'roast' – although there are dishes such as *Wiener Rostbraten* and *Esterhazy Rostbraten* which are not roast at all. *Schweinsbraten*, however, *is* roast: deliciously so.

Serves 4 – 6

boned loin of pork
  weighing about 3 lbs
  (1½ kilos), scored
coarse salt
1 crushed garlic clove
French mustard (optional)
pepper
paprika

1 teaspoon caraway seeds
2 – 3 tablespoons olive oil
1 – 2 carrots
1 medium-sized onion
½ small celeriac
2 tablespoons double or
  sour cream

Best with young pork and of course the rind should be left on the meat. Get the butcher to bone the meat for you, and ask to keep the bones – it will greatly improve the flavour of the roast and the bones will also make a good basis for stock.

Choose a roasting tin which is only slightly larger than the meat – this is important. Heat some water in the roasting tin to the depth of the fat on the meat. Plunge the meat, skin side down, into the hot water and leave to poach very gently for three to four minutes. Lift the pork occasionally during that time to make sure it does not stick to the tin and make sure that the water does not touch the actual meat. Take out the pork, pat dry with a cloth or paper towel and score with a sharp knife. Put garlic, salt, pepper, paprika, French mustard and caraway seeds into a small bowl and stir in enough olive oil to give a thick paste. Brush over the pork and well into the scored rind. Set aside the meat in a cool place for at least an hour (if you are putting the meat into a refrigerator, cover it loosely with foil).

Preheat the oven to Gas Mark 7, 425°F, 220°C. Pour away the water from the roasting tin and rinse, then wipe dry. Heat about a tablespoon oil in the tin, lightly brown bones and vegetables – no need to cut up the latter, unless carrot and celeriac are very large. Place the meat on top, skin side up, and put roasting tin in the oven. Roast for about eight minutes, then turn down heat to Gas Mark 4 – 5, 350°F – 375°F, 180°C – 190°C. Roast the meat until well done, basting frequently – this will take between 1 – 1½ hours. (If the fat in the roasting tin gets too hot, remove vegetables and throw in one or two peeled potatoes to cool it down.)

When the meat is cooked, remove from the pan and set it on a wire rack or trivet, either on a foil-lined baking sheet or in another roasting tin. Turn up the oven heat to Gas Mark 8, 450°F, 230°C and return the meat to the oven for five to ten minutes for the crackling to crisp.

Meanwhile carefully pour off the fat from the tin in which the meat was roasted. Add a little water to the tin and scrape up all the residue over low heat. Bring liquid to boil in the tin and stir in the sour cream or cream (or 1 teaspoon flour slaked with a little water). Simmer until thickened. Pour into a gravy-boat and serve with the meat.

SCHWEINSJUNGFER IN RAHMSAUCE

Fillet of Pork in Cream Sauce

Fillets of pork sold in one piece are used for this recipe, one fillet usually weighing about 12 oz (340g). Two of these fillets will do nicely for four people.

Serves 4

2 pork fillets in one piece, each weighing about 12 oz (340 g)
a few rashers streaky bacon
pepper
grated lemon rind
chopped marjoram
1 cup good clear stock

dash of brandy or apple brandy
3 tablespoons double cream
chopped parsley

Wipe the fillets and remove any skin or fat adhering to them. Cut the rinds off some streaky bacon rashers and flatten the rashers with a mallet or rolling pin. Rub the fillets with coarsely ground black pepper and sprinkle with a little grated lemon rind and chopped marjoram. Wrap each fillet in bacon rashers, fastening them with small wooden sticks where necessary. Put the wrapped fillet in a roasting tin, add the rind and roast the fillets for about forty-five minutes at Gas Mark 5, 375°F, 190°C, turning them over once.

Remove and chop the bacon, put on a baking sheet and return it to the oven to crisp.

Cut the fillets into medallions, slicing them downwards, and keep them on a warmed dish. Discard the bacon rind, pour off the fat from the roasting tin and pour in a cupful of good stock. Stir over brisk heat, making sure to take up all the sediment from the roasting tin. Add a dash of brandy or, preferably, apple brandy and cook briskly to reduce. Add the sliced pork fillets and the cream. Reduce heat and stir until well blended, then arrange meat and sauce on a serving dish. Sprinkle the crisped bacon over the top as well as a little chopped parsley.

SCHWEINSKARREE BÄCKERINNEN ART

Loin of Pork in Cheese Pastry

Serves 6 – 8
For the pastry
9 oz (250 g) curd cheese
salt
nutmeg
9 oz (250 g) butter
9 oz (250 g) plain flour
egg for glazing

For the filling
3½ lbs (1½ kg) boned loin
  of pork
salt and pepper
paprika
1 medium-sized onion
9 oz (250 g) mushrooms
2 oz (50 g) butter
chopped parsley
2 eggs

Score the pork, rub all over with salt, pepper and paprika and set aside for about an hour.

Sift together flour, nutmeg and salt. Cut butter into the flour, then crumble in the curd cheese, handling the mixture as lightly and as little as possible. Pat into a round, cover with a cloth and chill for at least half an hour.

Roast the pork at Gas Mark 6, 400°F, 200°C for 1¾ hours, basting frequently. Remove from heat and set aside to cool.

Meanwhile chop the onion and soften it in the butter. Add parsley and mushrooms and simmer gently until the mushrooms are soft. Add salt and pepper. Remove from heat and leave to cool a little, then stir in the beaten eggs. If possible chill before use.

Put the pork, fat side down, onto a working surface and cover with the mushroom mixture. Roll out the pastry on a floured board to about ¼ inch thickness and large enough to enclose the pork. Put the pork in the centre and wrap pastry over the meat. Secure the ends and trim away pastry. Press edges firmly together to seal. Cut small shapes from the pastry trimmings and use these to cover pastry joins. Set the meat on a baking sheet and brush all over with lightly beaten egg. Place in a hot oven (Gas Mark 6, 400°F, 200°C) and bake for about thirty to forty minutes.

Lean smoked loin of pork – available at most supermarkets – is excellent if treated this way. Roast or boil the meat for twenty minutes to the pound and then proceed as above.

STEIRISCHES WURZELFLEISCH

Styrian Pork with Root Vegetables

Serves 6 – 8

1 shoulder of pork, weighing about 4 lbs (1.8 kg)	salt
	1 crushed garlic clove
	3/4 cup white wine vinegar
5 oz (100 g) each of carrots, celeriac, onion, parsley root, all coarsely grated	freshly grated horseradish
a few juniper berries and peppercorns	
1 bayleaf	

Put the meat into a large saucepan, together with the vegetables and seasonings. Cover with water, add the vinegar and bring to the boil, then lower the heat and simmer until the meat is tender, allowing thirty to thirty-five minutes per pound plus another twenty minutes. Remove the meat from the saucepan and cut it into thick slices. Arrange the meat on a heated serving dish, surround with the vegetables and keep hot.

Strain some of the cooking liquid into a separate saucepan, bring to boil and cook rapidly until reduced to half the quantity. Pour over the meat and sprinkle plenty of freshly grated horseradish over the top. Serve with plain boiled potatoes.

This is the way the dish is usually cooked in Austria – simply and economically – and although the vegetables will have absorbed all the flavour from the meat, they will not look their radiant best. For a more elegant touch, proceed as follows: when the meat is nearly tender, strain about three or four ladlefuls of the liquid in which it is cooking into a separate saucepan. Add a fresh lot of root vegetables – cut into convenient chunks if you like – and cook until tender. Surround the meat with the freshly cooked vegetables, reduce the stock in which vegetables were cooked and pour over the meat. The remaining stock and vegetables can be used to make excellent soup.

SZEKELY GULASCH

Many years ago – so my friend Peter Esterhazy tells me – a Mr Szekely appeared rather late in the day (history does not relate how late) at a famous Budapest restaurant, wishing to dine. All that was left in the kitchen was a meagre portion of *Gulyas* – or possibly *Pörkölt* – and some cooked Sauerkraut which they hardly dared offer to their valued customer, but Mr Szekely was hungry and agreed to try out this unusual combination. It proved a great success, so much so that he returned the next day, accompanied by friends, and asked for a repeat performance. Thus *Szekely Gulasch* was born – quickly adopted by the Viennese who at some time re-named it *Szegediner Gulasch* in order to pay lip service to its Hungarian origin (Szeged is a town in Hungary). Just to make the story complete, my recipe for *Szekely Gulasch* comes from a Mrs Szekely – no relation!

Serves 6 – 8

2¼ lb (1 kg) Sauerkraut
4 oz (110 g) lard or pork dripping
pinch of sugar
1 heaped teaspoon caraway seeds
½ green pepper, de-seeded and cut into strips
stock
salt

2¼ lbs (1 kg) pork (shoulder, shank, leg, knuckle or hand)
2 – 3 medium onions
1 clove garlic
1 tablespoon paprika
pepper
generous ¼ pint (200 ml) sour cream
½ tomato

It may seem strange that for a dish of this type the meat and Sauerkraut should be cooked separately, but this really gives the best results and it is of course exactly how the dish was first created. Drain any liquid off the Sauerkraut and retain it. Cut two or three times through the Sauerkraut with a sharp knife to shorten the strands. Melt half the lard or dripping in a thick saucepan, add the Sauerkraut and brown it very lightly. Add a pinch of sugar and just enough of the drained-off liquid to prevent burning (if there is not enough liquid – some Sauerkraut is packed very dry – add a little stock). Season with caraway seeds and a pinch of salt. (Sometimes Sauerkraut contains caraway seeds, in which case adjust quantity accordingly.) Simmer over low heat for fifty minutes, then add the green pepper and cook for another ten minutes – one hour in all.

Trim the pork and cut it into cubes. Sprinkle with salt. Thinly slice the onions and crush the garlic under the blade of a knife with a little salt. Heat remaining fat in a saucepan or flameproof casserole, add the onion and garlic, stir and cover with a lid. Leave to simmer over very low heat until the onion is soft and transparent. Remove from heat, stir in the paprika and a pinch of pepper, add the meat and stir again. Add the tomato, broken up into smaller pieces and just enough water to prevent burning. Return pan or casserole to very low heat and leave to simmer until the meat is tender – about one hour, though this depends on the cut and quality of the meat – adding a little more water only if necessary.

Stir the Sauerkraut into the meat and finally add the sour cream. Reheat gently, but do not stir too much – the sour cream should be visible in generous streaks.

TIROLER SCHWEINSSTELZE

Knuckle of Pork

Stelze is the knuckle just above the trotter. One knuckle of pork is usually sufficient for two people, but much depends on the size of the knuckle and the appetite of the people concerned – which is why in restaurants *Stelze* is always sold according to weight and not per portion.

Serves 2

1 knuckle of pork
  (unsmoked)
1 garlic clove
1 teaspoon coarse salt
1 teaspoon caraway seeds
1 clove
3 juniper berries
French, preferably
  tarragon, mustard
6 rashers unsmoked bacon

3 tablespoons lard or pork
  dripping
good stock
about 3 tablespoons
  double cream

Blanch the knuckle of pork in 1 inch boiling water for 2½ minutes on each side. Take out of the water, wipe with a cloth or kitchen paper. Crush the garlic with the salt under the blade of a knife, then add the other seasonings and pound everything together. I have found that putting the caraway seeds, clove and juniper berries into my small electric coffee mill works extremely well – but the garlic has to be crushed separately or the coffee grinder would smell of garlic forever after!

Make criss-cross incisions in the surface of the pork. Rub with the crushed spices, garlic and finally spread with the French mustard.

Put 3 of the bacon rashers in a roasting tin, place the knuckle on top and cover with the remaining bacon rashers. Heat the lard or dripping and pour over the top. Roast at Gas Mark 7, 425°F, 220°C for ten to fifteen minutes, then lower the heat to Gas Mark 4, 350°F, 180°C and roast for a further thirty to forty minutes until well done, basting frequently with its own fat and a little stock. For the last five to ten minutes increase to maximum heat to crisp the surface.

Take out the knuckle of pork and the bacon and keep warm. Pour off surplus fat, then add a little stock to the roasting tin and set over medium heat. Take up all the scrapings from the tin, stir and then add cream to thicken the sauce.

BUTTERSCHNITZEL

Veal Meatcakes

Serves 4

3/4 lb (350 g) veal
2 day-old rolls without
    crust
a little milk
salt
nutmeg
about 2 fluid oz (60 ml)
    double cream

2 egg yolks
about 3 tablespoons
    clarified butter for
    frying
a little veal stock
lemon juice

Soak the rolls in milk to soften, then squeeze out all moisture. Mince veal and rolls twice or put through the blender, but do not allow the texture to become too fine. Season with salt and nutmeg and beat in the egg yolks and finally the cream. Shape into four oblong meatcakes.

Heat the butter, add the meatcakes and seal quickly on one side, then fry gently on both sides. Arrange meatcakes on a warmed serving dish, add a little veal stock to the frying pan and stir to take up all the residue from the pan. Let the sauce reduce a little, add lemon juice and pour over the meatcakes.

EINGEMACHTES KALBFLEISCH

Veal Ragout

Serves 4

1½ lbs (700 g) boneless
    veal, preferably shoulder
½ onion
2 carrots
parsley root
½ celeriac
½ small cauliflower
1 bayleaf
salt
5 peppercorns

4 oz (110 g) green peas
6 oz (170 g) mushrooms
1½ oz (40 g) butter
1 oz (30 g) plain flour
2 fluid oz (60 ml) double
    cream
1 – 2 egg yolks
lemon juice
small knob of butter
chopped parsley

Wipe the meat with a damp cloth and cut into convenient pieces. Put the meat into a large saucepan, cover with cold water (to get amount of water right), then pour off the water into another saucepan. Add onion, carrots, parsley root, celeriac, bayleaf, peppercorns and salt. Bring to boil, then add the meat which should just be covered with water and simmer gently until the meat is tender.

Cook cauliflower and peas separately in salted water. Separate cauliflower into florets. Wipe and slice the mushrooms. Melt the butter in a large saucepan, add the mushrooms, cover with a lid and simmer until the mushrooms are tender. Sprinkle with flour and stir, then gradually strain in the stock from the meat, stirring constantly. Slice the carrots and the celeriac, chop parsley root. Discard onion and bayleaf.

Add meat and vegetables to the sauce and simmer gently for ten minutes. Stir egg yolk(s) into cream, add to meat, stirring all the time and taking care that the mixture does not boil. Add nutmeg and a little lemon juice and adjust seasoning if necessary. Just before serving stir in a small knob of butter and sprinkle with chopped parsley.

Markknöderl – small dumplings made with bone marrow (see page 38) – are usually served in the ragout.

GEBRATENE KALBSSTELZE

Roast Knuckle of Veal

Serves 4

2 knuckles of veal	1 – 2 tablespoons butter or
strips of pork fat	dripping
salt and pepper	stock or water

Lard the knuckles of veal neatly, sprinkle with salt and a little pepper. Melt butter or dripping in a baking dish, turn the knuckles in melted fat and then roast them at Gas Mark 5, 375°F, 190°C, basting them frequently with the fat in the tin and a little stock or water. When the meat is tender and nicely browned, set it on a warmed serving dish. Pour off any surplus fat from the baking tin, add a little stock or water and cook over fierce heat, taking up all the scrapings from the baking tin. Let the liquid reduce a little, then pour over the meat and serve.

Another favourite way of dealing with a knuckle of veal is to turn it into *Kalbsvögerl* (literally little veal birds) by removing the bone altogether – cutting right down to the bone first and shaving carefully all round it. You will find that the meat falls into several oblong portions according to the fibres of the meat. Separate meat into these portions, lard them with strips of bacon fat and you can then take your choice from several good ways of cooking them. You can roll up the meat, tie it securely and simmer it gently with onions, tomatoes and a few small carrots, plus some finely chopped herbs and seasoning. Or you can roast them in the oven with a little dripping – cover the baking dish with foil to start with – and finish with a sauce made from the residue in the baking dish and a little sour cream. Or, probably most satisfying of all, you can spread the meat with your preferred stuffing (or prepare a stuffing as for breast of veal), roll up the meat as before and roast or braise it.

GEFÜLLTE KALBSBRUST

Stuffed Breast of Veal

The recipe for the stuffing is my own favourite, used over many years. It is very light and delicate and consequently a bit difficult to handle. Adding a little more bread makes handling easier, but the stuffing loses some of the lightness.

Serves 4 – 6
3 lbs (1 kg 400 g) breast of
  veal
salt and pepper
paprika
a little butter
7 fluid oz (200 ml) clear
  veal or chicken stock
3 tablespoons double or
  sour cream

For the stuffing
½ lb (225 g) day-old bread
  without crusts
7 fluid oz (200 ml) milk
6 – 8 oz (170 g – 225 g) mushrooms
½ small onion or shallot
2 oz (50 g) butter
salt and pepper
1 egg
chopped parsley

Prepare the stuffing in advance and chill it, as this will make it easier to handle. Break the bread into a bowl or dice it, cover it with the milk and leave to soak. Wipe the mushrooms and slice them very thinly. Chop the onion or shallot. Melt the butter, add the onion or shallot and cook gently in the butter until softened. Add the mushrooms, cover pan with a lid and simmer until the mushrooms are cooked. Squeeze out all moisture from the bread. Add the bread to the mushrooms and onion, stir constantly with a wooden spoon until the mixture is well blended and leaves the sides of the pan clean. Remove from heat and tip mixture into a bowl. Lightly whisk the egg with a fork and stir into the mixture. Add salt, pepper and chopped parsley. Cover bowl and set to chill.

Loosen the rib bones of the breast, but do not remove them. Make an incision between top layer of meat and the layer containing the bones to form a pocket. Sprinkle the meat inside and out with salt, pepper and paprika. Fill the meat 'pocket' with the stuffing and sew up the opening. Place the meat in a buttered roasting tin and spread with butter. Add a little stock and cover with a lid or kitchen foil. Roast at Gas Mark 3, 325°F, 160°C, basting from time to time and adding a little more stock as necessary.

At the end of roasting time increase oven heat to Gas Mark 8, 450°F, 230°C. Remove cover, baste the meat again and add a little more butter if necessary. Allow meat to brown for five to ten minutes. Remove meat from the roasting tin and set on a warmed serving dish. Add remaining stock to the meat residue in the roasting tin and bring to the boil, taking up all the scrapings from the tin. Add the cream and cook until thickened. Take out thread from the meat and slice the meat downwards between the bones. Serve sauce separately.

KALBSGULASCH

Veal Goulash

Serves 4

2 lbs (900 g) veal, preferably shoulder	salt
3/4 lb (300 g) onions, finely sliced	1/2 pint (280 ml) sour cream
2 oz (60 g) lard	1 scant tablespoon tomato purée
1 heaped tablespoon paprika	1 tablespoon plain flour

Cut the meat into cubes. Fry onions in fat until golden brown, dust with paprika, stir and immediately add about four tablespoons of water. Add salt and tomato purée and then add the meat. Leave to simmer over very low heat until the meat is tender, stirring from time to time. Mix the flour with the sour cream, add to the meat and simmer for another five to ten minutes until well blended.

Cooks more elegant than I transfer the meat to another dish as soon as it is tender, then add the sour cream slaked with the flour to the onions and cook this until well blended, after which they sieve the resulting gravy over the meat. Looks better, I admit, but whether it is worth the extra trouble . . .?

NATURSCHNITZEL

Serves 4

4 veal escalopes weighing about 5 oz (140 g) each	a little stock
salt and pepper	knob of butter
flour (optional)	a little lemon juice
2 oz (60 g) butter or oil	

Trim the escalopes, beat with a mallet and then make a few incisions around the edges. Dust both sides of each with salt and pepper, and dust one side lightly with flour (the latter being a question of taste). Heat butter or oil in a frying pan and fry escalopes on both sides (floured side first). Keep them hot on a warmed dish. Pour off surplus fat, stir in a little stock, bring to boil, taking up all the scrapings from the pan. Add a knob of butter and a dash of lemon juice, let the mixture bubble and pour over the escalopes. Serve at once.

PARISER SCHNITZEL

Serves 4

4 veal escalopes	3 eggs
salt	lard or clarified butter for
flour	frying

Trim escalopes neatly, make a few incisions round the edges and beat well. Sprinkle them with a little salt, dust lightly with flour and shake off surplus. Dip escalopes separately into lightly beaten seasoned egg and slip them at once into hot fat which should be deep enough for the escalopes to float. Shake the pan gently whilst they are frying on one side, then turn them over to fry on the other side until golden brown. Drain on kitchen paper and serve at once.

RAHMSCHNITZEL

Veal Escalopes with Cream Sauce

Serves 4

4 veal escalopes	juice ½ lemon
flour	1 tablespoon chopped
clarified butter for frying	capers
4 fluid oz (120 ml) sour	salt and pepper
cream	1 teaspoon French
4 fluid oz (120 ml) clear	mustard
stock	

Trim escalopes, beat to flatten and make a few incisions round the edges. Dust with salt and pepper on both sides and dust one side with flour. Fry the escalopes in clarified butter, lift out and keep warm. Pour off any surplus fat from the frying pan, add sour cream, stock, lemon juice, French mustard, capers, salt and pepper. Bring to boil, taking up all the scrapings from the pan. Cook to reduce and strain over meat.

WIENER SCHNITZEL

Buried in Vienna's archives is a report from Field Marshal Radetzky, dated 1848, in which he not only reports on the political and military situation in Lombardy, but also records that the kitchens of Milan were producing an extraordinary dish (*aussergewöhnlich* was his word): a veal cutlet dipped in egg and breadcrumbs and fried in butter. Legend has it that immediately upon his return to Vienna he was summoned to the Imperial Court – I'd like to say that this was because the Emperor wanted to ask him to procure the recipe, but that would be an exaggeration. Radetzky was, however, *also* asked to procure the recipe, presumably after he had made his military report.

As it happens, the Milanese did not invent the dish. It probably came to Italy via Byzantium and Andalusia – but there's no doubt that the Viennese perfected it and that a *Wiener Schnitzel* is seldom, if ever, perfect if ordered in a restaurant outside Austria (some say outside Vienna, but that is probably going too far).

The reasons for this are manifold, starting with the right cut of meat. Fillet of veal which I admit I advocated in *Austrian Cooking* because you are most likely to get it cut in the right way, is expensive and not necessarily the best. *Schlegel* (upper leg) or *Frikandeau* (cut from the lower leg) are better – if you can get them – the latter containing the so-called *Kaiserteil* (the Emperor's share) which gives a fair indication of its suitability. Franz Ruhm, a noted expert and Austria's very first Radio Cook in days gone past, insists on *Frikandeau,* stipulating 'rectangular pieces of meat which in turn consist of two connected parts'. If you can get your butcher to work to that specification you are well on your way to a perfect *Wiener Schnitzel.*

Quality of breadcrumbs (called *Semmelbrösel* – crumbs from a roll – in Austria) is of the utmost importance. These must be good, fine and fresh and it is just as well to remember that *semmelblond* (blonde like a roll) is a much-used colour definition in Austria, meaning that the crumbs should not be toasted (and certainly not dyed).

Thirdly, the fat for frying: it can be good olive oil or lard, but it must be deep enough for the *Schnitzel* to float in the pan. (I always add a good-size knob of butter to the fat in the pan.)

Prepare everything but the meat well in advance – under no circumstances should *Schnitzel* be kept before frying or they will dry out in the most unattractive way. (An American editor once altered my instructions and banished my *Wiener Schnitzel* to the fridge for half an hour before frying, with dreadful consequences.)

The garnish must be a decent wedge of lemon, not a coyly crimped slice, and possibly a sprig of parsley. Nothing else. There is a disdainful note at the end of Olga Hess's recipe for *Wiener Schnitzel* which says 'in Germany *Wiener Schnitzel* is sometimes served with gravy' – and I can still hear the shudder in her voice when we discussed the subject.

Hallmarks of a good *Wiener Schnitzel:* the coating should be golden brown and blistered – almost ruched – and you should be able to slip your knife easily between the coating and the meat. The coating should be crisp and the meat soft and succulent. And the *Wiener Schnitzel* should about cover your plate.

Serves 4

4 veal escalopes weighing 4 – 5 oz (120 g – 140 g) each	2 oz (60 g) plain flour 3 – 4 oz (80 g – 100 g) breadcrumbs
1 large or 2 small eggs	lard or oil for frying
1 teaspoon olive oil	1 dessertspoon butter
salt	

Trim the escalopes neatly, make a few incisions round the edges. Pound them with a mallet but not too fiercely; they should be about the thickness of a pencil. Have ready three soup plates – one with the flour, one with egg beaten lightly with a pinch of salt and the olive oil, and one with breadcrumbs.

Dip the escalopes first into flour, shake off surplus, then into the beaten egg and finally into the breadcrumbs. Do not press down the crumbs, just shake off the surplus. Drop the escalopes into hot fat. Do not fry too many escalopes at the same time – they must have room to float in the hot fat. Fry until golden on one side, shaking the pan very gently so that the hot fat 'washes over' the top of the *Wiener Schnitzel*, then turn the *Schnitzel* over and fry the other side (at most it should take $1\frac{1}{2} - 2$ minutes for each side). Lift out carefully and drain on kitchen paper. Serve at once.

GAME AND POULTRY

GAME

FASAN IN ROTWEIN

Pheasant Cooked with Red Wine

Even the toughest pheasant will succumb if cooked this way.

1 pheasant weighing about 3 lbs (1½ kg)	about 2 cups red wine
salt and pepper	2 tablespoons double cream
paprika	
about 2 tablespoons butter	

Clean the pheasant, then rub inside and out with salt, pepper and paprika and put in a cool place for about one hour.

Put a small lump of butter inside the pheasant, then lift the skin over the breast very gently and slip a lump of butter between skin and flesh on each side. Spread a little softened butter over the outside of the bird.

Put the pheasant, breast side down, into a roasting tin, pour in about a cupful of red wine and cover the tin with a lid or foil. Put the pheasant in the oven at Gas Mark 3, 325°F, 160°C until the pheasant is tender – about one hour (add a little more wine if necessary). Then turn up the heat to maximum and set the pheasant breast side up, on a rack in another roasting tin and leave to brown for another five minutes.

Meanwhile pour off any surplus fat from the juices which will have collected in the first tin, and if the pheasant looks a little dry, baste it with the fat thus collected. Add another cupful of wine to the remaining juices in the first pan, cook briskly on top of stove until reduced by half, making sure that all the scrapings from the pan are incorporated. Stir in the cream and cook gently until thickened. Serve sauce separately.

HASENBRATEN MIT RAHMSAUCE

Saddle of Hare in Cream Sauce

This method of cooking hare is also suitable for other game, particularly if the meat tends to be a little on the tough side.

1 saddle of hare	marjoram
strips of pork fat for	strips of lemon peel
larding	small piece root ginger
1 – 2 carrots	about ¾ pint (scant
1 medium-sized onion	½ litre) red wine
few peppercorns and	6 – 8 rashers unsmoked
juniper berries	bacon
1 – 2 bayleaves	double or sour cream
parsley and parsley root	1 tablespoon redcurrant or
thyme	cranberry jelly

Skin, trim and lard the saddle of hare with strips of pork fat. Slice the carrots and onion, crush peppercorns and juniper berries, gently bruise the ginger.

Put all the vegetables, spices and herbs into a saucepan, add a cupful of water and simmer gently for five minutes. Add the wine, heat through and pour over the meat. Leave covered in a cool place for one to two days, turning the meat over gently from time to time. The quantity of wine depends a little on the type of dish into which the meat is put: it is essential that the meat is completely covered.

Line a roasting tin with bacon rashers. Drain the meat, retaining the marinade, and pat dry with paper towels. Place meat on top of bacon rashers and roast at Gas Mark 5, 375°F, 190°C for about 1¼ hours, basting frequently with the juices from the roasting tin and with the strained marinade. Do not add all the marinade at once, but only as it becomes necessary. When the meat is tender, take it out and keep warm on a platter.

Remove bacon slices, add sliced onions, carrot and parsley root from the marinade to fat and juices in the pan. Brown these on top of the stove, then pour off fat, strain in remaining marinade and leave to simmer until vegetables are soft, which will only take a few minutes.

Pass vegetables through a sieve, return to pan and stir in enough cream or sour cream to thicken. Adjust seasoning if necessary, but usually the bacon will have provided enough salt.

I like to add about a tablespoon of cranberry or redcurrant jelly to the sauce, stirring well to blend, before pouring the sauce over the meat or serving it separately; but in any case cranberries are a 'must' as an accompaniment.

MARCHFELDER REBHÜHNER

Partridge à la Marchfeld

1 partridge serves 2

Some of the plumpest partridges in Austria come from the Marchfeld, the plains that stretch East of Vienna towards the Slovakian border. They are roasted very simply, after being rubbed with salt and pepper, and occasionally a sprig of thyme is put inside each bird. They are then wrapped in *Speck* (or bacon) and roasted at Gas Mark 5, 375°F, 190°C. Baste with a clear broth from time to time. As a rule partridges take no longer than twenty to twenty-five minutes.

Take off the bacon and cut it into small squares then crisp slightly in a frying pan. Put the partridges back into the oven to brown for a few minutes. Halve the partridges and arrange on a serving dish. Sprinkle with the crisped bacon. Pour a little stock into the roasting tin, bring to boil and reduce. Pour over the partridges.

POULTRY

BACKHENDL

Fried Spring Chicken

Although the preparation of *Backhendl* is very similar to that of *Wiener Schnitzel*, their culinary history is completely unconnected. *Backhendl* were known well before *Wiener Schnitzel* made its first appearance: my 1718 edition of Conrad Hagger's *Neues Saltzburgisches Koch-Buch* gives as precise a recipe as one would expect in those days, and there may have been published recipes even before that time. Biedermeier was the great era of the *Backhendl*, however – the period is also known as *goldene Backhendlzeit*, the golden era of Fried Spring Chicken.

The emphasis is on spring: *Backhendl* should weigh no more than 22 – 29 oz (600 – 800 g) and it is generally accepted that half a spring chicken per person is sufficient. After all, this means two portions, plus a share of the fried liver (in Vienna the liver and the stomach are treated in the same way as the chicken parts) . . . but I have known people with comparatively small appetites to polish off a whole *Backhendl* with the greatest of ease – between copious draughts of Heuriger, so be warned (or rather prepared)!

Backhendl is traditionally served with fresh cucumber salad – to celebrate the first glass of new wine, or the last bottle of an old vintage, or an anniversary, or simply gladness to be alive.

Serves 4

2 spring chickens	fine breadcrumbs
plain flour	lard or oil for frying
salt and pepper	parsley
1 – 2 eggs	lemon wedges

Clean and quarter the chickens. Twist back the wings, make an incision on top of the legs and twist them back. Some cooks remove all the skin; others consider this sacrilege, saying that if the skin is too tough the chicken is past the age when it should be used as *Backhendl*, but follow your own taste. Carefully remove all trace of gallbladder from the liver and remove lining from stomach. Halve stomachs and livers.

Heat the fat, which should be about 1 inch deep. Lightly beat the egg, or eggs, and season with salt and pepper. Dip chicken pieces first in flour, then in the beaten egg and finally in the breadcrumbs. Do not press down the crumbs, just shake off the surplus. Treat chicken livers and stomachs in the same way. Fry in smoking hot fat on both sides until golden brown. Drain and serve with crisply fried parsley and wedges of lemon.

HUHN IN SARDELLENSAUCE

Chicken in Anchovy Sauce

Anchovies were very much part of the Viennese culinary scene in the nineteenth century, when 'all Vienna' bought their anchovies at the *Grüne Fassl* at the Kohlmarkt (possibly not only because that is where the best anchovies were sold, but also for a fleeting glance at the owner of the shop, Anna Maria Spöttl, whose close links with the Metternichs, father and son, were the topic of Viennese gossip).

1 boiling fowl or capon cut into 8 pieces	1 teaspoon grated lemon rind
9 fluid oz (¼ litre) clear chicken stock	1 tablespoon finely chopped parsley
9 fluid oz (¼ litre) white wine	juice of 1 lemon
1½ oz (40 g) butter	4 tablespoons double cream
6 anchovy fillets, finely chopped	1 generous oz (30 g) butter
	1 tablespoon plain flour

Poach the chicken pieces in a mixture of chicken stock and wine until tender. Cream the 1½ oz butter, beat in the chopped anchovy fillets, parsley, lemon rind and juice and the cream. Melt the 1 oz butter, stir in the flour and gradually strain in the liquid in which the chicken was cooked. Cook gently, stirring constantly until well blended and thickened, then gradually add the anchovy mixture, but do not allow the liquid to come to the boil. Arrange chicken pieces on a warmed serving dish and pour the sauce over it.

HÜHNERLEBER IN ROTWEINSAUCE

Chicken Livers in Red Wine Sauce

Serves 4 as a first course, 2 as a main course

1 lb (450 g) chicken livers	1 shallot, finely chopped
about ½ pint (¼ l) red wine	salt and pepper
about 2 tablespoons clarified butter	a little plain flour
	2 – 3 tablespoons cream
	dash of brandy

Clean the chicken livers and cut off any sinews and discoloured bits. Cut the livers into fairly thick slices or chunks, put these into a bowl and cover with red wine. Leave for about half an hour.

Drain the livers (retaining the liquid) and pat them dry with kitchen paper. Dust livers very lightly with flour. Fry in clarified butter – do not overcook, they should still be pink inside – then lift them out with a slotted spoon and keep them in a warmed dish. Soften the chopped shallot in the same pan, adding a little more butter if necessary, and then pour in the wine in which the livers were marinated. Stir to take up all the bits from the bottom of the pan and cook briskly until the liquid has reduced by half. Add salt, pepper and a dash of brandy. Stir in cream, reduce heat and simmer until well blended, then add the chicken liver and simmer very gently for another one to two minutes. Serve immediately.

PAPRIKAHENDL

Paprika Chicken

Serves 4

1 medium-sized roasting chicken, weighing about 3 lbs (1.5 kg) or the equivalent in chicken joints
1 large onion, finely chopped
1 heaped tablespoon lard
1 green pepper, de-seeded and sliced
1 heaped tablespoon paprika

salt
1 peeled ripe tomato or 1 teaspoon tomato purée
3 tablespoons sour cream
2 tablespoons double cream
1 scant tablespoon plain flour

Joint the chicken into convenient pieces. Heat the lard in a large thick casserole, add the chopped onion and half the sliced green pepper, cover and soften them over gentle heat. Add the chicken, diced tomato or tomato purée, cover again and simmer for about ten minutes. Add paprika and salt and stir until well blended, then add about ½ cup water, cover and simmer very gently until the chicken is cooked, adding water only if necessary.

Transfer the chicken pieces to another casserole and keep warm. Blend together 2 tablespoons sour cream, flour and a teaspoon of water and stir into the onions and juice in the saucepan. Cook until thickened, then sieve contents of casserole over the chicken pieces. Add cream and cook very gently, uncovered, for a few minutes. Arrange chicken pieces and gravy in a deep serving dish (unless you prefer to bring the casserole to the table), then trickle the remaining tablespoon of sour cream over it and garnish with remaining strips of green pepper.

GEBRATENE ENTE

Roast Duck

Roast duck – roast goose too, for that matter – should have a crisp and crackly skin and meat as soft and succulent as good pâté. If your preference is for underdone slices of duck's breast with soft skin arranged fanwise on a plate, this recipe is not for you. On the other hand, if you have eaten and enjoyed freshly cooked duck or goose in a good Austrian restaurant, this is how it was most likely cooked (although they might have used water – or a dash of eau de vie – instead of the wine, this addition being my own invention).

Serves 4
1 duck
salt

paprika
a glass of red wine

Clean the duck well (I use eyebrow tweezers to remove any stubborn stubbles) then wash and pat it dry with paper towels. Rub it inside and out with salt and paprika, and as you do this, press down where the fat is thickest – at the leg joints – and pay special attention to the bit of skin which overlaps the neck opening. Remove any loose bits of fat: these make lovely dripping when rendered down. Do not truss the duck. Leave it in a cool place for as long as possible – overnight if you can.

Preheat the oven to Gas Mark 6, 400°F, 200°C. Put the duck into a roasting tin, breast side down, and add the red wine. Cover the tin with a lid, put it into the oven and immediately turn down the heat to Gas Mark 3, 325°F, 160°C. After about fifteen minutes the skin should be slightly transparent. Now prick the skin all over with a thin-pronged fork, being careful not to go further than the layer of fat. Turn the duck on its back, replace the lid and put back into the oven until the duck is tender. For a medium-sized duck this should take about forty-five to fifty minutes, but much depends on the distribution of the meat and the proportion of fat. Gently prick the skin every so often and if necessary, press down on the skin where the fat is thickest with the back of a fork to make the fat run.

When the duck is tender, turn up the oven heat to maximum and place the duck on a rack over another roasting tin or over the lid of the tin in which it was roasted (the fat which will have collected in the tin it was cooked in makes superb dripping, and the juices underneath, once the fat has been removed, a very good basis for soups or sauces). Have a good look at the skin of the duck and prick it once more where the fat is thickest. Let the duck cook – without lid, of course – breast side down for about five minutes, then turn it over and complete roasting for another five to eight minutes, until the skin is very crisp and brown.

The exact time depends on how quickly your oven will heat up to top heat and you will simply have to watch it.

In Austria poultry is not carved in thin slices (except in restaurants flirting with *nouvelle cuisine*) but is simply cut into convenient pieces with poultry shears. It tastes much better for it – try it!

GANSLEBER

Goose Liver

In Austria goose liver is rarely made into pâté or terrine. It is cooked very gently in its own fat, put into a jar or earthenware pot and the rendered goose fat is poured over so that it is completely covered and allowed to set. The goose liver is then served from the pot – you spread a little of the rendered goose fat on bread, a thin slice of goose liver and then, and only then, a sprinkling of salt is added. To cook the goose liver so that it literally 'melts' as you cut it is quite an art and this is the time-honoured method which I find best:

Clean the goose liver carefully and remove any adhering fat, thick skin, and sinewy or discoloured bits. Wash the liver and pat it dry with paper towels. Weigh it – you will need roughly the same weight in raw goose fat – the fat which lies between the outer skin and the flesh of the goose.

Poach the goose liver very gently in a mixture of milk and water which must completely cover the liver, for about two minutes. Take out the liver and pat dry with paper towels. Put half the diced goose fat into a small saucepan, set the liver on top and cover with the remaining diced goose fat. Cook gently over medium heat until all the fat has melted, by which time the liver will be cooked. Put the liver into a pot or earthenware jar and strain the melted goose fat over it. Allow to set.

The small crispy bits left in the strainer are called *Grammeln* and are delicious eaten with a sprinkling of salt or made into *Grammelpogatscherln* – (see page 324).

GEBRATENE GANS

Roast Goose

There are subtle differences between roasting a goose and roasting a duck, hence the separate recipes.

Clean and prepare the goose as for roast duck (see page 99), but as a goose is usually very much larger than a duck, mix together salt and paprika (3 parts salt to 1 part paprika) before rubbing the goose with the mixture. Rub inside of the goose with a little crushed marjoram or put a sprig of marjoram inside. Leave in a cool place for a few hours, overnight if possible.

Preheat the oven to Gas Mark 7, 425°F, 220°C. Weigh the goose and allow about half an hour for each pound (this will vary a little according to the ratio of meat to fat and also according to the thickness of the bones, but it is a pretty good guide).

Put the goose into a roasting tin, add a glassful of red wine and cover the tin with a lid or foil. Put the goose into the oven, lower heat to Gas Mark 4, 350°F, 180°C, and cook at this temperature until the skin starts to look transparent.

Remove the lid or foil, put a rack over the tin and put the goose on the rack, breast side upwards. Continue roasting at this temperature. Basting is not necessary, but prick the skin gently to make the fat run (making sure to prick only the fat and not the meat) and also press down gently with the back of a fork where the fat is thickest, round the top of the legs and the breast. If the wings brown too quickly, cover them lightly with foil. Towards the end of the roasting time, turn up the heat to maximum, turn the goose over and allow the back to crisp first, then turn it breast upwards again for a final crisping.

I do not use stuffing, but sometimes I put some small peeled apples inside the goose about half-way through the roasting time. Any stuffing is strictly reserved for the skin peeled off from the neck; sewn up at both ends so that it is like a thick sausage which can then be sliced. Favourite stuffings for the neck are minced lean pork, chestnuts and lightly fried mushrooms or – not traditionally Austrian, but very good – minced Hungarian salami, chopped black olives and cooked chopped chestnuts. The stuffed neck is put into the roasting tin half-way through the roasting time and it will emerge as a deliciously crisp sausage. Slice it to surround the goose which, like roast duck, is cut into portions with poultry shears.

GEBRATENE GANSLEBER

Fried Goose Liver

Serves 4 – 6

1 goose liver weighing about 1 lb (½ kg)
1 scant pint milk
1 generous oz (30 g) blanched almonds cut into strips

3 oz (80 g) rendered goose fat
salt

Put the goose liver into a bowl and cover with milk. Leave for one hour. Take out and dry with kitchen paper. Stud the goose liver with almonds cut into strips. Heat the goose fat and gently fry the liver, basting constantly with the hot fat. Slice the liver and arrange the slices on a warmed serving dish. Pour the hot fat over it and serve.

To serve the goose liver cold, proceed exactly as above but use a little extra rendered goose fat – say 4 oz (100 g). Set the cooked liver in a deep serving dish and pour the goose fat over it. Leave to set completely before serving.

OTHER
MAIN COURSE DISHES

OTHER MAIN COURSE DISHES

COMPOT VON KALBSHIRN

Ragout of Calves Brains

The inclusion of crayfish tails may at first seem odd, but the result is excellent, and the recipe dates back to a time, well over a hundred years ago, when crayfish tails were a favourite addition to all sorts of dishes, even sweet puddings! The original recipe naturally used fresh asparagus tips, but tinned or deep-frozen will do very well.

Serves 4 – 6

2 pairs of calves brains	2 heaped tablespoons
salt and pepper	butter
10 – 12 button mushrooms	chopped parsley
1 small tin asparagus tips	1 tablespoon plain flour
or	$\frac{1}{2}$ pint ($\frac{1}{4}$ litre) veal or
1 small packet deep-	chicken stock
frozen asparagus tips	20 cooked crayfish tails

Soak the brains in cold water for two to three hours, changing the water three or four times and removing any blood clots and as much skin as possible. Poach the brains gently in boiling salted water for eight minutes. Pour off the water. Remove skin from the brains and cut them into slices.

Wash and wipe the mushrooms and cut them into slices. Melt half the butter in a saucepan, add the sliced mushrooms and parsley and simmer gently for ten minutes.

In a separate saucepan melt the remaining butter, stir in the flour and gradually add the stock. Add the mushrooms, the sliced brains and the drained asparagus tips. (If using deep-frozen asparagus, do not pre-cook it, just leave it to thaw and cut it into convenient pieces. A little less stock may be required in this case.) Add the cooked crayfish tails. Leave to simmer very gently for another fifteen minutes, add pepper and adjust seasoning if necessary.

According to the original recipe, the dish should be served surrounded by a ring of puff pastry, but a ring of rice goes very well with it too.

HIRN MIT EI

Calves Brains with Eggs

Serves 4

1 lb (450 g) calves brains	salt and pepper
1 shallot	4 eggs
3 oz (80 g) butter	chopped parsley

Soak the brains for two hours in cold water, changing the water frequently. Blanch brains briefly in boiling salted water, rinse under cold running water and then remove skin. Melt the butter in a thick frying pan, add the finely chopped shallot and soften it, then add the brains and cook them gently, pushing with a wooden spoon as they cook so that eventually they will have the consistency of a thick purée.

Lightly beat the eggs with salt and pepper. When the brains are cooked, add the beaten eggs, stirring constantly until just set. Transfer to a heated serving dish, sprinkle with chopped parsley and serve immediately.

There is another way of serving this dish in which the brains are treated as before, but only the egg whites are added to the frying pan and lightly scrambled. The brains are then arranged in mounds on each separate plate, or on a large serving dish, and the raw egg yolks are put in the centre of each serving, or presented in a row on the large dish. The egg yolk is stirred into each separate portion on the plate, and the heat of the cooked brains should be just enough to set the egg. This version is quite often adopted in restaurants. For home use I would go so far as putting the egg yolks on people's plates, but I'd shy away from setting them out on a serving dish, since the transfer to individual plates demands considerable dexterity.

HIRNPOFESEN

'Poor Knights' filled with Calves Brains

A favourite addition to clear beef broth, but also a dish in its own right, served with a crisp green salad or creamed spinach.

Serves 4

1 small onion or shallot	1 egg yolk
1 tablespoon butter	1 – 2 eggs
1/2 lb (225 g) calves brains	8 slices bread cut fairly
salt and pepper	thin
nutmeg	a little milk
chopped parsley	clarified butter

Chop the onion or shallot very finely and soften in the butter. Clean brains and remove skin. Chop the brains, add to the onion and fry gently. Remove from heat, stir in egg yolk and seasoning and leave to cool. Spread mixture on half the de-rinded bread slices, top with remaining bread and press together gently. Dip 'sandwiches' first into milk, then into lightly beaten whole eggs, and fry in clarified butter.

ERDÄPFELKOCH MIT SCHINKEN

Potato and Ham Pudding

Serves 4

2½ oz (70 g) butter
4 egg yolks
1 egg white
5½ oz (150 g) mashed
   potatoes
5½ oz (150 g) finely
   chopped ham

butter for the pudding
   basin
grated Parmesan cheese
   and melted butter to
   serve

Butter a pudding basin. Cream butter and gradually beat in the yolks. Beat in mashed potatoes. Whisk whites until stiff and fold into the mixture. Finally fold in the chopped ham. Pile mixture into the pudding basin, cover and steam for about fifty minutes. Turn out onto a heated serving dish, sprinkle with grated Parmesan cheese and serve with melted butter.

JÄGERBRATEN

Hunter's Roast

Serves 4

½ lb (250 g) lean minced
   beef
½ lb (250 g) lean minced
   pork
½ lb (250 g) minced veal
2 rolls
4 eggs
1 small onion, finely
   chopped
1 tablespoon lard or butter
   or oil

chopped parsley
1 tablespoon finely
   chopped bacon
salt and pepper
strips of streaky bacon
1 tablespoon plain flour
5 fluid oz (140 ml) sour
   cream
1 tablespoon chopped
   capers

Hard-boil two of the eggs. Remove rind from rolls and soak in milk or water. Squeeze out all moisture from the rolls and add to the meat. Soften the onion in lard (or butter or oil) and add to the meat.

Mix together well, add finely chopped bacon, remaining eggs, salt, pepper and parsley. Mix everything together well, then press out into a rectangle. Put the two hard-boiled eggs down the centre, then close the meat over them and shape into a roll.

Set the roll in a baking dish, cover with overlapping strips of streaky bacon. Cover and cook at Gas Mark 5, 375°F, 190°C, removing lid and bacon (keep the bacon warm) towards the end to brown the meat. Arrange meat on a heated dish, surround with bacon strips. Pour off surplus fat from baking dish and sprinkle in about a tablespoon of flour. Stir well, gradually add sour cream, scraping up all the bits from the baking dish. Simmer until well blended, stir in the capers and serve sauce separately.

JÄGERWECKEN

Hunter's Loaf

This is used as an appetizer and for picnics. At an elegant nightclub in the Salzkammergut they used to serve large platters of sliced *Jägerwecken* which they displayed on stabilized rocking-horses around the room. For a picnic, chill well before slicing, then reshape into a loaf and wrap in kitchen foil.

Serves 4

2 large French loaves or 4 – 5 small ones	6 – 8 black olives
6 oz (160 g) lean ham	¼ red or green pepper
6 oz (160 g) cooked smoked tongue	8 oz (225 g) butter
6 oz (160 g) Hungarian salami	1 tablespoon anchovy paste or
2 oz (60 g) Gruyère cheese	2 – 3 mashed anchovy fillets
2 hard-boiled eggs	2 teaspoons French or Austrian mustard
2 – 3 small pickled cucumbers	

Cut off each end of the loaves and carefully scoop out the insides. (If the loaves are very long cut them in half first.) Chop the ham, tongue, salami and cheese. This is best done by hand – a food processor may be used, but do not cut the ingredients too fine. Dice the hard-boiled eggs, pickled cucumbers and the pepper, and cut the olives into slivers.

Cream the butter with the anchovies or anchovy paste and beat in the mustard. Gradually add the other ingredients. Stuff the hollow loaves with this mixture and wrap each loaf in kitchen foil. Chill well before cutting into thin slices.

LAVANTTALER LEBERLAN

A speciality from Carinthia – small buns with a spicy meat filling, to be eaten warm with Sauerkraut or cold with a salad. In Carinthia they are made fist-size, before allowing the dough to rise, but I make mine slightly smaller. When I bake them as a savoury to serve with drinks (and they are excellent for this), I make them smaller still.

Wholemeal flour is better than white flour for the dough. Traditionally the filling consists of cooked lung, heart and pork, including some crackling as well as raw liver, but you can of course use cooked beef or veal, as long as there is a little fat pork and crackling included. The latter may be replaced with a slice or two of lightly fried bacon, but go very easy on the salt in that case.

For about 15 medium-sized rolls

For the dough
9 oz (250 g) wholemeal
  flour
pinch of salt
½ oz (10 g) fresh yeast
6 tablespoons water
pig's caul or melted butter
For the filling
½ lb (200 g) cooked meat
  (see above)
¼ lb (100 g) pig's or calves
  liver

pinch of salt
1 teaspoon finely chopped
  onion
½ crushed clove garlic
chopped basil or savory
chopped mint
pinch of powdered
  rosemary

Sift flour and salt onto a wooden pastry board and make a well in the centre. Dissolve yeast in lukewarm water, pour into centre of flour and knead to a smooth dough. Set to rise in a warm place until doubled in bulk – about fifty minutes.

Prepare filling by mincing the meat and liver twice, or use a food processor, then mix in the other ingredients. If the mixture appears too dry, add a little milk or egg. Shape the mixture into small balls.

Knead the dough again lightly and shape into a roll. Cut into about fifteen equal-sized pieces and flatten each piece with your hands.

Enclose each lot of filling completely with dough, smoothing over the joins. Set them side by side, not too closely, in a buttered and floured roasting tin. Wrap each roll loosely with pig's caul or brush with melted butter. Cover the roasting tin with a cloth and set to rise again for about forty minutes. Bake in a preheated oven at Gas Mark 8, 450°F, 230°C for five minutes, then lower the heat to Gas Mark 6, 400°F, 200°C for a further thirty to thirty-five minutes. As they expand before and during baking, the little rolls will touch and this is as it should be, resulting in a crusty top and soft surrounds. Leave for a few minutes in the pan, then break apart to serve.

SCHINKENSTRUDEL

Strudel Filled with Ham

Strudel paste (see page 275)	2 eggs
melted butter	salt
1 lb (450 g) finely minced ham	nutmeg
8 fluid oz (225 ml) sour cream	2 tablespoons fine breadcrumbs

Pull out the *Strudel* paste as described on page 276 and brush with melted butter. Mix together all the ingredients for the filling – be careful about the salt in case the ham is too salty. Spread filling over two thirds of the *Strudel* dough, then proceed as for Apple *Strudel*, i.e. start rolling up the *Strudel* at the filled end. Set on a buttered and floured baking sheet, brush with melted butter and bake at Gas Mark 4 – 5, 350 – 375°F, 180 – 190°C for about three quarters of an hour.

SPECKLABERLN

Meat Cakes

Serves 4

1 medium onion	1 egg
½ clove garlic	3 – 4 tablespoons oil for frying
salt	paprika
2 oz (50 g) bacon	8 fluid oz (225 ml) sour cream
pepper	a little clear broth
2 day-old rolls	
milk	
11 oz (300 g) lean beef	
11 oz (300 g) pork	

Chop the onion finely. Crush the garlic under the blade of a knife with a little salt. Chop the bacon and put it into a frying pan over a low heat. When the bacon has turned transparent and the fat starts to run, add onion and garlic and lightly fry everything together.

Soak the rolls in milk to soften, then squeeze out all moisture. Mince the beef and the pork. Add fried onions, rolls, garlic and bacon to the meat, as well as the egg, a little pepper and a small pinch of salt. Mix together well and shape into rounds.

Heat oil in a frying pan, fry the rounds until nicely browned on both sides. Remove and keep warm. Add sour cream and paprika to the residue in the frying pan, stir and add a little clear broth, then return the rounds to the pan. Cover frying pan and leave to simmer for about twenty-five minutes.

ERDÄPFELGULASCH

Potato Goulash

2 lb (900 g) potatoes	1 crushed garlic clove
½ lb (225 g) finely sliced onions	1 teaspoon caraway seeds
	about 8 fluid oz (225 ml) clear stock
2 oz (50 g) lard, dripping or olive oil	½ green pepper, thinly sliced
1 tablespoon paprika	
1 tablespoon wine vinegar	1 tablespoon tomato purée
salt and pepper	2 pairs Frankfurter sausages
1 teaspoon finely chopped marjoram	2 tablespoons sour cream

Peel the potatoes and cut them into thickish slices. Soften the onions gently in the lard over low heat. When the onions are soft and slightly transparent, turn up the heat, stir until they are nicely browned, then stir in the paprika. Let it froth up, then add a dash of wine vinegar. Add the potatoes, salt, pepper, tomato purée, marjoram, caraway seeds and garlic. Cover with stock, stir and add the sliced green pepper. Cover and simmer over low heat until the potatoes are soft and just beginning to fall apart. Add sliced Frankfurter sausages and heat gently. Swirl in the sour cream just before serving.

G'RÖSTL

Known in the Tyrol as *G'röschl*, and in the rest of Austria as *Tiroler G'röstl*. The meat used may well be a mixture of beef, pork and veal and quite often cooked meat is used to make *G'röstl* – though the original recipe starts from scratch with raw meat. Whether using cooked or raw meat, the potatoes must be cooked separately since it is the difference in textures – meat melting into a sauce and crisply fried potatoes which are added just before serving – which are the hallmark of a good *G'röstl*.

Serves 4 – 5

1 medium-sized onion	1 teaspoon caraway seeds
1 lb (450 g) lean meat (see above)	1 bayleaf
	a little chopped marjoram
3 lbs (1.35 kg) potatoes	4 tablespoons meat gravy or stock
4 oz (100 g) pork dripping	
salt and pepper	

Slice the onion finely. Cut the meat into fairly small pieces. Boil, peel and slice the potatoes. Heat about a third of the dripping in a frying pan, add the onion and soften, then increase the heat, add the meat and brown everything together. Add salt, pepper, bayleaf, caraway seeds and marjoram, stir, then cover and leave to simmer gently with the meat gravy or stock until the meat is cooked.

Melt the remaining dripping in another frying pan, add sliced potatoes and fry until nicely crisp and brown on both sides, turning them with a fish slice from time to time. If necessary reduce liquid with the meat, then add potatoes to meat, remove bayleaf and serve at once.

KALBSBEUSCHERL

Ragout of Lights and Heart

Kalbsbeuscherl was once a 'poor people's' dish: good, economical and filling, at its best at a simple inn where much care was taken with its preparation. In more prosperous restaurants – or at home if you felt prosperous – cream, sour cream or rich gravy were added and simple *Kalbsbeuscherl* was turned into *Rahmbeuscherl* ('with sour cream') or *Salonbeuscherl* ('fit for higher social strata').

Then labour became expensive (cooking *Beuscherl* is a somewhat time-consuming process), and suddenly *Beuscherl* could be found only in the very best – and mostly expensive – restaurants, where it suddenly became fashionable. Today there is hardly an exclusive restaurant in Austria which does not pride itself on its special *Beuscherl*. You can still find it in country inns, but as Günther Sanin, one of my favourite Austrian chefs, is fond of saying: '*Beuscherl* is a matter of trust', meaning that it is only as good as the raw materials and the care and attention that have gone into its preparation.

Serves 4

½ calves lights and ½ calves heart, weighing together about 1¾ lbs (750 g)
1 bayleaf
1 onion
1 carrot
1 parsley root
sliver celeriac or a few celery tops
sprig of thyme
clove
few peppercorns
salt
dash of wine vinegar

2 oz (60 g) butter or good dripping
2 oz (60 g) plain flour
2 cucumbers pickled in brine
2 anchovy fillets
1 shallot
1 heaped teaspoon capers
1 teaspoon French mustard
rind of ½ lemon, finely grated
little lemon juice
¼ pint (140 ml) sour cream

Wash the lights and the heart well, put in a saucepan with bayleaf, onion, carrot, parsley root, celeriac, thyme, clove and peppercorns. Cover with cold water, add a pinch of salt and a dash of vinegar and simmer gently for about 1½ hours. After that time the lights should be cooked. Take out the lights and refresh with lightly salted cold water.

The heart will take a little longer to cook – leave to simmer until tender. Cut heart and lights into short, thin strips, discarding any tubes or gristle.

Melt the butter or dripping, add the flour and prepare a light brown roux. Chop the pickled cucumbers, shallot and capers very finely and add to the roux with the anchovies and mustard. Stir until well blended, then add a dash of wine vinegar and slowly add the strained liquid in which the lights and heart were cooked. Leave to simmer gently for twenty to thirty minutes, stirring from time to time, then add heart and lights, lemon rind and juice. Leave to simmer for another fifteen minutes, adjust seasoning if necessary and stir in the sour cream. Reheat gently and serve in deep soup plates. Semmelknödel (see page 139) are the usual accompaniment.

When *Kalbsbeuscherl* is elevated to *Salonbeuscherl* – indicating that it is *salonfähig* (fit for the best tables) – the sour cream is left out, but a large spoonful of good *Gulasch* gravy is spooned into the centre of each plate just before serving.

STEIRISCHES RAHMFLEISCH

Styrian Ragout

Serves 2

2 oz (50 g) veal	2 fluid oz (50 ml) white
2 oz (50 g) lean pork	wine
2 oz (50 g) boned chicken	4 tablespoons meat glaze
leg	3 tablespoons double
1 tablespoon butter	cream
salt and pepper	1 teaspoon cooked
rosemary	cranberries
2 oz (50 g) mushrooms	lemon juice
1 teaspoon finely chopped	
onion	

Cut the meat into thin slices. Melt the butter, throw in the meat, add salt, pepper and a dash of rosemary and fry quickly on both sides. Take out and keep warm. Soften the onion very gently in the same pan as the meat, adding a little more butter if necessary, then add the mushrooms, cover and simmer gently until the mushrooms are cooked – about five minutes. Add the wine and cook without a lid to reduce. Add the meat glaze, cream and cranberries. Bring to boil quickly, stirring constantly, then add the meat. Bring to boil again, then lower the heat and simmer for two to three minutes. Add the lemon juice and adjust seasoning.

Erdäpfelschmarrn (see page 160) and a fresh green salad are the traditional accompaniments.

SERBISCHES REISFLEISCH

Serbian Risotto

There are a great number of variations concerning this traditional dish, the main point at issue being whether the meat should be veal or pork. No hard and fast rules about this – you can use either, or both, and even add beef if you like: but if pork is used it should be fairly lean.

Serves 4

1¼ lb (500 g) stewing veal or lean pork	salt and pepper
1 large onion	1 tablespoon paprika
1 green or red pepper	about 3 cups water
4 oz (100 g) fat bacon or 2½ oz (60 g) lard or dripping	chopped marjoram
	1 tablespoon tomato purée
	9 oz (250 g) arborio rice
	grated Parmesan cheese

Cut the meat into bite-sized cubes. Peel and chop the onion finely. Remove the seeds from the pepper and cut the flesh into strips. De-rind and dice the bacon.

Heat the bacon in a thick saucepan over low heat until transparent and the fat starts to run, then add the onion and brown in the fat with the bacon (if using lard or dripping, heat gently and lightly brown the onion in this). Add the green pepper, stir, and then add salt, pepper, paprika and a cupful of water and simmer for five minutes. Add the meat, marjoram and tomato purée. Cover and simmer gently for about twenty-five minutes. Add a little more water during this time only if necessary – there should be enough juice from the meat.

Rinse and drain the rice and stir into the dish, together with 2 scant cups of water. Cover and simmer until rice is tender. Add more water if necessary, but you should find that after fifteen to twenty minutes meat and rice are tender and that all the liquid has been absorbed. This is not a 'dry' risotto, though the grains of rice should be separate.

In Austria the risotto is usually pressed into dariole moulds which are then inverted onto a plate, but you can serve it just as it is, piled into a serving dish. Sprinkle liberally with grated Parmesan cheese and serve more Parmesan separately.

LEBERWÜRSTE OHNE DARM

Liver Sausages without Skin

I found this recipe in a cookery book dated 1846 which, like most cookery books of that time, was rather vague about quantities. After experimenting with several variations I think this is a recipe well worth resurrecting. If the sausages are made small enough, they are excellent as a snack to serve with drinks, but they also make a good main course served with vegetables or a salad.

½ lb (225 g) calves liver	finely chopped fresh
milk	marjoram
½ small onion	pinch of nutmeg
3 – 4 tablespoons fine	tiny pinch of chopped
fresh breadcrumbs	thyme
1 egg	6 large or 12 small slices
salt and pepper	bacon
paprika	

Put the liver in a dish and cover with milk. Leave for one to two hours, then remove from the milk and pat dry with kitchen paper. Peel and grate the onion, mince the liver finely, then mix together with the breadcrumbs, egg, seasonings and herbs. The quantity of breadcrumbs depends on the size of the egg and on how long the mixture is subsequently left in a cool place. Beat the mixture really well with an electric whisk until it begins to thicken. Cover and set aside in a cool place for one hour.

If the bacon slices are large, cut them in half. Place 2 teaspoons of the mixture on each slice of bacon and roll up. Place the rolls close together in an ovenproof dish, folded edges underneath. Cover with a lid or foil and bake for one hour at Gas Mark 4, 350°F, 180°C. Uncover, increase heat to Gas Mark 8, 450°F, 230°C and bake for a few more minutes until crisp. Drain on kitchen paper before serving.

GEFÜLLTE KOHLRABI

Stuffed Kohlrabi

Serves 4

4 kohlrabi	1 roll soaked in milk
2 shallots	1 – 2 eggs
1 tablespoon butter or lard	clear beef broth
salt and pepper	sugar
marjoram	chopped parsley
7 oz (200 g) minced veal or pork (or a mixture of both)	

Peel the kohlrabi, cut off lid and scoop out insides, leaving only a shell. Chop the scooped-out flesh, and the shallots. Melt lard or butter and soften shallots, then add chopped kohlrabi and finely chopped kohlrabi tops, salt, pepper and marjoram. Blend well, then allow to cool a little. Mix with meat and roll from which all moisture has been squeezed. Work in the egg(s) and stuff the kohlrabi shells with this filling.

Set them side by side in a casserole, add enough clear broth to come about half-way up the kohlrabi, then season with salt and a pinch of sugar. Cover and either simmer on top of the stove or put the dish into a medium oven (Gas Mark 3, 325°F, 160°C) until kohlrabi are cooked. Lift them out and keep them warm on a heated dish. Reduce liquid in the casserole to half by boiling rapidly and pour over kohlrabi. Sprinkle with chopped parsley.

GEFÜLLTES KRAUT

Stuffed Cabbage Leaves

Serves 4
8 large cabbage leaves
1 small onion, finely
  chopped
1 heaped tablespoon
  butter
½ lb (225 g) lean minced
  beef
½ lb (225 g) lean minced
  pork
salt and pepper
caraway seeds
marjoram
8 bacon rashers

For the sauce
1 small onion, finely
  chopped
1 large or 2 small red or
  green peppers
butter or lard for frying
a little good stock
salt and pepper
paprika
sour cream (optional)

Scald the cabbage leaves with boiling salted water and leave for about five minutes. Drain, pat dry with paper towels and cut out the thick stems if necessary. Fry the chopped onion in butter, add meat and seasonings. Blend well. Spread out the cabbage leaves, put some of the filling in the centre of each leaf and roll up. Wrap a thin slice of de-rinded bacon around each roll and tie up with thread or fix with a small wooden cocktail stick.

De-seed the peppers and chop coarsely. Gently fry the onion and peppers in butter or lard until softened. Add stock to cover. Season with paprika.

Set the stuffed cabbage leaves in a casserole, pour over the peppers and stock. Cover with a lid or foil and leave to cook gently either in the oven at Gas Mark 3, 325°F, 160°C or over low heat for about 1½ hours, adding more stock if necessary. Just before serving remove cover and increase oven heat to brown the tops of the bacon or place for a few minutes under a hot grill. Adjust seasoning if necessary. The sauce may be pushed through a sieve and thickened with sour cream. Serve the stuffed cabbage leaves in the dish in which they were cooked.

GEFÜLLTE PAPRIKA

Stuffed Green Peppers

Serves 4	*For the sauce*
4 large green peppers	1 small onion
1 small onion	1 lb (450 g) ripe tomatoes
1 tablespoon butter or	1 tablespoon butter or oil
good dripping	salt and pepper
2 oz (50 g) rice	good pinch of sugar
3/4 lb (350 g) minced meat	1 teaspoon plain flour
(see note below)	dash of wine vinegar
chopped parsley	thyme
salt and pepper	marjoram

The best mixture is pork and lean beef in about equal quantities. Beef and veal is good too, but in that case it should be two parts beef and one part veal.

Begin by preparing the tomato sauce: chop the onion finely, heat butter or oil in a thick saucepan, add onion and brown very lightly. Throw in the tomatoes, chopped coarsely or broken in half. Add salt, pepper and a good pinch of sugar. Toss the tomatoes in hot butter with the onion, then add flour and stir. Barely cover tomatoes with water (or good stock), add a good dash of vinegar and the herbs and simmer very gently until the tomatoes are pulpy.

Meanwhile cut the tops off the green peppers. Remove seeds and white inside parts and pour boiling water over the peppers. Leave to stand for three to five minutes, then drain. Peel and chop the onion finely. Melt butter or dripping, soften the chopped onion in the fat, then add the rice and fry until rice is transparent. Add 3/4 cup water, cover and leave to simmer until the water has been absorbed by which time the rice will be half-cooked. Add the minced meat, chopped parsley, salt and pepper and mix everything together.

Fill the green peppers with this mixture – do not pack too tightly – and replace lid on each pepper. Stand the peppers in a deep casserole. If any of the meat and rice mixture is left over – this depends entirely on the shape of the peppers – form it into small balls and place around the peppers.

Sieve the tomatoes, adding all the cooking liquid. The sauce should be fairly thin – add a little more water, stock or tomato juice if it is too thick. Pour the sauce over the stuffed peppers in the casserole, cover with a lid and either put it in the oven at Gas Mark 3 – 4 (325 – 350°F, 160 – 180°C) or let it simmer very gently on top of the stove for 1 1/4 – 1 1/2 hours until tender. Adjust seasoning if necessary and serve with rice or plain boiled potatoes.

There is, as always, a short cut to the tomato sauce: fry the onion as described, then add a large tin of peeled tomatoes (14 oz) and leave to simmer for a little while. Sieve the tomatoes, add seasonings and herbs, then add a large tin (1 lb 12 oz) tomato juice and a tin (12½ oz) of V.8. Pour over green peppers as described and cook as before – little, if any, seasoning will be required. Slake a scant teaspoon of flour with a little of the liquid, stir into the sauce and leave to cook for another five minutes.

SÜSSES FASCHIERTES KRAUT

Stuffed Cabbage

A very old recipe – opulent to the point of being slightly wicked: imagine using half a goose liver as a stuffing for cabbage! Except that geese and their livers were plentiful and cheap in those days. The recipe is typical of all that was good in life under the Austro-Hungarian Monarchy . . .

My original recipe left one to guess the weight of 'half a goose liver'. The largest goose liver I have ever seen taken out of a goose (as against those bought at special shops in Vienna which could, of course, weigh much more) was weighed with great ceremony by my grandmother watched over by what seemed to me half the population of our village, and tipped the scales at 960 g. All that was missing was a round of applause! Coming back to the recipe however, I find that the same weight as the cooked veal – or simply 250 g (9 oz) – is about right – and chicken or duck's liver can be used instead, but soak it in milk for an hour or so before use as it greatly improves the flavour.

Incidentally, this is one of the few recipes which does not call for a 'firm white cabbage'. In fact, the looser the leaves are packed, the better.

Serves 4

1 white cabbage	salt and pepper
salt	1 – 2 tablespoons double
	or sour cream
For the filling	3 egg yolks
9 oz (250 g) goose liver (or	10 oz (280 g) chopped veal
chicken or duck's liver)	
fine white breadcrumbs or	*For the sauce*
plain flour	½ pint (280 ml) veal or
rendered goose fat or	chicken stock
dripping for frying	4 – 5 peppercorns
½ small onion	pinch of powdered mace
chopped parsley	1 tablespoon butter
½ day-old roll	1 scant tablespoon plain
milk	flour

Remove outer leaves of cabbage if necessary, make a few incisions across the stalk with a sharp knife. Pat the cabbage into a bowl and pour boiling salted water over it. Leave to stand until the water has cooled.

Meanwhile prepare the filling. Slice the goose liver and dust very lightly with fine breadcrumbs or flour. Quickly fry the goose liver on both sides, either in rendered goose fat or in dripping.

Soak the roll in milk. Chop the onion very finely. Squeeze out all moisture from the roll. Mince the goose liver and the veal. Blend together veal, goose liver, roll, chopped onion and parsley, salt, pepper, egg yolks and cream.

Separate leaves of the cabbage. Cut off the stalks and set them aside. Butter a soufflé dish or deep ovenproof dish. Line with cabbage leaves and spread a layer of filling on the leaves, cover with more cabbage leaves and continue in this way until all the filling has been used up, ending with a layer of cabbage leaves. Cover with buttered foil and either steam for three quarters of an hour or stand the dish in a baking dish with water half-way up the sides and bake at Gas Mark 5, 375°F, 190°C for the same time.

To prepare the sauce, add the cabbage stalks, peppercorns and mace to the stock and simmer gently for fifteen minutes. Melt the butter, stir in the flour and gradually strain in the stock. Simmer until well blended and thick. When the cabbage is ready, turn it out onto a heated serving dish and either surround with the sauce or serve it separately.

Incidentally, the name of the dish means 'sweet minced cabbage' though no sugar is added and only the filling is minced. Nor was it meant to be a complete course – it was surrounded by fried or grilled cutlets and 'for special occasions' the filling was further enriched with crayfish tails!

CHEESE AND EGG
DISHES

CHEESE

KÄSE TIMBALEN

Cheese Timbales

Schloss Sighartstein near Salzburg was the family home of Countess Palffy who, helped by her husband and entire family, ran it for many years as a superbly comfortable castle hotel. The cooking was outstandingly good; there was a large and treasured collection of recipes started by Countess Palffy's mother (some handwritten by Frau Anna Sacher) and I found – or rather re-discovered – marvellous dishes at every visit. *Diplomatenpudding* (see page 255) was one such discovery, *Käse Timbalen* another.

Quantities are sufficient for 8 1/4 pint (140 ml) moulds or 1 large mould holding 2 – 2 1/4 pints

9 fluid oz (250 ml) double cream	3 oz (80 g) grated Parmesan cheese
3 eggs	pinch of salt

Heat the cream in a thick saucepan and bring to the boil, then remove from heat and leave to cool. Whisk in the eggs and a pinch of salt, then fold in the cheese. Half-fill eight buttered 1/4 pint (140 ml) timbale or dariole moulds with the mixture, or pour into a buttered 2 – 2 1/4 pint savarin ring.

Stand the mould (or moulds) in a baking tin half filled with cold water and put into a preheated oven at Gas Mark 7, 425°F, 220°C. Baking time for individual moulds is thirty-five to forty minutes, for one large mould fifty to sixty minutes. Turn out onto warm plates or dish and serve at once.

LIPTAUER

There must be as many variations of *Liptauer* as there are cooks who swear that it is their speciality. Some say that chives have no place in a genuine *Liptauer*, only finely chopped onions being allowed; others insist that a dash of beer adds that special touch; and you could, of course, take the easy way out and serve *Liptauer* as it is served in many Austrian restaurants with the basic butter/curd cheese mixture in the centre, dusted with a sprinkling of paprika and surrounded by small piles of the other ingredients so that everyone can mix it according to their own preference. Using a low fat soft cheese, the proportions of butter and cheese should be equal, but if you use a medium fat soft cheese the butter should be halved in quantity and if you use a full fat cream cheese the addition of butter will be barely necessary – perhaps just a token quantity. The following is my own recipe, which can of course be varied at will.

Serves 8

½ lb (¼ kg) low fat soft cheese
½ lb (¼ kg) butter
1 teaspoon caraway seeds
2 teaspoons paprika
⅕ oz (5 g) chopped capers
1 heaped teaspoon mustard
2 anchovy fillets, finely scraped

pinch of salt
1 shallot, finely chopped or equal quantity of chopped chives
1 heaped teaspoon finely chopped pickled cucumber

Beat together butter and cheese, then mix in all the other ingredients. Arrange on a serving dish or in a bowl and decorate by making a few indentations with the back of a knife.

PARMESANDUNSTKOCH

Cheese Ring

Serves 6 – 8

4½ oz (120 g) butter
salt
6 eggs
3 oz (80 g) grated Parmesan cheese
9 fluid oz (¼ l) sour cream

5½ oz (150 g) plain flour
butter and flour for the savarin ring
finely chopped ham for garnish

Cream butter with a pinch of salt until light and fluffy. Separate eggs. Beat yolks into creamed butter, alternately with the grated Parmesan cheese. Gradually add the sour cream and beat in the flour. Whisk whites until stiff and fold into the mixture. Butter and flour a large savarin ring and pile the mixture into this. Steam for three quarters of an hour. Turn the ring onto a warmed serving dish. Surround with finely chopped ham.

A sharp tomato sauce goes well with this.

TOPFENKAS

A favourite spread for thick country bread, particularly in Lower Austria.

1 - 2 floury potatoes, cooked in their skin	1 clove garlic, crushed
9 oz (250 g) curd cheese	salt and pepper
1 generous oz (30 g) melted butter	paprika
	a little sour cream

Peel the potatoes and allow to cool. Grate rather finely, then mix with the curd cheese. Add crushed garlic clove to butter, beat into the potato mixture and season with salt, pepper and a generous quantity of paprika. Add a little sour cream to give a soft spreading consistency.

EIERTANZ (OR 'TANZENDE EIERSPEIS' – DANCING EGGS)

This recipe for *Eiertanz* comes from *Wienerisches bewährtes Kochbuch* by Ignaz Gärtler and Barbara Hikmann, in the 1812 edition which also gives a recipe for '*Eierspeise auf englische Art*' with anchovies and mushrooms.

Hardboil 14 eggs, cut 12 of these into rounds and mash the remaining ones. Soak a 4-Kreuzer roll [as one might say a 'twopenny roll'] in milk, squeeze out the liquid and mix with 2 eggs, some finely cut crayfish tails, 1 Seitel (about 1/3 litre) cream, nutmeg, 1 Vierting (140 g) crayfish butter. Reserve a little of the butter and the cream. Mix everything together well, use the reserved butter to grease a dish, spread mixture into the dish and cover with the sliced eggs, cover with a layer of the mixture and repeat until sliced eggs and mixture are used up, finishing with a layer of the creamed mixture. Trickle reserved cream over the top, dot with butter, sprinkle with breadcrumbs and bake slowly.

A more recent version is as follows:

Serves 4

4 hardboiled eggs	2 tablespoons fine breadcrumbs
1 roll (crumb only)	salt
2 oz (50 g) butter	6 oz (170 g) morels
2 eggs	
8 tablespoons double cream	

Mix hardboiled egg yolks with the moistened crumbs of the roll. Cream butter, add egg and roll mixture, eggs, 3 tablespoons cream, breadcrumbs and a pinch of salt. Slice morels and the hardboiled egg whites.

Butter a flameproof dish and pour in a tablespoon of cream. Spread a third of the butter mixture into the dish, sprinkle with half the morels and egg whites, cover with more butter mixture then remaining morels and egg white and top with the remaining butter mixture, moistening the morel mixture with 2 – 3 tablespoons cream. Pour a little cream over the top and dot with butter.

Bake at Gas Mark 5, 375°F, 190°C until golden brown.

WIENER EIERSPEIS'

Not scrambled eggs and not an omelette, but a typically Viennese speciality which lies somewhere between the two. A favourite light luncheon dish to order at a Viennese coffeehouse where – if it is a good, old-fashioned coffeehouse – they will ask whether you would like your *Eierspeis'* cooked in butter or dripping.

Eierspeis' is always served in and eaten from the dish in which it was cooked, called *Eierspeispfandl* in Vienna: a small, round enamel or flameproof porcelain pan with short handles, just large enough for 2 – 3 eggs.

For *Wiener Eierspeis'* allow 2 – 3 eggs per person and beat them lightly with a pinch of salt. Melt a large lump of butter or dripping in the pan and when the butter starts to froth, pour in the eggs. Leave to set for a few seconds, then stir very lightly – the whites should be clearly discernible. Grind a little pepper over it, sprinkle with chopped chives and serve at once.

Good dark bread – what they call *Hausbrot* in Austria – spread thickly with fresh country butter, is the best accompaniment.

SARDELLEN SOUFFLE MIT SCHNITTLAUCH SAUCE

Anchovy Soufflé with Chive Sauce

'Vice President and Corporate Executive Chef of Cunard Lines' sounds quite a mouthful (no pun intended), but that is the official title of Rudi Sodamin, a brilliant chef and author of several cookery books. A native of Styria, his recipes have a typical Austrian touch, also shown by his preference for anchovies and yet another version of chive sauce.

Serves 6

For the soufflé	*For the sauce*
½ pint (300 ml) milk	⅓ pint (200 ml) white wine
5 oz (150 g) plain flour	⅓ pint (200 ml) double
1 generous oz (30 g) butter	cream
1 7 oz (200 g) tin	2 finely chopped shallots
anchovies	1 scant oz (20 g) butter
6 egg yolks	1½ oz (40 g) red caviar,
8 egg whites	lightly smoked
2 tablespoons cornflour	salt and pepper
butter and flour for the	about 2 tablespoons
soufflé dish	chopped chives

Slake flour with milk and bring to boil, stirring constantly. Cook gently until thickened, remove from heat and stir in cold butter. Gradually stir in egg yolks and finally the drained and chopped anchovies. Whisk egg whites until stiff and fold cornflour into them. Fold whites into anchovy mixture. Bake in a buttered and floured soufflé dish at Gas Mark 6½, 410°F, 210°C for fifteen to twenty minutes. Serve at once.

The anchovies usually provide enough salt, but just to be on the safe side, taste a little of the mixture after the egg whites have been added and adjust if necessary.

For the accompanying chive sauce cook the finely chopped shallots in the wine until liquid is reduced to half. Add cream and again reduce quantity to half. Whisk in the butter and sieve the sauce. Add seasoning, chopped chives and caviar and serve separately.

DUMPLINGS AND
PASTA DISHES

DUMPLINGS AND PASTA DISHES

A *Knödel* is a dumpling, sometimes large, sometimes smallish. A *Knöderl* is a small dumpling, used mainly in soups. *Nudeln* are noodles, of course – but this is where things can get slightly confusing: *Topfennudeln*, a favourite country dish, are broad noodles served with curd cheese, sour cream and crackling, but *Kärntner Topfennudeln* (or their more elegant version of *Bleiberger Topfennudeln*) are not noodles at all, but pasta envelopes filled with curd cheese and herbs. Nor do *Schlutzkrapfen* bear any resemblance to *Krapfen* of the fried pastry type but are small pasta rounds with a savoury meat filling. They are all delicious – best to enjoy them all and forget about the definition!

BLEIBERGER TOPFENNUDELN

The Bleibergerhof at Bad Bleiberg in Carinthia is a Spa hotel at its Austrian best, situated nearly 1000m above sea level with marvellous views, and the cooking – until fairly recently reserved for hotel guests only – is definitely worth a detour. Alfred Süssenbacher makes much use of traditional Carinthian recipes to which he gives his own inimitable touch. *Bleiberger Topfennudeln* are a typical example – a smaller and lighter version of the more robust *Kärntner Kasnudeln*.

Makes 20 – 24
For the dough
7 oz (200 g) plain flour
2 – 3 eggs
1 tablespoon olive oil
salt
a little egg white

For the filling
7 oz (200 g) very dry and
    crumbly curd cheese
    (see note below)
3 medium-sized potatoes,
    cooked and sieved
2 egg yolks
2 rolls (crumb only)
    soaked in milk
salt
2 tablespoons chopped
    fresh chervil
2 tablespoons chopped
    fresh mint
1 teaspoon potato flour
melted butter for serving

Sift flour with salt and work to a dough with the eggs and oil. Cover with a bowl and leave for half an hour.

For the filling mix together all the ingredients, having first squeezed out all moisture from the rolls. Shape filling into small balls about the size of a walnut.

Divide dough into two equal parts and roll out as thinly as possible. Set the filling at even intervals on one part of the rolled out dough. Brush with a little egg white round the filling and cover with remaining dough. Cut into squares of about 1¼ – 1½ inches (3 – 4 cm) with a zig-zag cutting wheel. Press down around the filling to seal edges. Drop into boiling salted water, leave to simmer for five to six minutes. Drain and serve with melted butter.

Note: the cheese normally used for this recipe is *Bauerntopfen* (farmer's curd cheese) which is a full fat curd cheese, exceptionally dry and crumbly. Ricotta can also be used. If using cottage cheese, drain off all moisture first and add a tablespoon of cream.

BREGENZERWALD GRIESSKNÖDEL

Semolina Dumplings from the Bregenzerwald

Excellent in clear beef broth or – in slightly larger form – served with *Schwammerlsauce* (see page 193).

Serves 4

5 – 7 oz (150 g – 200 g)
   cooked ham
2½ oz (70 g) butter
1 egg yolk
1 egg
1 tablespoon water
salt

1½ oz (45 g) coarse
   semolina
chopped chives

Chop the ham very finely. Cream butter with egg yolk, egg and water. Beat in the salt and half the semolina. Leave to stand for fifteen minutes. Stir in the remaining semolina, then leave to stand for two hours. Add the chopped ham and the chives. Form dumplings and drop them into boiling salted water. Cover and leave to simmer – with the lid slightly tilted – for about fifteen minutes. Drain well.

BRÖSELKNÖDEL

Dumplings made with Breadcrumbs

Serves 4

1 tablespoon butter
1 egg
salt
nutmeg

¼ lb (110 g) fine
   breadcrumbs
1 dessertspoon plain flour

Cream butter, beat in the egg, salt and nutmeg. Stir in breadcrumbs and flour. Cover and leave to stand for half an hour. Form small dumplings and – as always – cook a test dumpling first. Drop dumpling into boiling, salted water and leave to simmer until the dumpling rises to the top – only a matter of minutes.

EIERNOCKERL

A favourite light luncheon dish, particularly good if accompanied by a crisp green salad.

Prepare *Nockerl* as described on page 136. Break two or three eggs into a bowl, add a pinch of salt and a little white pepper and beat lightly. Melt a tablespoon butter in a frying pan, add the *Nockerl* to reheat, shaking pan from time to time, then pour the eggs over them and stir – rather like making scrambled eggs. When the eggs have just set, stir again and serve at once, sprinkled with chopped chives.

ERDÄPFELKNÖDEL

Potato Dumplings

The mixture for potato dumplings varies according to region. This particular recipe comes from the Waldviertel, the 'forest region' of Lower Austria which borders Czechoslovakia.

Makes 5 – 6 dumplings

1 lb (450 g) potatoes, cooked and sieved	salt
1 lb (450 g) raw, peeled potatoes	about 3 tablespoons strong flour

Grate the raw potatoes and squeeze out moisture. Add to the cooked sieved potatoes, together with a pinch of salt and enough flour to give a firm paste. (If mixture is too firm, add a little softened butter, if too soft, add a little more flour or fine semolina).

Make a small test dumpling and drop into boiling salted water. Cook gently until dumpling rises to the top. Shape remaining mixture into dumplings, drop into boiling salted water and cook for about twenty minutes.

GEBACKENE LEBERKNÖDEL

Fried Liver Dumplings

Accompanied by a salad in summer or a dish of more substantial brown lentils or Sauerkraut in winter, these dumplings make a very good main course. They are, of course, excellent as an addition to clear beef broth: pour the soup over them at the last minute, just before serving.

For 24 dumplings

3 thick slices bread or 3
   rolls
milk or water
6 oz (160 g) calves liver
4 oz (110 g) butter
½ teaspoon chopped onion
1 heaped teaspoon finely
   chopped parsley

1 egg
3 oz (80 g) fine
   breadcrumbs
salt and pepper
¼ teaspoon finely chopped
   marjoram
¼ teaspoon finely chopped
   thyme
lard or oil for deep frying

Soak the bread or rolls in water or milk, then squeeze out all moisture. Mince the liver. Heat about a quarter of the butter in a frying pan, add the onion and allow to soften over low heat, then add bread and parsley. Blend well, remove pan from heat and tip contents into a bowl.

Add the minced liver and put it all through a blender or push through a sieve. Cream remaining butter, beat in liver mixture and then add remaining ingredients. Leave to stand for at least half an hour.

As with all dumplings it is best to test one dumpling before shaping all the others. Fry the test dumpling: if the mixture is too soft, add a little more breadcrumbs to the mixture or, if too firm, a little more egg or milk. Shape the remaining mixture into dumplings and fry in deep oil or fat. Drain well on kitchen paper. (The dumplings can also be fried in shallow fat – in which case they lose a little of their round appearance. Not for the perfectionist, but quite successful.)

GRIESSKNÖDEL

Semolina Dumplings

Serves 4

2½ oz (70 g) butter
1 tablespoon water
1 egg yolk
1 egg

pinch of salt
5 oz (140 g) coarse
   semolina

Cream butter, add the water gradually. Beat in the yolk and the lightly beaten whole egg with a pinch of salt, then stir in 3 oz (85 g) of the semolina. Cover bowl and leave to stand for a quarter of an hour. Add remaining semolina and leave for two hours.

Scoop out medium-sized portions with the help of a dessertspoon and shape into balls, handling very lightly. Drop into boiling salted water, cook until dumplings rise to the top. Drain and rinse carefully under cold water. Heat very gently in sauce or gravy for scrving.

They go well with most sauces, but I find that they are particularly delicious with Dill Sauce – another favourite 'Friday' dish of my childhood.

IMSTER SCHLUTZKRAPFEN

'Z'Imscht in der Poscht da gibt's a guate Koscht' goes an old saying in the Tyrol, meaning that you will fare well at the lovely Hotel Post at Imst. *Schlutzkrapfen* exist – with variations – all over the Tyrol, but this is the treasured recipe from the Post.

Serves 4

For the dough	*Filling*
7 oz (200 g) strong flour	3½ oz (100 g) cooked liver
pinch of salt	3½ oz (100 g) cooked
3 eggs	potatoes
water	½ clove garlic, crushed
egg for sealing	with salt
	chopped marjoram
	salt and pepper
	2 oz (50 g) chopped bacon
	grated Parmesan cheese
	and browned butter to
	serve

Sift together flour and salt, make a well in the centre and drop in the eggs. Work to a smooth dough, adding water as necessary. Cover with a cloth and leave to stand for half an hour.

For the filling, lightly fry the bacon in its own fat, add it to liver and potatoes, and mince everything. Season with marjoram, crushed garlic, salt and pepper.

Roll out the dough as thinly as possible and stamp into rounds about 3 inches (8 cm) in diameter. Put a teaspoonful of filling in the centre of each round, brush edges with beaten egg and fold over dough to form half-circles. Pinch together edges of pastry to seal. Bring a large saucepan of lightly salted water to boil, drop in filled dough mounds. Simmer until *Schlutzkrapfen* rise to the top. Drain, rinse under hot water and serve with grated Parmesan and browned butter.

KÄSKNÖPFLE, KÄSSPÄTZLE

Cheese buttons

It has been said that a true native of Vorarlberg would readily sell his soul for a dish of *Käsknöpfle*, though the dish is by no means a native of Vorarlberg – it hails from Swabia. The cheese varies according to personal preference: it may be a sturdy *Bergkäse* from the Bregenzerwald or it could be a mixture of mild and sharp. Good Emmenthal is also very suitable, but experiment for yourself.

7 oz (200 g) plain flour	butter for frying
salt	about 7 oz (200 g) grated
1 egg	cheese
1 medium-sized onion	melted butter

Sift flour and salt onto a pastry board and make a well in the centre. Add the egg and sufficient cold water to make a smooth paste – no kneading required. Ideally the paste should be pushed through a large-holed sieve straight into boiling salted water. Failing that, scoop out small portions with a teaspoon frequently dipped into hot water. Bring to boil once, fish out one of the 'buttons' with a slotted spoon and taste. If you have used a sieve, they will probably be ready – if using a teaspoon they may require another minute. Pour a ladleful of cold water into the saucepan, then drain carefully.

Chop the onion finely and fry in butter according to taste, either golden brown or dark brown and crisp. Arrange layers of the 'buttons' in a large warmed dish, sprinkling cheese between each layer and moistening with melted butter. Top with fried onions and hot melted butter.

Sometimes the fried onions are replaced by breadcrumbs fried in butter, and instead of cheese hot Sauerkraut is used, in which case the dish is called *Krutspätzle*.

NOCKERL (MEHLNOCKERL)

All *Nockerl* look more or less the same – small and oblong – but their texture varies. *Butternockerl* and *Griessnockerl* (see pages 33 and 35), both favourite additions to clear beef broth, are very light and airy. *Mehlnockerl*, which are sometimes just called *Nockerl*, are a little more solid, much like their German and Swiss cousins, *Spätzle*, and they are often served with *Gulasch*. In Austria all *Nockerl* based on flour are made with the help of a *Nockerlbrett*, a small wooden board which is slightly bevelled at one end. The *Nockerl* dough is spread on the board, one end of which is held firmly in one hand, and is then snipped off with a knife, straight into the boiling water into which the knife is dipped from time to time. Scooping out the dough with a teaspoon frequently dipped into boiling water does, however, work perfectly well. As with dumplings, it is best to cook a sample *Nockerl* first and if necessary add a little melted butter to the mixture if the dough is too firm, or flour if too soft, before cooking the remaining mixture.

Serves 4

9 oz (250 g) plain flour	9 fluid oz (¼ l) milk
1 oz (25 g) butter	1 egg
salt	

Sift flour and salt into a bowl. Melt butter in milk, remove from heat and leave to cool a little. Whisk egg into milk, then stir milk mixture into the sifted flour and beat well with a wooden spoon. The dough should be fairly soft – adjust with more milk or flour if necessary.

Bring a large pan of slightly salted water to boil. Cut out a small *Nockerl* with the help of a teaspoon, throw into boiling salted water and cook for two minutes. Fish out with a perforated spoon and test. If necessary add a little more flour or melted butter to the dough. Cut small *Nockerl* with the aid of a teaspoon and throw into boiling salted water, dipping the spoon frequently into the boiling water. Cook for two to three minutes, no more. Drain well, then rinse carefully under cold running water.

To serve Nockerl with Goulash and other stews
Melt 1 tablespoon butter in a saucepan, add *Nockerl* and heat carefully, shaking pan from time to time.

PALFFY KNÖDEL

Palffy Dumpling

When emperors, kings and princes went visiting, chefs would excel themselves not only in creating new dishes, but also in decorating them strictly according to protocol. So Conrad Hagger's *New Salzburg Cookery Book for Princely Courts*, published in 1718, gives beautifully detailed drawings, all in their proper order, starting with a pâté embellished with the imperial coat of arms and ending with one where the space for the coat of arms has been left blank, for the last-minute addition of *einen unverhofften Fürsten* (a prince dropping in unexpectedly).

The recipe for *Palffy Knödel* was created more recently for one such occasion. It dates back from just before the First World War, when the head of the house of Palffy visited a neighbouring prince. It consists of a dumpling. Yes, just one. Not the heavy-handed compliment you may think, but the lightest, fluffiest dish of a dumpling ever to be set before a prince. It is served sliced to accompany stews and casseroles, but makes a very good light luncheon dish on its own (add 3 – 4 oz grated cheese or the same quantity of chopped ham or lightly fried bacon to the basic mixture), accompanied by a crisp green salad. And use your sharpest knife for slicing – Josef Wechsberg once told me that in his family even the sharpest knife was considered too clumsy for so delicate a dumpling and a violin string was used – he failed to specify the key!

Serves 4
6 day-old rolls or 11 oz
(300 g) white bread
4½ oz (125 g) butter

5 eggs
salt
a little melted butter

Wring out a large tea towel in cold water and brush one side of it with melted butter. Bring a large saucepan of salted water to the boil while preparing the dumpling.

Cut bread or rolls into ½ inch (1 cm) cubes. Some cooks remove the crust first. I don't bother with this, but if you do, weigh the bread after the crust has been removed. If the bread is too fresh (two days old is ideal), set the cubes on a baking sheet and dry them a little in a warm oven.

Separate eggs. Cream butter with a pinch of salt, beat in the yolks one by one. Whisk whites until stiff, fold into butter mixture alternately with the cubed bread. Put the mixture into the centre of the tea towel, gently shape it into a large dumpling and tie the ends of the towel loosely to allow the dumpling to expand during cooking.

Choose a wooden spoon with a handle longer than the width of your saucepan, slot its handle under the tea towel's knot, and rest spoon on the saucepan's rim so that the dumpling hangs down into the boiling water, being careful that it does not touch the bottom of the saucepan. Replace saucepan lid – there will be a little gap because of the spoon, which is exactly as it should be. Cook the dumpling gently for forty-five to fifty minutes.

Remove from saucepan and take off the cloth. Put on a warmed serving dish and cut into slices. Failing a violin string use the sharpest, lightest knife you can find (or a wire cheese cutter).

PINZGAUER PRESSKNÖDEL

Pinzgau Cheese Dumplings

Hearty, and heart-warming. One or two or these dumplings in a cup of clear consommé and there is little room left for anything else.

Makes 8 dumplings

1 lb (500 g) day-old white bread	1 medium-sized potato
6 – 7 oz (150 g – 200 g) goats cheese or Tilsiter cheese	2 cloves garlic
	3 eggs
	1 tablespoon plain flour
1 medium-sized onion	salt and pepper
½ oz (15 g) butter	lard or oil for frying
	clear beef broth

Dice the bread and the cheese. Chop the onion finely and fry gently in butter until light brown. Crush the garlic. Grate the potato. Mix together all ingredients and shape into dumplings the size of golf balls, flattening them a little between your hands. Fry in shallow fat or oil until golden brown all over, then drop them into hot broth and simmer over low heat for about eight minutes. Serve in soup bowls with the clear broth poured over them.

SEMMELKNÖDEL

Bread Dumplings

Makes 4 dumplings

4 day-old rolls or equivalent quantity of bread	1 egg
	milk
	salt and pepper
1 heaped tablespoon butter	4 tablespoons plain flour

Dice the rolls or bread. Melt the butter and fry the breadcubes until light golden brown. Sprinkle with the flour, stir and empty contents of frying pan into a bowl.

Break egg into a cup, add salt and pepper and fill up cup with milk. Stir with a fork and pour over rolls and flour in the bowl. Mix and leave to stand for half an hour.

Form dumplings, adding a little more flour if necessary and drop into boiling salted water (lift with a cooking spoon, making sure that the dumplings do not settle at the bottom of the pan). Cook very gently for about ten minutes (the dumplings will rise to the top when cooked). Lift out with a perforated spoon and drain well.

Knödel mit Ei – sometimes just called *geröstete Knödel* – are simply left-over *Semmelknödel*, sliced thinly and fried in a little butter or good dripping until brown and crisp. Two or three eggs are then lightly beaten with a pinch of salt and a little pepper and poured over the *Knödel* in the frying pan and stirred. Serve straight from the pan, sprinkled with chopped chives and accompanied by a green salad. Very simple – and very delicious.

SERVIETTENKNÖDEL

Dumpling Cooked in a Napkin

A more mundane version of the princely *Palffy Knödel*, this dumpling is served sliced and sometimes sprinkled with breadcrumbs fried in butter, as an accompaniment to meat instead of potatoes. Sliced, moistened with melted butter and sprinkled with sugar, it can also be served as a pudding of the 'sweet pasta' variety, usually accompanied by a fruit compote.

2 eggs	2 oz (60 g) semolina
1½ oz (45 g) butter	½ lb (240 g) curd cheese
salt	melted butter for the cloth
sugar	

Separate eggs. Cream butter with a pinch of salt and sugar, add yolks gradually and then the semolina. Whisk whites until stiff, fold into the yolk mixture, alternately with the cheese.

Shape into a large dumpling and place in the centre of a napkin (or tea towel) previously wrung out in cold water and brushed with melted butter. Tie ends loosely over the dumpling. Have ready a pan of boiling slightly salted water. Slot the handle of a wooden spoon through the tied napkin ends and rest it on the saucepan's rim so that the dumpling hangs into the boiling water. Cover saucepan with a lid, leaving a slight gap for the spoon, and lower the heat. Simmer the dumpling for half an hour. Lift dumpling from the saucepan and remove cloth. Set dumpling on a warmed serving dish and cut into slices for serving.

SPECKNOCKERLN

Bacon Dumplings

Excellent on their own, accompanied by a salad – cucumber or lamb's lettuce are particularly suitable. Or they can be served with a more robust dish such as *Bierfleisch* (see page 73) or *Gefüllte Schweinsschnitzel* (see page 75). The recipe is by Herbert Hüpfel, Chef de Cuisine at the Intercontinental, Vienna.

Serves 4

11 oz (300 g) plain flour	3½ oz (100 g) *Speck* or
3½ fluid oz (100 ml) milk	streaky bacon in one
salt	piece
3 eggs	chopped chives

Sift flour into a bowl. Mix together milk and eggs with a pinch of salt. Add to flour and mix to a light dough with a wooden spoon. Scoop out small gnocchi with the help of a teaspoon and drop into boiling salted water. Bring to boil again and drain. Dice the bacon and brown in its own fat. Add the drained gnocchi and mix with the bacon. Arrange on a warmed serving dish and sprinkle with chopped chives.

TIROLER SPECKKNÖDEL

Tyrolean Dumplings

Bauernschmaus, though served throughout Austria, has its home in the Tyrol. It consists of a large platter of smoked pork, sausages, roast pork, Sauerkraut, pickled cucumber and – most important of all – *Tiroler Speckknödel*: at least one per person.

In the old days, on Sundays, a large piece of beef would be cooked very gently with vegetables to make good clear beef broth; a worthy recipient in which to serve the dumplings. That would be the main course. Quality and cut of the meat were of secondary importance – very unlike the Viennese, who might take hours pondering the particular cut of meat which should go into the pot for their beloved boiled beef. In the Tyrol the beef would simply be dished up, finely chopped and sitting on a bed of Sauerkraut, as a starter. The star of the meal would be – and still is – the dumpling.

'The best thing in life is *der gedachte Idealfall* [the imaginary ideal situation]' said one of my Tyrolean friends, 'and that doesn't exist. But I can assure you that the second best thing is Tyrolean dumplings, and the ones you are going to eat now are the very best Tyrolean dumplings you'll ever taste.' The place happened to be a hotel kitchen in the province of Salzburg, but the hotel owner was Tyrolean and I must admit that I have never had better *Speckknödel*. I noted down the recipe as the dumplings were being made.

The sausage used is called *Extrawurst* in Austria. It can be bought in this country, where it is sold under various names ranging from Polish Ring to Jubilee Sausage. The texture is smooth, rather like Frankfurter. Failing *Extrawurst* use skinless Frankfurters.

Makes 6 dumplings

7 – 8 oz (200 – 225 g) day-old bread (about 5 rolls)	1 tablespoon olive oil or dripping
½ small onion	1 tablespoon chopped parsley
¼ lb (100 g) cooked ham	2 eggs
¼ lb (100 g) *Extrawurst* or Frankfurter sausages	salt and pepper
¼ lb (100 g) *Speck* or streaky bacon	1 – 2 tablespoons plain flour

Dice the bread or rolls. Chop the onion. Also chop the ham, sausage and *Speck* (or bacon). Heat oil or dripping in a frying pan, add the onion and allow it to soften over low heat. Add meats and parsley and fry until very lightly browned. Add bread cubes and continue frying until the bread is golden brown and crisp. Transfer contents of frying pan to a bowl.

Beat the eggs lightly, add salt and pepper and pour over the mixture in the bowl. Mix well with a fork and stir in the flour. Divide the mixture equally and shape into 6 dumplings with your hands (it helps if you dip your hands into cold water from time to time). If the mixture seems too dry, add a little more milk or, if too soft, a little more flour, but go easy on either and handle the dumplings very gently.

Heat a large saucepan of salted water. When the water boils, drop in the dumplings. Reduce heat so that the water just bubbles gently. Cover pan with a lid, tilted to leave a little space and allow the dumplings to poach for about ten minutes – they will rise to the top when they are cooked. Lift out with a perforated spoon and drain carefully.

PASTA

KRAUTFLECKERL

Pasta Squares with Cabbage

Typical of Lower Austria and the Burgenland, and the nearer you
get to the Hungarian border, the sweeter the flavour. In some parts
of the Burgenland *Krautfleckerl* are even served with a fine dusting
of icing sugar, in the old 'sweet pasta' tradition, like noodles with
poppyseeds (or ground walnuts) sprinkled with cinnamon and sugar,
or small pasta envelopes filled with thick sweet plum jam. In other
parts of Lower Austria, and also in Vienna, the savoury taste prevails
and the onion is fried in rendered *Speck* and *Krautfleckerl* are served
as an accompaniment to meat; but in all cases the cabbage will
be unrecognisable as such, cooked almost to the consistency of a
sauce. *Krautfleckerl* are possibly an acquired taste – but delicious once
you've acquired it – and rumour has it that guests at the famous
Zu den 3 Husaren in Vienna order the special pot-roast largely for
the accompanying *Krautfleckerl*.

Serves 4

Fleckerl (see page 34)	1 small onion, finely sliced
1 small, firm white	1 tablespoon icing sugar
cabbage weighing about	salt and pepper
1¼ lb (560 g)	dash of wine vinegar
3 oz (80 g) lard or oil	1 teaspoon caraway seeds

Shred cabbage finely after removing outer leaves and any woody parts.
Sprinkle with salt. Melt the fat, add the finely sliced onion and allow
it to soften over low heat. Sprinkle with sugar, increase heat for the
onion to brown and the sugar to caramelize, stirring constantly. Add the
vinegar – carefully, as it is apt to splutter – add the cabbage. Sprinkle
with caraway seeds and pepper, cover and allow to simmer very gently,
adding water (or stock) only if absolutely necessary. Stir frequently and
cook until the cabbage is reduced to an almost sauce-like consistency
and is soft brown in colour.

Cook pasta in plenty of boiling lightly salted water until just tender
and rinse under cold running water. Drain well and add to the cabbage.
Reheat gently and serve.

SCHINKENFLECKERL

Pasta with Ham

As the name implies, these should be made with *Fleckerl* (see page 34), but any good pasta can be used provided it is small enough, which includes most of the pastina minestrone family. At a pinch you could even break up broad noodles – before cooking, of course.

My recipe for *Schinkenfleckerl* is a very old one which has certainly been in my family for over three generations. I was amused to find a recipe for *Schinkenflecken, ganz ordinär* (rather common) in *Die Baierische Köchin in Böhmen* by Maria Anna Neudecker, née Ertl, published in 1819. It goes as follows: Prepare a noodle dough with 3 eggs and cut into small squares. Cook the squares in salted water, then toss them in hot butter until very lightly browned and add a pinch of salt. Put into a buttered dish, mix with 1 lb finely chopped ham, add ½ Mass (700 ml = 1¼ pints) sour cream and put into a hot oven. Serve in the dish in which they are baked.

Not all that far removed from my own recipe – and I swear that my grandmother had never heard of the admirable Maria Anna Neudecker, née Ertl.

Serves 3 – 4

½ lb (225 g) *Fleckerl* or
    other pasta
salt
1 heaped tablespoon
    butter
2 eggs
5 oz (140 g) chopped
    cooked ham

8 fluid oz (225 ml) sour
    cream
salt and pepper
butter for the baking dish

Cook the pasta in plenty of boiling salted water until just tender, being careful not to overcook. Drain and rinse under cold water.

Meanwhile butter a gratin dish and preheat the oven to Gas Mark 5, 375°F, 190°C. Cream the butter. Separate eggs and beat the yolks into the butter, then stir in the sour cream. Whisk whites until stiff, then fold into the butter together with the chopped ham. Taste and adjust seasoning with salt and pepper, depending on the saltiness of the ham. Finally fold in the drained pasta. Bake until nicely browned on top. A green salad goes well with this.

As with all traditional recipes, there are numerous variations – the most usual one is to leave out the creaming of the butter and just toss the pasta in melted butter (as Maria Anna Neudecker suggested) then stir in the remaining ingredients. The top may be sprinkled with a little grated cheese and/or breadcrumbs which makes for a good brown crust.

VEGETABLES AND VEGETABLE DISHES

VEGETABLES AND VEGETABLE DISHES

When the Austrians feel virtuous about their vitamins, they cook their vegetables in what they fondly believe to be the 'English' way. They do not feel virtuous very often and even then they compromise by sprinkling a plainly cooked vegetable liberally with crisply fried breadcrumbs (or ground walnuts for special occasions). This applies particularly to cauliflower, French beans and tiny Brussel sprouts which are usually served as a separate dish when prepared this way.

Vegetables cooked the 'Viennese' way are something else again – cream, herbs and spices play an important part in the preparation. There are also some hearty vegetable dishes from Austria's provinces and recipes for potatoes too good to miss.

GEDÜNSTETES KRAUT

Red or White Cabbage

1 firm red or white cabbage	1 heaped teaspoon caraway seeds
3 tablespoons butter or good dripping	1 – 2 cooking apples
2 tablespoons caster sugar	wine vinegar (red for red cabbage if possible)
salt and pepper	little water, stock or wine

Trim the cabbage and shred finely. Put into a colander and rinse under cold running tap. Sprinkle cabbage with salt. Melt butter or dripping in a large saucepan. Add the sugar and stir until sugar has dissolved and turned golden brown. Throw in the shredded cabbage very quickly – stand away from the pan as it will splutter – then turn down the heat and stir briefly. Add caraway seeds, pepper, a good dash of wine vinegar and just enough stock or water to prevent burning.

Peel, core and quarter the apples and add these as well.

Simmer very slowly in a covered pan, stirring from time to time and adding a little more stock or water if necessary. Taste and adjust seasoning if necessary – it should have a distinctly sweet/sour flavour.

If using wine instead of water or stock, less vinegar is needed. I do not thicken cabbage cooked in this way, but this is more often than not done in Austria – just slake about a tablespoon flour with cold water or stock and add to the hot cabbage, then leave to simmer until well blended. This is one of those dishes which improves every time it is warmed up!

KARL ESCHLBÖCK'S ROTKRAUT

Karl Eschlböck's Red Cabbage

Landhaus Plomberg at Mondsee is famed for its fine cooking and for Karl Eschlböck's versions of traditional dishes. His specialities are numerous – and new ones are constantly brought to the table for his admiring guests to sample. Of the more recent inventions, I thought his way of cooking red cabbage well worth capturing.

11 oz (300 g) red cabbage	salt and freshly ground
4½ fluid oz (⅛ l) red wine	black pepper
1 tablespoon cranberries	1 tablespoon soft brown
4½ fluid oz (⅛ l) orange	sugar
juice	1 apple
pinch each of powdered	1 medium-sized onion
cinnamon, nutmeg,	4 tablespoons butter
allspice and cloves	½ tablespoon granulated
1 scant oz (20 g) plain	sugar
chocolate, grated	
grated rind of ½ lemon	

Wash the cabbage, remove any 'woody' parts of the stem and shred the cabbage finely. Mix together red wine, cranberries, orange juice, spices, chocolate, lemon rind, salt, pepper and brown sugar. Peel and core the apple and grate into the above ingredients. Mix with the shredded cabbage and leave, covered, in a cool place for twenty-four hours.

Finely slice the onion. Melt 2 tablespoons of the butter, add onion and let it soften, then add granulated sugar and let it caramelize lightly. Add the red cabbage including all liquid and leave to simmer gently until it is cooked but still has some 'bite' to it. Adjust seasoning if necessary. Cream the remaining butter and stir in just before serving.

PARADEISKRAUT

White Cabbage Cooked with Tomatoes

1 small white cabbage	salt and pepper
(about 2 lbs/900 g)	1 teaspoon caraway seeds
½ green pepper	6 tomatoes, peeled
1 small onion	and chopped or 3
2 oz (50 g) lard, dripping	tablespoons tomato
or oil	purée
1 tablespoon sugar	about 4 fluid oz (⅛ l)
dash of wine vinegar	water or good stock
	1 teaspoon plain flour

Trim and quarter the cabbage, then shred it finely. De-seed the green pepper and cut it into strips. Slice the onion. Heat the fat, add the onion and allow it to soften, then add the sugar. Stir over low heat until the sugar turns golden brown, then throw in the cabbage – stand away from the pan as contents are apt to splutter. Stir, then add vinegar, salt, pepper, caraway seeds, tomatoes or tomato purée and water or stock. Simmer gently until cabbage is cooked, but still crisp. Slake flour with a little water, add to the cabbage and simmer for another few minutes until well blended.

SPECKKRAUT

White Cabbage with Bacon

A splendid way of serving cabbage which I first encountered at Zell am See in the province of Salzburg. I was assured that it was a local dish – but I'm not convinced.

1 small firm white cabbage	streaky bacon
salt	1 ladleful of clear beef broth
butter for the dish	

Remove the outer leaves from the cabbage. Make a few incisions in the stalk and if necessary, remove any woody parts. Steam or boil the cabbage – whole – in a pan of salted water until the stalk end is barely tender. Drain well. Preheat the oven to Gas Mark 4, 350°F, 180°C. Butter a soufflé dish. Cut the rinds off enough bacon rashers to cover the cabbage and flatten the rashers with a rolling pin. Put the cabbage in the soufflé dish and press it down a little. Pour about a ladleful of beef broth over the cabbage and cover the top with bacon, cutting the rashers to size if necessary. Cook in the oven until the bacon is nicely browned. Serve cut into wedges.

For an even simpler method of preparation, steam or boil the cabbage and put it in the buttered soufflé dish. Add the beef broth and cover cabbage with buttered foil. Place it in the oven at Gas Mark 4, 350°F, 180°C. Meanwhile dice the bacon and fry it until crisp. Take off the foil, pour rendered bacon fat over the cabbage and return it to the oven for a few minutes. Sprinkle the fried bacon over the top just before serving.

WIENER KOHL

Savoy Cabbage Viennese Style

2 lbs (900 g) savoy cabbage	about ¾ pint (450 ml)
4 oz (110 g) streaky bacon	clear beef broth
1 small onion, finely	4 potatoes, parboiled
chopped	salt and pepper
1 garlic clove, crushed	caraway seeds
1 tablespoon chopped	marjoram
parsley	
1 heaped tablespoon plain	
flour	

Wash and shred the cabbage and blanch it in lightly salted water.
Refresh under cold tap. Dice the bacon, heat in a thick saucepan until
the fat starts to run, then lightly fry the chopped onion in the fat. Add
garlic and parsley, and stir, then sprinkle in the flour. Stir over low
heat and gradually add enough beef broth to make a thick sauce –
about ¾ pint (450 ml). Add the savoy cabbage, the parboiled cubed
potatoes, salt, pepper, caraway seeds and marjoram. Simmer gently for
about ten minutes, adding a little more beef broth if necessary.

KAROTTEN AUF WIENER ART

Carrots Viennese Style

1 lb (450 g) carrots	salt and pepper
2 heaped tablespoons	about 8 fluid oz (225 ml)
butter	clear broth
1 small onion, finely	1 scant tablespoon plain
chopped	flour
1 teaspoon sugar	chopped parsley

Wash and scrape the carrots and cut into slices. Soften the onion in the
butter, sprinkle with sugar and caramelize lightly. Add carrots, salt and
pepper. Cover with stock and simmer until carrots are almost tender.
Slake the flour with a little cold water or clear broth and add to the
carrots, then allow to simmer for another eight to ten minutes, adding
a little more broth if necessary. Sprinkle with chopped parsley before
serving.

GEBACKENER KARFIOL

Cauliflower 'In a Hood'

1 medium-sized cauliflower	1 tablespoon fine breadcrumbs
2½ oz (70 g) butter	4 tablespoons sour cream
3 eggs	butter for the dish
2 heaped tablespoons grated Parmesan cheese	

Cook the cauliflower in boiling salted water, or steam it until just tender. Butter a gratin dish.

Cream butter. Separate eggs. Beat yolks into creamed butter, then add Parmesan cheese, breadcrumbs and sour cream. Whisk whites until stiff and fold into mixture. Spread one third of the mixture in the buttered gratin dish and sit the drained cauliflower on top. Completely mask the cauliflower with remaining mixture. Bake at Gas Mark 5, 375°F, 190°C until nicely browned on top.

GEBACKENER ZELLER

Celeriac Fritters

1 large celeriac	1 – 2 eggs, lightly beaten
salt	fine breadcrumbs
1 medium-sized onion	1 tablespoon grated Parmesan cheese
1 – 2 tablespoons oil	deep oil for frying
seasoned plain flour	

Wash and peel the celeriac and cut it into slices about ¼ inch thick. Sprinkle with salt. Chop the onion finely and sauté it gently in the hot oil until softened and barely coloured. Add the celeriac slices and a dash of water. Cover and simmer gently until the celeriac is tender, shaking the pan from time to time. Leave to cool in the pan.

Lift out the slices very carefully so that some of the onion purée will cling to each slice and turn the slices first in seasoned flour, then in lightly beaten egg and finally in breadcrumbs to which the Parmesan cheese has been added. Fry the slices – not too many at the same time – in hot oil which should be deep enough for the slices to float. Drain on kitchen paper and serve while still hot.

ZELLER PUREE

Celeriac Purée

1 large or 2 medium-sized celeriac	1 large apple, peeled, cored and quartered
milk and water	2 tablespoons double cream
salt and white pepper	

Peel the celeriac and cut it into chunks. Cook the celeriac in a lightly salted mixture of milk and water to cover. Towards the end of the cooking time add quartered apple. Drain off the liquid and purée apple and celeriac. Add warmed cream and white pepper.

GURKENGEMÜSE

Stewed Cucumber

1 large cucumber	finely chopped dill
1 small onion, finely chopped	salt and pepper
	a little clear broth
2 tablespoons butter	1 tablespoon tomato purée

Peel cucumber, halve lengthways and remove seeds then chop or slice. Melt the butter, and soften onion. Add cucumber, stir then add dill, salt and pepper. Cover with a lid and simmer gently, adding a little clear broth, until cucumber is cooked. Add tomato purée and adjust seasoning if necessary.

GRÜNE FISOLEN AUF WIENER ART

French Beans in Cream Sauce

Fisolen is the Viennese name for French beans, which are often cooked briefly in salted water and then served with crisply fried buttery breadcrumbs (or ground walnuts for high days and holidays). The following recipe is for French beans when served with *Tafelspitz* – and all the other variations of boiled beef. It works equally well with shelled broad beans.

1 lb (450 g) French beans (or shelled broad beans)	1 scant tablespoon plain flour
1 small onion or shallot	clear beef broth
1 heaped tablespoon butter	1 – 2 tablespoons chopped fresh dill

about ¼ pint (150 ml)
  double or sour cream
small pinch of sugar

dash of lemon juice or
  white wine vinegar
salt and pepper

String the beans and cut or break into 1 inch pieces. Throw beans into a cupful of boiling salted water, cook until just tender, drain and reserve the liquid. Chop the onion or shallot finely, soften in the butter, but do not allow it to brown. Sprinkle in the flour, stir and then gradually add the water from the beans and enough clear beef broth to make a thick sauce. Add the cooked beans, chopped dill, salt, pepper, sugar and lemon juice or vinegar. Finally stir in the cream or sour cream. Adjust seasoning if necessary – the flavour should be mildly sweet and sour.

WIENER KOHLRABI

Kohlrabi Viennese Style

4 – 6 Kohlrabi
salt and pepper
2 oz (50 g) finely chopped
  onion
1 generous tablespoon
  butter
1 scant tablespoon plain
  flour

chopped parsley
about 18 fluid oz (½ litre)
  beef broth or water
1 teaspoon sugar
nutmeg
lemon juice

Peel Kohlrabi and cut into slices. Cook in beef broth or lightly salted water until almost tender, drain well, retaining the water.

Chop the green Kohlrabi tops finely. Melt butter, add onion and allow it to soften. Add Kohlrabi tops and parsley, stir and then add the flour. Blend well and then add liquid gradually. Blend again and simmer gently, stirring constantly, until thickened. Add Kohlrabi, pepper, nutmeg and a little lemon juice. Simmer for another five minutes and serve.

SAURE LINSEN

Brown Lentils Sweet and Sour

1 lb (450 g) brown lentils
1 – 2 medium-sized
  carrots
1 medium-sized onion
1 bayleaf
thyme
grated lemon rind
good pinch of sugar
dash of wine vinegar

black pepper
1 ham bone (or a few
  bacon rinds tied
  together)
about 1½ pints (scant litre)
  water
3 oz (85 g) fat bacon (optional)
1 tablespoon plain flour
  (optional)

Pick over the lentils, rinse them in a sieve under cold running water, then put them in a bowl and cover them with cold water. Leave to soak for a few hours or overnight.

Pour away the water, put lentils into a large saucepan, together with the carrot, halved onion, bayleaf, thyme, lemon rind, sugar and vinegar. Add the ham bone or, failing that, a few bacon rinds tied together. Cover with about $1\frac{1}{2}$ pints cold water and simmer very slowly until the lentils are tender. Take out the ham bone – or bacon rinds – and remove bayleaf and onion. Adjust seasoning if necessary – the flavour should definitely be sweet and sour and have quite a sharp tang.

Now you can either reduce the liquid or – for the authentic version – dice the bacon, then throw it into a frying pan and render down the fat. Crisp the remaining bits of bacon and drain them on kitchen paper. Brown the flour lightly in the bacon fat and add to the lentils. Fish out the carrots and slice them into the lentils. Simmer for a few minutes until well blended and sprinkle with the crispy bits of bacon.

Whatever else is served with the lentils – they go exceedingly well with smoked pork, ham and the Vorarlberg sausages called *Schübling* – a *Tiroler Speckknödel* or *Semmelknödel* (see page 140) is almost obligatory.

KOCHSALAT MIT GRÜNEN ERBSEN

Braised Lettuce with Peas

1 lb (450 g) cos lettuce	1 scant tablespoon plain
7 oz (200 g) shelled peas	flour
salt	1 tablespoon chopped
1 heaped tablespoon	parsley
butter	pepper
1 small onion or shallot,	nutmeg
finely chopped	beef or veal stock

Wash the lettuce and cook briefly in a minimum of salted water. Drain, retaining the liquid, and put lettuce in a colander. Refresh under cold tap and leave to drain well. Chop the lettuce coarsely. Cook the peas in salted water. Drain and retain liquid.

Melt the butter, add the finely chopped onion and allow it to soften without browning. Add the chopped parsley, stir and then sprinkle in the flour. Stir again and let it take colour lightly – the roux should be biscuit-coloured. Pour in the liquid in which the vegetables were cooked and enough stock to make a thin sauce. Add lettuce and peas, pepper and nutmeg. Taste and adjust seasoning if necessary. A spoonful of cream is a good addition, though not part of the 'classic' recipe.

KÜRBISKRAUT

Marrow in Cream Sauce

1 medium-sized marrow	1 heaped tablespoon finely
salt	chopped fresh dill
1 small onion	dash of wine vinegar
2 tablespoons butter	pinch of caster sugar
2 scant tablespoons plain	¼ pint (140 ml) sour
flour	cream
about ¼ pint (140 ml)	
clear beef stock	
paprika	

Peel and quarter the marrow, remove all seeds and fibre. Shred the marrow coarsely. Sprinkle with salt and set aside for at least forty-five minutes – longer if possible.

Peel and finely chop the onion. Melt the butter in a thick saucepan, add the onion and fry very gently until lightly browned. Stir in the flour and the stock. Simmer for a few minutes until well blended, then stir in a pinch of paprika and the chopped dill. Squeeze out all moisture from the marrow and add to the pan together with a dash of wine vinegar and a pinch of sugar. Cover and leave to simmer for about forty-five minutes. Add sour cream, leave to simmer for a further ten to fifteen minutes, adjust seasoning and serve.

This is the 'approved' way of cooking *Kürbiskraut*. I prefer to add the sour cream at the same time as the marrow and then leave everything to simmer together. This may well be frowned upon in the strictest culinary circles in Austria, but I think it tastes much better.

PAPRIKAKÜRBIS

Marrow with Paprika Sauce

1 marrow weighing about	pinch of sugar
3¼ lbs (1½ kg)	pinch of ground caraway
2 generous oz (60 g) lard	seeds
1 large onion, finely	2 tablespoons tomato
chopped	purée
1 garlic clove, crushed	4 fluid oz (⅛ l) sour cream
with salt	1 tablespoon plain flour
1 tablespoon chopped dill	dash of vinegar
1 heaped teaspoon paprika	a little clear beef broth
salt and pepper	

Peel marrow, cut in half and remove seeds and fibres. Shred the marrow or cut it into thin slivers, using a mandoline cutter or the coarse-holed disc of a food processor. Sprinkle with salt and leave to stand for about ten minutes, then squeeze out all moisture.

Melt the fat, add the onion and soften a little then add dill, paprika and the marrow. Stir, add garlic, caraway seeds, tomato purée and a pinch of sugar. Leave to simmer gently for about fifteen minutes. Mix together sour cream and flour, add to marrow and season with salt, pepper and a dash of vinegar as well as a little beef broth. Simmer gently for another five minutes until well blended and thickened.

SCHWAMMERLGULASCH

Mushroom Goulash

In my native Lower Austria the mushrooms for this were almost always chanterelles which grow there in profusion. Boletus would have been considered a luxury. Of course, button mushrooms will do, but I lately discovered that slices of puffball are best of all – if you can find one!

Serves 2
2 oz (60 g) butter
1 small onion, finely
    chopped
1 lb (450 g) mushrooms,
    cleaned and sliced
salt and pepper
1 tablespoon paprika
about 4 fluid oz (100 ml)
    clear beef broth

1 scant tablespoon plain
    flour
9 fluid oz (250 ml) sour
    cream

Melt the butter, add the onion and soften it gently. Add the mushrooms, stir and then add salt, pepper and paprika. Cover the saucepan and simmer gently until the mushrooms are cooked. Sprinkle with flour, stir to blend and then add about 4 fluid oz clear beef broth. Cook gently for a few minutes, then add the sour cream. Simmer until well blended and adjust seasoning if necessary.

Semmelknödel (see page 139) go particularly well with this.

SCHWAMMERLPUDDING

Mushroom Pudding

The best mushrooms for this are boletus, known as *Steinpilze* in Austria. Dried boletus can be used (about scant 2 oz would be sufficient for this recipe) but they have to be soaked in warm water first and the water has then to be strained in case of any sand residue.

1 lb (450 g) mushrooms
3 tablespoons butter
1 shallot, finely chopped
2 rolls
about 1 cup milk
2 eggs
salt

butter and flour for the
   pudding basin
browned butter for serving

Clean and chop the mushrooms. Melt 2 tablespoons of the butter, add the mushrooms and simmer until tender, then leave to cool. Soften the shallot in remaining butter, add the rolls previously soaked in milk and all liquid squeezed out. Simmer for a few minutes to blend. Leave to cool.

Separate eggs. Add cooled mushrooms to onion mixture, then beat in the yolks, salt and 1 tablespoon milk (or strained water in which the dried mushrooms were soaked). Whisk whites until stiff and fold into the mixture. Pile mixture into a buttered and floured pudding basin and steam for about half an hour. Turn out onto a warmed serving dish and serve with hot browned butter.

BÖHMISCHE ERBSEN

Bohemian Peas

11 oz (300 g) dried yellow
   peas
salt
chopped marjoram
3 tablespoons lard or
   dripping
2 oz (50 g) breadcrumbs

1 medium-sized onion,
   finely chopped
fat and breadcrumbs for
   the dish

Soak the peas overnight in cold water. Pour away the water, put peas into a large saucepan, cover with plenty of fresh water and cook them, skimming off the outer skins as they rise to the top. Pour off surplus water, season peas with salt and a little chopped marjoram.

Grease a gratin dish with lard and dust with breadcrumbs. Fry the 2 oz (50 g) breadcrumbs in about a third of the lard and sprinkle over peas. Fry onion in remaining lard until pale golden brown and sprinkle over peas, together with any fat from the frying pan. Put into oven at Gas Mark 5, 375°F, 190°C for fifteen to twenty minutes, until nicely browned on top.

EINGEMACHTE ERBSEN

Green Peas and Bacon

18 oz (500 g) shelled green
  peas
5 oz (140 g) bacon
4 oz (110 g) button onions
  or spring onions
chopped parsley
salt and pepper
about ½ pint (250 ml)
  water or clear beef or
  veal stock

1 tablespoon butter
1 scant tablespoon plain
  flour

Dice the bacon and heat it in a thick saucepan until the fat starts to run. Add the onions and brown them very lightly. Add peas and chopped parsley and enough clear stock or water to cover. Season with salt and pepper. Cover saucepan with a lid and simmer gently until peas are cooked. Mix together butter and flour with a fork and add in small flakes. Cook until well blended and thickened.

ERBSENPUREE

Purée of Dried Yellow Peas

12 oz (350 g) dried yellow
  peas
salt and pepper
parsley and parsley root
a few bacon rinds

2 tablespoons butter
1 tablespoon double cream
1 small onion, finely sliced
2 tablespoons butter

Soak the peas overnight in cold water. Pour away the water, put the peas into a saucepan, together with a small bunch of parsley and some parsley root, a few bacon rinds and water to cover. (If you are lucky enough to have some ham stock, use this – de-greased – instead of the water and leave out the bacon rinds). Cook until the peas are quite soft. Drain, then sieve. Add salt and pepper, beat in butter and cream.

Melt the other two tablespoons butter and fry the thinly sliced onion until brown and crisp. Pile purée into a warmed serving dish, sprinkle with browned onions and trickle the melted butter over it.

EINGEBRANNTE ERDÄPFEL

Potatoes in a Cream Sauce

1¼ lb (600 g) potatoes
2 small onions or shallots,
    finely chopped
2 tablespoons good
    dripping
4 – 5 small cucumbers
    pickled in brine
1 scant teaspoon caraway
    seeds

18 fluid oz (½ litre) good
    stock
1 bayleaf
salt
1 tablespoon plain flour
dash of vinegar
4 fluid oz (⅛ l) sour cream

Peel and slice the potatoes. Melt 1 tablespoon of the fat, add chopped onion or shallot and soften it gently. Add sliced potatoes and brown lightly with the onions. Pour in the stock, add caraway seeds, bayleaf and salt and simmer gently until the potatoes are half-cooked.

Melt remaining fat, stir in the flour and make a light roux. Add it to the potatoes. Chop the cucumbers finely, add to potatoes and simmer until potatoes are cooked. Stir in the sour cream and a dash of vinegar and reheat gently. Instead of the vinegar you can add a dash of the pickling liquid from the cucumbers.

ERDÄPFEL PUDDING

Potato Pudding

Good as an accompaniment to meat, and also as a dish in its own right.

2½ oz (70 g) butter
4 eggs
2 tablespoons plain flour
4½ fluid oz (⅛ l) sour
    cream
1 heaped tablespoon
    grated Parmesan cheese
9 oz (¼ kg) cooked sieved
    potatoes

salt
butter and flour for the
    pudding basin
breadcrumbs fried in
    butter for serving

Separate eggs. Cream butter, beat in yolks one by one, add salt then beat in flour and sour cream. Whisk whites until stiff, fold into the mixture together with the grated Parmesan and cooked sieved potatoes. Steam in a buttered and floured pudding basin for about half an hour. Turn onto a heated serving dish and sprinkle with breadcrumbs browned in butter.

ERDÄPFELSCHMARRN

There has always been controversy about the type of potatoes which should be used for this very Austrian dish: some cooks insist on floury potatoes whilst others swear that they have to be waxy and that anything less than a genuine Austrian *Kipfler* will not do. The preparation varies according to the type of potato – if using floury potatoes they are lightly squashed with a fork whilst frying, whilst *Kipfler* and other waxy specimens retain their elegant sliced shape.

2 lbs (900 g) potatoes boiled in their skins	salt and pepper
1 small onion, finely sliced	caraway seeds
	about 2 tablespoons lard or dripping

Peel potatoes whilst still hot, leave to cool and cut into thin slices. Heat fat in a large frying pan, add the onion and soften, then brown very lightly. Add potatoes and fry with the onion, turning frequently so that there are plenty of crispy bits. Season with salt, pepper and caraway seeds whilst frying.

GESTÜRZTE ERDÄPFEL

Spiced Potato Pudding

1 lb (500 g) waxy potatoes	2 eggs
¼ lb (100 g) spiced sausage or de-rinded bacon	9 fluid oz (250 ml) sour cream
butter for the dish	salt and pepper

Preheat the oven to Gas Mark 5, 375°F, 190°C. Boil the potatoes in their skins until just tender then drain, peel and slice. Dice the bacon or slice the sausage and fry lightly. Butter a deep gratin dish.

Whisk together the eggs and sour cream and season with salt and pepper. Gently mix potatoes with sausage or bacon and transfer to the buttered gratin dish. Pour the sour cream mixture over and bake until nicely browned on top – about twenty-five minutes.

A crisp green salad goes well with this dish.

KAISERERDÄPFEL

Emperor's Potatoes

1 lb (450 g) cooked, peeled potatoes	2 eggs
3½ oz (100 g) butter	6 tablespoons sour cream
	salt
	butter for the dish

Let the potatoes get quite cold, then grate them quite finely on a cheese grater. (Do not use a food processor for this – it does not work.)

Cream the butter until light and fluffy. Separate eggs. Add the yolks to the creamed butter, one by one, beating well after each addition. Stir in the sour cream and the potatoes. Whisk whites with a pinch of salt until stiff, then fold them into the potato mixture. Pile the mixture into a buttered gratin dish and bake at Gas Mark 5, 375°F, 190°C until nicely browned on top (about thirty to thirty-five minutes).

KÜMMELERDÄPFEL

Potatoes Roasted with Garlic and Caraway Seeds

Sometimes known as *falscher Schweinsbraten* – 'pretending to be roast pork' – this could make quite a substantial course in its own right, accompanied by a crisp green salad. Or serve the potatoes as an accompaniment to hot or cold roast meat.

2 lbs (900 g) fairly large potatoes	2 heaped tablespoons good pork dripping
2 – 3 cloves garlic	1 teaspoon caraway seeds
salt	

Wash and dry, but do not peel the potatoes. Cut them into halves or quarters. Crush the garlic with salt under the blade of a knife. Melt the dripping in a large roasting tin, add the garlic and potatoes. Shake the tin so that the potatoes are covered all over with the fat. Sprinkle with caraway seeds. Arrange the potatoes, cut side up, in the roasting tin and sprinkle with salt. Roast at Gas Mark 6, 400°F, 200°C until nicely browned – roasting time depending on size.

MAJORANERDÄPFEL

Marjoram Potatoes

1½ lbs (650 g) cooked,   salt and pepper
  peeled potatoes   4 fluid oz (⅛ litre) sour
2 oz (60 g) butter   cream
1½ oz (40 g) plain flour
1 pint (good ½ litre) clear
  beef broth
1 heaped tablespoon finely
  chopped fresh marjoram

Best cooked in an flameproof dish from which the potatoes can also
be served.

Slice the potatoes to about the thickness of a fifty pence piece. Melt
the butter over low heat, blend in the flour and gradually stir in the
beef broth and the chopped marjoram. Leave to simmer for about five
minutes until well blended, stirring from time to time. Add the potatoes
and cook gently until the potatoes are warmed through – if you are
using freshly cooked potatoes, cook only as long as it takes for them to
be incorporated into the sauce. Add the sour cream and stir. Taste and
adjust seasoning if necessary. Excellent even without the sour cream,
though it does lend a special touch.

PAPRIKA ERDÄPFEL

Paprika Potatoes

2 onions   salt
5 large potatoes, peeled   1 teaspoon paprika
  and quartered   1 tablespoon tomato purée
3 oz (80 g) lard or
  dripping

Peel and slice the onions finely. Melt the lard in a thick saucepan and
soften the onions, then turn up the heat to brown them lightly. Add a
pinch of salt and the potatoes, paprika and tomato purée. Stir, then
add a little water. Cover and simmer gently until potatoes are cooked,
adding more water as necessary – about 9 fluid oz (¼ l) in all.

SARDELLENERDÄPFEL

Anchovy Potatoes

1½ lb (¾ kg) peeled raw potatoes	1 heaped tablespoon chopped parsley
3 oz (80 g) olive oil or good dripping	4 anchovy fillets, finely chopped
1 shallot or 1 teaspoon finely chopped onion	8 fluid oz (225 ml) sour cream

Slice the potatoes fairly thinly. Heat the oil or dripping. Finely chop the shallot and lightly brown in the fat. Add the parsley, stir and then add the potatoes, turning them over so that they are well blended with the shallot and parsley. Cover and simmer over very low heat, shaking the pan from time to time, until the potatoes are cooked. Mix the sour cream with the chopped anchovies, pour over the potatoes and reheat gently. Serve sprinkled with chopped parsley.

SAURE ERDÄPFEL

Sweet and Sour Potatoes

2 lbs (900 g) waxy potatoes	1 bayleaf
1 small onion	winter savory, chopped
½ garlic clove	parsley root, finely chopped
1 tablespoon chopped parsley	18 fluid oz (½ litre) good stock, preferably veal
2 tablespoons olive oil or good dripping	dash of wine vinegar
2 scant tablespoons plain flour	pinch of sugar
salt	1 finely chopped cucumber pickled in brine or 1 dessertspoon chopped capers
6 peppercorns	

Cook the potatoes in their skins, peel and cut into slices. Chop the onion finely, crush the garlic. Heat the fat, add onion, garlic and parsley and brown very lightly. Add the flour, stir until very lightly coloured, then stir in the stock, salt, peppercorns, bayleaf, winter savory and parsley root. Add a dash of wine vinegar and a pinch of sugar. Simmer very gently for about twenty minutes. Add potatoes and stir to blend. Finally stir in chopped pickled cucumber or capers – but not both!

SENFERDÄPFERL

Mustard Potatoes

When the Viennese really take something to their hearts they add the diminutive 'r' by way of endearment – as in roast goose which is often called Ganserl and as in *Senferdäpferl*, a wonderful old-fashioned way of preparing potatoes with a warm mustard dressing. Marvellous with cold meats. Failing the typical Viennese *Estragon Senf* (mild mustard scented with tarragon), Dijon mustard will do very nicely, provided you use tarragon vinegar.

1 lb (450 g) slim, waxy potatoes (*Kipfler* for preference)	dash of wine vinegar
	1 heaped tablespoon Dijon or tarragon mustard
salt and pepper	4 tablespoons olive oil
2 egg yolks	finely chopped chives

Boil the potatoes in their skins, then peel and slice them into a bowl whilst still hot. Sprinkle with salt.

Put the egg yolks into a bowl, add a small pinch of salt and a little finely ground white pepper, a dash of wine vinegar (or tarragon vinegar if using Dijon mustard) and the mustard. Stand the bowl over a pan of simmering water and gradually add the olive oil. Stir over steam – making sure that the water underneath does not touch the bowl – until thickened, which will happen almost immediately. Pour over the potatoes and mix very lightly. Cover and leave to stand for about five to ten minutes. Sprinkle with chives before serving.

TOPFENERDÄPFEL

Potatoes with Curd Cheese

Claimed by Carinthia as its very own, but equally at home in Lower Austria and Burgenland – in fact wherever there is plenty of good curd cheese (*Topfen*) and *Speck* – a favourite combination.

1¾ lb (800 g) potatoes	good pinch of salt
14 oz (400 g) curd cheese	3½ oz (100 g) bacon in one piece

Boil potatoes in their skins, peel and slice. Sprinkle with salt. Dice bacon and fry until brown. Butter a gratin dish and arrange alternate layers of potatoes, cheese and bacon. Brown at Gas Mark 6, 400°F, 200°C.

REIS

Rice

The following two ways of cooking rice are the ones mainly favoured in Austria. Rice and liquid are always measured in cups, making the exact size of the cup immaterial.

First method
2 cups rice
3 cups good beef broth

2 tablespoons butter
salt

Put the rice in a sieve and rinse it under hot running water, then shake dry. Add butter to beef broth, salt to taste and bring to boil. Throw in the rice, let it boil up once, then lower the heat immediately. Simmer very gently in a covered saucepan until the rice is cooked and has absorbed all the liquid.

Second method
2 cups rice
2 tablespoons butter or
   good dripping or oil
1 medium-sized onion

salt and pepper
4 cups water or good
   stock

Wash the rice as before, drain well and shake dry. Heat the fat in a thick saucepan, add the rice and stir over low heat until the rice looks transparent. Add boiling water or stock, salt, pepper and the onion. Cover and simmer very gently until the rice is tender and has absorbed all the liquid – about twenty minutes. Remove saucepan lid, discard onion, put a clean napkin over saucepan and re-cover for a few minutes to absorb any extra moisture.

In either method, the rice can be cooked in the oven instead, using a covered casserole, at Gas Mark 3 – 4, 325 – 350°F, 160 – 180°C. For the second method you can also chop the onion finely and soften it in the butter before adding the rice.

RISI BISI

You will sometimes find this listed as *Risipisi* – all one word – on restaurant menus. It is, of course, the barely disguised Venetian *Risi e Bisi* – but not quite: in Austria *Risi Bisi* – whichever way you spell it – is served as an accompaniment to meat and it does not contain bacon or ham. If ham is added, the dish disclaims its Italian origins altogether and becomes Austrian *Schinkenreis*, often served as a separate course.

Serves 4

1 small onion
2 heaped tablespoons
  butter
4 heaped tablespoons
  shelled young peas
9 oz (250 g) arborio rice

18 fluid oz (500 ml) good
  meat broth or water
salt and pepper
Parmesan cheese
  (optional)

Chop the onion very finely. Melt half the butter in a thick saucepan, add the onion and allow it to soften over low heat. Rinse the rice under a hot tap and shake it dry. Add the rice to the onion and toss it in the butter until the rice is transparent. Add the meat broth and the peas and simmer gently until the rice is cooked – about twenty minutes – by which time all the liquid will have been absorbed. Adjust seasoning if necessary.

Remove saucepan lid and place a clean napkin over the saucepan and re-cover for a minute or two, then stir in the remaining butter. Depending on the main course – and the vegetables served with it – sprinkle the rice with grated Parmesan or serve as it is.

This is not a dish for marrowfat peas – if you cannot get young, tender and above all small peas, use frozen petit pois and stir them in, defrosted, about five minutes before the rice is cooked.

ANANASKRAUT

Sauerkraut with Pineapple

Particularly good with game.

Serves 6

2 lbs (900 g) Sauerkraut
salt

about 1 tablespoon sugar
1 lb (450 g) pineapple cut
  into small chunks

Cut through the Sauerkraut with a sharp knife to shorten the strands. Cook the Sauerkraut in its own liquid or in white wine with a good pinch of salt and a little sugar, then add the pineapple chunks and simmer until heated through. Or, if using tinned pineapple, drain the Sauerkraut and cook it in the pineapple liquid, adding a pinch of salt. Cut the pineapple into cubes and add to the Sauerkraut when it is cooked, then heat through.

GABELKRAUT

'Forked' Sauerkraut

During cooking, and serving, the Sauerkraut is loosened with a fork, hence the name.

1½ lbs (¾ kg) Sauerkraut	1 small onion, finely
salt	chopped
½ teaspoon caraway seeds	1 teaspoon sugar
2 oz (60 g) fat bacon or	
Speck	

Drain the Sauerkraut and press out all remaining liquid. Cut three or four times through the Sauerkraut to shorten strands. Put the Sauerkraut into a saucepan, add a little water, salt and the caraway seeds. Cover and simmer gently for about half an hour, lifting it with a fork from time to time to loosen it.

Dice the *Speck* or fat bacon, having cut off the rind. Put bacon or *Speck* into a thick saucepan and heat until the fat begins to run, then add the onion. Brown onion and cubed bacon in its own fat, then add the sugar and let it caramelize. Add the Sauerkraut, stir and then leave it to simmer for another five minutes. Loosen the Sauerkraut with a fork as you arrange it in a serving dish and moisten with a little of the cooking liquid.

SAUERKRAUT

My Tyrolean cousin swears that this is the only authentic way to cook Sauerkraut – certainly in the Tyrol. It differs quite a bit from the more usual method, but it is excellent, particularly if served as an accompaniment to roast pork, smoked pork and, of course, Tyrolean dumplings.

2¼ lb (1 kg) Sauerkraut	salt
1 ladleful water	1 medium-sized onion
1 bayleaf	2 dessert apples, peeled,
3 juniper berries	cored and quartered
	2 ladlefuls clear beef broth

Put the Sauerkraut into a large pan, add the water, bayleaf, juniper berries, salt, quartered apples and the onion, peeled but left whole. Simmer gently for half an hour, then add 2 ladlefuls of clear beef broth and simmer for another half an hour. If necessary add a little more stock.

I have not forgotten the pepper – my cousin says that this must not be added on any account!

SPINATPUDDING

Spinach Pudding

1 lb (450 g) spinach	1 oz (28 g) fresh
2 day-old rolls	breadcrumbs, plus a
milk	heaped tablespoon for
3½ oz (100 g) butter	garnish
4 eggs	1 heaped tablespoon
salt	butter
nutmeg	butter and flour for the
1 tablespoon chopped	pudding basin
parsley	
3 fluid oz (85 ml) sour cream	

Butter and flour a pudding basin. Steam or cook the spinach in its own steam i.e. just the water clinging to the leaves, shaking the pan from time to time and turning over the spinach leaves. Drain off all liquid, then squeeze out excess moisture. Sieve the spinach or put through a blender or food processor. Grate the crust off the rolls and soak the crumb in a little milk to soften.

Cream the butter. Separate eggs, beat the yolks into the creamed butter, one by one, then add the sieved spinach, salt, grated nutmeg, chopped parsley and sour cream. Whisk whites until stiff and fold into the mixture alternately with the breadcrumbs. Pile mixture into buttered and floured pudding basin and steam for one hour.

Melt the heaped tablespoon butter and fry the tablespoon breadcrumbs until crisp and golden.

Turn out the pudding onto a warmed serving dish and sprinkle with the fried breadcrumbs. Serve at once.

For a slightly more substantial dish surround the pudding with finely chopped lean ham and serve with a sharp tomato sauce.

SPINATROULADE I

Spinach Roulade I

For the roulade	*For the filling*
½ lb (225 g) spinach,	1 tablespoon butter
cooked and drained	½ lb (225 g) mushrooms,
2 oz (60 g) butter	cleaned and sliced
2 level tablespoons plain	1 tablespoon plain flour
flour	9 fluid oz (¼ l) milk
6 fluid oz (170 ml) milk	salt and pepper
salt and pepper	chopped parsley
mace	½ lb (225 g) lean chopped
4 eggs	ham
butter and flour for the	
baking sheet	

Frozen spinach is quite suitable for this dish, but use either leaf or chopped spinach – 'creamed' spinach does not work. If you are using a food processor, there is no need to cook the spinach first – just leave it to defrost, press out all water by placing it in a clean tea towel and then purée it. If you are not using a food processor or blender, it is best to cook the spinach lightly first.

Preheat the oven to Gas Mark 5, 375°F, 190°C. Line a baking sheet with two layers of greaseproof paper and butter the paper well. Dust with flour or with fine breadcrumbs.

Reduce spinach to a purée either in a blender or food processor, or sieve it. Melt butter in a saucepan and stir in the flour. Gradually add milk and stir over a low heat until you have a thick sauce. Add the spinach, salt, pepper and a pinch of mace. Remove from heat.

Separate eggs. Beat yolks gradually into the sauce, leave to cool. Whisk whites until stiff and fold into the mixture. Spread the mixture to about the thickness of a finger, or a little thicker over the prepared baking sheet and bake for twenty to twenty-five minutes.

Meanwhile prepare the filling. Melt the butter in a saucepan and add mushrooms. Cover and leave to simmer very gently until the mushrooms are cooked. Dust with flour, stir and then blend in the milk. Add salt, pepper and a little chopped parsley. Stir over low heat until thickened, then stir in the ham.

Remove spinach pastry from the oven and carefully turn it out onto a warmed serving dish. Peel off the paper – it may need a little easing with a palette knife. Spread the filling to within 1/2 inch of the edges and roll up the pastry as for Swiss roll, then serve.

The filling can of course be varied – chopped hardboiled eggs in a thick bechamel sauce are very good, sharpened with finely scraped anchovies, but I prefer the mixture of ham and mushrooms which I think blends perfectly with the spinach.

If the spinach is intended as a second course, set it on an ovenproof dish and put it back into the oven at Gas Mark 5, 375°F, 190°C whilst you have your first course – the roulade will puff up slightly and brown a little.

Spinatroulade II

4 eggs	salt and pepper
4½ oz (120 g) cooked mashed potatoes	nutmeg
	2 scant oz (50 g) plain flour
4½ fluid oz (⅛ l) sour cream	butter and breadcrumbs for the baking sheet
9 oz (¼ kg) spinach, cooked and sieved	

Separate eggs. Cream mashed potatoes with yolks and sour cream. Whisk whites until stiff and fold into the mixture, then fold in the

sieved spinach seasoned with salt, pepper and nutmeg and finally fold
in the flour. Spread mixture on a buttered baking sheet sprinkled with
breadcrumbs and bake at Gas Mark 6, 400°F, 200°C for about ten
minutes. Carefully turn onto a kitchen towel previously wrung out in
warm water. Spread with filling, roll up and put back into the oven for
a few more minutes.

For the filling use the one described in the previous recipe, or a light
bechamel sauce into which chopped ham has been folded.

SPINAT SOUFFLÉS

Spinach Soufflés

The mixture could, of course, be used to make one large soufflé, but
using small individual soufflé dishes not only reduces the baking time
(if you are serving the spinach soufflés as a first course you can prepare
the basic mixture in advance and just whisk the egg whites and slip
the soufflés into the oven while your guests are having an aperitif).
And small individual soufflés, all nicely puffed up, make a splendid
and festive start to any meal.

Serves 4 – 6

12 – 14 oz (340 g – 390 g) cooked spinach	4 fluid oz (110 ml) milk
salt	2 eggs
ground mace or nutmeg	1 oz (25 g) grated
1 heaped tablespoon butter	Parmesan cheese (optional)
1 lightly heaped tablespoon plain flour	butter and flour for the soufflé dishes

Press out all water from the spinach, then sieve it or pass it through a
blender or food processor so that you have a fine purée. Season with
salt and ground mace or nutmeg.

Melt the butter, stir in the flour and gradually add the milk. Cook to
a thick sauce. Add the spinach and stir to blend. Separate eggs. Beat the
yolks into the spinach mixture and fold in the grated Parmesan cheese
(I have made this 'optional' because the soufflé mixture is excellent
without it, but it adds a little more 'bite'). Whisk whites until stiff
and fold in the mixture. Divide between four or six small buttered
and floured soufflé moulds. Quantities are sufficient for four moulds
measuring 3 inches (7½ cm) in diameter, or six moulds measuring 2½
inches (5 cm) in diameter. Bake at Gas Mark 6, 400°F, 200°C until
nicely puffed up and browned on top (fifteen to twenty minutes for a
large soufflé, eight to ten minutes for small ones. But take this as a
rough guide because ovens vary a lot). Serve at once.

WIENER SPINAT

Spinach Viennese Style

2 lbs (900 g) spinach	salt and pepper
1½ oz (45 g) butter	nutmeg
1 tablespoon plain flour	little beef broth or milk
1 crushed garlic clove	

Wash the spinach well, then cook it in very little salted water until just tender – in fact the water clinging to the leaves is usually sufficient. But whatever you do, save any liquid remaining in the saucepan. Purée the spinach. Melt the butter, stir in the flour and gradually add any cooking water from the spinach and enough beef broth or milk to give a thick sauce. Season with salt, pepper and nutmeg and add the garlic. Simmer gently for eight to ten minutes, stirring constantly. Add the spinach, cook briefly until well blended and adjust seasoning if necessary.

SALADS

SALADS

KRAUTSALAT AUF KÄRNTNER ART

Carinthian Cabbage Salad

One of the many dishes typical of Carinthia which Lia Miklau taught me. It is essential that the actual mixing of the salad should take place at the last possible minute.

Serves 4

1 small firm white cabbage	caraway seeds
salt	sour cream

Quarter the cabbage and shred it finely – this is best done with a mandoline cutter. Sprinkle with salt, then work the salt well into the cabbage with your hands. Taste and add more salt if necessary. Mix in a good sprinkling of caraway seeds and as much sour cream as the cabbage will absorb.

WARMER KRAUTSALAT I

Warm Cabbage Salad I

A favourite accompaniment to roast pork. *Speck* – delicious cured and smoked fat pork – should really be used for this salad, but failing that, a thick piece of fat bacon will do nicely.

Serves 4

1 small firm white cabbage weighing about 18 oz (500 g)	3 tablespoons water
1 teaspoon salt	2 – 3 tablespoons wine vinegar
1 teaspoon caraway seeds	pepper
4 oz (100 g) *Speck* or fat bacon in one piece	

Discard coarse outer leaves, quarter cabbage and shred finely. Sprinkle cabbage with salt and caraway seeds and work the shredded cabbage with your hands to blend well. Dice the bacon or *Speck*, put the cubes into a frying pan over low heat to extract the fat and then increase the heat and fry the cubes until crisp. Drain fried bacon on kitchen paper. Pour water and vinegar into the frying pan – stand aside as it is apt to splutter – and pour over the cabbage. Mix well, add a little pepper and sprinkle with the bacon.

Warmer Krautsalat II

Serves 4

1 small firm white cabbage weighing about 18 oz (500 g)	1 teaspoon caraway seeds 6 oz (150 g) diced fat bacon or *Speck*
1 teaspoon salt	good dash of wine vinegar

Remove coarse outer leaves and shred cabbage finely. Pour boiling salted water over the cabbage, cover with a lid and leave to stand for five minutes. Pour off the water and repeat the process twice more. Sprinkle drained cabbage with caraway seeds. Fry diced bacon until crisp. Lift out with a slotted spoon and drain on kitchen paper. Pour a good dash of wine vinegar into the frying pan (careful, it is apt to splutter), swill it round the pan and pour over cabbage. Sprinkle crispy bacon or *Speck* over the top and serve at once.

GURKENSALAT

Cucumber Salad

The traditional accompaniment for *Backhendl* (see page 96), but also excellent with *Wiener Schnitzel* and lots of other Austrian dishes.

Serves 4

1 large cucumber	paprika
salt and pepper	1/2 teaspoon French or Austrian mustard
3 tablespoons olive oil	1/2 clove garlic (optional)
1 tablespoon wine vinegar	

Slice the cucumber very thinly, using a mandoline cutter or the thinnest slicer on a food processor. Whether or not you peel the cucumber first is a question of personal taste (with me it is often also a question of time). Sprinkle with salt, cover and leave to stand for at least half an hour.

Prepare the salad dressing by mixing together the oil, vinegar, salt, pepper and the mustard. In Austria a tablespoon of water – sometimes even two – and a small pinch of sugar would also be added and, according to taste, half a crushed garlic clove. Drain all moisture from the cucumber by putting the slices into a clean cloth or kitchen paper and squeezing gently. Toss cucumber in the dressing and sprinkle a little paprika over it.

FISOLENSALAT

French Bean Salad

Serves 4

1 lb (450 g) French beans
1 small slice rye bread
  without crust
3½ oz (100 g) finely
  chopped walnuts
1 tablespoon chopped
  fresh herbs according
  to season

1 crushed garlic clove
salt and pepper
4 tablespoons olive oil
1 tablespoon wine vinegar

String the beans and, according to size, break in half. Cook the beans briefly in lightly salted boiling water. Drain and refresh. Meanwhile soak the bread in water, squeeze out all moisture. Mix bread with herbs and walnuts. Whisk together oil and vinegar, add salt, pepper and crushed garlic. Stir walnut mixture into oil and vinegar, pour over beans and mix well.

WIENER HERINGSALAT

Viennese Herring Salad

Herring salads are very popular in Austria, particularly during the carnival season which culminates in a herring feast (*Heringschmaus*) on Ash Wednesday – a giant hot and cold buffet featured by practically every restaurant in the country. There are a great many variations on the theme of Herring Salad and every Viennese household, to say nothing of restaurants, has its own treasured recipe. Some add diced cooked celeriac, others cooked dried white beans or diced beetroot. My own version is fairly basic – vary it according to your taste.

Serves 4

4 salted herrings,
  preferably with soft roes
2 – 3 tart eating apples
1½ lbs (700 g) cooked waxy
  potatoes
1 tablespoon finely
  chopped capers
1 very small, finely grated
  onion or shallot

9 fluid oz (250 ml) sour
  cream
2 – 3 pickled cucumbers,
  finely chopped
about 4 tablespoons olive
  oil
salt and pepper
dash of tarragon vinegar
chopped chives

Soak herrings overnight in milk or water, then scale and clean them and cut into squares. Peel, core and dice the apples. Slice the potatoes.

Sieve the soft herring roes, mix with the sour cream and stir in the oil gradually. Add salt, capers, pepper and a dash of vinegar, then fold in the herrings, apples, potatoes, onion and pickled cucumbers. Chill for a few hours before serving. Sprinkle with chopped chives.

This recipe is based on using salted herring which has to be soaked and scaled before it can be used. Using Matjes herring fillets is a perfectly permissible short cut, but you will not get the soft herring roes which are a necessary part of the dressing. A tablespoon or two of good mayonnaise can be used instead.

BRAUNER LINSENSALAT

Brown Lentil Salad

Serves 4
½ lb (225 g) brown lentils
1 medium-sized onion
1 carrot
1 bayleaf
sprig of thyme
a few bacon rinds tied
    together
salt

Dressing
3 tablespoons olive oil
1 tablespoon wine vinegar
Dijon mustard
salt and pepper
1 shallot, finely chopped

Soak the lentils in cold water for a few hours or overnight. Pour away the water. Put the lentils into a saucepan, together with onion, carrot, bayleaf, thyme, bacon rind and a small pinch of salt. Cover with cold water and cook until the lentils are tender. Drain and remove vegetables, herbs and bacon rind.

Make a dressing by dipping a fork into the mustard and using this to blend oil and vinegar. Season with salt and pepper. Pour over the lentils while they are still hot. Sprinkle with shallot.

SCHWAMMERLSALAT

Mushroom Salad

Serves 4
¾ lb (330 g) button
    mushrooms
salt and white pepper
cayenne pepper
1 tablespoon lemon juice
dash of white wine vinegar

4 tablespoons sour cream
    and 1 tablespoon
    Greek yoghurt (or
    5 tablespoons Greek
    yoghurt)
1 – 2 tablespoons olive oil
2 tablespoons chopped
    chives

Clean the mushrooms and slice them into a bowl. Whisk together the lemon juice, vinegar, sour cream, yoghurt and oil until well blended.

Season with salt, white pepper and a flick of cayenne. Add a tablespoon chopped chives and mix the dressing with the mushrooms. Cover and chill for at least half an hour. Serve sprinkled with the remaining chives.

ERDÄPFEL MAYONNAISE

Potato Mayonnaise

Not a 'real' mayonnaise, but a sauce always used in our family for making a very light potato salad.

Serves 4

2 lbs (1 kg) waxy salad potatoes	1 heaped teaspoon tarragon mustard
1 egg	salt and pepper
1 egg yolk	small pinch of sugar
4 tablespoons vinegar	1 tablespoon olive oil
2 tablespoons water	

Boil potatoes in their skins, peel and slice them, still warm, into a bowl.

Prepare dressing while potatoes are cooking. Put all ingredients except the oil in a bowl, and whisk over steam until thick and frothy. Remove from fire, whisk in the oil and continue whisking until cool, then fold in the sliced potatoes.

ERDÄPFELSALAT

Potato Salad

In Austria *Kipfler* potatoes are the only ones used for potato salad, but failing these, small waxy 'salad' potatoes can be used, provided that they are not much thicker than a thumb.

Mixing a Viennese potato salad is quite unlike mixing any other salad – ordinary rules simply do not apply.

Cook 1 lb (½ kg) potatoes in their skins, peel and slice into a bowl while still hot. Sprinkle with salt. Carefully stir 2 tablespoons hot clear beef broth into the potatoes, then mix in 1 tablespoon wine vinegar and finally add 2 – 3 tablespoons olive oil – as much as the potatoes will absorb. Add a twist or two from the peppermill and – if you wish – some very finely chopped or grated onion.

And let me add, just as a matter of interest, that Viennese cooks advocated the use of raspberry vinegar for potato salad well over a hundred years ago. So much for its being an invention of *nouvelle cuisine*!

SAUCES, RELISHES AND ACCOMPANIMENTS

SAUCES, RELISHES AND ACCOMPANIMENTS

Some Austrian sauces – like tomato sauce or mushroom sauce, which is more of a creamed vegetable than a sauce – are worthy recipients of featherlight dumplings, the latter having a natural affinity with *Semmelknödel*, and dill sauce being particularly good with fluffy semolina dumplings. Serve in deep soup plates with the dumpling sitting in the centre surrounded by generous helpings of the sauce.

Gekochtes Rindfleisch, Vienna's famous boiled beef (see page 57), calls for accompaniments which are really more of a relish than a sauce, the most usual ones being horseradish and apple, as well as chive sauce of which there are literally dozens of variations (which explains the large selection of recipes). In old country inns – and traditional ones in Vienna as well – you will often get *Rindfleisch fein garniert*, when the boiled beef is served in the centre of a large dish, surrounded by small compartments holding different accompaniments such as creamed vegetables and potatoes and anything up to five different sauces and relishes. There is no reason however why some of the traditional boiled beef accompaniments should not be served with other meat or indeed fish dishes!

SARDELLENSAUCE I

Anchovy Sauce

Serves 4
4 – 6 anchovy fillets
2 egg yolks
6 tablespoons olive oil
juice of 2 lemons
dash of wine vinegar

dash of brandy
pepper

Scrape the anchovies finely or pound them to a paste. Add to yolks and gradually beat in the oil. Add lemon juice and vinegar. Season with a dash of brandy and a little pepper – salt should not be necessary because of the anchovies, but taste and adjust seasoning if necessary.

Sardellensauce II

Serves 4

1 heaped tablespoon
   butter
1 small finely chopped
   onion or shallot
1 tablespoon chopped
   parsley
1 scant tablespoon plain
   flour
10 fluid oz (280 ml) clear
   beef broth

6 anchovy fillets, finely
   chopped
salt and pepper
a little lemon juice
2 tablespoons double or
   sour cream

Melt the butter and soften the onion or shallot. Add the parsley and fry lightly. Sprinkle in the flour, stir and then gradually add the beef broth. Cook gently until well thickened, sieve and reheat carefully, adding the anchovies. Season with salt, pepper and a little lemon juice and stir in the cream or sour cream just before serving.

WARME RINDFLEISCH SAUCE

Sauce to Serve with Boiled Beef

Serves 4

2 tablespoons clear beef
   broth
3 oz (90 g) melted butter
2 egg yolks

3 tablespoons double
   cream
juice of ½ lemon

Put all ingredients except the melted butter into the top of a double boiler, or in a bowl set over steam, and whisk, adding the melted butter gradually. As soon as the sauce has thickened, serve at once.

   A little salt may have to be added, but as a rule the seasoning of the stock combined with the sharpness of the lemon juice is all that is required.

KASTANIENPUREE

Chestnut Purée

An excellent accompaniment to game.

Serves 6

1 lb (450 g) chestnuts
¼ pint (⅛ l) milk
¼ pint (⅛ l) single cream
1 – 2 tablespoons butter

1 tablespoon sugar
salt
½ small celeriac
a little lemon juice

Cut across the chestnuts with a sharp knife and set them on a baking tray. Put them into a hot oven (Gas Mark 6, 400°F, 200°C) until the shells burst open. Meanwhile heat milk and cream with sugar and about 1 tablespoon butter. Shell the chestnuts, drop them into the hot milk and cook until soft.

Cook peeled and sliced celeriac in salted water to which a little lemon juice has been added and drain well. Purée chestnuts and celeriac together with a little butter and add salt to taste. The chestnuts can also be cooked in clear bouillon, in which case stir a little cream into the purée.

SCHNITTLAUCHSAUCE

Chive Sauce

Schnittlauchsauce is one of the traditional – and almost revered – accompaniments to the equally traditional and revered boiled beef (see page 57), and consequently there are dozens of varieties. Here are just a few:

Schnittlauchsauce I

Serves 4

2 eggs
1/4 teaspoon plain flour
5 fluid oz (140 ml) clear
  beef broth
2 teaspoons icing sugar
2 tablespoons white wine
  vinegar

salt and pepper
chopped chives
2 tablespoons olive oil

Mix together the eggs, flour and a tablespoon of the beef broth. Blend until smooth. Put sugar and remaining beef broth in a saucepan, set over low heat and stir until the sugar has dissolved. Add salt, pepper and a tablespoon of the vinegar. Remove from heat and pour into the egg mixture, whisking constantly. Pour the mixture into a double saucepan or a bowl set over a saucepan of simmering water. Heat gently, whisking constantly, until the mixture is thick. Stir in the remaining vinegar and the oil and remove from heat. Stir in plenty of chopped chives and serve warm.

Schnittlauchsauce II

> *Serves 4*
>
> 2 tablespoons clear beef
>   broth
> 4 tablespoons olive oil
> 2 tablespoons white wine
>   vinegar
> 1 tablespoon French or
>   Austrian (Estragon)
>   mustard
>
> salt and pepper
> pinch of sugar
> 2 eggs
> chopped chives

Remove any trace of fat from the beef broth. Put all the ingredients except the chives into a double boiler and whisk over steam until thickened. Remove from heat and whisk until cold. Add plenty of chopped chives and serve cold.

Schnittlauchsauce III

> *Serves 4*
>
> 3 hardboiled eggs
> 9 fluid oz (¼ l) sour cream
> salt and pepper
>
> 1 tablespoon olive oil
> chopped chives

Shell the eggs and remove yolks – the whites can be chopped and sprinkled over salads. Crush the yolks and blend with the oil. Gradually stir in the sour cream and salt and pepper to taste. Just before serving add a good handful of chopped chives.

Schnittlauchsauce IV

> *Serves 4*
>
> 3 hardboiled egg yolks
> 2 raw egg yolks
> 2 day-old rolls
> about 8 fluid oz (250 ml)
>   olive oil
>
> salt
> pinch of sugar
> dash of wine vinegar
> 2 heaped tablespoons
>   chopped chives

Grate the crust off the rolls and soak crumb in water. Squeeze out all moisture and sieve the softened crust. Blend together hardboiled and raw egg yolks, stir in the sieved crusts and gradually add the olive oil, exactly as if making mayonnaise. Season with salt, sugar and a good dash of wine vinegar and stir in the chopped chives.

Schnittlauchsauce V

Serves 4

2 hardboiled egg yolks
1 teaspoon French
   mustard
salt and pepper
dash of wine vinegar
olive oil
1 tablespoon chopped
   chives

½ tablespoon chopped
   capers
1 tablespoon good meat
   jelly

Mix the egg yolks to a smooth paste with mustard, salt, pepper and a dash of wine vinegar. Gradually add sufficient olive oil to give the consistency of whipped cream. Stir in chives and capers, also meat jelly and adjust seasoning if necessary.

Schnittlauchsauce VI (the cheat's way)

Stir chopped chives into good mayonnaise, then stir in a tablespoon cream or sour cream. If anyone clamours for the recipe, say it is a family secret!

GURKENSAUCE I

Fresh Cucumber Sauce

Like *Marillentörtchen* (see page 246), this is one of Lisl Wagner-Bacher's 'Specials'. She invented the sauce for one of her fish dishes, but I find it goes equally well with roast meat, particularly lamb.

Serves 4

1 flat coffeespoon mustard
   seeds
4 fluid oz (110 ml) good
   clear stock
1 large cucumber
1 tablespoon butter

dash of wine vinegar
2 tablespoons double
   cream
1 tablespoon chopped dill
salt and pepper

Soak the mustard seeds in the stock for one to two hours. De-seed but do not peel the cucumber and chop it finely. Simmer the cucumber in the butter, then add the strained stock and leave to cook, uncovered, until most of the liquid has been reduced and the cucumber is only just tender – do not allow to overcook. Add the cream, dill, salt, pepper and a dash of wine vinegar. Blend well and adjust seasoning if necessary.

GURKENSAUCE II

Sauce Made with Pickled Cucumbers

Serves 4

2 – 3 medium-sized
  cucumbers pickled in
  brine
1 tablespoon finely
  chopped fresh dill
1 shallot, finely chopped
1 anchovy fillet
2 hardboiled eggs

3 tablespoons olive oil
1 tablespoon French
  mustard
salt and pepper
dash of vinegar
1 coffeespoon tomato
  purée

Chop the cucumbers finely. Scrape the anchovy with a knife. Mix the egg yolks with the scraped anchovy and the olive oil. Combine with all the other ingredients, including the finely chopped egg whites.

In Austria the vinegar would be diluted with water for a milder taste – I prefer the undiluted sharpness of the vinegar, but use it with restraint!

WARME GURKERLSAUCE

Warm Sauce made with Pickled Cucumbers

Serves 4

2 – 3 cucumbers pickled
  in brine
2 tablespoons butter
1 tablespoon plain flour
½ pint (9 fluid oz) clear
  beef broth

salt and pepper
dash of pickling liquid
1 tablespoon sour cream
1 tablespoon finely
  chopped fresh dill

Slice the cucumbers thinly. If they are very fat, halve them lengthwise before slicing. Melt butter, stir in flour, then add broth and cook gently until thickened. Add cucumbers, salt, pepper and a dash of the liquid in which the cucumbers were pickled. Simmer very gently for half an hour. Stir in a tablespoon of sour cream and sprinkle with chopped dill.

DILLENSAUCE

Dill Sauce

Excellent with boiled beef, dill sauce is also a favourite sauce for serving with dumplings – in fact I have fond childhood memories of a featherlight semolina dumpling surrounded by dill sauce – a typical 'meatless Friday' luncheon dish, invariably preceded by *Stoss Suppe* (see page 19) in my native Lower Austria.

1 heaped tablespoon
  butter
1 scant tablespoon plain
  flour
¼ pint (150 ml) clear beef
  broth
1½ tablespoons lemon
  juice or white wine
  vinegar
salt and pepper
sugar

2 – 3 tablespoons finely
  chopped fresh dill
¼ pint (150 ml) sour
  cream

Melt the butter in a small thick saucepan. Stir in the flour and cook gently until well blended. Gradually stir in the beef broth. Add salt, pepper, sugar, lemon juice (or vinegar) and the chopped dill. Cook until thickened, stirring all the time, then add the sour cream and simmer gently until well blended. Adjust seasoning if necessary, adding extra sugar or vinegar. The sauce should have a distinctly sweet and sour flavour. Serve hot.

BOHNENSAUCE

Dried Bean Sauce

Serves 4

1 cupful dried white
  butter beans
2 tablespoons olive oil
salt and pepper
dash of white wine vinegar
1 finely chopped small
  onion or shallot

1 tablespoon chopped
  parsley
1 – 2 tablespoons clear
  beef broth

Soak the beans overnight in cold water. Pour away the water, put the beans in a saucepan, cover with water and cook until soft. Drain well and sieve. Stir in the other ingredients, adding enough clear beef broth to achieve a thick, creamy consistency.

APFELKREN

Horseradish Sauce with Apples

Serves 4

1 lb (450 g) tart cooking
  apples
lemon juice
pinch of sugar

2 tablespoons white wine
  vinegar
salt
about 2 oz (50 g) freshly
  grated horseradish

Peel, core and quarter the apples. Place in a saucepan, add a squeeze of lemon juice and a pinch of sugar. Cook over very low heat, stirring frequently, until the apples are soft. Do not add any water unless absolutely necessary. Sieve the apples, add vinegar, freshly grated horseradish and a pinch of salt. Mix well and serve cold.

ERDÄPFELKREN

Potato and Horseradish Cream

1½ lbs (¾ kg) potatoes
salt
8 fluid oz (¼ l) clear beef
  broth
4 fluid oz (⅛ l) double
  cream

3 tablespoons freshly
  grated horseradish
2 oz (50 g) butter
grated nutmeg

Peel and quarter the potatoes and cook them in salted water until tender. Drain, then return potatoes to the pan in which they were cooked. Cover and leave for two to three minutes. Stir in beef broth and cream and reheat gently, adding the butter cut into small pieces. Finally stir in the horseradish and a little grated nutmeg.

ESSIGKREN

Horseradish with Vinegar Dressing

Serves 4

2 tablespoons clear beef broth
3 tablespoons finely grated
  horseradish
3 tablespoons olive oil

pinch each of salt, sugar
  and pepper
1 tablespoon white wine
  vinegar

Heat the beef broth and pour over grated horseradish. Leave to cool. Mix together remaining ingredients as for a salad dressing, then stir in the horseradish. Serve cold.

GEFRORENER MEERRETTICH

Iced Horseradish

A very elegant accompaniment to meat and not just to the famous boiled beef. The fact that it counts as a rather superior accompaniment can be gathered from the fact that it is described as *Meerrettich*, and not the Austrian *Kren* (which is the same thing).

Quantities are a matter of taste, depending on how 'hot' you want this to be: basically it consists of freshly grated horseradish stirred into whipped cream, together with a good dash of lemon juice, a small dash of vinegar and a pinch of salt. Either chill in the refrigerator for at least half an hour or let it freeze into a soft mousse in the ice-cube tray, having first set the control to maximum.

MANDELKREN

Horseradish with Almonds

Serves 4

¼ pint (150 ml) double cream
1 oz (30 g) ground blanched almonds

1 – 2 heaped tablespoons horseradish
pinch of icing sugar

Whisk cream until stiff with a pinch of icing sugar. Fold in the ground almonds and the grated horseradish (quantity varies according to taste and strength of horseradish). Chill before serving.

This is not really a sauce, much more of a savoury mousse, and it can be frozen in the ice-cube tray of a refrigerator (previously set at maximum) and served cut into slices, or scooped into small mounds.

OBERSKREN

Horseradish Cream

Serves 4

4 tablespoons double cream
2 tablespoons white white vinegar

1 teaspoon icing sugar
pinch of salt
grated horseradish

Mix together cream, wine vinegar, sugar and salt and stir in sufficient finely grated horseradish to give a thick and smooth consistency.

Note: horseradish must be freshly grated – it loses strength if left for any length of time.

PREISELBEERKREN

Cranberry Sauce with Horseradish

Serves 4

4 tablespoons cooked cranberries	salt
1 – 2 tablespoons freshly grated horseradish	a little lemon juice
1 tablespoon French or Austrian mustard	5 fluid oz (⅛ l) double cream

Blend together cranberries, horseradish, mustard, and lemon juice – in a food processor, if possible. Whisk cream with a pinch of salt until thick and fold cranberry mixture into it.

RAHMKREN MIT EIERN

Eggs with Horseradish Cream

An ideal accompaniment to farmhouse sausages, smoked pork and grilled meat.

4 hardboiled eggs	1 tablespoon freshly grated horseradish
¼ pint (125 ml) sour cream	salt

Shell and chop the hardboiled eggs. Gently stir in the sour cream, grated horseradish and salt to taste.

ROTER RÜBENKREN

Beetroot and Horseradish Relish

½ lb (225 g) cooked beetroots	salt and pepper
1 small cooking apple	pinch of sugar
1 heaped tablespoon freshly grated horseradish	1 tablespoon wine vinegar
	2 tablespoons olive oil

Peel and grate the beetroot. Core and grate the apple, with or without the skin. Mix together the beetroot, apple and horseradish. Blend vinegar, sugar, salt and pepper with the oil to make a dressing and add to the beetroot mixture. Adjust seasoning if necessary. Serve cold.

It will keep well if stored in a cool place, preferably in a screw-topped jar – in fact it matures well. The apple may be omitted.

SEMMELKREN

Bread Sauce with Horseradish

Very good with boiled beef or roast pork.

Serves 4

4 day-old rolls	1 tablespoon butter
13 fluid oz (375 ml) clear beef broth	3 – 4 tablespoons freshly grated horseradish
1 teaspoon sugar	2 tablespoons double cream or 1 – 2 egg yolks
salt and pepper	(optional)
nutmeg	

Grate the rind off the rolls and cut the crumb into slices. Remove every speck of fat from the beef broth. Bring broth to the boil, pour over rolls and leave for the rolls to soften. Sieve the mixture, then heat it in a small thick saucepan, whisking all the time. Still whisking, add sugar and seasonings and then whisk in the butter. Cook until thickened, then add the horseradish and stir in the cream or egg yolks. Blend until smooth but do not allow the mixture to boil.

SCHWAMMERLSAUCE

Mushroom Sauce

Served with dumplings, this makes a very satisfying main dish, but it is equally good with boiled beef. Field mushrooms, particularly ceps, are best, but cultivated mushrooms will do very nicely.

1/2 lb (225 g) mushrooms	sprig of thyme
1 heaped tablespoon butter	1 tablespoon plain flour
1/2 teaspoon caraway seeds	scant 1/2 pint (250 ml) clear beef broth
pepper	5 fluid oz (125 ml) double or sour cream
juice of 1/2 lemon	salt
1 tablespoon chopped parsley	

Clean but do not peel the mushrooms. Slice them finely. Melt butter in a thick saucepan, add the mushrooms, caraway seeds, parsley, thyme, pepper and lemon juice. Cover and simmer gently until the mushrooms are tender – about twenty minutes. Dust with the flour, stir and then add the beef broth gradually, stirring all the time. Simmer for another five to ten minutes, then stir in the cream or sour cream. Continue cooking until the sauce has thickened again. Adjust seasoning if necessary.

SENFSAUCE

Mustard Sauce

Serves 4

3 eggs	3 tablespoons French
1½ oz (40 g) softened	mustard
butter	1 scant dessertspoon
4 fluid oz (⅛ l) clear beef	redcurrant jam
broth	salt
1 teaspoon lemon juice	

Put eggs, softened butter, mustard and clear broth into a bowl and whisk over steam until thickened. Remove from heat, add salt, lemon juice and finally redcurrant jam. Serve at once.

PARADEISSAUCE

Tomato Sauce

2 lbs (900 g) tomatoes	sugar
1 medium-sized onion,	parsley root
coarsely chopped	lemon juice or vinegar
1 crushed clove garlic	1 heaped tablespoon
2 cloves	butter
few lovage leaves	1 scant tablespoon plain
salt	flour

Wash the tomatoes, do not dry them. Break up the tomatoes and put them into a thick saucepan with about 9 fluid oz (¼ litre) water, onion, garlic, cloves, lovage, parsley root, and simmer gently until the tomatoes are soft. Melt the butter, add flour and stir gently until light golden brown. Sieve tomatoes, strain liquid, and add to the roux with the salt, sugar and lemon juice or vinegar. Simmer until well blended and thickened.

PUDDINGS,
HOT AND COLD,
WITH
THEIR SAUCES

PUDDINGS, HOT AND COLD, WITH THEIR SAUCES

Austrian puddings are marvellous, from the simplest to the most extravagant. You may think that I have been over-generous with stating 'serves four' on some of the recipes which could well serve six. They could in theory, but in practice I have found that second helpings are nearly always accepted and indeed called for and for this reason I have swayed towards generosity.

SCHWARZBROTPUDDING MIT ROTWEINSAUCE

Bread Pudding with Red Wine Sauce

Serves 4

For the pudding
1½ fluid oz (40 ml) red wine
1 heaped tablespoon icing sugar
2 egg yolks

For the sauce
2½ oz (75 g) brown breadcrumbs
2 fluid oz (60 ml) red wine
2½ oz (75 g) butter
3 oz (80 g) icing sugar
2 eggs
1 oz (25 g) ground hazelnuts
cinnamon
vanilla sugar
grated orange rind
butter and ground hazelnuts for the dish

Moisten breadcrumbs with red wine. Cream butter and sugar until light and fluffy. Separate eggs.

Beat yolks into creamed butter. Whisk whites until stiff and fold into yolk mixture, alternately with ground hazelnuts and moistened breadcrumbs. Add cinnamon, vanilla sugar and a little grated orange rind.

Butter 4 ramekins or dariole moulds and dust with ground hazelnuts. Divide mixture between the four dishes and put them into a roasting tin with water to come half-way up the ramekins or dariole moulds. Bake at Gas Mark 6, 400°F, 200°C for about twenty to twenty-five minutes.

Carefully turn out the puddings onto warmed plates and cover with the sauce. A small teaspoonful of preserved cranberries on top of each pudding is a nice, though optional, addition.

To make the sauce whisk together red wine, egg yolks and sugar over steam until frothy.

SILBERNUDELN

Bohemian Bun Pudding

Small yeast buns served warm with ice-cold *Kanarienmilch* (see page 254) make an excellent pudding for a cold day. *Silbernudeln* are a rich relation of the more mundane *Dukatennudeln*, the difference being that the latter are made without almonds (use 30 g – 40 g extra flour), cooked in milk instead of cream and slightly smaller – the size of an old ducat, in fact.

For about 50 buns, 2 – 2¹/₂ inches in diameter

9 fluid oz (250 ml) milk
³/₄ oz (20 g) fresh yeast
³/₄ oz (20 g) caster sugar
18 oz (500 g) plain flour
4 teaspoons vanilla sugar
1 egg
2 egg yolks
good dash of dark rum
1 tablespoon grated orange rind
1 generous oz (30 g) ground almonds

5 oz (140 g) melted butter
1 generous oz (30 g) caster sugar
9 fluid oz (250 ml) single cream (or half milk and half double cream)
1¹/₂ oz (40 g) butter
2 – 3 tablespoons melted butter for brushing over buns

Heat the milk until lukewarm. Cream yeast with a teaspoon of the sugar, add about a cupful of the milk and sprinkle with a teaspoon of flour. Sift remaining flour, sugar and 2 teaspoons of vanilla sugar into a bowl. Make a well in the centre and pour in the yeast mixture. Set in a warm place for the yeast to rise.

When the yeast starts to bubble, add the remaining milk, draw in the flour, then beat in the egg, egg yolks, rum, orange rind, ground almonds and finally the melted butter. Beat well with a wooden spoon, by hand or use the dough hook attachment of the electric mixer. The mixture should be very smooth, shiny and come away clean from the sides of the bowl. Cover with a cloth and leave to rise in a warm place until about doubled in bulk – about forty minutes.

Tip the contents of the bowl onto a warmed pastry board or kitchen table and knead lightly. Roll out to about the thickness of a finger. I do not usually bother to use a rolling pin for this, I just press the dough out gently with my knuckles. Cut into rounds with a 2 – 2¹/₂ inch cutter.

Add the 1 oz caster sugar, remaining vanilla sugar and butter to the cream and heat gently, stirring all the time until sugar and butter have dissolved. Divide liquid between two or three deep ovenproof dishes – ideally ones with sides about 2 – 3 inches high – so that each dish has about ¹/₂ inch of cream in it. Test temperature of cream mixture (it should be lukewarm) and if necessary allow it to cool. Set rounds of dough side by side in the dishes, brush with some of the melted butter, cover with a cloth and leave in a warm place for thirty to forty minutes until doubled in bulk. Brush very gently with remaining melted butter and bake in preheated oven at Gas Mark 5, 375°F, 190°C until nicely browned on top – about forty minutes. Serve warm with *Kanarienmilch* (see page 254).

APFELKNÖDEL IN MOSTSAUCE

Apple Dumplings with Apple Wine Sauce

Tschebull at Egg, on Faaker See, styles itself as 'a Carinthian inn with rooms to let', which is rather an understatement. The rooms are infinitely more comfortable than one would expect of a simple country inn and the cooking – though obviously specialising in regional dishes – is quite exceptional. Their apple dumplings were so much in demand that they've now had the recipe printed to hand out to guests. The original uses local apple wine, but still dry cider can be used instead.

Serves 4
For the pudding
9 oz (250 g) apples, peeled
   and cored
2 oz (50 g) butter
1½ oz (40 g) caster sugar
2 pinches of powdered
   cinnamon
1 pinch each of ground
   cloves and allspice
2 oz (50 g) fine
   breadcrumbs
1 generous oz (30 g)
   ground hazelnuts
1 oz (25 g) raisins
1 egg
flour, egg and breadcrumbs
   for coating
oil for frying

For the sauce
11 fluid oz (300 ml) apple
   wine or dry still cider
⅓ oz (10 g) cornflour
2 eggs
4 oz (120 g) caster sugar
2 cloves
a small piece cinnamon
   bark

Cube the apples. Melt half the butter and lightly sauté the apples in it. Sprinkle with sugar and spices, stir and set aside.

   Melt remaining butter and fry the breadcrumbs in it, then add hazelnuts and raisins. Mix with the apples and bind with lightly beaten egg.

   Form small dumplings, dip them first in flour, then in lightly beaten egg and finally in the breadcrumbs. Fry in deep oil. Drain on kitchen paper and keep warm.

   To make the sauce heat 7 fluid oz (200 ml) of the apple wine with the sugar, cloves and cinnamon bark. Mix remaining apple wine with eggs and cornflour. Add to hot apple wine and whisk over low heat (or over steam) until frothy and thickened. Pour over apple dumplings just before serving.

GERMKNÖDEL (POWIDLKNÖDEL)

Yeast Dumplings Filled with Dark Plum Jam

Light and airy when properly prepared, these dumplings make a very good – if rather filling – pudding for cold days. There are hand-written instructions by the Empress Maria Theresia – mother of Marie Antoinette – that *Powidlknödel* had to appear on the imperial nursery menu at least four times every month, and *Powidl* was supplied to the imperial court in huge wooden tubs from Bohemia. More recently – since it was discovered that yeast dough freezes extremely well – *Powidlknödel* of almost unbelievable size and lightness can be found in mountain huts throughout Austria, where they have become a favourite food of hungry skiers and climbers.

Makes 20 – 24 dumplings
1 lb (500 g) plain flour
½ oz (15 g) fresh yeast
1 tablespoon icing sugar
about 6 tablespoons
   (125 ml) lukewarm milk
2 oz (60 g) butter
2 eggs
1 tablespoon dark rum
½ teaspoon grated lemon
   rind
pinch of salt
Powidl (see page 2)

For serving
1 tablespoon vanilla sugar
4 oz (100 g) melted butter
3 tablespoons ground
   poppyseeds
or
5 tablespoons breadcrumbs
   fried in butter
1 tablespoon vanilla sugar

Sift the flour into a bowl. Cream the yeast with sugar, add about half the lukewarm milk and a teaspoon of the flour and set to prove in a warm place. Melt the butter in the remaining milk.

When the yeast has started to bubble, add to flour, together with the butter/milk mixture and the eggs. Beat in the rum, lemon rind and the salt. Knead well – the dough should be 'smooth as silk and soft like velvet', it says in my old cookery book. When you feel your dough is living up to that description, shape it into a round, cover it with a cloth and leave to rise in a warm place until doubled in bulk.

Knead the dough lightly, then shape into a roll about 1½ –2 inches in diameter. Cut into 20 – 24 equal parts. Flatten each round very slightly, make a little hollow in the centre and fill with a spoonful of *Powidl*. Close dough well over the filling and seal all openings. Set the dumplings on a floured cloth, dust with flour, cover lightly and leave to rise again for about twenty-five minutes, or until doubled in size.

Heat a large pan with very lightly salted water, drop in the dumplings, upside down, leaving plenty of room for expansion. Leave to simmer – tilt the saucepan lid so that the saucepan is not completely covered – for six minutes, then turn over the dumplings carefully and prick each dumpling with a needle or a fine toothpick. Leave to simmer for another six minutes, then lift out carefully.

Keep cooked dumplings warm over steam and cook remaining dumplings as described. Serve at once, covered either with melted butter, ground poppyseeds and vanilla sugar or with fine breadcrumbs fried in butter and vanilla sugar.

Warning: the dumplings are apt to collapse a little – hence the piercing with a fine needle – and should therefore be served as soon as possible. Instead of boiling they may be steamed; butter the steamer in advance, and avoid steaming too many dumplings at the same time.

MARILLENKNÖDEL

Apricot Dumplings

Dumplings filled with fruit – most often plums or apricots, but occasionally cherries and in recent years also strawberries – are characteristic Austrian puddings. For reasons best known to themselves all the cooks in my family maintained that plum dumplings should be made with a potato paste while for *Marillenknödel* the type of choux pastry given below was obligatory. (Cherry dumplings – never a great favourite – would be made with curd cheese pastry like *Topfenknödel*.) The explanation, if forthcoming, was usually the typically Austrian '*das ham ma immer so g'macht*' – we've always done it that way. But it was sometimes muttered that when plums are ripe, potatoes are usually of the right floury consistency for making potato pastry ... hardly a conclusive argument when you come to think about it. There is in fact no reason why the pastes cannot be switched, and you may care to try this paste for the plum dumplings on page 203, or vice versa.

Makes about 12 dumplings

about 1 lb (450 g) apricots	1 large or 2 small eggs
lump sugar	4 oz (110 g) butter
11 fluid oz (300 ml) milk	4 oz (110 g) fine fresh
or water	breadcrumbs
1 tablespoon butter	icing sugar sifted with
pinch of salt	vanilla sugar
9 oz (250 g) plain flour	

Stone the apricots and replace the stones with lumps of sugar. This is best done by easing out the stone gently with the handle of a wooden spoon, without having to cut open the apricots.

Heat water or milk with a pinch of salt and the tablespoon of butter. When the butter has melted turn up the heat and bring liquid to the boil. Tip in the sifted flour and stir over low heat until the mixture leaves sides of the saucepan clean. Remove from heat, beat in the egg. Beat well with a wooden spoon until quite smooth, then tip the mixture into a bowl or onto a pastry board and leave to cool. When cold knead briefly until quite smooth. Roll the dough into a sausage shape about 2 inches (5 cm) in diameter (or into two rolls if you find it easier) and cut into about 12 equal pieces.

Flatten each piece between your hands and wrap each apricot in a piece of dough, taking care that there should not be any gaps. Bring a large pan of water to the boil, add a pinch of salt and drop the dumplings into the boiling water one by one. They will sink to the bottom at once – lift them carefully with a slotted spoon so that they do not stick. Cover saucepan and bring water to boil once again, then reduce heat so that the dumplings cook very gently, tilting the saucepan lid so that there is a small gap. The dumplings will rise to the top when ready – after about eight to ten minutes. Leave to simmer for another minute, then lift out carefully and set them to drain in a colander.

Melt the butter in a large pan, add the breadcrumbs and fry them until lightly browned, stirring all the time. Add the drained dumplings and toss them with the crumbs until the crumbs are really crisp. Arrange dumplings in a warmed dish and sprinkle with icing sugar sifted with vanilla sugar. Serve immediately.

For high days and holidays replace the breadcrumbs with ground hazelnuts or walnuts.

TOPFENKNÖDEL

Dumplings Made with Sieved Curd Cheese

Very light dumplings which are always served with breadcrumbs fried crisply in butter, sprinkled with sugar and accompanied by stewed fruit or fruit purée. Sometimes the dough is wrapped round soft fruit such as strawberries or cherries and for special occasions the breadcrumbs are replaced by ground walnuts or hazelnuts.

Makes about 16 dumplings
3 eggs
3 generous oz (90 g) butter
pinch of salt
1 teaspoon sugar
11 oz (300 g) curd cheese
4½ oz (120 g) coarse
   semolina

3½ oz (100 g) butter
3 oz (80 g) fresh
   breadcrumbs
vanilla sugar

Separate eggs. Cream the butter with the sugar and salt, beat in the yolks one by one, then add curd cheese and continue creaming until smooth. Fold in the semolina. Cover bowl and leave to stand for about two hours.

Whisk egg whites until stiff, fold into the mixture. Make a test dumpling and drop it into plenty of boiling very slightly salted water and simmer gently for twelve to fifteen minutes. If this test shows that the mixture is too soft, add a little more semolina; if too firm, a little more cheese or a little cream. Form mixture into dumplings and cook like the test dumpling for twelve to fifteen minutes. Drain well. Melt the butter and fry breadcrumbs until golden brown and crisp. Serve the dumplings sprinkled with breadcrumbs and vanilla sugar.

ZWETSCHKENKNÖDEL

Plum Dumplings

The best plums to use are the small blue plums which look rather like outsize damsons. Sometimes they are even labelled *Zwetschken*, spelled in one of about ten different ways. Opinions differ as to whether the plums should be stoned and the stone replaced with a lump of sugar (moistened with a drop or two of Slivowitz, as one of my favourite cooks insists) or whether they should be left whole. If you prefer the former, push out the stone with the handle of a wooden spoon – the loss of juice will be considerably less.

The quantity of flour needed for this recipe varies according to the potatoes and as with all dumplings it is best to make a test with one dumpling before covering the rest of the plums with dough. If the dough is too soft, add more flour, if too stiff, add a little more softened butter.

Makes 15 – 20 dumplings

1 lb 11 oz (750 g) floury potatoes
pinch of salt
1 egg or 2 yolks
1 – 2 tablespoons cream
2 oz (50 g) slightly softened butter
about 9 oz (250 g) plain flour

about 1¼ lb (600 g) plums
3½ oz (100 g) butter
4½ oz (120 g) fine fresh breadcrumbs
vanilla sugar mixed with icing sugar
cinnamon

Choose floury potatoes and cook them in their skins. Peel while still hot and push them through a sieve, or a potato ricer, straight onto a pastry board. Leave to cool, then add a pinch of salt, the egg (or yolks), the softened butter, cream and enough flour to make a dough which does not stick to the pastry board.

Shape the dough into one or two rolls, about 2 inches thick. Cut off a small piece of dough, flatten with your hands and wrap it round one of the plums, making sure that there is no gap. Drop the dumpling into a pan of lightly salted boiling water, lift gently from the bottom of the pan (to which it will sink immediately) and cover the pan with a lid, leaving a small gap. Simmer gently for ten to twelve minutes, until the dumpling rises to the top. Remove with a perforated spoon and cut it open. If the dough is too soft, add a little more flour or fine semolina to your mixture. If it is too stiff, work in a little more softened butter.

Cover each plum with a little of the dough, being careful to seal all openings. Roll each dumpling between the palms of your hands to ensure it is quite smooth. Drop dumplings into boiling water, and cook as before, lift carefully from the bottom of the pan so that they do not stick. Cover pan with a lid, bring water to the boil again, then lower heat and tilt the lid so that a small gap remains open. Simmer gently for ten to twelve minutes, until the dumplings rise to the surface and allowing another thirty seconds. Drain in a colander or a sieve.

Melt the second lot of butter, fry breadcrumbs until pale golden brown, then throw in the dumplings and toss them in the crumbs, crisping the crumbs at the same time. Dust with icing sugar (to which a little vanilla sugar has been added) and cinnamon. Serve immediately.

HIMBEER CHAUDEAU

Raspberry Chaudeau

A fruity and non-alcoholic version of *Weinchaudeau*.

Serves 6

11 fluid oz (300 ml) unsweetened raspberry juice	dash of lemon juice 5½ oz (150 g) caster sugar 6 egg yolks

Whisk together egg yolks and sugar in a bowl. Gradually add the lemon juice and raspberry juice. Set bowl over steam and whisk until thickened. Spoon into glasses and serve at once.

WEINCHAUDEAU

Zabaglione Viennese Style

This is fluffier than Italian zabaglione because whole eggs, or a combination of yolks and whole eggs, are used rather than egg yolks only. But it is made and usually served in the same way, in individual glasses with a sponge finger or two to keep it company. It is a favourite accompaniment to steamed or baked puddings, and also used to be one of my childhood treats when convalescing from illnesses: the combination of egg yolks, sugar and wine was credited with restorative powers. In those days no one worried about barely-cooked eggs, or about giving wine to a child – and it's too late to start worrying now.

Serves 2 – 3

2 eggs	dash of lemon juice
4½ fluid oz (⅛ l) white wine	2½ oz (70 g) caster sugar

Put the ingredients into a bowl and whisk over steam until fluffy. Serve at once.

The above is my family's recipe, but quantities can be varied according to personal taste. For a slightly denser version you can use 3 yolks and 1 whole egg, with 9 fluid oz (¼ l) white wine and 3½ oz (100 g) sugar, but no lemon juice. It is a matter of experimenting to find out which suits you best.

KAISEROMELETTE

Emperor's Omelette

Although the name refers to the singular, the batter is enough for at least four omelettes. The 'Kaiser' stands for 'fit for an Emperor' – and so they are!

Serves 4

3 eggs	1 teaspoon vanilla sugar
5⅓ fluid oz (125 ml) milk	butter for frying
1 oz (30 g) butter	jam or vanilla custard for
2 oz (50 g) plain flour	filling
2 oz (50 g) caster sugar	icing sugar for dusting over top

Separate eggs. Put milk into a saucepan, add butter and half the sugar, heat slowly to dissolve then bring to the boil and tip in the sifted flour. Stir mixture over medium heat until smooth and until it leaves the sides of the pan clean. Remove from heat. Beat in the egg yolks gradually. Leave to cool. Whisk whites until stiff, whisk in remaining sugar and vanilla sugar. Fold whites into yolk mixture.

Heat butter in an omelette pan, pour in a ladleful of the mixture and fry gently on one side until golden brown. Turn omelette over carefully, cover frying pan with a lid and complete frying on the other side (leave room for expansion). Fill with jam or vanilla custard, dust with icing sugar and serve at once. Use up remaining mixture as before.

STEPHANIE OMELETTE

Named in honour of Crown Princess Stephanie whose husband, Crown Prince Rudolf, sought his untimely death at Mayerling. Crown Princess Stephanie's lot at the Austrian Imperial Court was not a happy one – but she did have an unfortunate knack for saying the wrong thing, such as forever complaining that 'the food in Vienna is coarse and unappetizing'. By way of response – or rather as an act of self-defence – Viennese chefs created a great many dishes in her honour, including Stephanie Omelette, the lightest, fluffiest omelette, just to prove a point. (They also invented Gateau Stephanie – the richest, most complicated and most unsubtle combination of flavours – by way of 'sweet revenge'.)

For two greedy people or three moderate appetites
3 eggs
2 tablespoons icing sugar   2 tablespoons butter
2 tablespoons plain flour   apricot jam
3 tablespoons double   vanilla sugar
  cream

Preheat the oven to Gas Mark 6, 400°F, 200°C. Set an ovenproof omelette pan over a very low heat. Separate eggs. Whisk yolks with all but 1 teaspoon of the sugar until thick and creamy. Lightly beat in the cream.

Whisk whites until stiff, then whisk in remaining sugar. Fold whites into yolks, then fold in the flour.

Put the butter into the omelette pan – it should melt at once. Do not let it colour – as soon as it melts turn the pan round and round so that bottom and sides are coated. Pile the omelette mixture into the pan, spread it with a spatula so that it is slightly higher round the sides than in the middle – this makes it easier to fold.

Put the omelette into the hot oven as quickly as possible and leave for about eight minutes, until puffed up and golden brown. Spread quickly with warmed apricot jam and slide onto a warmed dish sprinkled with vanilla sugar, folding the omelette over at the same time. Dust top with more vanilla sugar and serve at once.

SCHLOSSERBUAM

Prune Fritters ('Locksmith's Apprentices')

Batter as for *Wiener*   16 whole blanched
  Wäschermädln (see page   almonds
  207)   deep fat or oil for frying
16 large prunes   grated chocolate
weak cold tea

Soak the prunes in the tea for one to two hours, remove the stones and replace with almonds.

Coat each prune with batter and drop into hot fat. Fry until golden brown. Drain on kitchen paper and serve sprinkled with grated chocolate.

WIENER WÄSCHERMÄDLN

Apricot Fritters ('Viennese Laundresses')

Wiener Wäschermädln were known for their charm and their wit and to this day there is the Ball of the Viennese Laundresses during Carnival season. Why apricot fritters should be named after them is a mystery. But then, there is no explanation as to why prune fritters should be called *'Schlosserbuam'* – 'Locksmith's Apprentices'.

Serves 4

2 eggs
5 oz (150 g) plain flour
4½ fluid oz (125 ml) white
   wine, beer, milk or soda
   water
pinch of salt
1 tablespoon icing sugar
2 teaspoons oil
12 ripe apricots

4 oz (100 g) marzipan
2 tablespoons apricot eau
   de vie
2 tablespoons icing sugar
vanilla sugar
deep fat or oil for frying

Stone the apricots and put them in a bowl. Pour apricot eau de vie over them and dust with icing sugar. Cover and leave to stand whilst preparing the batter.

Separate eggs. Sift flour with a pinch of salt into a bowl, add yolks and wine (or beer, milk or soda water) and the oil. Mix to a smooth batter. Whisk whites until stiff, whisk in the icing sugar and fold into the batter.

Fill cavity in each apricot with a small ball of marzipan. Coat each apricot with batter, drop into hot fat and fry until golden brown on all sides. Lift out with a slotted spoon and drain on kitchen paper. Serve hot, sprinkled with icing sugar scented with vanilla sugar and – for special occasions – with a good vanilla sauce (see page 254). A dash of apricot eau de vie or rum in the batter does not come amiss!

MOHNNUDELN

Poppyseed Noodles

Recipes for this very popular and hearty 'pudding' – a typical example of the 'sweet pasta' family – vary considerably. In Carinthia *Mohnnudeln* consist of small pasta envelopes filled with poppyseeds, ground dried pears and curd cheese, flavoured with lemon balm and served with melted butter and honey, sprinkled with cinnamon. In my native part of Lower Austria – due east of Vienna in the large plains known as the Marchfeld – *Mohnnudeln* are just ordinary broad noodles served with ground poppyseeds and sugar, much the same as *Nussnudeln* which are served with ground walnuts, sugar and cinnamon. In the Waldviertel, the Northern region of Lower Austria near the Czech border where poppyseeds are grown, *Mohnnudeln* are something quite different again and there is a definite distinction between *Weitraer Mohnnudeln* made with rye flour (supposedly the 'real thing') and *Waldviertler Mohnnudeln* which are made with potatoes and rye flour, as well as just ordinary *Mohnnudeln* made with potato paste similar to the one used for plum dumplings. Except that in the Waldviertel these are known as *Wiener Mohnnudeln* (of course). Respectable *Mohnnudeln* made with potato paste (with or without rye flour) have to be *handgewuzelt* – a very Austrian term which means 'rolled by hand' – and in small country inns where lunch may well consist of soup followed by a substantial pudding, particularly on Fridays, you will often find *handgewuzelte Mohnnudeln* listed with great pride.

Serves 6

18 oz (500 g) potatoes	2 generous oz (60 g) butter
4 oz (120 g) plain flour	2 generous oz (60 g)
pinch of salt	ground poppyseeds
1 scant oz (20 g) semolina	2 generous oz (60 g) sifted
1 generous oz (30 g)	icing sugar
softened butter	
1 egg yolk	

You will need floury potatoes for this – new potatoes will not do. Boil the potatoes in their skins, peel and whilst still warm push them through a potato ricer. Sift flour with a pinch of salt, add to potatoes and quickly work to a dough with semolina, softened butter and egg yolk. Divide the dough into several portions and form each portion into a roll, about the thickness of a thumb, then cut off walnut-sized pieces.

Roll each piece between your hands to form elongated gnocchi, pointed at each end, and drop these into boiling salted water. Cook gently for about five minutes – they will rise to the surface when they are cooked. Drain, rinse with cold water, then toss in hot butter, but do not brown. Sprinkle with a mixture of ground poppyseeds and sifted icing sugar, and serve.

TOPFENTASCHERL

Typical of the 'sweet pasta' family, these small envelopes filled with sweetened curd cheese (or with thick plum jam called *Powidl*, in which case they are called *Powidltascherl*) are often made with potato paste like the one used for *Zwetschkenknödel* (see page 203). My preferred version is the one using a good noodle paste, for instance 7 oz (200 g) flour, 1 – 2 eggs, salt and if necessary, a little water to make a firm dough. Roll out thinly, stamp into rounds with a pastry-cutter.

Serves 4
Filling

2½ oz (70 g) butter	double or sour cream
1 heaped tablespoon icing sugar	egg for brushing over pastry
6 oz (170 g) curd cheese	melted butter
1 tablespoon raisins	sugar sifted with
1 – 2 egg yolks	cinnamon for serving

Cream butter with sugar, beat in egg yolk, cheese and raisins and, if necessary, a little cream or sour cream to give a stiffish paste. Put a good dab of filling in the centre of each pastry round, brush round the filling with lightly beaten egg, fold over pastry and press down the edges. Cook in boiling salted water for about eight minutes, drain and rinse under cold tap. Toss in hot butter and serve sprinkled with sugar sifted with cinnamon.

BÖHMISCHE DALKEN

Bohemian Pancakes

Not pancakes in the strict culinary sense – *Dalken* are nicely rounded top and bottom about 2 – 2½ inches in diameter and eaten warm, sandwiched together with – what else, for anything called 'Bohemian'? – *Powidl*, thinned down with a little rum.

Makes about 24 Dalken

½ oz (15 g) fresh yeast	1 tablespoon rum
9 oz (240 g) strong flour	2 eggs
1 flat tablespoon caster sugar	1½ oz (40 g) melted butter butter for frying
2 teaspoons vanilla sugar	*Powidl* (see page 2) or other jam
13 fluid oz (375 ml) lukewarm milk	rum and icing sugar for sprinkling over top
pinch of salt	
little grated lemon rind	

The proper way to cook Dalken is to fry them in a special pan, called *'Dalkenpfanne'*, which is simply a frying pan with three, four or more small hollows, large enough to hold an egg in each (in fact it is sometimes used for frying eggs). The nearest equivalent is a muffin pan or a baking tin used for making small individual cakes or buns – usually about nine to twelve at a time. This works perfectly well if placed on the solid plate of an electric or solid fuel cooker – almost better than the original *Dalken* pan, because you can fry more *Dalken* at one time. On a gas cooker the procedure is slightly more complicated, but still feasible: just put one of the heat-preserving plates over the top of the burner and the baking sheet over it – but you will only be able to use the centre hollows. *Dalken* can, of course, be fried on a griddle – but

I hesitate to suggest this because it robs them of their nicely rounded appearance.

Cream yeast with a teaspoon of the caster sugar, stir in about half a cupful of the lukewarm milk and sprinkle a teaspoon of the flour over the top.

Sift remaining flour and sugar with the salt and vanilla sugar into a bowl and make a well in the centre. Pour the yeast mixture into the well, cover bowl with a cloth and set to prove in a warm place. Separate eggs.

When the yeast starts to bubble add the remaining milk, drawing in the flour from the sides of the bowl. Beat well with a wooden spoon or an electric beater, also beating in egg yolks, rum, lemon rind and finally melted, cooled, butter. The mixture should be the consistency of a thick batter.

Whisk egg whites until stiff, fold into the mixture. Cover bowl with a cloth and leave to rise for thirty minutes in a warm place. (It may sound against every culinary rule in the book to do this *after* the whipped egg whites are added, but this is how it is done, and it works.)

Melt a little butter in each hollow (see above) until it begins to froth, then spoon in the batter. Fry on both sides until golden brown – about three minutes on each side. Repeat until all the batter has been used. Mix *Powidl* with a little rum (or thin down firm jam with rum) and sandwich the *Dalken* together in pairs. Dust top with icing sugar and serve at once.

RAHMDALKEN

A quicker version of the previous recipe, since the batter does not contain yeast. *Dalken* are usually served as a rather substantial pudding, but they are also marvellous with tea or coffee, particularly on a frosty winter's day.

Serves 4

3 eggs	4 oz (100 g) butter for
4½ fluid oz (125 ml)	frying
double cream	jam for filling
1 generous oz (30 g) caster	icing sugar
sugar	
5½ oz (150 g) plain flour	

Separate eggs. Whisk together yolks with cream. Whisk whites until stiff, then whisk in the caster sugar. Fold whites into yolks, then fold in the flour. Fry as for *Böhmische Dalken*, then sandwich in twos together with jam. Dust top with icing sugar.

KAISERSCHMARRN

The word *Schmarrn* – if there is such a thing as 'pure' Viennese, this is it – is untranslatable into German, to say nothing of any other language. It can mean a mere nothing, a trifle tossed off easily, a favour denied – or just plain 'no'. Much depends on the circumstances and on the way in which it is said.

Culinary *Schmarrn* are easier to explain. They are based on a very light batter, made lighter still by the addition of whipped egg whites and torn up when half cooked. They date back to the sixteenth century and were originally food for shepherds and herdsmen – easily prepared and allowing plenty of variation. The batter can be made with flour, semolina, soaked rolls or *Kipfel* (the Austrian version of *croissants*), and can be sweet or savoury. They can be soft and almost melting inside, or crisped more or less to a frazzle, depending on taste. And you have the consolation that absolutely nothing can ever go wrong with a *Schmarrn* – in fact it has been suggested that *Schmarrn* originated when a soufflé went wrong or a pancake got torn in turning.

Kaiserschmarrn is probably the best-known *Schmarrn* and legend has it that it was one of the favourite dishes of the Emperor Franz Josef, as befitted his simple tastes. But the truth is that the 'Kaiser' in *Kaiserschmarrn* is not imperial: it probably stems from the word *Koaserer* – cheesemaker.

For two greedy people

4½ oz (120 g) plain flour	4 eggs
pinch of salt	1 oz (30 g) caster sugar
9 fluid oz (¼ l) milk	1 oz (30 g) raisins or
3½ oz (100 g) butter	sultanas
	vanilla sugar

Preheat the oven to Gas Mark 6, 400°F, 200°C. Put half the butter in a cup or small jug and melt it by standing it in a saucepan of hot water. Whisk together milk, flour and salt and set aside. Separate eggs. Beat yolks gradually into batter.

Put the remaining butter into a gratin dish and heat in the oven. Whisk egg whites until stiff, whisk in the sugar. Add the first lot of melted, but not hot, butter to the batter, fold in the whisked egg whites.

By that time the butter in the oven should be hot and frothy, but not brown. Pour the batter into the dish, sprinkle with raisins or sultanas and return the dish to the oven.

Whilst the dish is baking in the oven you will have to make a decision: do you want the *Kaiserschmarrn* to be soft inside, with just a little brown crust, or do you want it really crisped? In either case you will have to wait until it has browned on top. If you want it very crisp, turn it over with a fish slice – it does not matter if it breaks in the process – and return it to the oven for a few minutes so that there is a nice brown crust top and bottom, then tear it into small pieces with two forks and return it to the oven for another two or three minutes. If you want it to be fairly soft, do not turn it over but tear it into smallish pieces as soon as it is browned on one side and return it to the oven for about five minutes. Serve dusted thickly with vanilla sugar.

Traditional accompaniments are raspberry syrup or *Zwetschkenröster* (see page 3).

GRIESS SCHMARRN

Serves 4

3/4 pint (420 ml) milk
1 teaspoon vanilla sugar
1 heaped tablespoon
   butter
1 tablespoon caster sugar
5 oz (140 g) coarse
   semolina

little grated lemon rind
1 egg
1 heaped tablespoon
   raisins
2 tablespoons butter
icing sugar for sprinkling
   over the top

Put the milk, vanilla sugar, caster sugar and butter into a saucepan and bring to boil. Sprinkle in the semolina, stirring constantly. Cook until thickened, remove from heat and cover saucepan. Leave to stand for about five minutes, then stir in the raisins and the egg. Melt the 2 tablespoons butter in a baking dish, pour in the semolina mixture and put into the oven at Gas Mark 5, 375°F, 190°C until nicely browned on top, then tear into smallish pieces with two forks. Return dish to the oven for the whole thing to crisp nicely, then turn it onto a warmed dish and sprinkle liberally with icing sugar.

Serve with stewed fruit – cranberries or *Zwetschkenröster* (see page 3).

PALATSCHINKEN

Pancakes

Austrian pancakes are rather plumper and larger than their cousins, the French *crêpes*. They are always served with a filling which can vary from a savoury ragout to jam made from apricots ripened on the banks of the Danube – with a good dash of local apricot brandy added for good measure.

Serves 4

approximately 5 oz (140 g)
   plain flour
pinch of salt

1 – 2 eggs (or 1 egg plus 1
   egg yolk)
9 fluid oz (250 ml) milk
melted butter

Sift flour and salt into a bowl, add eggs and enough milk to give a fairly thin batter and whisk briskly. (Some cooks swear that the addition of a dash of soda water makes all the difference.) Have ready a small jug with melted butter. Pour a little butter into an omelette pan, move the pan so that the butter coats the pan evenly, and when it is hot pour in a little of the batter. Tilt the pan quickly so that the mixture spreads evenly. Fry over moderate heat until golden brown on one side, then turn the pancake over (never toss an Austrian pancake – it would resent such treatment bitterly) and fry the other side. Use up rest of the batter in the same way. Stack cooked pancakes on top of each other to keep warm.

The pancakes will be even better if you replace some of the milk with single cream.

JÖRG WÖRTHER'S PALATSCHINKEN MIT GRIESSCREME

Pancakes with Cream Filling

Jörg Wörther was nominated 'Cook of the Decade' by Gault Millau, and his Villa Hiss at Badgastein is certainly one of the best restaurants in Austria. The following recipe is one of his deceptively simple specialities.

Makes about 12 small pancakes

For the pancakes	For the filling
9 fluid oz (¼ l) milk	4½ fluid oz (⅛ l) milk
pinch of salt	vanilla pod
4½ fluid oz (⅛ l) double cream	1 scant oz (25 g) fine semolina
3 eggs	3 tablespoons granulated sugar
4½ oz (125 g) plain flour	1 egg
clarified butter for frying	3 egg yolks
	5 egg whites
	butter for the dish

Start with the cream filling. Split vanilla pod and add to the milk, together with a tablespoon of the sugar. Heat gently, bring to the boil and sprinkle in the semolina. Cook over low heat, stirring constantly, until thickened. Remove from heat, and allow to cool, stirring occasionally.

Mix together ingredients for the pancakes, blend well and fry small pancakes in clarified butter.

Remove vanilla pod from semolina mixture and beat in whole egg and egg yolks. Whisk egg whites until stiff, then whisk in the rest of the sugar and fold into the mixture.

Spread a little of the filling over each pancake, roll up very carefully and set in a lightly buttered gratin dish. Bake at Gas Mark 3½, 340°F, 170°C for about ten minutes. Serve at once.

PALATSCHINKENAUFLAUF

Pancake Pudding

Serves 6 – 8
For the pancakes
2 oz (60 g) butter
5 eggs
2 oz (60 g) icing or caster
  sugar
1 teacup milk
2 oz (60 g) sifted self-
  raising flour

For the filling
3 eggs
3 tablespoons icing sugar
a little grated lemon rind
$\frac{1}{2}$ teaspoon vanilla sugar
4 oz (115 g) ground
  almonds
butter and breadcrumbs
  for the cake tin
butter for frying
about 3 fluid oz (85 ml)
  sour cream and icing
  sugar for topping

Butter a 9-inch spring-clip cake tin and dust lightly with fine breadcrumbs.

Put the butter for the pancakes into a cup and stand it in a small pan of hot water until the butter melts. Separate eggs. Whisk yolks with the sugar until very thick and creamy. Whisk in the milk. Whisk whites until stiff and fold into the batter, alternately with the sifted flour. Finally fold in the melted, but not hot, butter.

To make the filling, separate eggs. Whisk yolks with sugar until thick and creamy, add the grated lemon rind and vanilla sugar. Whisk the whites until stiff and fold into the yolk mixture, alternately with the ground almonds.

Melt a small knob of butter in a frying pan – if possible one which is the same size as the cake tin, but it does not matter if it is slightly smaller. Pour in a quarter of the batter and fry the pancake until it is golden brown underneath. Slip the pancake – upside down so that the uncooked side rests on the bottom – into the cake tin.

This is quite easy with the first pancake as you can simply invert the tin over the frying pan, but gets a little more difficult with the subsequent pancakes, though it is in fact easier than it sounds. (If necessary, push the pancakes gently into place.) Spread the cooked side of each pancake with filling before placing the next pancake on top. The top layer should be a pancake with no filling. Spread the top thickly with sour cream and bake the pudding at Gas Mark 6, 400°F, 200°C, until the cream is just tinged with colour – about twenty to twenty-five minutes. Take the pudding out of the oven, release the spring-clip and dust the top thickly with icing sugar. Do not attempt to remove the pudding from the bottom of the cake tin – just set it on a large serving dish with the cake tin base still underneath. Serve cut into wedges like a cake.

RAHMPALATSCHINKEN

Cream Pancakes

Makes 4 pancakes

5 eggs
3 tablespoons icing sugar
4 tablespoons double or
   sour cream
4 tablespoons plain flour
butter for frying

jam for filling
icing sugar scented with
   vanilla

Separate eggs. Whisk yolks with icing sugar until thick and creamy. Add cream and sifted flour and finally fold in the stiffly beaten whites. Melt a walnut-sized lump of butter in a frying pan, pour in a quarter of the mixture and fry pancake over fairly brisk heat on both sides. Use up remaining mixture in the same way. Fill pancakes with jam, fold over and serve dusted with icing sugar scented with vanilla.

TOPFENPALATSCHINKEN

Pancakes with Curd Cheese Filling

4 – 6 pancakes (see page 212)

Filling

9 oz (250 g) curd cheese
2 oz (50 g) butter
2 oz (50 g) icing sugar
2 oz (50 g) raisins
2 eggs

4½ fluid oz (125 ml) sour
   cream
grated lemon rind
a little milk
butter for baking sheet
vanilla sugar for sprinkling

Cream butter with half the icing sugar until light and fluffy. Separate eggs and beat the yolks into creamed butter gradually. Beat in grated lemon rind. Stir in the cheese and sour cream. Add raisins. Whisk egg whites until stiff, whisk in remaining sugar. Fold whisked whites into mixture.

Divide mixture between the pancakes, placing it down the centre of each pancake, then fold over the sides. Place pancakes, folded side down, on a buttered baking sheet, leaving space between each pancake. Brush with a little milk and bake at Gas Mark 5, 375°F, 190°C until well risen. Sprinkle with vanilla sugar and serve at once – the filling will still be a little creamy inside.

GEBACKENE TOPFENPALATSCHINKEN

Baked Pancakes with Curd Cheese Filling

8 thin pancakes about 8
  inches in diameter

For the filling
1 oz (30 g) raisins
a little rum
1½ oz (40 g) butter
1½ oz (40 g) caster sugar
2 eggs
4½ fluid oz (120 ml) sour
  cream
7 oz (200 g) curd cheese
grated lemon rind
1 teaspoon vanilla sugar
pinch of powdered
  cinnamon
butter for the dish

For the topping
5 fluid oz (140 ml) sour
  cream
2 tablespoons milk
1 egg
1 oz (30 g) icing or caster
  sugar
icing sugar for the top

Soak the raisins in a little rum to make them swell up. Cream the butter with the sugar until light and fluffy. Separate eggs. Beat yolks into the butter mixture, then beat in the sour cream and the curd cheese. Add lemon rind, vanilla sugar and cinnamon. Whisk the whites until stiff and fold into the mixture, then fold in the raisins.

Butter a deep gratin dish. Cut the pancakes in half and spread thickly with the mixture. Fold the pancakes over so that the filling is in the centre and arrange them – overlapping like tiles – in the gratin dish.

Whisk together all the ingredients for the topping and pour over the pancakes. Bake at Gas Mark 4, 350°F, 180°C, for twenty-five to thirty minutes, until the creamy mixture has set. Serve warm sprinkled with icing sugar.

KUKURUZKOCH

Polenta Pudding

Kukuruz is the Austrian name for corn or maize (as well as corn-on-the-cob) but in some parts of the country, just to confuse matters, it is also known as *Türken*. Cornmeal, also known as *Türkenmehl* or Polenta – the latter giving its name to the basic ingredient and the finished dish – is used for a number of delicious puddings, of which this is a fine example. See also *Türkentommerl* (page 217).

4 – 6 generous helpings

1 pint (550 ml) milk	1 teaspoon grated lemon
¼ pint (140 ml) cornmeal	rind
(polenta)	juice of ½ lemon
2 teaspoons vanilla sugar	pinch of cinnamon
5 tablespoons caster sugar	3 eggs
3 heaped tablespoons	butter for the dish
butter	

The cornmeal will be poured into the hot milk, so it is best to measure it in a jug from which it can then be poured.

Heat the milk with 1 tablespoon of the sugar and the vanilla sugar. When the milk starts to boil, pour in the polenta gradually and cook until thickened. Set aside to cool. Cream butter with remaining sugar, beat in lemon rind, lemon juice and cinnamon. Separate eggs. Beat yolks gradually into the creamed butter mixture, then stir in the cooled cornmeal mixture. Whisk whites until stiff and fold into the mixture. Pile mixture into a buttered deep gratin dish and bake at Gas Mark 4, 350°F, 180°C for about an hour.

The pudding is delicious just on its own or – as served in Austria – with a little fruit syrup; but quite often fruit in season is added. Cherries are particularly good, and in the unlikely case of there being any of the pudding left over, it tastes very good cold too. Although I prefer it baked, it can also be steamed and served with a fruit sauce.

TÜRKENTOMMERL

Türken or *Türkenmehl* is what they call cornmeal in some parts of Austria, because for centuries it was believed that the Turks had first introduced maize to the country. And when the hot summer wind brushes through the maize fields they call it *Türkenwind*, as it makes the maize grow particularly well. *Tommerl* is simply the name for a dish baked in the oven – at least in some regions. It gives no indication how good a pudding this is, particularly on a cold winter's day.

Serves 6 – 8

7 oz (200 g) butter (a little	2 teaspoons vanilla sugar
less may be used, but	pinch of ground cinnamon
the buttery taste is an	4 eggs
integral part of the dish)	12 fluid oz (330 ml) milk
4 oz (120 g) cornmeal	3 dessert apples
(polenta)	2 oz (50 g) raisins or
3 tablespoons caster sugar	sultanas
1 teaspoon grated lemon	icing sugar sifted with
rind	vanilla sugar
pinch of salt	

Preheat oven to Gas Mark 7, 425°F, 220°C. Place the butter in a large baking dish and heat in the oven until the butter has melted.

Mix together cornmeal, sugar, lemon rind, salt, vanilla sugar and cinnamon in a bowl. Add the eggs and milk and mix well. Peel and core the apples. Beat the cornmeal mixture once again to make sure that it is well blended, then pour into the baking dish containing the melted butter – the cornmeal mixture should only half fill the dish. Grate the apples over the top and sprinkle with raisins. Bake for twelve to fifteen minutes – some cooks like to give the mixture a good stir after about five minutes to ensure even blending.

Sprinkle thickly with icing sugar which has been sifted with vanilla sugar and serve warm, not hot.

REISAUFLAUF

Baked Rice Pudding

Reisauflauf has always been one of my favourite puddings, and when I was a child there would be earnest discussions as to the special form it would take. Since the rice for an Austrian rice pudding is cooked in milk before any additions and embellishments are made, there was ample time for this. Would it just be a simple *Reisauflauf* – a little solid perhaps, but heavily scented with vanilla and lemon, and served with a rich vanilla custard? Or a lighter, creamier version with lots of fruit and perhaps topped with meringue? Or *Schönbrunner Reisauflauf* – part plain, part chocolate?

Since Austrian *Reisauflauf* is so different from English rice pudding (which incidentally I love just as much), I have given two versions, which still leaves plenty of scope for variations.

'Classic' Reisauflauf

Serves 4

3½ oz (100 g) arborio rice	1 generous oz (30 g)
18 fluid oz (½ l) milk	raisins
1 vanilla pod	butter and biscuit, or fine
2 generous oz (60 g) butter	breadcrumbs for the
1½ oz (40 g) caster sugar	dish
2 eggs	icing sugar for sprinkling
grated rind of ½ lemon	over the top

Butter a deep gratin dish and dust it lightly with biscuit crumbs or fine breadcrumbs.

Rinse the rice under a hot tap and shake it dry. Cook the rice gently in the milk with a vanilla pod and leave to cool.

Cream butter and sugar. Separate eggs. Beat yolks into the creamed butter mixture and add the grated lemon rind, then add the cooled rice, having removed the vanilla pod. Whisk whites until stiff and fold into the mixture, then fold in the raisins. Pile the mixture into the prepared gratin dish and bake at Gas Mark 4, 350°F, 180°C for thirty-five to forty minutes. Sprinkle with icing sugar and serve.

Excellent as it is, but better still if served with a good vanilla custard.

Reisauflauf (according to family tradition)

Serves 6

6 oz (170 g) arborio rice	2 eggs
3/4 pint (420 ml) milk	raspberries or strawberries
vanilla pod	a little icing sugar
rind of 1/2 lemon	butter and fine
1 tablespoon butter	breadcrumbs for the
3 oz (90 g) caster sugar	dish

Butter a soufflé or deep gratin dish and sprinkle with fine breadcrumbs. Put the rice in a sieve and rinse it under the hot tap. Shake dry, put rice into a saucepan with vanilla pod and a few slivers of lemon rind. Cover with milk, add the butter and cook gently until the rice is soft, but not mushy. Remove from heat and leave to cool slightly.

Separate eggs. Whisk the yolks with half the sugar until thick and creamy. Whisk whites until stiff, then whisk in remaining sugar. Fold whites into yolk mixture. Remove vanilla pod and lemon rind from the cooked rice. Fold egg mixture into rice, which should be just tepid by now. Pile half the rice into the prepared dish, arrange a layer of raspberries or strawberries over it, dust with a little icing sugar and top with remaining mixture. Bake at Gas Mark 3½, 340°F, 170°C for about forty minutes. Serve raspberry syrup separately.

There are a great many variations on this theme – we used apples when raspberries and strawberries were out of season (personally I prefer soft fruit, and frozen raspberries or strawberries are very good for this pudding), and sometimes the fruit was left out altogether and one or two tablespoons of raisins were stirred into the mixture instead.

Alternatively, about 3 oz (80 g) melted chocolate would be stirred into half the rice mixture. This would then be piled on top of the plain mixture and the whole pudding topped with a meringue made with 2 egg whites and 2 oz (50 g) granulated sugar. The rice pudding would be first baked as before (fastidious cooks use rice paper to separate the two layers of rice) and then topped with the meringue mixture and put back into a very hot oven for a few minutes to set the meringue. This was known as *Schönbrunner Reisauflauf.*

ERDBEER SOUFFLÉ

Strawberry Soufflé

Serves 4

7 egg whites
5½ oz (150 g) granulated
   sugar
2 tablespoons granulated
   sugar
6 oz (170 g) strawberry
   purée (made from
   about 11 oz/300 g fresh
   strawberries)

1 tablespoon plain flour
butter and icing sugar for
   the soufflé dish
ground hazelnuts or
   almonds

Butter a soufflé dish and dust with icing sugar. Preheat oven to Gas Mark 7, 425°F, 220°C. Put 2 egg whites, the strawberry purée and 5½ oz sugar into a bowl and stir, like creaming butter and sugar for a cake, until the mixture is thick and almost stiff.

Whisk remaining 5 whites until stiff, fold in the 2 tablespoons sugar and whisk until smooth. Fold whisked whites into the strawberry mixture and sift in the flour. Pile into the soufflé dish and sprinkle with ground hazelnuts or almonds. Bake at Gas Mark 7, 425°F, 220°C for ten minutes, then turn down heat to Gas Mark 5½, 390°F, 195°C without opening oven door. Bake for another seven minutes and serve at once.

OBST SOUFFLÉ

Jam Soufflé

Delicious and foolproof, this can be baked in a soufflé dish in the usual way, but it is even better – and more impressive too – when baked in a flat dish.

Serves 4

3 good tablespoons firm
   seedless jam (apricot,
   or redcurrant jelly, for
   instance)
6 egg whites
1 tablespoon rum
8 oz (225 g) icing or caster
   sugar

3 tablespoons blanched
   almonds cut into strips
butter and ground
   almonds for the dish
a little extra icing sugar

Preheat the oven to Gas Mark 7, 425°F, 220°C. Butter an ovenproof dish – a flan or gratin dish with a low rim is ideal – and dust it lightly with flour or, better still, with ground almonds. Cream the jam with the rum until light and airy. Whisk the egg whites until stiff, then whisk in the sugar gradually until the mixture is very smooth and shiny. Fold the egg whites into the jam. Pile the mixture into the dish, making it higher in the centre (or, for a professional touch, use the largest plain nozzle on the icing bag and pipe the mixture in a huge mound onto the dish). Scatter the slivered almonds over it and dust very lightly with a little sifted icing sugar.

Bake for eight to ten minutes. Serve at once – the soufflé will be just set inside and the almonds give a deliciously crisp finish, but it is likely to collapse very quickly.

SCHOKOLADE SOUFFLÉ

Chocolate Soufflé

'Not so much a soufflé as a delicious treat to have at teatime', one of my favourite aunts used to say, though why at teatime, and why she rejected the word 'soufflé' for this feathery light dish, I never found out.

Serves 4

4 egg whites	1 scant tablespoon boiling
2½ oz (70 g) icing sugar	hot black coffee
2½ oz (70 g) softened plain	butter and sugar for the
chocolate	dish.

Preheat the oven to Gas Mark 7, 425°F, 220°C. Butter a soufflé dish and dust it lightly with icing sugar. Cream 1 egg white with sugar and the softened chocolate until very thick, then stir in the boiling coffee. Whisk the remaining 3 egg whites until stiff and fold into the mixture. Bake for approximately ten minutes – it should be crisp outside and very creamy inside. Serve at once – it collapses faster than almost any other soufflé – preferably with a rich dark chocolate sauce or with ice-cold whipped cream.

ZITRONEN SOUFFLÉ

Lemon Soufflé

Serves 4

5 eggs	butter and sugar for the
3 oz (85 g) icing sugar	soufflé dish
juice and grated rind of	icing sugar for sprinkling
1 lemon	over top

Butter a soufflé dish and dust with icing sugar. Preheat the oven to Gas Mark 6, 400°F, 200°C.

Separate eggs. Whisk the yolks with sugar and lemon juice until thick and creamy. Add grated lemon rind. Whisk whites until stiff. Fold whites into yolks. Pile mixture into the prepared soufflé dish and bake for about ten to twelve minutes. Dust with icing sugar and serve at once.

B'SOFFENE LIESL

Drunken Lizzie

Also known as Drunken Kathi or – more irreverently – Drunken Capucine. A wonderful pudding for a cold winter's day.

Serves 4 – 6

3 eggs	3 tablespoons sugar
3 lightly heaped tablespoons icing sugar	2 teaspoons vanilla sugar cinnamon rind
3 – 4 lightly heaped tablespoons ground walnuts, moistened with 1 tablespoon rum	1 – 2 cloves pared or finely grated orange rind
butter and flour for the cake tin	
½ pint (¼ l) red wine, medium-dry	
¼ pint (⅛ l) water	

Butter and flour an 8 inch or 9 inch cake tin. Preheat the oven to Gas Mark 4, 350°F, 180°C.

Separate eggs. Whisk the yolks with the sugar until thick and pale in colour. Whisk whites until stiff then fold into the yolks, alternately with the ground walnuts. If you do not have any walnuts, you can use fine breadcrumbs instead, but be generous with the rum in that case. (You can of course also use a mixture of walnuts and breadcrumbs.) Tip the mixture into the prepared cake tin and bake for about forty-five minutes – until the top feels slightly firm and the cake has shrunk slightly away from the sides of the tin.

Whilst the mixture is baking, put the wine into a saucepan together with the water, sugar, orange rind and the spices. Heat gently until the sugar has dissolved.

Carefully remove the cake from the tin and allow it to cool a little on a rack, then set it in a warmed deep dish. Slow strain the hot wine mixture over cake allowing it to soak it all up. Serve warm – with whipped cream if you want to be extravagant.

FÜRSTENKOCH

Princes' Pudding

Early in the nineteenth century, Maria Anna Neudecker, née Ertl, wrote *Die Baierische Köchin in Böhmen* (The Bavarian Cook in Bohemia) in which the following recipe appeared. Today, as on the day the book was first published, it is still indeed 'a pudding fit for princes'.

Serves 4 – 6

3½ oz (105 g) boudoir biscuits (sponge fingers)	8 egg yolks
3½ oz (105 g) macaroons or Italian almond biscuits (Amaretti)	6 egg whites
½ pint (300 ml) double cream	butter and icing sugar for the baking dish

Butter a deep baking dish and dust with icing sugar. Preheat the oven to Gas Mark 3, 325°F, 160°C.

Crush the sponge fingers and the macaroons to the texture of very coarse breadcrumbs. Bring the cream to the boil, add the crushed biscuits and cook gently, stirring all the time, until the mixture is thick. Remove from heat, stir until cool, then beat in the egg yolks gradually. Whisk whites until stiff, fold into the mixture and bake until golden brown and firm – about 1 – 1¼ hours.

In the original version the pudding is turned onto a warmed platter, but I find it better served straight from the dish, with the sauce poured either over the whole pudding or over the individual helpings.

For the sauce, use either the Wine Sauce on page 225 or – since the pudding is rather rich – simply heat 9 fluid oz red wine with a stick of cinnamon, 1 – 2 cloves and a little sugar, depending on the wine. Strain and serve.

GRAZER TRIET

Triet based on white bread – with or without raisins – is known in other Austrian provinces, particularly in Lower Austria and Burgenland, as well. The Styrian (Graz) version, based on a light sponge mixture, sometimes known as *Grazer Zwieback*, is particularly delicious. Use the recipe on page 267 for *Grazer Zwieback* as a basis, or the following:

Serves 6 – 8

For the sponge
8 eggs
1 tablespoon vanilla sugar
14 oz (400 g) icing sugar
18 oz (500 g) sifted plain
  flour
3½ oz (100 g) melted
  butter
butter and flour for the
  baking sheet
icing sugar

For the mulled wine
18 fluid oz (500 ml) red
  wine
2 tablespoons sugar
grated rind of ½ lemon
cinnamon
cloves

Whisk eggs with sugar and vanilla sugar until thick and creamy. Lightly fold in the sifted flour and finally stir in the melted, but not hot, butter. Spread over a large (or two smaller) baking sheets, previously buttered and floured. Bake for twenty-five to thirty minutes at Gas Mark 4, 350°F, 180°C. Leave to cool, then cut into slices. Put the slices back into the oven to brown very lightly, then dust with icing sugar on all sides.

Prepare the mulled wine: put the wine with sugar, spices and lemon rind into a saucepan, and heat to just below boiling point. Remove from heat and cover with a lid.

Just before serving the first course, arrange slices of sponge in a large deep plate and strain the wine over them. By the time it is to be served, *Triet* will have reached exactly the right consistency – but it is a question of taste whether the wine should be cold, hot or merely warm when it is strained over the sponge.

GRIESS-NIEGEL

A marvellous old-fashioned pudding, the preparation of which may sound complicated, but in fact the most important ingredients are two gratin dishes, one of which should be slightly larger and deeper than the other. After that it is very simple and the result is definitely worthwhile.

Serves 4

7 fluid oz (200 ml) coarse
  semolina
3 eggs
2 heaped tablespoons
  caster sugar
1 teaspoon vanilla sugar
1 heaped tablespoon
  butter
27 fluid oz (750 ml) cold
  milk

3 tablespoons caster sugar
pinch of vanilla sugar
2 teaspoons grated orange
  rind
butter for the dishes
sugar for sprinkling over
  the top

Butter the two gratin dishes well. Preheat oven to Gas Mark 4, 350°F, 180°C. Measure out the semolina – it is quicker and easier to use a measuring jug than to weigh it. Whisk together the eggs with the 2 tablespoons caster sugar and the teaspoon of vanilla sugar until light and frothy, then fold in the semolina. Bake in the smaller of the two dishes until golden brown on top and just firm to the touch – about fifteen minutes. Meanwhile put the heaped tablespoon of butter in a cup and stand this in a pan of hot water until it melts.

As soon as the semolina mixture is golden brown, tip it carefully into the larger dish. Mix together the cold milk, the 3 tablespoonfuls of sugar, the pinch of vanilla sugar, and the grated orange rind and stir in the melted butter. Pour this over the baked pudding – it should cover it completely. Lower heat to Gas Mark 3, 325°F, 160°C and put the dish into the oven until the milk has been completely absorbed. Serve sprinkled thickly with sugar.

It is intended to be eaten hot, but is also delicious cold, particularly if served with a good fruit syrup.

GRIESSTORTE ALS MEHLSPEISE

Semolina Cake Served as Pudding

I am quite sure this pudding was a culinary accident rather than an intended creation – probably a cake which failed to rise; but it is so delicious that I would not worry about its origin.

Serves 4 – 6
2½ oz (75 g) sugar
2 eggs
2 oz (55 g) ground
   almonds
1 oz (30 g) coarse semolina
butter and ground
   almonds for the cake tin

White wine sauce
¼ pint (150 ml) white wine
2 eggs
juice of ½ lemon
2½ oz (75 g) caster sugar

Separate eggs. Whisk together yolks and sugar until light and fluffy. Whisk whites until stiff, then fold into yolk mixture, alternately with the ground almonds and semolina. Butter cake tin and lightly dust with ground almonds. Bake the mixture for about half an hour at Gas Mark 4, 350°F, 180°C. Leave for a few minutes in the tin, then set the cake carefully in a warmed dish. Pour the sauce over it and serve warm, not hot.

For the sauce whisk together all ingredients over steam until light and frothy.

KASTANIEN PUDDING

Chestnut Pudding

Serves 4 – 6

10 oz (280 g) peeled, cooked and puréed chestnuts (equivalent of about 1 lb/450 g raw, unpeeled chestnuts)	4 oz (110 g) ground almonds
	pinch of cinnamon
	finely grated rind of 1 lemon
5 oz (140 g) butter	icing sugar for dusting over the pudding
4 oz (110 g) icing or caster sugar	butter and sugar for the dish
6 eggs	

Preheat the oven to Gas Mark 5, 375°F, 190°C. Butter a deep gratin dish and dust it lightly with sugar.

Cream the butter with the sugar until light and fluffy. Separate eggs. Beat the yolks into the sugar and butter mixture, one by one, beating well after each addition, adding a little of the ground almonds if the mixture shows any sign of curdling. Beat in the puréed chestnuts, cinnamon and lemon rind. Whisk the whites until stiff and fold into the mixture with the rest of the almonds and bake for about thirty minutes, until nicely browned on top.

Serve warm rather than hot, sprinkled thickly with icing sugar. A frothy wine sauce (see page 225) goes well with this, as does a simple chocolate sauce (see page 233).

LEBZELTER AUFLAUF

Honeycake Pudding

Lebzelten – or *Lebkuchen* – is the name for honeycakes, whether in the shape of cakes, or biscuits (usually baked for Christmas as part of the traditional *Weihnachtsbäckerei*) or of huge hearts saying 'Be Mine Forever' or some similar message in sugared icing, mostly sold at local fairs. *Lebzelter* is a maker of honeycakes. Lebzelter-Obauer at Werfen, in the province of Salzburg, is one of the best restaurants in Austria, and *Lebzelter Auflauf* is one of their specialities. The original uses honeycake spice (*Lebkuchengewürz*), a blend of allspice, cloves and cinnamon which is available, blended and packaged, in Austria and sometimes also at delicatessens in this country. You can of course make up your own blend, or use grated honeycake instead of breadcrumbs.

Serves 4 – 6

For the pudding	For the sauce
5 eggs	3 fluid oz (80 ml) white
3 oz (80 g) caster or icing	wine
sugar	2 egg yolks
3 generous oz (90 g)	3 tablespoons granulated
melted butter	sugar
1 fluid oz (20 ml) rum	
2 oz (50 g) ground	
almonds	
2 oz (50 g) grated	
chocolate	
1 scant oz (20 g) fresh	
breadcrumbs	
1 teaspoon honeycake	
spice (see above)	
butter and icing sugar for	
the dish	

Separate eggs. Whisk yolks with 2 oz (50 g) of the sugar. Whisk whites until stiff, whisk in remaining sugar. Fold whites into yolks, alternately with ground almonds, chocolate, breadcrumbs and the honeycake spice. Finally fold in the melted, but not hot, butter and the rum. Arrange mixture in a buttered and sugared soufflé dish and stand it in a baking dish with warm water to come half-way up the pudding basin. Bake at Gas Mark 3½, 340°F, 170°C for about thirty-five minutes.

Serve immediately, with wine sauce made by whisking together wine, sugar and egg yolks over steam until frothy.

LINZER KOCH

Spiced Pudding

Serves 4 – 6

3½ oz (100 g) ground	1 teaspoon finely grated
walnuts	lemon rind
3½ oz (100 g) butter	5 eggs
3½ oz (100 g) icing or	2 oz (50 g) redcurrant jam
caster sugar	butter and flour for the
½ teaspoon each powdered	pudding basin
cloves and cinnamon	

Butter and flour an ovenproof pudding basin. Preheat the oven to Gas Mark 5, 375°F, 190°C.

Mix together walnuts, spices and lemon rind. Cream butter with two-thirds of the sugar until light and fluffy. Separate eggs. Add yolks to creamed butter, one by one, beating well after each addition. Whisk whites until stiff, whisk in remaining sugar. Fold whites into yolks, alternately with the walnut mixture.

Spoon half of this mixture into the prepared pudding basin, carefully add redcurrant jam and top with remaining pudding mixture (if the redcurrant jam is very firm, warm it a little first). Bake until well risen and golden brown on top – about forty-five minutes. Carefully turn out onto a warmed serving dish and serve with *Weinsauce* (see page 225).

MARILLEN AUFLAUF

Apricot Pudding

Serves 4

1 lb (450 g) ripe apricots
4½ fluid oz (125 ml) white
  wine
2 tablespoons caster or
  icing sugar
4 eggs
3 oz (80 g) icing sugar
2 oz (60 g) ground walnuts
  or hazelnuts

1 scant oz (25 g) fine
  breadcrumbs
1½ oz (40 g) melted butter
butter and fine
  breadcrumbs or
  hazelnuts for the dish

Butter a large gratin dish and dust with fine breadcrumbs or ground hazelnuts. Stone the apricots and poach them in the wine with 2 tablespoons sugar until they are just tender – do not overcook them. (Two or three crushed apricot stones – the brown skin comes off quite easily – poached with the apricots greatly improves the flavour.)

Separate eggs. Whisk the whites until stiff, then whisk in half the icing sugar. Whisk in the yolks, one by one, and then whisk in the remaining sugar. Fold in the ground walnuts or hazelnuts and the breadcrumbs. Finally fold in the melted, but not hot, butter.

Put half the mixture into the buttered gratin dish, cover with the apricots and pile the remaining mixture on top. Bake at Gas Mark 5, 375°F, 190°C and for the first ten minutes of the baking time leave the oven door very slightly ajar. After that time close the oven door and bake the pudding until it is golden brown on top. It tastes equally good hot or cold, but I prefer it when it is just warm, with a fine sprinkling of vanilla sugar on top.

MUSCAZIN KOCH

Brown Almond Pudding

This pudding can be steamed or baked – personally I prefer it baked. For special occasions put a layer of tinned and drained morello cherries into the baking dish, sprinkle with rum and then top with the pudding mixture.

Serves 4 – 6

6 egg yolks
3½ oz (100 g) caster sugar
1 egg
2½ oz (70 g) unblanched
   almonds, not too finely
   ground
pinch each of allspice,
   cinnamon, nutmeg and
   ground cloves

juice and grated rind of
   ½ lemon
3 egg whites
butter and ground
   almonds (or fine
   cakecrumbs) for the
   dish

Whisk egg yolks and whole egg with sugar until thick and creamy, add lemon juice and rind and the spices. Whisk egg whites until stiff and fold into the mixture. Finally fold in the almonds. Bake for about thirty minutes at Gas Mark 5, 375°F, 190°C in a deep gratin dish, previously buttered and dusted with ground almonds or fine cakecrumbs. The mixture should still be a little runny inside. Serve at once.

SCHOKOLADEKOCH

Chocolate Pudding

Serves 4

2½ oz (75 g) butter
2½ oz (75 g) icing sugar
2 oz (50 g) softened
   chocolate
4 egg yolks
2 egg whites
2½ oz (75 g) ground
   almonds
butter and flour for the
   cake tin

Topping

4 egg whites
5½ oz (150 g) caster sugar

Cream butter and sugar until light and fluffy. Beat in the egg yolks and softened chocolate. Whisk egg whites until stiff and fold into the mixture alternately with the ground almonds. Bake in a buttered and floured spring-clip cake tin at Gas Mark 4, 350°F, 180°C for fifty minutes.

Whisk the 4 egg whites until stiff, then whisk in the caster sugar. Pile on top of the chocolate base and bake at Gas Mark 9, 475°F, 240°C for about five minutes, until lightly tinged on top. Serve immediately.

SCHWARZER KIRSCHENPUDDING

Black Cherry Pudding

Serves 4

4 – 5 day-old rolls
9 fluid oz (250 ml)
  lukewarm milk
1½ lbs (700 g) black
  cherries
4 oz (110 g) butter
4 oz (110 g) icing sugar
3 eggs
1 teaspoon powdered
  cinnamon

1 scant teaspoon grated
  lemon rind
2½ oz (70 g) ground
  almonds
vanilla sugar
butter for the baking dish

Preheat the oven to Gas Mark 5, 375°F, 190°C. Butter a fairly deep gratin dish.

Grate the crust off the rolls and then slice the rolls fairly thinly. Pour the milk over the rolls and leave to soak. Wash and dry the cherries, remove the stalks, but do not stone them.

Cream 3½ oz of the butter with the sugar. Separate eggs. Beat the yolks into the creamed butter, one by one. Add cinnamon and lemon rind. Beat in the softened rolls. Whisk the egg whites until stiff, fold into the mixture alternately with half the ground almonds. Fold in the cherries.

Spoon the mixture into the buttered gratin dish and sprinkle with the remaining ground almonds. Dot with small flakes of remaining butter. Bake for forty-five to fifty-five minutes, until well browned. Dust with vanilla sugar and allow to cool a little before serving.

TOPFEN AUFLAUF

Baked Pudding Made With Curd Cheese

Serves 4 – 6

butter and ground walnuts
  for the dish
3½ oz (100 g) curd cheese
6 eggs
3½ oz (100 g) butter
3½ oz (100 g) caster or
  icing sugar

3½ oz (100 g) ground
  walnuts
3½ oz (100 g) raisins
a little grated lemon rind
1 teaspoon vanilla sugar
icing sugar scented with
  vanilla for the top

Butter a deep gratin dish and dust with ground walnuts. Preheat the oven to Gas Mark 5, 375°F, 190°C.

Separate eggs. Cream butter and sugar until very light and fluffy, then beat in the cheese and the egg yolks, adding them one by one and beating well after each addition. Whisk the whites until stiff and fold into the mixture, alternately with the ground walnuts. Finally fold in the raisins, grated lemon rind and the vanilla sugar. Spoon into the prepared gratin dish and bake until nicely browned on top – about thirty-five to forty minutes. Dust thickly with icing sugar.

The pudding tastes best when eaten warm, not hot. Serve with raspberry syrup or stewed fruit.

WEINKOCH

Wine Pudding

Serves 4
4 eggs
2 generous oz (60 g) caster
  sugar
2 generous oz (60 g)
  ground unblanched
  almonds
1 generous oz (30 g)
  biscuit crumbs
grated lemon rind
butter and ground
  almonds for the dish

For the sauce
¼ pint (⅛ l) white wine
2½ oz (75 g) caster sugar
1 clove
¼ pint (⅛ l) water
juice of ½ lemon
1 teaspoon vanilla sugar

Butter a deep gratin dish and sprinkle with ground almonds. Separate eggs.

Whisk yolks with half the sugar until thick and creamy. Whisk whites until stiff, then whisk in remaining sugar. Fold whites into yolks, then fold in ground almonds, biscuit crumbs and grated lemon rind. Bake at Gas Mark 6, 400°F, 200°C until nicely browned – about twenty to twenty-five minutes.

Meanwhile put the sugar for the sauce into a thick saucepan and melt over low heat. When the sugar turns pale yellow, add the wine, water, vanilla sugar, clove and lemon juice. Bring to boil slowly and strain hot over the baked pudding. Serve at once.

ZWETSCHKEN UND MANDEL PUDDING

Plum and Almond Pudding

Serves 4

1 lb (450 g) plums	3½ oz (100 g) ground
2 – 3 tablespoons soft	unblanched almonds
brown sugar	3 eggs
pinch each of powdered	2½ oz (70 g) icing or caster
cinnamon and cloves	sugar
3 oz (85 g) boudoir	1 teaspoon vanilla sugar
biscuits (sponge fingers)	1 tablespoon rum

Halve the plums and remove stones. Put the plums into a fairly deep gratin dish and sprinkle with the brown sugar, cinnamon and cloves. Cover and leave to stand for as long as possible – the longer the better. Put the dish, still covered, into the oven at Gas Mark 3, 325°F, 160°C until the plums are just cooked, but still retain their shape.

Crush the sponge fingers with a rolling pin (or use a coffee grinder or food mill) until they are the consistency of rather coarse breadcrumbs. Mix together the crushed biscuits and ground almonds. Separate eggs. Whisk together yolks, icing (or caster) and vanilla sugar until thick and creamy. Add the rum. Whisk the whites until stiff. Fold the whites into yolks, alternately with the biscuit crumbs and ground almond mixture. Pile on top of the plums and bake at Gas Mark 4, 350°F, 180°C until nicely browned on top – about thirty minutes.

Serve hot with thick ice-cold cream – though it is pretty good cold, too, even without the cream.

BAUMWOLLKOCH

'Cotton Wool Pudding' seems much too mundane a name for a pudding as delicious as this, but this is exactly what Katharina Prato called it.

Serves 4 – 6

5 oz (140 g) butter	4 egg whites
5 oz (140 g) caster or icing	1 tablespoon plain flour
sugar	2 heaped tablespoons
8 egg yolks	apricot jam
grated rind and juice of	butter and icing sugar for
½ lemon	the dish

Cream butter and sugar until light and fluffy, then beat in the yolks one by one. Add lemon juice and rind. Whisk whites until stiff, fold into the mixture, and finally fold in the flour. Bake or steam in a buttered and sugared gratin dish at Gas Mark 4, 350°F, 180°C for about fifty minutes. Turn out onto a warmed serving dish and cover with melted apricot jam.

BISCUITPUDDING

Glacé Fruit Pudding

Serves 4

8 oz (250 g) boudoir biscuits (sponge fingers)	5 oz (150 g) mixed glacé fruit cut into small pieces
¼ pint (150 ml) double cream	4 tablespoons apricot jam
vanilla pod	1 tablespoon Cointreau
3½ oz (100 g) butter	butter for the pudding mould
3½ oz (100 g) caster sugar	
3 eggs	

Crumble the sponge fingers into a bowl. Heat cream with vanilla pod and pour over crumbled sponge fingers. Cover and leave to cool.

Cream butter and sugar until light and fluffy. Separate eggs and beat yolks into creamed butter, one by one. Beat in the sponge fingers, having removed the vanilla pod. Add the glacé fruit. Whisk whites until stiff and fold into the mixture. Arrange mixture in buttered pudding basin, cover with foil or lightly buttered waxed paper and steam for about one hour, until set.

Heat the jam until melted and press through a sieve, then reheat gently with the Cointreau. Turn the pudding out onto a warmed serving dish and trickle the warm apricot jam over it.

GELBER PUDDING MIT SCHOKOLADE SAUCE

Yellow Pudding with Chocolate Sauce

Serves 4	*Chocolate Sauce*
3½ oz (100 g) butter	5 oz (140 g) chocolate
4½ oz (120 g) icing sugar	5 oz (140 g) icing sugar
3 eggs	½ pint (280 ml) water
juice and grated rind of ¼ lemon	
3 tablespoons plain flour	

Cream butter and sugar until light and fluffy. Separate eggs and beat yolks into the creamed butter mixture, one by one. Whisk whites until stiff and fold into the creamed butter, alternately with the flour. Finally add lemon rind and juice. Steam for about three-quarters of an hour. Serve with chocolate sauce.

For the chocolate sauce break the chocolate into small pieces. Dissolve it in the water together with the sugar, and cook until thickened, stirring constantly.

HASELNUSS PUDDING

Hazelnut Pudding

Serves 4 – 6

For the pudding
3 oz (80 g) hazelnuts
3½ oz (100 g) butter
3½ oz (100 g) icing sugar
5 eggs
1 teaspoon vanilla sugar
1 generous oz (30 g) fine
    biscuit crumbs
2 oz (50 g) plain flour
grated rind of ½ lemon
butter and ground
    hazelnuts for the
    pudding basin

For the sauce
½ pint (280 ml) milk
2 egg yolks
2 oz (50 g) sugar
2 oz (50 g) hazelnuts
1 teaspoon vanilla sugar
1 good tablespoon rum

Butter a pudding basin and dust it with ground hazelnuts. Put the whole hazelnuts on a baking sheet and brown them in the oven at Gas Mark 6, 400°F, 200°C until the skins rub off easily. Put the hazelnuts into a clean kitchen towel and rub the skins off. Grind the hazelnuts.

Cream the butter with two-thirds of the icing sugar until light and fluffy. Separate eggs. Add the yolks, one by one, to the creamed butter, beating well after each addition. Whisk the whites until stiff, then whisk in the remaining sugar and the vanilla sugar. Fold the whipped whites into the yolk mixture, alternately with the ground hazelnuts, biscuit crumbs and the flour. Finally fold in the grated lemon rind. Pile the mixture into the pudding basin and steam for about forty minutes. Turn out onto a heated serving dish and serve with the following sauce.

Put the hazelnuts for the sauce on a baking sheet and brown lightly in the oven until the skins rub off easily. Rub the skins off, grind the hazelnuts and then spread them on a baking sheet and return them to the oven until they are nicely browned. Whisk together egg yolks, sugar and a little of the milk. Heat remaining milk, then stir into yolk mixture. Whisk over steam – or over very low heat – until thickened, then add vanilla sugar, rum and hazelnuts.

HIMBEER KOCH

Raspberry Pudding

Serves 4

7 oz (200 g) raspberries
7 oz (200 g) icing sugar
1 generous oz (30 g) butter
1 egg
3 egg yolks
2 egg whites
3½ oz (100 g) ground
   almonds

1 generous oz (30 g)
   breadcrumbs moistened
   with milk
a little lemon juice
butter and sugar for the
   pudding basin

Sprinkle raspberries with icing sugar, leave to stand for a little while until the sugar has melted and there is quite a bit of juice. Purée the raspberries (or use a food processor) and then sieve to remove the pips. Cream butter and beat in the whole egg and the egg yolks gradually, then add the lemon juice and raspberry purée. Beat in the moistened breadcrumbs. Whisk egg whites until stiff and fold into the mixture, alternately with the ground almonds. Spoon mixture into buttered and floured pudding basin and steam for about fifty minutes. *Weinchaudeau* (see page 204) goes particularly well with this.

KAFFEE PUDDING

Coffee Pudding

Serves 4

3 oz (80 g) rolls (weight
   after cutting off crust)
¼ pint (140 ml) strong
   black coffee
3 oz (80 g) butter

3 oz (80 g) icing sugar
3 eggs
2½ oz (70 g) ground
   unblanched almonds
butter and sugar for the
   pudding basin

Slice the rolls thinly, pour hot coffee over the slices. Stir, then pass the mixture through a sieve. Cream butter and sugar until fluffy. Separate eggs and beat the yolks into the butter mixture, then beat in the puréed rolls. Whisk whites until stiff and fold into the mixture, alternately with the ground almonds. Pile into the prepared pudding basin and steam for about three-quarters of an hour. Serve with *Weinchaudeau* (see page 204).

KAISER PUDDING

Emperor's Pudding

The Emperor in this particular case was Franz I, father-in-law of Napoleon, about whom he said: 'Now that I've met him I like him even less.'

Serves 4
For the pudding
2½ oz (70 g) ground
  almonds
1 tablespoon fresh orange
  juice
3 eggs
2½ oz (70 g) icing sugar
1 heaped tablespoon finely
  chopped candied peel
butter, icing sugar
  and halved blanched
  almonds for the pudding
  basin

For the sauce
½ pint (¼ l) double cream
2 egg yolks
1 heaped tablespoon sugar
1 teaspoon vanilla sugar
2 – 3 tablespoons Orange
  Curaçao

Butter a pudding basin and dust it lightly with icing sugar. Arrange halved almonds in circles or in a pattern at the bottom of the basin. Moisten the ground almonds with orange juice.

Separate eggs. Whisk the yolks with the icing sugar until very thick and fluffy, and pale yellow in colour. Whisk the whites until stiff and fold into the yolk mixture, alternately with the moistened ground almonds. Fold in the finely chopped peel. Pile the mixture into the prepared pudding basin and steam for thirty to forty minutes. Turn out carefully onto a hot dish and serve.

A simple hot orange sauce goes well with this pudding, but for special occasions serve it with a rich custard made by cooking the cream, egg yolks, sugar and vanilla sugar in a double saucepan until thick. Remove from heat, stir in the Orange Curaçao and serve.

KASTANIENKOCH

Steamed Chestnut Pudding

Serves 4 – 6
5 eggs
7 oz (200 g) icing sugar
2 oz (60 g) plain or bitter
  chocolate, softened

7 oz (200 g) cooked sieved
  chestnuts (equivalent of
  12 – 13 oz, 350 g – 380 g
  uncooked chestnuts)
1 teaspoon vanilla sugar
butter and vanilla sugar
  for the pudding basin

Separate eggs. Whisk yolks with two-thirds of the icing sugar until thick and creamy, then stir in softened, but not hot, chocolate. Whisk whites until stiff, then whisk in remaining sugar and vanilla sugar. Fold into yolk mixture, alternately with the sieved chestnuts. Pile mixture into buttered and sugared pudding basin and steam for about one hour. Serve with chocolate sauce (see page 233).

MANDEL PUDDING I

Almond Pudding I

Serves 4
2½ oz (70 g) ground
  almonds
orange juice to moisten
3 eggs
2½ oz (70 g) icing sugar
1 heaped tablespoon
  chopped mixed peel or
  glacé fruit
butter and icing sugar for
  the pudding basin

Orange Sauce
½ pint (280 ml) single
  cream
2 egg yolks
1 tablespoon icing sugar
2 – 3 tablespoons Orange
  Curaçao

Butter a pudding basin and dust with icing sugar. Moisten the ground almonds with a little orange juice.

Separate eggs. Whisk yolks with sugar until thick and creamy. Whisk whites until stiff. Fold whites into yolks, alternately with ground almonds. Finally fold in mixed peel or glacé fruit. Steam for thirty to forty minutes, covered, leaving room for expansion. Carefully turn out onto a hot platter and serve with Orange Sauce.

For the orange sauce whisk together cream, egg yolks and icing sugar over steam until frothy, then add the Curaçao, whisk again and serve.

Mandel Pudding II

Serves 4
4 eggs
2½ oz (70 g) icing sugar
2 oz (50 g) plain flour
2½ oz (70 g) ground
  almonds

1 oz (30 g) melted butter
butter and sugar for the
  pudding basin

Separate eggs. Whisk yolks with half the sugar until fluffy. Whisk whites until stiff, and whisk in remaining sugar. Fold whites into yolks, alternately with flour and ground almonds. Fold in the melted butter. Steam in a buttered and sugared pudding basin for about fifteen to twenty minutes. Serve with *Weinchaudeau* (see page 204) or chocolate sauce (see page 233).

MOHR IM HEMD

The supreme chocolate pudding, and my favourite way of serving it is to top it with great mounds of ice-cold whipped cream scented with vanilla sugar and very hot chocolate sauce poured over the lot. If you pour the chocolate sauce over at the last moment and the whipped cream has been properly chilled (and also added just before serving), the chocolate sauce will gently slide off the snowy peaks, presenting not only a pretty picture but also a marvellous mixture of textures and flavours.

Serves 4 – 6
For the pudding
4 eggs
2½ oz (70 g) butter
2½ oz (70 g) icing sugar
2½ oz (70 g) grated plain
    chocolate
2½ oz (70 g) ground
    almonds
butter and icing sugar for
    the pudding basin
whipped cream lightly
    sweetened with vanilla
    sugar

For the sauce
5 oz (140 g) plain
    chocolate
5 oz (140 g) icing sugar
½ pint (280 ml) water

For the pudding, separate eggs. Cream butter with the sugar until very light and fluffy, beat in the yolks one by one. Whisk whites until stiff. Fold whites into the yolk mixture, alternately with the grated chocolate and almonds. Steam in buttered and sugared pudding basin covered with a lid or foil, folded with a pleat to allow room for expansion, for about three-quarters of an hour.

For the sauce grate the chocolate or break it into small pieces. Put sugar and chocolate into a thick saucepan, add the water and cook gently over low heat, stirring constantly, until the chocolate and sugar are dissolved, then cook more briskly, still stirring to prevent burning, until thick.

Turn the pudding out onto a warmed serving dish. Top with chilled whipped cream, lightly flavoured with vanilla sugar, and pour the hot chocolate sauce over it.

NACKTER PUA

Naked Boy

Typical of Carinthia, this is an excellent pudding for a cold day. Ingredients may be varied according to what is in the larder.

Serves 4 – 6

7 oz (200 g) white bread, *brioche* or *Kärntner Reinling* (see page 317)	a little finely chopped lemon balm
9 fluid oz (¼ l) double or sour cream	pinch of salt
4 – 5 eggs	softened butter for the cloth
4 tablespoons caster sugar	cloves or sultanas
2 oz (50 g) raisins or sultanas (or dried cranberries)	2 – 3 tablespoons eau de vie (Schnaps)

Cut the bread (crumb only) into fairly thin, small slices. Put into a bowl, add the cream or sour cream and leave to soak. Whisk together eggs and sugar, add the soaked bread with all the liquid, then stir in the raisins, lemon balm and a pinch of salt. If the mixture appears too dry, add a little milk.

Wring out a napkin or tea towel in cold water and spread with softened butter. Place the pudding mixture in the centre of the napkin, tie the four corners loosely over it and slot a wooden spoon through the top. Hang the pudding over a pan of boiling water with the wooden spoon resting across the saucepan. Steam, covered, for one hour, taking care not to let the water boil over or boil dry.

Turn the pudding onto a heated serving dish, stud with cloves or sultanas, pour over some warmed eau de vie and set alight. Hot spiced apple juice can be used instead of the eau de vie (but it cannot be set alight, of course). Mulled wine – though not traditional – is also very good.

NUSS PUDDING

Walnut or Hazelnut Pudding

Particularly good when served with raspberry syrup and topped with whipped cream. The mixture can of course be steamed in individual small pudding moulds, in which case the cooking time should be reduced to thirty-five or forty minutes.

Serves 4 – 6

2 small day-old *brioches* or bridge rolls	1 scant teaspoon finely ground coffee
a little milk	4 eggs
3½ oz (100 g) butter	raspberry syrup and sweetened whipped cream for serving
2½ oz (70 g) icing sugar	
5 oz (140 g) ground walnuts or hazelnuts	butter and flour (or ground walnuts) for pudding basin
1 heaped tablespoon fine breadcrumbs	

Butter a 1½ pint pudding basin and dust lightly with flour or ground walnuts. Grate the crust off the *brioches* or bridge rolls. Dice or break up the crumb and soak in milk.

Separate eggs. Cream butter and sugar and beat in the yolks one by one, beating well after each addition. Squeeze out moisture from rolls and beat the pulp into the butter mixture. Whisk egg whites until stiff, fold into butter mixture, alternately with ground coffee and nuts. Finally fold in the breadcrumbs. Pile mixture into prepared pudding basin and steam for three quarters of an hour. Serve with raspberry syrup and whipped cream.

RAHMKOCH

Cream Pudding

Serves 4

1 scant oz (20 g) butter	4 tablespoons icing sugar
4 eggs	3 tablespoons plain flour
4 tablespoons double cream	butter and flour for the pudding basin

Separate eggs. Cream butter, beat in the yolks one by one, alternating them with a tablespoon cream and a tablespoon sugar. Whisk egg whites until stiff. Fold into the yolk mixture alternately with the flour. Pile mixture into buttered and floured pudding basin, leaving room for expansion. Cover basin and steam for about forty-five minutes. Serve with lightly sweetened fruit purée.

RUM PUDDING

Serves 4

For the pudding	*For the sauce*
2½ oz (70 g) butter	3 tablespoons rum
2½ oz (70 g) icing or caster sugar	2 egg yolks
3 eggs	2 scant tablespoons caster sugar
1 scant oz (20 g) breadcrumbs moistened with rum	
2½ oz (70 g) ground unblanched almonds	
2½ oz (70 g) raisins	
1 oz (25 g) grated plain chocolate	
butter and icing sugar for the pudding basin	

Butter a pudding basin and dust it lightly with icing sugar. Separate eggs. Cream the butter and the sugar until light and fluffy, then beat in the yolks, one by one, alternately with the moistened breadcrumbs. Whisk the whites until stiff and fold into the mixture, alternately with the ground almonds and the grated chocolate. Finally fold in the raisins. Pile the mixture into the prepared pudding basin and steam for thirty-five to forty-five minutes.

Turn out onto a hot dish and serve with rum sauce, made by whisking together the rum, egg yolks and sugar over steam until light and frothy.

SCHMANKERL

Schmankerl is a Viennese expression for especially delectable titbits, whether a juicy bit of gossip or some culinary delight saved by cook especially for you (some restaurant menus have a separate heading for *Schmankerl* listing specialities of the house or the region). There is a recipe for *Schmankerl*, or rather *Schmankerlmasse (Schmankerl* mixture), dating back well over a hundred years – a light, biscuity batter which was baked and crumbled into slivers as it was removed from the baking sheet. The resulting crumble – *Schmankerl* in fact – was used in a number of recipes such as *Schmankerlkoch*, which are enjoying a recent revival.

1 scant oz (20 g) icing sugar	7 fluid oz (200 ml) plain flour
1 heaped teaspoon butter	single cream
	melted butter

Crumble butter into sugar, add the flour and enough single cream to give a thick batter. Spread thinly on buttered and floured baking sheet and bake at Gas Mark 5, 375°F, 190°C, brushing with melted butter as the edges brown. Remove from baking sheet with a palette knife – the mixture will crumble, resulting in *Schmankerl*. Store in an airtight container.

SCHMANKERLKOCH

Pudding made with *Schmankerl*

Schmankerl are not weighed for this recipe, but measured out in a measuring jug: volume is more important than weight.

Serves 4

7 fluid oz (200 ml) double cream	1 heaped tablespoon butter
11 fluid oz (300 ml) *Schmankerl* (see above)	4 egg yolks
	2½ oz (70 g) sugar
	3 egg whites

Bring the cream to the boil, sprinkle in the *Schmankerl*, stirring constantly. Bring to boil again, pour into a bowl and set to cool. Cream the butter, beat in the sugar and the egg yolks, then add the *Schmankerl* mixture. Finally fold in the stiffly beaten egg whites. Steam in a buttered and sugared pudding basin for about thirty-five minutes. Serve with fruit purée or fruit sauce.

SCHOKOLADE PUDDING

Chocolate Pudding

Serves 4

3 rolls
a little milk
6 eggs
3 oz (80 g) icing sugar
3½ oz (100 g) butter
2 oz (50 g) grated
    chocolate

3 oz (80 g) ground
    unblanched almonds
butter and icing sugar for
    the pudding basin

Grate the crust off the rolls, cut rolls into cubes and soak in milk. Separate eggs. Cream butter and sugar then add yolks one by one. Drain rolls, squeeze out all moisture and beat into sugar mixture. Whisk whites until stiff, fold into mixture, alternately with ground almonds and grated chocolate. Steam for about an hour.

Chocolate Sauce with Whipped Cream

8 oz (225 g) plain
    chocolate
8 tablespoons sugar

4 tablespoons water
½ pint (280 ml) double
    cream

Break chocolate into small pieces and set to melt over steam or in the oven. Dissolve sugar in water over low heat, then cook to 'small thread' stage. Remove from heat and stir into melted chocolate. Stir until cool, but still spreadable, then fold into whipped cream.

TIROLER NUSSKOCH MIT WEICHSELN

Walnut Pudding with Morello Cherries

Like the recipe for *Imster Schlutzkrapfen*, this comes from the famous Hotel Post at Imst.

Serves 4 – 6

5 eggs
3½ oz (100 g) icing sugar
grated rind of ½ lemon
3½ oz (100 g) ground
   walnuts
2 oz (50 g) fine
   breadcrumbs

1 oz (25 g) melted butter
1 small jar or tin
   preserved morello
   cherries
butter and ground walnuts
   for pudding basin

Separate eggs. Whisk yolks with half the sugar until thick and creamy. Whisk whites until stiff. Whisk in remaining sugar. Fold whites into yolks, alternately with walnuts and breadcrumbs. Fold in grated lemon rind. Finally fold in melted butter and chopped and drained morello cherries. Pile mixture into the pudding basin, previously buttered and sprinkled with ground walnuts. Steam pudding for about an hour. Serve with the juice from the morello cherries.

TOPFENKOCH

Pudding Made with Curd Cheese

Serves 4

4½ oz (120 g) curd cheese
2½ oz (70 g) butter
4 egg yolks
2 egg whites
2½ oz (70 g) ground
   almonds

2 oz (60 g) icing sugar
1 teaspoon vanilla sugar
2½ oz (70 g) raisins
butter and flour for the
   pudding mould

Sieve the curd cheese to make sure it is absolutely smooth and dry. Cream butter and sugar until light and fluffy, beat in the egg yolks, one by one. Add curd cheese and vanilla sugar. Whisk egg whites until stiff. Fold whites into curd cheese mixture, alternately with ground almonds and raisins. Steam in a buttered and floured pudding mould with a lid (or covered with foil, pleated to allow room for expansion) for one hour.

Very lightly sweetened strawberry or raspberry purée goes well with this.

WIENER PUDDING

Viennese Almond Pudding

Serves 4

5 oz (140 g) butter
3½ oz (100 g) caster sugar
1 tablespoon vanilla sugar
7 egg yolks
4 egg whites
4½ oz (120 g) ground
   almonds
butter and ground
   almonds for the pudding
   basin

For the sauce
¼ pint (140 ml) white wine
juice of ½ lemon
2½ oz (70 g) caster sugar
2 eggs

Butter a pudding basin and dust with ground almonds. Cream butter, sugar and vanilla sugar until very light and fluffy. Beat in the egg yolks one at a time. Whisk whites until stiff, fold into butter mixture, alternately with the ground almonds. Spoon the mixture into the prepared pudding basin, cover with lid or with foil, pleated to allow room for expansion. Steam for forty-five to sixty minutes. Turn onto a warmed serving dish and serve with the following sauce.

Put all the ingredients into a bowl and set it over a pan half filled with simmering water. Whisk over steam until the mixture is very hot and frothy. Serve at once.

CREME KOCH

A more luxurious, and even more delicious version of *Wiener Koch* (see page 254).

Serves 4 – 6

2½ oz (70 g) slivered
   almonds
2½ oz (70 g) icing sugar
14 fluid oz (400 ml) single
   cream
6 eggs

3½ oz (100 g) caster sugar
1 teaspoon vanilla sugar
1 scant tablespoon plain
   flour
butter for the dish

Gently brown almonds and icing sugar together, allow to cool and then crush.

Separate eggs. Heat cream with vanilla sugar and caster sugar. Whisk in yolks and the flour and cook until well thickened. (If you are careful you can cook this over very low heat, otherwise use a double boiler.) Remove from heat and stir until cool (plunge saucepan into a large bowl of ice-cold water to speed up the process).

Whisk whites until stiff. Add crumbled almonds to the egg cream, then fold in whisked whites. Pile mixture into a buttered deep gratin dish and bake at Gas Mark 5, 375°F, 190°C for about fifteen minutes.

CREME PUDDING

Quantities given should be enough for three, but this pudding is so light and delicious that I have known two people polish it off without any difficulty whatsoever.

3 eggs	1 tablespoon plain flour
2 tablespoons icing or	a little grated orange rind
caster sugar	butter and flour for the
1 teaspoon vanilla sugar	dish
3 tablespoons double	
cream	

Butter and lightly flour a deep gratin or soufflé dish. Preheat the oven to Gas Mark 5, 375°F, 190°C.

Separate eggs. Whisk together yolks, sugar and vanilla sugar until thick and creamy, then whisk in the cream. Whisk the whites until very stiff, then fold them into the yolks, alternately with the flour. Finally add the grated orange rind. Pile the mixture into the prepared dish and bake until nicely browned on top – about twelve to fifteen minutes. Serve at once, spooning out from the sides.

The mixture should still be a little runny inside and it will go on cooking slightly in the hot dish so that second helpings will be just right when you get to them.

FLAMBIERTE BRATÄPFEL

Apple Flambé

Serves 4

5 eating apples	1 small wine glass of
1 tablespoon butter	white wine
2 heaped tablespoons icing	2 generous liqueur glasses
sugar	of Calvados

Peel, core and halve the apples. Melt the butter in a shallow flameproof dish, add the apples and the wine. Simmer gently until the apples are cooked but not mushy, then turn up the heat so that the syrup from the apples will thicken and slightly caramelize. Gently warm the Calvados, pour over the apples and set alight. Serve at once, preferably accompanied by Chestnut Ice Cream (see page 261) or *Geeiste Kastanienmousse* (see page 255).

KAISERKOCH

Emperor's Pudding

A delicious light pudding, worthy of its imperial prefix. The original recipe, dating back to the last century, uses Austrian *Kipfel* for the crumbs. They are very special, much drier and crisper than French *croissants*. When Marie Louise, second wife of Napoleon and Viennese by birth, became Duchessa di Parma, she took her Viennese pastry chef Gippritsch to Parma, so as not to be deprived of *Kipfel*, and to this day, *croissants* – alas, not necessarily the Viennese kind – are known in Parma as *Giprini*. Since you are unlikely to get an Austrian *Kipfel* (at least not without difficulty), use *brioche*, or even plain, crustless white bread instead. *(Croissants* will not do as they contain too much fat.)

Serves 4 – 6

10 oz (280 g) fresh raspberries	little cream or top milk
10 oz (280 g) caster sugar	2 oz (50 g) butter
7 fluid oz (200 ml) water	5 oz (140 g) ground almonds
2½ oz (70 g) white bread or *brioche* crumbs	6 eggs

Sieve the raspberries, retaining the juice. Dissolve sugar in water over low heat, bring to boil and cook to small pearl stage (200°F). Add raspberries and juice and cook until well thickened. Set aside to cool.

   Moisten the crumbs with a little cream or top milk. Cream butter until light and fluffy and beat in almonds and two of the eggs. Beat in the moistened crumbs. Separate remaining eggs and gradually add the yolks to the butter mixture. Whisk whites until stiff. Fold them into mixture alternately with the cooled raspberries. Bake in a buttered soufflé dish at Gas Mark 4 – 5, 350° - 375°F, 180° – 190°C for fifty to sixty minutes.

MARILLENTÖRTCHEN

Apricot Tartlets

Lisl Wagner-Bacher, of Landhaus Bacher at Mautern in Lower Austria, is the First Lady of Austrian Cooking, proclaimed Chef of the Year in 1983, the year the award was first made. Her culinary creations are many and varied (she has also written an excellent cookery book) and her apricot tartlets are one of my favourites, worth every minute of the effort.

For the pastry
7 oz (200 g) strong flour
4½ oz (120 g) butter
2 flat tablespoons icing
  sugar
2 egg yolks
1 tablespoon water
pinch of salt
butter and flour for the
  tartlet tins

For the glaze
2½ fluid oz (65 ml) milk
2½ fluid oz (65 ml) double
  cream
4½ fluid oz ((120 ml) sour
  cream
2 egg yolks
1 generous oz (30 g)
  granulated sugar
1 teaspoon vanilla sugar

For the filling
4½ oz (120 g) curd cheese
1½ oz (40 g) butter
1 generous oz (30 g) icing
  sugar
⅔ oz (20 g) granulated
  sugar
2 eggs
pinch of salt
1 teaspoon vanilla sugar
1 teaspoon grated lemon
  rind
8 apricots
2 tablespoons apricot eau
  de vie
2 tablespoons apricot
  liqueur
For the sauce
10 apricots
a little sugar
5 fluid oz (125 ml) double
  cream

For the pastry, sift flour with a pinch of salt and the icing sugar. Cut butter into flour and quickly work to a dough with the egg yolks and water. Wrap dough in foil and chill for half an hour, no longer. Roll out to the thickness of about ⅛ of an inch (2 mm), and line four buttered and floured tartlet tins with it. Prick with a fork and bake at Gas Mark 4, 350°F, 180°C until golden brown. Remove carefully from tins and set to cool on a rack.

For the filling, wash and stone apricots, and cut into slices. Cover with apricot eau-de-vie and apricot liqueur and set aside. Separate eggs. Cream butter with icing sugar, beat in the yolks gradually, then add vanilla sugar and grated lemon rind. Gradually add the cheese. Whisk egg whites until stiff, whisk in granulated sugar. Fold whites into cheese mixture. Divide apricot slices between the tartlets and three-quarters fill tartlets with the cheese mixture, flattening the top with a palette knife. Bake for about ten minutes at Gas Mark 4, 350°F, 180°C.

Whilst the tartlets are baking, prepare the glaze. Mix together all ingredients, top tartlets with the glaze. Bake until top is golden brown.

For the sauce scald apricots with hot water, then dip them into cold water and remove skin. Remove stones and purée the apricots. Sweeten with sugar to taste and add vanilla sugar. Put a spoonful of apricot purée on each plate, with a blob of cream in the centre, drawing a pattern through with a fork.

NUISCHMALZ

A speciality from the Tyrol where it is served on high days and holidays.

1½ oz (40 g) fine cake flour	1½ oz (40 g) butter
1½ oz (40 g) strong flour	pinch of salt
18 fluid oz (½ l) milk or single cream	about 1 lb (450 g) butter warmed honey

Sift together the two kinds of flour. Slake flour with a little of the milk (or cream) and bring remaining milk to boil with the 1½ oz butter and a pinch of salt. Pour over the slaked flour, return mixture to stove and cook to a thick cream over low heat. Remove from heat, stir until just warm to the touch (in Austria this is called *lippenwarm* – as warm as your lips), then whisk in butter in small flakes until the mixture is the consistency of whipped cream. Pile onto plates – in the Tyrol these are invariably made of pewter – and trickle warmed honey over each pile.

OBSTAUFLAUF

Pudding Made with Fresh Fruit

Almost any soft fruit can be used for this delicious pudding, but I find it best when made with morello cherries or small blue plums.

Serves 4

For the pudding
1½ lbs (750 g) morello cherries or plums
3 tablespoons caster or icing sugar
½ teaspoon each vanilla sugar, cinnamon and allspice
1 oz (30 g) ground almonds
1 tablespoon double cream
dash of rum
butter for the dish

For the topping
3 eggs
2 oz (60 g) butter
2½ oz (70 g) caster or icing sugar
5 fluid oz (140 ml) milk or single cream
3½ oz (100 g) plain flour
grated lemon rind
vanilla sugar

Lightly butter a soufflé or deep gratin dish. Stone the fruit, or if using plums, halve them. Put fruit into the prepared dish, sprinkle with sugar, vanilla sugar, spices and ground almonds. Add the cream and the rum and stir lightly, then cover the dish with foil and leave to stand for at least half an hour.

Preheat the oven to Gas Mark 2, 300°F, 150°C and put the dish – still covered with foil – into the oven whilst preparing the topping.

Separate eggs. Cream butter and sugar until light and fluffy, then beat in the yolks one by one. Gradually beat in the milk or cream and the flour. Whisk whites until stiff, then fold into the butter mixture, together with the grated lemon rind and vanilla sugar. Pile the mixture on top of the fruit which should be heated through by now. Bake for fifteen minutes at Gas Mark 2, 300°F, 150°C, then increase heat to Gas Mark 4, 350°F, 180°C and bake for another thirty to forty-five minutes.

The juice at the bottom of the dish may at first suggest that the pudding has not quite baked through, but it is in fact a delicious sauce which the pudding has produced for itself. This dish tastes equally good served hot, cold or just warm.

POFESEN

Poor Knights

This classic old dessert, found in many countries, has several names in Austria. It is *Pofesen* in Vienna and Lower Austria (*Pofesen, Pofesen, wo bist so lang g'wesen*, runs an old children's rhyme – Pofesen, where have you been for so long?). In most other parts of the country the name is *Arme Ritter* (Poor Knights) while in the Tyrol the Knights are *versoffene* (drunk) because there they are dipped in mulled red wine instead of milk (which is sometimes done in Lower Austria, too, after which they are dipped in a yeast batter before being fried).

In Carinthia and Styria the name is more often than not just *Schnitten* (slices) and they may be sprinkled with dried pears, honey and cinnamon. *Arme Ritter* always have a sweet filling, whilst *Pofesen* comes in savoury versions as well – see *Hirnpofesen* (page 106).

Serves 4

1 day-old small French loaf or 8 slices cut from a French loaf without crust	2 eggs, or batter as for *Wiener Wäschermädln* (see page 207)
good firm jam	lard or oil for frying
about ¼ pint (⅛ l) milk or wine	icing sugar

Trim or grate the crust off the French loaf. Cut the loaf into slices about the thickness of a finger, then cut down the centre of each slice to within ⅛ inch of edge and spread some good, firm jam into the opening (cherry or redcurrant are particularly suitable, though in Austria it is often *Powidl*). Press together the slices over the jam and dip them into milk or wine, taking care that they should not get too wet. Dip the moistened slices into lightly beaten egg or batter and fry in smoking hot fat until golden brown on both sides. Drain on kitchen paper and serve hot, dusted with sugar. Fruit syrup – particularly raspberry syrup – is often served separately, as a sauce.

SALZBURGER GOLDHÜHNER

'Golden Hens' from Salzburg

Maria Anna Neudecker, née Ertl, gave explicit instructions for this dish in her cookery book first published in 1810, omitting only one thing: the actual recipe. Since it is now impossible to ascertain exactly what she would have accepted as *Brandteig mit vielen Eiern* (choux pastry with many eggs), I can only hope that she would have approved of my interpretation.

Serves 4 – 6

4½ fluid oz (125 ml) water
4½ oz (125 g) butter
pinch of salt
4½ oz (125 g) plain flour
4 eggs
fat or oil for deep frying
2 – 3 tablespoons icing
   sugar

1 heaped teaspoon vanilla
   sugar
½ teaspoon cinnamon
butter and flour for the
   baking sheet

Put water, butter and salt into a saucepan and bring to the boil. Do not do this too quickly – the butter must have time to dissolve completely. Then tip in the sifted flour, all at once. Beat well with a wooden spoon, remove from heat and beat in the eggs one by one.

Butter and flour a baking sheet. Spread the mixture to the thickness of a finger (about ½ an inch) and bake at Gas Mark 6, 400°F, 200°C for three to five minutes, until the mixture has just set.

Using a teaspoon, scoop out small rounds and drop them into hot fat and fry until golden brown. Fry only a few at a time, leaving room for expansion. Drain on kitchen paper and sprinkle with a mixture of icing sugar, vanilla sugar and cinnamon.

SALZBURGER NOCKERLN

No visitor to Salzburg could possibly miss them: great golden globes of vanilla-scented froth, a barely perceptible crust enveloping a soft and creamy centre. One reliable Austrian cookery book, claiming to give 'the original recipe', states that they are extremely difficult to prepare. In fact, as served in Austrian restaurants today, *Salzburger Nockerln* – though very impressive and absolutely delicious – are no more difficult to prepare than a soufflé.

The 'real thing' was called *Salzburger Nocken* – the diminutive 'rl' was added only when dimensions became huge – and was made from choux pastry, cooked in milk, covered with an egg custard and baked. This dish was certainly known in the eighteenth century and probably as far back as the sixteenth (legend has it that it was first served to Prince Archbishop Wolf Dietrich von Raitenau). The first published recipe appears to be in Maria Anna Neudecker's *Die Baierische Köchin in Böhmen* (The Bavarian Cook in Bohemia), and my 1819 edition contains a recipe for *Salzburger Nocken* made with choux pastry into which whipped egg whites were folded for extra lightness. The mixture was then scooped out in small portions – about the size of a hazelnut – and poached in cream, where they greatly increased in size.

The recipe developed from there. Sometimes the cooked *Nocken* would be masked with a soufflé mixture and baked, thus creating a series of small soufflés within a soufflé. One of my favourite versions consists of very light yet moist *Nocken* made with a sponge mixture and baked in an egg custard – a recipe which certainly dates back well into the last century.

More and better ways of creating these very popular golden mounds were constantly sought, until *Salzburger Nockerln* became great balloons of soufflé mixture containing the merest flick of flour, fried, and then piled in towers on a warmed serving dish. These were, indeed, difficult to prepare, to say nothing of threatening to collapse as soon as they came out of the frying pan. And it also became increasingly difficult to find cooks capable of making them.

Then someone rediscovered *Pongauer Nocken* (Pongau is a region in the province of Salzburg), also known as *Salzburger Nockerln in der Schale* ('in the dish'): a method of preparation that is almost foolproof. After that there was no holding the popularity of this dish. Almost every restaurant has its special recipe. The one I have chosen is signed, sealed and approved by the appropriate Salzburg authorities. Quantities are for two, according to Salzburg. I think they are sufficient for four – all right, three if you are greedy!

3 tablespoons butter	3 egg yolks
4 tablespoons icing sugar	little grated lemon rind
1 tablespoon vanilla sugar	(optional)
2 tablespoons milk or	1 teaspoon plain flour
single cream	vanilla sugar for dusting
5 egg whites	over top

This is not as complicated as it sounds, but good timing is essential and the principle of the recipe must be understood: i.e. a very light soufflé mixture (practically no flour) is dropped in separate portions into a hot mixture of butter, a little sugar and milk (or single cream). The butter must be really hot and frothing, but not brown.

Get all the ingredients together and preheat the oven to Gas Mark 9, 475°F, 240°C. Choose a shallow ovenproof dish, preferably oval in shape, about 12 inches long and about 2¼ inches deep. Put the dish into the oven to heat. Cream butter with 1 tablespoon of the icing sugar and beat in the milk or cream. Set aside.

Whisk egg whites until very stiff, whisk in remaining icing sugar and vanilla sugar and whisk again until smooth. Lift up the whisk with some of the white still clinging to it and insert it into the yolks and whisk for a second or two. This will ensure an even blend. Now fold the yolks into the whites – not the other way round as in most recipes. Fold in the flour and the grated lemon rind.

Put the butter mixture into the heated dish – it should melt at once and froth slightly. If not, return the dish to the oven for a second or two. Arrange the egg mixture in four separate mounds, side by side. I use a flexible spatula for this, but use whatever suits you best and allows you to work fast, for speed is the essence of the whole operation. Put the dish into the hot oven as near the top as possible, but leaving room for the mixture to rise. Bake until just set and golden brown – about seven minutes. Dust with vanilla sugar and serve at once.

Salzburger Nockerln II

Not the original version, which used choux paste, but my favourite amongst the old recipes. It is very light, yet moist and succulent, and not all that difficult to prepare. All that is required is a little patience!

Serves 4 – 6

8 eggs	2 egg yolks
4 oz (120 g) butter	1 tablespoon vanilla sugar
3 oz (90 g) icing sugar	icing sugar sifted with
1¾ pints (1 litre) milk	vanilla sugar for
1½ oz (45 g) plain flour	sprinkling over top

Preheat oven to Gas Mark 5, 375°F, 190°C. Butter a deep (2-quart) ovenproof dish. Separate eggs. Cream butter and sugar until light and fluffy. Beat in the yolks of the eight eggs gradually, beating well after each addition. Reserve ¼ cup of the milk and pour the remainder into a fairly large, but not too deep saucepan and heat gently.

Meanwhile whisk the whites until stiff. Fold the whites into the yolk mixture alternately with the flour. Drop spoonfuls of the mixture into the hot milk and allow to poach gently for about four minutes, until set. The size of the *Nockerln* depends entirely on your taste – you can use teaspoons or tablespoons for scooping out the mixture, but leave space for the *Nockerln* to expand in the hot milk. Remove with a slotted spoon and place in the buttered dish. Continue until all the mixture has been used up.

Blend the two egg yolks with vanilla sugar and the reserved milk. Stir in the milk left from poaching the *Nockerln* and strain the mixture over the *Nockerln* in the baking dish. Place in the preheated oven and bake for ten to fifteen minutes until nicely browned. Dust with icing sugar sifted with vanilla sugar and serve immediately.

SCHNEEBALLEN

Snowballs

Serve them with a little raspberry syrup or fruit purée as a pudding, or sprinkle them lightly with icing sugar sifted with a pinch of cinnamon, and serve with tea or coffee.

Serves 4

3 generous oz (90 g) plain flour	1 – 2 tablespoons white wine
2 oz (50 g) butter	dash of rum
3 egg yolks	deep fat for frying
½ tablespoon double cream	sifted icing sugar
	cinnamon

Sift the flour onto a pastry board, make a well in the centre and drop in the yolks. Work to a smooth dough with the butter, cream, white wine and rum. Pat into a round, cover with a cloth and leave for half an hour.

Roll out to about ⅛ inch thickness, cut into squares measuring about 4½ inches by 4½ inches (11 cm × 11 cm) with a zig-zag cutter. Run the pastry cutter three or four times down each square, from within half an inch of the edge to half an inch of the opposite edge. Heat the fat and, when smoking hot, drop in each 'snowball' separately, picking up alternate strips with the handle of a wooden spoon, thus letting each snowball slide into the hot fat. Fry until golden brown, drain on kitchen paper and dust with icing sugar and cinnamon while still hot. Serve as soon as possible after frying.

VANILLA AUFLAUF

Vanilla Pudding

Serves 4

11 fluid oz (300 ml) double cream	2 tablespoons potato flour
1 teaspoon vanilla sugar	butter and flour for the dish
3½ oz (100 g) icing sugar	vanilla sugar for sprinkling over top
6 eggs	

Butter and flour a deep gratin dish. Separate eggs. Whisk together cream, sugars and yolks until well blended. Whisk whites until stiff. Fold whites into yolks, then fold in potato flour. Pile mixture into prepared dish and bake at Gas Mark 6, 400°F, 200°C until puffed up and golden brown on top. Sprinkle with vanilla sugar and serve at once.

WIENER KOCH

Viennese Pudding

Serves 4
6 eggs
2 tablespoons plain flour
15 fluid oz (420 ml) milk
3 oz (90 g) butter

4 oz (110 g) caster sugar
1 teaspoon vanilla sugar
butter and sugar for the
dish

Preheat oven to Gas Mark 7, 425°F, 220°C. Butter a soufflé or deep
gratin dish and dust with sugar. Separate eggs. Blend together flour,
yolks and a little cold milk. Heat remaining milk with sugar, vanilla
sugar and butter, and stir into the yolks. Cook mixture very gently in
a double boiler, stirring constantly until thick. Remove from heat, stir
until cool. Whisk egg whites until stiff, fold into the mixture and bake
for about twelve minutes.

KANARIENMILCH

Canaries Milk

A very old Viennese name for a light and frothy vanilla sauce, served
with a great number of puddings.

2 egg yolks
4 oz (110 g) caster sugar

2 teaspoons vanilla sugar
18 fluid oz (½ litre) milk

Whisk together egg yolks, sugar, vanilla sugar and half the milk. Heat
remaining milk, pour onto the yolk mixture, whisking all the time. Pour
into the top of a double boiler or into a bowl set over a saucepan
half-filled with simmering water, and whisk until very frothy. Serve
at once.

If you want a thicker sauce – and there are some puddings where this
is preferable – add about two tablespoons finely ground almonds to the
egg yolks and proceed as above.

COLD PUDDINGS

DIPLOMATENPUDDING

Serves 4 – 6

2½ oz (75 g) plain chocolate	dash of rum
1 teaspoon butter	18 fluid oz (½ litre) double cream
½ oz (15 g) gelatine	1 tablespoon chopped mixed peel or glacé fruit
6 egg yolks	
6½ oz (180 g) icing or caster sugar	

Lightly butter a sheet of cooking foil. Break the chocolate into small pieces and set it to melt either in a low oven or over steam. As soon as the chocolate has melted, remove it from the heat, allow it to cool a little and then stir in the butter. Spread the chocolate over the cooking foil and leave to set in a cool place or in the refrigerator. When the chocolate has set, cut or break it into small pieces. Treated this way, the chocolate incorporated into the pudding will literally melt in the mouth – very superior to just using chopped up pieces of chocolate!

Dissolve gelatine in a little warm water – this is best done by putting the gelatine into a small bowl, adding the water and stirring until the gelatine has dissolved completely. Whisk together over steam the egg yolks, sugar, rum and a little of the cream, until thick and fluffy. Remove the mixture from heat, stir in dissolved gelatine and whisk until cool. Fold in lightly whipped cream, the chocolate pieces and the chopped mixed peel.

Put mixture into a pudding mould previously rinsed with cold water, and chill until set. Unmould pudding before serving and serve with raspberry syrup. Incidentally, I find that chopped preserved stem ginger instead of the mixed peel adds a delicious touch, but then I love stem ginger!

GEEISTE KASTANIENMOUSSE

Iced Chestnut Mousse

Serves 4

9 oz (250 g) canned sweetened chestnut purée	1 tablespoon rum
	5 fluid oz (140 ml) double cream

I use a French brand of chestnut purée which is not only sweetened but also lightly scented with vanilla. If necessary, add a little vanilla sugar to the purée.

Set the refrigerator control to maximum. Tip the chestnut purée into a bowl, add the rum and stir to mix.

Whisk the cream until it is about the same consistency as the purée. Fold the whipped cream into the purée and taste it – the sweetness of the various brands varies a little; if the mixture tastes absolutely marvellous and you want to go on eating it, that's about it. It should be slightly too sweet, in fact, as some of the sweetness is lost in the freezing. If it tastes much too sweet, stir in a little cream or even top of the milk.

Take out the partitions from an ice-cube tray and tip the mixture into the tray. Cover lightly with kitchen foil and put it into the ice-cube compartment of the refrigerator. If the compartment is very large and you have an ice cream bombe mould, you can use this instead of the ice-cube tray. The mixture will not quite freeze, it merely sets into the most delicious creamy mousse. On one occasion I put the mixture, absentmindedly, into my ice cream-maker and that way it turned out delicious, too. Marvellous if served with small sponge fingers or macaroons, but absolutely sensational with Apple Flambé (see page 245).

KASTANIENREIS

Sometimes Known as 'Mont Blanc'

Serves 4

1 lb (450 g) chestnuts
2 oz (60 g) icing sugar
1 tablespoon rum
9 fluid oz (250 ml) double
  cream

about 1 tablespoon icing
  sugar
1 teaspoon vanilla sugar

Slit the chestnuts across with a sharp knife and place them on a baking sheet previously rinsed in cold water and not wiped dry. Put into a hot oven (Gas Mark 5, 375°F, 190°C) for five to ten minutes, until both skins come away easily. Peel the chestnuts and drop them into hot water. Cook until tender, drain and then purée. Beat in the sugar and the rum and then push the purée through a potato ricer or a medium-sized grater straight into individual serving dishes so that the resulting strands are piled up in a pyramid. Whisk cream with the icing sugar and vanilla sugar. Top each pyramid with a large blob and, if possible, a cherry preserved in brandy (but – please – not a glacé cherry!), then surround with remaining whipped cream.

KASTANIEN DESSERT

Chestnut Slab

Serves 4 – 6

My own chestnut favourite – an old recipe which has been amended and improved by practically every member of my family as it was passed on. Like most recipes using chestnuts, it is a lengthy job, but it requires no special skill – just a lot of patience which will be well rewarded by the result.

You will need 1 lb (450 g) chestnuts. Make an incision across the top of each chestnut and put them into a hot oven for a few minutes until shells come away easily. Have ready a saucepan of hot milk with a vanilla pod and drop the shelled chestnuts into this as you remove the skins (known in my family as 'fetching chestnuts out of the fire').

Simmer gently until the chestnuts are quite soft. Drain, retaining the milk, and sieve the chestnuts – or use a blender. Heat $\frac{1}{8}$ pint (70 ml) of the milk with 5 oz (140 g) sugar and a teaspoon butter and cook to the 'small pearl' stage (220°F, 105°C). Pour over the chestnut purée and beat well with a wooden spoon. Add juice of 1 lemon and finely grated rind of $\frac{1}{2}$ lemon, and a dash of Cointreau, and fold in 1 oz (30 g) chopped almonds or walnuts, and 1 – 2 oz (30 g – 60 g) chopped glacé cherries. Mould the purée into a slab with the help of a palette knife. Chill well.

For the icing, cream $1\frac{1}{2}$ oz (45 g) butter with $2\frac{1}{2}$ oz (65 g) icing sugar. Add $\frac{1}{2}$ oz (15 g) cocoa and 1 egg yolk. Beat well until very light and fluffy and add a teaspoon or two of cream. Spread over the chestnut slab and chill again, then cover with a thin layer of chocolate icing as used for *Sachertorte* (see page 365). A light sprinkling of fine biscuit or cake crumbs will keep chocolate cream and icing separate. Keep in a cold place until required and cut into thin slices before serving.

KIRSCHENCREME

Cherry Cream

Serves 4 – 6

1 lb (450 g) black or
   morello cherries
3 – 4 oz (85 g – 110 g)
   icing or caster sugar
16 fluid oz (450 ml) milk
3 tablespoons sugar
vanilla sugar
4 egg yolks

2 fluid oz (60 ml) milk
1 heaped teaspoon
   cornflour
2 egg whites
5 fluid oz (140 ml) double
   cream
5 – 6 crushed Amaretti
   biscuits or 2 crushed
   meringues

Stone the cherries and sprinkle with icing or caster sugar. (Morello cherries will need a little more sugar than black cherries.) Leave them to stand in a cool place for about an hour. Gently simmer the cherries in their own juice for about five minutes. Put the cooked cherries into a bowl or into individual bowls and chill.

Gently heat the 16 fluid oz milk with the 3 tablespoons sugar and a pinch of vanilla sugar. Whisk together the egg yolks, the 2 fluid oz milk and the cornflour. Pour on the warmed milk, whisking all the time. Return the mixture to the stove and cook it very gently until thick (you can use a double saucepan for this, but it is not really necessary, provided a little care is taken). Remove from heat, allow to cool, stirring from time to time. When the mixture is quite cold, whisk the egg whites until stiff. Also whisk the cream. Fold whites and cream into the egg custard, together with the crushed Amaretti biscuits or the meringues. Spoon the cream over the cherries and chill before serving.

MOZART BOMBE

A very grand pudding from Vienna's Zu den 3 Husaren restaurant. Do not be put off by the long list of ingredients – the pudding is remarkably easy to prepare. It only *looks* complicated!

Serves 6 – 8

For the sponge mixture
3 eggs
2½ oz (70 g) granulated sugar
2½ oz (70 g) plain flour
1 generous oz (30 g) melted butter
pinch of salt
1 teaspoon vanilla sugar
1 teaspoon grated lemon rind
butter and fine breadcrumbs for the cake tin

For the cover
5½ fluid oz (150 ml) double cream
5½ oz (150 g) plain or bitter chocolate

For the filling
9 oz (250 g) stoned and preserved morello cherries
7 fluid oz (200 ml) juice from the cherries
12 fluid oz (⅓ l) double cream
1 scant teaspoon cornflour
2 tablespoons brandy or rum

For decoration
2 generous oz (60 g) double cream
¾ oz (20 g) toasted almond slivers
¾ oz (20 g) chopped pistachio nuts

The sponge mixture is baked in a cake tin shaped as a half-sphere. An ovenproof pudding basin can be used, but baking time might have to be adjusted. A metal basin for whisking egg whites, now sadly going out of fashion, would also be suitable.

Butter the cake tin and dust lightly with fine breadcrumbs. Whisk eggs, salt, sugar and vanilla sugar over steam until thick, remove from heat and whisk until cool. Carefully fold in the flour and finally the melted, but not hot, butter.

Bake at Gas Mark 6, 400°F, 200°C for about eighteen minutes. Leave to cool, then turn onto a wire rack to cool further.

Slake the cornflour with a little of the cherry juice. Bring remaining cherry juice to the boil and reduce by one third. Add the slaked cornflour and cook until thickened. Add brandy or rum.

Whisk the cream until thick. Chop the cherries. Cut the sponge horizontally into as many thin slices as possible. Put the smallest slice into the form in which the sponge was baked, sprinkle with a little of the thickened cherry juice. Add a little whipped cream, some chopped cherries and a few drops of the cherry juice. Put the next sized sponge slice on top, sprinkle with cherry juice etc. and repeat until the form has been filled, finishing with the largest round of sponge. Cover and chill for several hours.

Grate the chocolate. Bring the cream to the boil, remove from heat and add the chocolate. Stir until chocolate has melted. Dip the Bombe into hot water for a second or two and then turn it out onto a wire rack. Pour the chocolate sauce over it, sprinkle with almonds and pistachios and decorate with whipped cream.

REIS TRAUTTMANSDORFF

Rice Trauttmansdorff

There has always been quite a bit of controversy concerning this recipe: some experts say that the addition of fruit amounts to heresy and that 'real' *Reis Trauttmansdorff* should be served with good thick raspberry syrup and nothing else, whilst others insist that the inclusion of fruit is *de rigueur* and whoever heard of raspberry syrup! I do not see why it cannot be eaten with both fruit and syrup. My own preference is for raspberries, fresh or deep-frozen without sugar. If using the latter, leave them in a bowl until they are just de-frosted but still firm and cold, drain off any juice and sprinkle lightly with raspberry liqueur or Cointreau, then fold into the rice. Alternatively, use a small jar or tin of mixed fruit – peaches, apricots, cherries – drained of all syrup, diced and sprinkled with Maraschino.

Serves 4 – 6

9 oz (250 g) arborio rice	1/2 lb (250 g) fruit (see above)
1³/₄ pints (1 litre) milk	good dash Maraschino,
7 oz (200 g) caster sugar	raspberry liqueur or
1 tablespoon vanilla sugar	Cointreau
grated lemon rind	whipped cream and
1/2 oz (15 g) powdered gelatine	Maraschino cherries for decoration
1¹/₄ pint (³/₄ litre) double cream	raspberry syrup (see above)

Rinse the rice, shake dry and cook in the milk with sugar, half the vanilla sugar and lemon peel until soft but not mushy. Dissolve the gelatine in a little hot water and stir into the rice. Pour into a bowl and chill until just beginning to set. Whisk the cream until stiff, fold in remaining vanilla sugar. Fold whipped cream and fruit into the rice. Rinse a large mould or several small moulds or ramekin dishes with cold water and fill with the rice mixture. Chill until well set. Dip mould, or moulds, into hot water for a second, then invert over a dish or individual plates. Decorate with whipped cream and Maraschino cherries. Trickle a little raspberry syrup over the top.

SCHNEENOCKERL

Floating Islands

Serves 4

4 egg whites	3 egg yolks
4 oz (110 g) icing sugar	1 scant tablespoon plain
³⁄₄ pint (420 ml) milk	flour
¹⁄₄ pint (140 ml) water	3¹⁄₂ oz (100 g) caster sugar
1 vanilla pod	about ¹⁄₂ cup milk
cream (see recipe)	
1 teaspoon vanilla sugar	

Whisk egg whites until stiff, and gradually whisk in the icing sugar. The mixture should be very stiff, smooth and shiny.

In a large saucepan – ideally a deep frying pan with a lid – heat milk and water with a vanilla pod. When the milk begins to rise, lower heat at once and drop in the egg white mixture with the help of a tablespoon, taking care that the 'islands' do not touch as they swell during the cooking. Cover pan with a lid and simmer gently for three minutes – do not allow the liquid to boil. Remove the lid, carefully turn the islands with a slotted spoon and poach them for another minute or two, this time minus the lid.

Lift them out with a perforated spoon and arrange them in a dish. Use up remaining egg white mixture in the same way.

Strain liquid in which they were cooked into a measuring jug and make it up to three-quarters of a pint (420 ml) with cream. Pour into a saucepan, add sugar and vanilla sugar, and heat. Slake flour with half a cup of cold milk, whisk in the egg yolks. Gradually pour on the hot milk. Cook in a double boiler, stirring constantly, until thickened. Carefully pour the cream over the islands and chill well before serving.

I list flour among the ingredients, because it is considered essential in Vienna. Personally, having always resented it and having long replaced it with arrowroot or potato flour in diminishing quantities, I now leave it out altogether.

SÜDTIROLER KASTANIENEIS

Chestnut Ice Cream

Serves 4

1¼ lb (500 g) chestnuts	1 liqueur glass rum
2¼ pints (1¼ litre) milk	9 fluid oz (250 ml) double
1 vanilla pod	cream
1 lb (450 g) caster sugar	2 teaspoons vanilla sugar
10 egg yolks	

If using a refrigerator, set it at maximum before starting to cook the chestnuts.

Make an incision across the chestnuts and set them on a baking sheet. Put into a hot oven (Gas Mark 7, 425°F, 220°C) until the chestnuts split open and the skins come away easily.

Heat ½ pint (¼ litre) of the milk with a vanilla pod and about 2 tablespoons of the sugar. Remove both skins from the chestnuts whilst they are still hot and drop them into the hot milk as they are being shelled. Cook chestnuts gently until soft. Remove vanilla pod, sieve the chestnuts and reserve the milk.

Heat the remaining milk and the milk from the chestnuts and stir into the sieved chestnuts. Whisk together remaining sugar, egg yolks and rum and gently pour the milk/chestnut mixture into it whisking all the time. Beat over steam until very thick. Remove from heat, leave to cool, stirring from time to time, then put into ice cream machine or into freezing trays (if using the latter, cover with kitchen foil). When the mixture is half frozen, whisk the cream to the thickness of the half-frozen ice cream, whisk in vanilla sugar and fold into the chestnut mixture. Return to freezing trays or ice cream machine to complete freezing.

There is a better, though slightly more tedious way of shelling and cooking the chestnuts. Remove outer shell of chestnuts and put the chestnuts into a saucepan. Cover with cold water in which a little flour has been dissolved (about 1 oz/25 g flour for 4½ pints/2 litres water). Bring to boil slowly and cook until the inner skin can be removed easily – about thirty minutes.

Fish out the chestnuts one by one – do *not* rinse. Remove inner skin and drop chestnuts into hot milk and sugar as described above. Cooked in this way the chestnuts are in no way toughened – there is always a slight danger of 'roasting' them if you put them in the oven – and the addition of the flour to the water helps to retain their flavour.

For a less rich, and infinitely quicker, version of this recipe see *Geeiste Kastanienmousse* (page 255).

WEINÄPFEL

Apples Cooked in Wine

Very popular in the eighteenth century as an accompaniment to meat or game, apples cooked this way also make an excellent pudding. As an accompaniment they are best served slightly warm, but as a pudding they are at their most delicious served chilled and accompanied by thick cream.

9 oz (250 g) caster sugar	a small stick cinnamon
½ pint (280 ml) white wine	a few slivers lemon peel
8 fluid oz (225 ml) water	generous 2 lbs (1 kg) small
juice of 1 lemon	eating apples
2 cloves	cranberry preserve or jelly

Peel, core and halve the apples and sprinkle with half the lemon juice. Put sugar, wine, water and the remaining lemon juice into a saucepan, bring gently to the boil and simmer for seven to eight minutes, removing any scum rising to the top. Add cinnamon, cloves and lemon peel, and gently poach the apples in the liquid until they are transparent. Lift out with a slotted spoon and arrange in a dish. Leave the cooking liquid to cool a little and spoon over the apples. Put a small portion of cranberry jelly or preserve into the cored centre of each halved apple.

CAKES, PASTRIES
AND BISCUITS

CAKES, PASTRIES AND BISCUITS

The culinary repertoire of Austria is abounding in cake, pastry and biscuit recipes. Some are rich and rare and require an army of helpers to reach perfection. Others are so simple that it seems presumptuous to even write down the recipe. Most of them are widely known and where this is the case, there are many variations regarding the preparation of one and the same thing. Thus there are numerous recipes for *Bischofsbrot*, cakes made with fresh fruit or the hundred and one different yet similar nut and almond biscuits.

I have tried to be discriminating and yet fair to recipes which I have known and loved for as long as I can remember, as well as to those which I have come to love in recent years (with recipes culled from kind friends all over Austria). If I have seemingly repeated myself, it was done in the firm belief that each and every one of them is too good to be left out!

BISCHOFSBROT I

Bishop's Bread

A very good light fruit cake, always baked in a loaf tin or the special ridged tin used for *Rehrücken* (see page 359). The fruit and nut mixture can be varied according to taste – walnuts or hazelnuts (pistachio nuts if you feel in an extravagant mood), glacé cherries, candied peel or glacé fruit. But in my opinion the most important addition is the chocolate, broken into small lumps which retain, or rather regain, their shape when the cake has cooled.

3 eggs	grated lemon rind
1 generous oz (30 g) plain chocolate	4½ oz (120 g) icing sugar
1 generous oz (30 g) walnuts, hazelnuts or unblanched almonds	2 teaspoons vanilla sugar
	4½ oz (120 g) plain flour
	icing or vanilla sugar for dusting over the top
¾ oz (20 g) raisins	butter and flour for the cake tin
¾ oz (20 g) sultanas or glacé cherries	
¾ oz (20 g) candied peel or glacé fruit	

Butter and flour a loaf tin measuring about 9 × 5 inches. Preheat the oven to Gas Mark 4, 350°F, 180°C.

Separate eggs. Coarsely chop the chocolate, hazelnuts, walnuts or unblanched almonds. Chop the glacé cherries and glacé fruit. Pick over the raisins or sultanas. Mix together all the fruit, nuts and chocolate and add candied peel and grated lemon rind.

Whisk together egg yolks with a generous three-quarters of the icing sugar until very thick and creamy. Whisk whites until stiff, then whisk in the remaining icing sugar and the vanilla sugar. Fold whites into yolks, alternately with the flour and the fruit and nut mixture. Pile mixture into the prepared loaf tin and bake at Gas Mark 4, 350°F, 180°C for forty-five to fifty minutes.

Turn out onto a rack, sprinkle with icing or vanilla sugar while still warm. Leave for twenty-four hours before cutting if possible.

Bischofsbrot II

2 eggs
3½ oz (100 g) butter
3½ oz (100 g) icing sugar
3½ oz (100 g) plain flour
a little grated lemon rind
2 oz (50 g) raisins
2 oz (50 g) coarsely
  chopped chocolate

2 oz (50 g) chopped
  walnuts or almonds
2 oz (50 g) chopped glacé
  cherries
butter and flour for the
  cake tin

Separate eggs. Cream butter with half the sugar, beat in the yolks. Whisk whites until stiff, whisk in the remaining sugar. Fold whites into yolks alternately with the flour. Fold in lemon rind, raisins, glacé cherries almonds (or walnuts) and chocolate gradually. Bake at Gas Mark 4, 350°F, 180°C for about forty-five minutes.

Cool on a rack and dust with icing sugar sifted with a little vanilla sugar. Slice when cold, preferably the next day.

Bischofsbrot III

3 eggs
4½ oz (120 g) icing sugar
1 teaspoon vanilla sugar
1 scant oz (20 g) coarsely
  chopped candied peel
1 generous oz (30 g)
  chopped walnuts
1 generous oz (30 g)
  chopped almonds

1 scant oz (20 g) raisins
1 generous oz (30 g)
  chopped chocolate
4½ oz (120 g) plain flour
butter and flour for the
  baking tin

Separate eggs. Whisk yolks with sugar and vanilla sugar until thick and fluffy. Gradually add fruit, nuts and chocolate. Whisk whites until stiff and fold into the mixture, alternately with the flour. Bake at Gas Mark 4, 350°F, 180°C for about forty-five minutes. Cool on a rack and dust with icing sugar. Cut into slices when cold, preferably the next day.

GRAZER ZWIEBACK

A very light cake mixture, always baked in an oblong cake tin – quite often the tin used for *Rehrücken* (see page 359) is used. The cake is cut into slices, toasted in the oven and dusted lightly with sugar. Sometimes known as *Kinderzwieback* – presumably because it is a suitable reward for a good child – it can also form the basis of *Grazer Triet* (see page 223).

Makes about 24 slices

1 generous oz (30 g) melted butter	3 oz (80 g) plain flour butter and flour for the
5 egg whites	cake tin
3½ oz (100 g) icing sugar	2 oz (50 g) icing sugar
1 teaspoon vanilla sugar	

Butter and flour an oblong cake tin measuring about 11 × 7 inches (28 cm × 17½ cm). Whisk egg whites until stiff. Whisk in the 3½ oz icing sugar, then sift in the flour and the vanilla sugar.

Finally stir in the melted, but not hot, butter.

Bake at Gas Mark 3½, 340°F, 170°C for about fifty minutes, until set and golden brown. Carefully turn cake onto a rack and leave to cool. When the cake is quite cold – preferably the next day – cut it into slices. Set on a baking sheet and sprinkle with a little icing sugar. Bake at Gas Mark 5, 375°F, 190°C to dry. Dust with icing sugar on both sides and store in an airtight tin when quite cold.

GRÜNER WEINBEERKUCHEN

Cake Made with Green Grapes

The recipe is taken from the hand-written cookery book of Anna Plochl, daughter of a local postmaster, who married Archduke Johann, brother of the ruling Emperor Franz I. The book was lent me by Count Franz Meran, a descendant of Anna Plochl and the Archduke (they were created Counts of Meran by Imperial decree). It is charming, full of asides and interspersed with love poems, which Anna Plochl must have written down during her many solitary hours before the marriage was given Imperial approval. After I had duly returned the book it was displayed at an exhibition about the life and times of Archduke Johann, who is almost the Patron Saint of Styria.

The recipes had all the hallmarks of good genuine cooking – I would have loved to try more of them but the book had to be returned for the exhibition. This one is marked *ist sehr gutt* (very good indeed) in Anna Plochl's own handwriting, and having tried it, I can only endorse her opinion. Probably in her time grapes which were not quite up to eating standard were used – Archduke Johann was also Mayor of Stainz in the centre of one of Styria's wine regions – but small seedless grapes are excellent for the recipe. If you use Muscat grapes you'll have a cake fit not just for an Archduke, but an Emperor!

Makes two cakes

4½ oz (125 g) green grapes	dash of lemon juice and
4 eggs	lemon rind
4½ oz (125 g) butter	⅓ oz (10 g) fine fresh
4½ oz (125 g) caster sugar	breadcrumbs
4½ oz (125 g) ground	butter and flour or ground
unblanched almonds	almonds for cake tin

Butter two loaf tins measuring about 7 × 4 inches (19 cm × 10 cm) and dust with flour or ground almonds. Wash and dry the grapes.

Separate eggs. Cream butter and sugar, beat in the yolks gradually, then beat in the lemon rind and juice. Whisk whites until stiff, fold into the mixture alternately with the washed and dried grapes and the ground almonds. Finally ('and swiftly' said Anna Plochl) fold in the breadcrumbs. Divide the mixture evenly between the two loaf tins, then bake at Gas Mark 6, 400°F, 200°C for about thirty-five minutes.

Using two loaf tins instead of a large cake tin was my own invention – I found it suits the cake best and only hope that Anna Plochl would have approved.

GUGLHUPF MIT BACKPULVER

Traditionally *Guglhupf* is made with yeast (see page 313, also for general remarks about *Guglhupf* moulds) but there are several delectable varieties which use plain flour with the addition of baking powder. I have always suspected Frau Katharina Schratt's famous 'breakfast' *Guglhupf*, which she used to bake for the Emperor Franz Josef, to be of the latter category, but Zauner's at Bad Ischl, who always baked an 'understudy' just to be sure, deny this and swear that the Emperor's *Guglhupf* was made with yeast. (Visitors to Frau Schratt's former residence just outside Bad Ischl, which is now a superb restaurant called simply Villa Schratt, are given a miniature *Guglhupf* with their coffee, in fond memory – and that is definitely made with baking powder rather than yeast.)

The recipe given below is an old family one – if you stir a little melted chocolate into half the mixture and then arrange it in alternate layers in the mould, you get *Marmorguglhupf* (marbled *Guglhupf*) and if you leave out the raisins and the almonds for the mould and cover the *Guglhupf* with chocolate icing, it is a *Sacherguglhupf*.

3½ oz (100 g) butter
10 oz (280 g) plain flour
2 teaspoons baking powder
5 oz (140 g) icing sugar
5 eggs
4 tablespoons milk
grated rind of ½ lemon

2 tablespoons raisins
butter, blanched almonds
    cut into strips and flour
    for the mould
icing sugar sifted with
    vanilla sugar for the top

Prepare *Guglhupf* mould as described on page 314. Cream butter and sugar until light and fluffy. Sift together flour with baking powder. Cream beaten eggs into butter and sugar mixture, alternately with flour and milk. Fold in grated lemon rind and raisins. Bake at Gas Mark 4½, 360°F, 185°C for about one hour. Unmould carefully and set on a rack or hair sieve. Dust with icing sugar sifted with vanilla sugar whilst still warm.

KIRSCHENKUCHEN

Fresh Cherry Cake

Some say that the best cherries in Austria grow in the province of Styria, others insist that they are even better in Upper Austria. Holders of these two opinions can never have tasted cherries in the Burgenland, or been to Fraxern in Vorarlberg where they grow twenty different kinds at an altitude of 1000 metres (though admittedly most of the Fraxern cherries go to make a pretty potent eau de vie). Cakes made with fresh cherries are popular throughout Austria. This recipe happens to be marked 'particularly good' in one of my family's handwritten books.

about 1 lb (450 g)
    unstoned black or
    morello cherries
2½ oz (70 g) unblanched
    almonds
5 eggs
2 oz (50 g) butter
4½ oz (120 g) icing sugar
1 teaspoon vanilla sugar

2 oz (50 g) fine fresh
    breadcrumbs
2½ oz (60 g) plain flour
grated lemon rind
pinch of ground cloves
butter and flour for the
    cake tin

This cake is usually baked in a loaf tin and the above quantities are sufficient for two cakes using loaf tins measuring about 7½ × 4 inches or for one cake using a loaf tin measuring about 9 × 5 inches. You can use whole, unstoned cherries, in which case roll them very lightly in flour to prevent their sinking to the bottom of the cake. If you stone the cherries first you will get a more moist cake – and there too, a light dusting with flour does not come amiss. The weight given in the recipe is for unstoned cherries with the stems removed, but it can vary a little according to the type of cherry used and also whether one or two cakes are to be baked from this mixture.

Preheat the oven at Gas Mark 4, 350°F, 180°C. Put the almonds on a baking sheet and brown them in the oven, then grind them. Separate eggs. Cream butter with half the sugar until soft and fluffy, then beat in the yolks, one by one. Whisk the whites until stiff, whisk in remaining sugar and vanilla sugar. Fold the whites into yolk mixture, alternately with sifted flour, almonds and breadcrumbs. Fold in the grated lemon rind and ground cloves.

Spoon mixture into buttered and floured loaf tin(s), place cherries – lightly dusted with flour – on top and smooth the top over with a palette knife or spatula. Bake at Gas Mark 4, 350 °F, 180°C for forty-five to fifty minutes for a large cake, about thirty-five minutes for the two smaller ones.

The cake is best kept for a day before cutting – if you can bear to wait that long, for the scent is irresistible.

MARILLENKUCHEN I

Apricot Cake

For the base
7 oz (200 g) plain flour
2 oz (50 g) icing sugar
3½ oz (100 g) butter
1 egg
butter and flour for the
    cake tin

For the topping
about 2 tablespoons
    apricot jam
1 lb (450 g) apricots
2 eggs
3½ oz (100 g) caster sugar
2 teaspoons vanilla sugar
8 fluid oz (¼ litre) milk
¾ oz (20 g) plain flour

To make the base, sift flour and sugar into a bowl or onto a pastry board. Cut the butter into the flour, work in the egg. Pat pastry into a round and chill for half an hour. Line bottom and sides of a buttered and floured 9 inch spring-clip cake tin with the pastry. Spread thinly with apricot jam and cover with halved and stoned apricots. Bake at Gas Mark 4, 350°F, 180°C for about fifteen minutes.

Meanwhile whisk together the eggs, caster sugar, vanilla sugar and the flour. Gradually add the warmed milk and cook in a double boiler until thickened. Leave to cool, then pour over the apricots and bake for another fifteen to twenty minutes.

There are various extra touches which make this cake even more delicious – use ground almonds instead of flour for the custard, or single cream instead of milk, or reserve a tablespoon of the sugar and whisk an egg white until stiff, then whisk in the sugar and fold the egg white into the cooled custard before masking the apricots.

Marillenkuchen II

4 oz (110 g) butter
3 egg yolks
1 egg
4 oz (110 g) icing
   sugar
2 oz (60 g) ground
   almonds
4 oz (110 g) plain
   flour
pinch each of
   ground cinnamon
   and cloves

about 1 lb (450 g)
   apricots
icing sugar sifted
   with vanilla sugar
butter and flour (or
   ground almonds)
   for the tin

Preheat oven to Gas Mark 5, 375°F, 190°C. Butter and flour a baking tin – a roasting tin is ideal – or sprinkle with ground almonds.

Cream butter and sugar until light and fluffy, then beat in the egg yolks and the whole egg gradually, beating well after each addition. Add the ground almonds and the flour mixed with the spices. Spread the mixture, which will be fairly stiff, over the prepared baking tin and cover thickly with halved apricots. Bake for twenty-five to forty minutes.

Leave to cool in the tin, dust thickly with sifted icing sugar to which a little vanilla sugar has been added and cut into slices or squares.

MOHNKUCHEN

Poppyseed Cake

A lovely moist cake which for some reason always seems best when baked in a loaf tin.

4½ oz (120 g) plain flour
3 flat teaspoons baking
   powder
2 eggs
5½ oz (150 g) icing sugar
5½ oz (150 g) ground
   poppyseeds
2 teaspoons vanilla sugar
little grated lemon rind
redcurrant jam or jelly
butter and flour for the
   cake tin

For the icing
7 oz (200 g) icing sugar
lemon juice

Butter and flour a loaf tin. Preheat oven to Gas Mark 2, 300°F, 150°C.

Sift together flour and baking powder. Whisk eggs with icing sugar until thick and creamy, then add ground poppyseeds, flour, vanilla sugar and grated lemon rind. Bake for approximately forty minutes.

Remove carefully from baking tin and set on a rack to cool. When quite cold, cut through once and sandwich the two layers together with redcurrant jam or jelly and spread a little warmed redcurrant jam (or jelly) over top and sides. Leave to dry, then cover with icing made by stirring enough lemon juice into the sifted icing sugar to give a thick paste. Whipped cream goes particularly well with this cake.

PFIRSICHKUCHEN

Peach Cake

4½ oz (120 g) plain chocolate	4½ oz (120 g) fine breadcrumbs
4 eggs	peaches
4½ oz (120 g) butter	vanilla sugar
4½ oz (120 g) caster sugar	butter and flour for the
4½ oz (120 g) ground unblanched almonds	baking dish

Break the chocolate into small pieces and set to melt in a warm place, either over steam or in a low oven. Butter and flour a large rectangular baking dish – a roasting tin will do nicely.

Separate eggs. Cream butter with sugar until light and fluffy. Beat in the yolks, one by one, and the melted, but not hot chocolate.

Whisk the whites until stiff, fold into the mixture, alternately with ground almonds and breadcrumbs. Spread the mixture in the prepared baking dish and cover thickly with slightly overlapping slices of skinned peaches (dip the peaches briefly into hot water and the skin will come off easily). Bake at Gas Mark 5, 375°F, 190°C for forty to forty-five minutes, allow to cool in the baking tin and dust with vanilla sugar. Cut into squares or slices when cold.

PINZGAUER HOFBROT

Chocolate and Raisin Loaf

Makes two loaves

5 eggs and their weight in caster sugar, ground unblanched almonds, raisins and flour	3½ oz (100 g) plain chocolate butter and flour for the cake tins

Butter and flour two loaf tins measuring about 8 × 4 inches. Break the chocolate into small pieces and set to soften in a warm place – either over steam or in a low oven. Pick over the raisins and dust them with a little of the flour to prevent them from sinking to the bottom of the cake.

Separate eggs. Whisk yolks with the sugar until thick and fluffy. Whisk whites until stiff. Fold whites into yolks, then gradually fold in the almonds, raisins and flour. Finally fold in the softened, but not hot chocolate. Divided mixture evenly between the two tins. Bake at Gas Mark 5, 375°F, 190°C for about forty minutes. Best kept for a day before slicing.

RAHMGUGLHUPF

'Only lazy cooks use baking powder,' a superb Viennese pastry cook once told me, meaning that a cake's lightness should come from whipping egg whites and creaming butter and sugar – not from the addition of baking powder. This is one of the few recipes which does use baking powder; but as if to make up for that 'lapse', the mixture also includes cream – for goodness!

9½ oz (270 g) plain flour
1 teaspoon baking powder
3 eggs
5½ oz (150 g) icing sugar
9 fluid oz (250 ml) double
    cream
3 oz (85 g) raisins
1 teaspoon grated lemon
    rind

butter, flour and slivered
    almonds for the
    Guglhupf mould
icing sugar sifted with
    vanilla sugar for
    sprinkling over the top

Carefully butter and lightly flour a *Guglhupf* mould, and sprinkle it with slivered almonds.

Sift together flour and baking powder, then sift again. Separate eggs. Whisk yolks with about two-thirds of the sugar, gradually add the cream and whisk until well blended and fluffy. Whisk whites until stiff, fold in remaining sugar and whisk until smooth. Fold whisked whites into the yolk mixture, alternately with the flour. Finally add lemon rind and raisins.

Bake in the prepared *Guglhupf* mould at Gas Mark 4½, 360°F, 185°C for about forty-five minutes. Carefully turn out of the mould, set on a rack or hair sieve to cool and dust with vanilla-scented icing sugar whilst still warm.

RIBISELKUCHEN

Redcurrant Cake

This cake is usually baked in a large baking dish – a roasting tin is ideal – and cut into squares or rectangles for serving.

3 oz (80 g) butter	1 teaspoon vanilla sugar
3 oz (80 g) caster sugar	grated lemon rind
3 oz (80 g) cake or biscuit	butter and flour for the
crumbs	baking sheet
2 oz (50 g) ground	9 oz (250 g) redcurrants
hazelnuts	with stems removed
4 eggs	icing sugar sifted with
dash of rum	vanilla sugar
pinch of ground cinnamon	

Mix together hazelnuts and crumbs. Butter and flour a baking or roasting tin. Cream butter with half the sugar, beat in the rum, cinnamon, vanilla sugar and grated lemon rind.

Separate eggs. Beat yolks into creamed butter mixture, one by one. Whisk whites until stiff, whisk in remaining sugar. Fold whites into yolk/butter mixture, alternately with the hazelnut/crumb mixture. Spread over the baking tin and cover closely with redcurrants (you can strip them with a fork directly onto the cake mixture).

Bake at Gas Mark 4, 350°F, 180°C for about forty minutes. Dust with icing sugar whilst still warm, cut into slices when cold and dust again with icing sugar sifted with vanilla sugar.

SCHWARZER KIRSCHENKUCHEN

Dark Cherry Cake

Professor Rudolf Bibl is a brilliant conductor who is also a superb cook, and his dark cherry cake is one of the best I have ever eaten.

5 oz (140 g) plain or bitter	5 oz (140 g) plain flour
chocolate	black cherries to cover top
5 oz (140 g) butter	of cake
5 oz (140 g) icing or caster	butter and flour for the
sugar	cake tin
4 eggs	

Whether or not you stone the cherries is a matter of personal preference, but if they are very juicy they are best left whole.

Preheat the oven to Gas Mark 4, 350°F, 180°C. Break the chocolate into small pieces and set it to melt either over steam or in the oven. Butter and flour a square or rectangular baking or roasting tin.

Cream the butter with the sugar until light and fluffy. Separate eggs, then beat the yolks into the butter mixture, one by one. Add the melted, but not hot chocolate. Whisk whites until stiff and fold into the mixture, alternately with the flour. Spoon the mixture into the cake tin, then cover the top with cherries. Do not press them down, they will sink into the cake of their own accord. Bake for about forty to forty-five minutes. Leave to cool in the tin and cut into slices when cold.

STEIRISCHE APFELTORTE

Styrian Applecake

For the pastry	*For the topping*
5 oz (140 g) plain flour	2 – 3 cooking apples
pinch of salt	good dash of rum
5 oz (140 g) butter	2 tablespoons icing sugar
1 egg yolk	1 teaspoon vanilla sugar
2 tablespoons double	2 eggs
cream	2½ oz (70 g) icing sugar
butter and flour for the	2½ oz (70 g) ground
baking sheet	almonds

Preheat the oven to Gas Mark 4, 350°F, 180°C. Butter and flour a baking tin measuring about 7 × 11 inches.

Sift together the flour and salt, cut in the butter and work quickly to a smooth paste with the egg yolk and cream. Press out the pastry into the baking tin with your fingers – no need to roll it out.

Peel, core and slice the apples and spread them over the pastry. Sprinkle with rum, the 2 tablespoons icing sugar and the vanilla sugar. Separate eggs. Whisk the yolks with the 2½ oz sugar until thick and fluffy, then whisk the whites until stiff. Fold whites into yolks, alternately with the ground almonds. Spread over the apples, masking them completely. Bake for thirty-five to forty-five minutes.

Leave to cool in the tin, but cut into slices whilst still warm. It is one of those cakes which seem to taste best when served straight from the tin.

STRUDELTEIG

Strudel Paste

There are *Strudeln* and *Strudeln*: baked and boiled; savoury and sweet; made with puff pastry and made with yeast. But when the talk is of *Strudelteig* (*Strudel* dough) it means only one thing – a recipe of the type quoted below. Sometimes it may contain an egg, sometimes only the yolk.

Strudel dough stems from Turkey, was perfected in Hungary, and was further improved by the Viennese – though Hungarians would take issue with the latter statement. In the nineteenth century the Ritz Hotel in Paris sent its head *patissier* to Budapest to study the preparation of *Strudel*, and thereafter imported special *Strudel* flour from Hungary. Hungarian *Strudel* makers – invariably female incidentally – use sour cream instead of water for the dough.

Strudel dough is not all that difficult to make, but it does require a little practice; a 'feeling' for the dough as it were. Do not be dismayed if you get a few tears and holes on your first – or even second and third – attempt. Everybody does. Just mutter something about the impossibility of finding *glattes* flour (which has a high gluten content) – which will mark you as an expert beyond any doubt – and there is more than a grain of truth in it.

8 oz (225 g) plain flour	1 heaped teaspoon butter
pinch of salt	about ¼ pint (140 ml)
1 teaspoon wine vinegar or	warm water
lemon juice	about ½ cup melted butter

Forget everything you have ever been told about keeping everything cool when making pastry. This does not apply to *Strudel* – everything should be nicely warmed: hands, liquid, pastry board. A wooden pastry board is preferable to any other kind, but if you have to use some other surface, wipe it over with a cloth wrung out in hot water before starting.

Sift flour and salt onto a clean pastry board. Make a well in the centre, pour in vinegar or lemon juice. Work in the teaspoon of butter with your fingers, but do not use butter straight from the fridge. Add enough warm water to make a soft dough and knead it well until it blisters. Bring it down onto the pastry board with a few smart slaps from time to time – *Strudel* paste seems to thrive on rough treatment.

When the dough has been worked really well, pat it into a round, brush it very lightly with melted butter and cover it with a warmed bowl – but make sure that the bowl does not touch the dough. Leave in a warm place for half an hour, renewing the covering bowl should it cool too rapidly. Prepare the filling during that time.

After half an hour the dough should be 'ripe' for pulling. Cover the kitchen table with a clean cloth and dust lightly with flour (if the kitchen table is not large enough, use the dining table – if it is larger, of course). Place the dough in the centre and carefully roll it out as far as it will go, then brush it with a little melted butter. Slip your hands underneath the dough and pull it out gently, using the balls of your thumbs, not your fingers and always work from the middle, being careful not to tear the dough.

When the dough has been pulled out as thin as parchment, brush it all over with melted butter and leave to dry for fifteen minutes. Fill and bake according to individual recipes.

APFELSTRUDEL

Apple Strudel

Serves 4
Strudel paste (see
    page 275)

Filling
2 lbs (900 g) cooking
    apples
1 tablespoon lemon juice
about 4 oz (110 g) caster
    or icing sugar
1 tablespoon vanilla sugar
pinch each of ground
    cinnamon, nutmeg and
    cloves
3 oz (85 g) raisins
3½ oz (100 g) fine
    breadcrumbs

3½ oz (100 g) butter
1 – 2 tablespoons apricot
    jam
2 oz (60 g) melted butter,
    plus melted butter for
    brushing over pastry
butter and flour for the
    baking sheet
icing sugar sifted with
    vanilla sugar

Prepare *Strudel* pastry as described on page 276.

Peel, core and thinly slice the apples into a bowl. Sprinkle with lemon juice, sugar (quantity will vary a little depending on the tartness of the apples), vanilla sugar and spices. Add the raisins and cover bowl.

Fry the breadcrumbs in the butter until golden brown. Sprinkle fried breadcrumbs evenly over the pulled-out *Strudel* pastry, then spread the apple and raisin filling over half the surface and dot with apricot jam.

Sprinkle melted butter over the entire surface.

Tear off the rather thick rim of pastry which overhangs the table and start rolling up the *Strudel* by lifting the cloth at the apple end. Roll up very carefully, like a Swiss roll and secure ends.

Transfer *Strudel* to a buttered and floured baking sheet by sliding it off the cloth straight onto the baking sheet, bending the *Strudel* gently so that it forms a horseshoe. Brush with melted butter and bake at Gas Mark 4, 350°F, 180°C for forty to forty-five minutes. If the top browns too quickly, cover it very lightly with buttered greaseproof paper for part of the baking time, but remove the paper towards the end.

Strudel is best when eaten warm, not hot. Sprinkle with icing sugar sifted with vanilla sugar whilst still warm.

KIRSCHENSTRUDEL

Cherry Strudel

Strudel pastry as
described on page 275.
Filling

2 lbs (900 g) morello
cherries or black
cherries
4½ oz (120 g) caster sugar
juice of ½ lemon
pinch each of ground
nutmeg, cinnamon and
cloves
2 heaped tablespoons
butter
4 oz (110 g) fine fresh
breadcrumbs

3 heaped tablespoons
chopped walnuts
2 tablespoons apricot jam
3 oz (80 g) melted butter
vanilla sugar
butter and flour for the
baking dish

Prepare and pull out the *Strudel* pastry as described on page 276. Stone the cherries and sprinkle with caster sugar, cinnamon, nutmeg, cloves and lemon juice.

Fry the breadcrumbs in the 2 tablespoons butter. Sprinkle fried breadcrumbs evenly over the pastry, then cover ½ – ⅔ of the pastry with cherries and chopped walnuts, adding any of the juice which will have collected. Sprinkle with some of the melted butter and dot with apricot jam. Tear off the rather thick rim of pastry which should overhang the table and start to roll up the *Strudel* by lifting the tablecloth at the cherry end. Roll up very carefully, seal the ends and slide the *Strudel* onto a buttered and floured baking sheet so that it forms a horseshoe. Brush with melted butter and bake at Gas Mark 4, 350°F, 180°C for forty to forty-five minutes. If the top begins to brown too quickly, cover with lightly buttered greaseproof paper for part of the baking time, but remove paper towards the end. Sprinkle with vanilla sugar.

MILCHRAHMSTRUDEL

Breitenfurt in Lower Austria is known less for the splendour of its Baroque church than for the excellence of its *Milchrahmstrudel*, the recipe for which – in all its variations – is kept a closely guarded secret. In Vienna, if a restaurant is justly proud of its *Milchrahmstrudel* it is referred to as 'Genuine Breitenfurter' – though Breitenfurters, who usually call it simply by its name, sometimes describe it as Viennese. Recipes for fillings vary considerably, some containing sour cream, and some even bread. Having tried a great many variations over the years, including several old family recipes, the one which I prefer above all others is Frieda Juza's as it was served at the Steiermärkische Weinstube in Graz.

Strudel pastry (see
   page 275)
For the filling
3½ oz (100 g) butter
5½ oz (150 g) caster sugar
4 eggs
1 lb 10 oz sieved curd
   cheese
dash of rum
1 teaspoon grated lemon
   rind
2 teaspoons vanilla sugar
2 oz (60 g) raisins
   (optional)
5½ oz (150 g) fine
   semolina
melted butter for the
   baking dish

For baking the Strudel
18 fluid oz (½ l) milk
18 fluid oz (½ l) double
   cream
3 eggs
1 tablespoon caster sugar
vanilla sugar

Prepare *Strudel* pastry as described on page 276. Butter a deep baking dish.

Cream butter and sugar. Separate eggs and beat the yolks into the creamed butter, one by one. Beat in the curd cheese. Add rum, lemon rind, vanilla sugar and raisins. Whisk egg whites until stiff and fold into the mixture, alternately with the semolina. Spread over two-thirds of the *Strudel* pastry. Tear off the thick rim of pastry which overhangs the table and roll up the *Strudel* by lifting the tablecloth at the filled end. Seal ends and set the *Strudel* in a coil in the baking dish and brush with melted butter. Bake at Gas Mark 4, 350°F, 180°C for twenty-five minutes.

Meanwhile whisk together milk, cream, eggs, sugar and vanilla sugar. Pour over the hot *Strudel*, return it to the oven and bake for another twenty minutes approximately, by which time it will have absorbed most of the milk mixture. Best eaten warm, not hot.

Sometimes served with *Kanarienmilch* (see page 254) but I feel that this is gilding the lily!

WEICHSELKUCHEN

Cake with Morello Cherries

4 eggs
7 oz (200 g) butter
7 oz (200 g) icing sugar
7 oz (200 g) plain flour
a little grated lemon rind

about 1 lb morello cherries
butter and flour for the
   baking tin
sifted icing sugar for
   dusting

Separate eggs. Cream butter and sugar until light and fluffy. Beat in yolks gradually. Whisk whites until stiff and fold into the mixture, alternately with the flour. Finally fold in the grated lemon rind.

Spread mixture over a deep buttered and floured baking tin – a roasting tin is ideal – and cover thickly with morello cherries. Bake at Gas Mark 5, 375°F, 190°C for about fifty minutes. Dust with sifted icing sugar whilst still warm. Leave to cool in the tin, then cut into slices when cold.

COGNAC RINGERL

Brandy Rings

5 oz (140 g) plain flour	grated rind of 1 lemon
2½ oz (70 g) icing sugar	pinch of cinnamon
5 oz (140 g) butter	2 tablespoons brandy
5 oz (140 g) ground almonds or walnuts	icing sugar and brandy topping
1 egg yolk	

Sift together sugar and flour, add the ground almonds (or walnuts). Cut butter into dry ingredients and work to a paste with the egg yolk, brandy, cinnamon and grated lemon rind. Chill for quarter of an hour.

Roll out to about ¼ inch thickness, cut into rings and set them on a buttered and floured baking sheet. Brush the rings with brandy and dust with icing sugar, then add a few more drops of brandy so that the rings are covered with a thick layer of sugar moistened with brandy. Bake at Gas Mark 4, 350°F, 180°C until golden brown.

GEFÜLLTE LEBKUCHEN

Filled Honeycakes

4 oz (125 g) honey	*Filling*
2 generous oz (60 g) sugar	2 generous oz (60 g) ground hazelnuts
1 dessertspoon cinnamon	2 generous oz (60 g) icing sugar
pinch of ground cloves	
9 oz (250 g) plain flour	
½ teaspoon baking powder	1 generous oz (30 g) chopped mixed peel
1 egg	
halved blanched almonds	little grated orange or lemon rind
egg white for brushing over pastry	1 egg
butter and flour for the baking sheet	

Heat the honey, then add cinnamon, cloves and sugar. Stir until the sugar dissolves and set aside to cool. Add flour sifted with the baking powder, and the egg. Work to a smooth paste, cover with a cloth and leave overnight.

Mix together all the ingredients for the filling. Roll out the dough to about ⅛ inch thickness and cut into shapes with a biscuit cutter. Put a little of the filling in the centre of half the cut-out shapes, cover with remaining pastry shapes and press down the edges to seal. Brush with egg white and decorate with halved almonds. Bake at Gas Mark 3½, 340°F, 175°C until nicely browned on top.

HASELNUSS STANGERL

Hazelnut Sticks

3½ oz (100 g) butter	5½ oz (150 g) plain flour
4½ oz (125 g) icing sugar	ground or finely chopped
2 egg yolks	hazelnuts

Cream butter with sugar until light and fluffy, then beat in one yolk and flour. Chill for twenty minutes, then roll out to ⅛ inch thickness on a floured pastry board. Cut into strips. Brush with the lightly beaten second yolk, and sprinkle with hazelnuts. Bake at Gas Mark 5, 375°F, 190°C on a buttered and floured baking sheet until golden brown.

HAUSFREUNDE

Sigisbées

Hausfreund (singular) translates as 'friend of the house' – always a bachelor who, it is clearly understood, is the devoted 'friend' of the lady of the house rather than to the whole family. Until he gets married, that is. *Sigisbée*, according to Larousse, stands for *cavalier servant d'une dame*. You'll find recipes for *Hausfreunde* (plural) in many Austrian cookery books, and in the case of serious books which also give descriptions of dishes in French, they'll be properly sub-titled *Sigisbées*.

As with all traditional recipes, there are a great many variations, but my favourite one is less complicated than most – a perfect *Hausfreund* in fact!

3 eggs
weight of 2 eggs in icing
   sugar, plain flour,
   walnuts or almonds,
   raisins

a little candied peel
butter and flour for baking
   sheet

Chop the almonds or walnuts. Whisk eggs with the sugar until thick and fluffy. Add nuts, raisins, finely chopped candied peel and finally the flour. Spread mixture about ½ inch (1 cm) thick on a buttered and floured baking sheet and bake at Gas Mark 5, 375°F, 190°C until golden brown. Cut into squares or slices when cold.

KASTANIENWÜRFEL I

Chestnut Squares

For the base
1 generous oz (30 g)
   chocolate
1 teaspoon butter
2 egg whites
2 generous oz (60 g) icing
   or caster sugar
2 generous oz (60 g) plain
   flour
butter and flour for the
   baking sheet

For the topping
5 fluid oz (140 g) double
   cream
9 oz (250 g) sweetened
   chestnut purée
grated chocolate for the
   top

Butter and flour a baking sheet measuring about 10 × 12 inches (25 cm × 30½ cm). Break the chocolate into small pieces and set to soften over steam or in a low oven. As soon as the chocolate has softened, stir in the butter. Whisk egg whites with sugar over steam until thick and creamy. Remove from heat and fold in the sifted flour and then the softened, but not hot chocolate. Spread on the prepared baking sheet and bake for ten to twelve minutes at Gas Mark 6, 400°F, 200°C.

Whisk cream until thickened, fold in chestnut purée. When the base is quite cold spread thickly with the chestnut mixture and sprinkle grated chocolate over the top. Chill a little to firm, then cut into squares with a hot knife.

Kastanienwürfel II

6 eggs
5 oz (140 g) icing sugar
5 oz (140 g) cooked, peeled
and sieved chestnuts
(yield from about
9 oz (250 g) uncooked
chestnuts)
3½ oz (100 g) grated
chocolate
¾ oz (20 g) plain flour

Filling
9 fluid oz (¼ l) double
cream
1½ oz (40 g) icing sugar
3½ oz (100 g) cooked,
peeled and sieved
chestnuts (yield from
about 6 oz (170 g)
uncooked chestnuts)
apricot jam
Chocolate icing (see
page 365)

Separate eggs. Whisk yolks with sugar until thick and creamy, whisk in sieved chestnuts, then add grated chocolate. Whisk whites until stiff, fold into yolk mixture and finally fold in the flour. Spread mixture to about the thickness of a finger on a baking sheet previously lined with lightly buttered and floured baking paper or baking parchment. Bake for about twenty minutes at Gas Mark 6, 400°F 200°C. Carefully remove baking paper and leave the pastry to cool.

For the filling whisk cream with sugar until thickened, then fold in the chestnuts.

Cut the pastry in half, spread one half with the filling, then place other half on top and chill a little, then cut into squares with a hot knife. Spread top of squares with warmed apricot jam, leave to dry and then cover with chocolate icing.

For a less rich version leave off the apricot jam and the chocolate icing and simply dust the top with a little icing sugar sifted with vanilla sugar.

KASTANIENSCHNITTEN

Chestnut Slices

Pastry base as for
Zigeunerschnitten (see
page 289)
a little cherry brandy
3 fluid oz (80 ml) double
cream
6 oz (170 g) sweetened
chestnut purée

chocolate icing (see
page 365)
biscuit crumbs

Bake pastry base as for *Zigeunerschnitten*, cut into 2 inch wide strips and sprinkle with cherry brandy. Whisk cream and fold into sweetened chestnut purée. Spread thickly over base, sprinkle with biscuit crumbs and chill to firm. Spread carefully with chocolate icing and cut into slices with a hot knife.

MANDELSCHNITTEN

Almond Slices

2 oz (70 g) icing sugar
4 oz (140 g) butter
6 oz (210 g) plain flour
5 egg whites
8 oz (220 g) granulated
  sugar
5 oz (150 g) chopped
  almonds

⅓ oz (10 g) plain flour
jam
melted chocolate
butter and flour for the
  baking sheet

Cream butter with icing sugar until fluffy, add the 6 oz of flour and quickly work to a dough. Line a buttered and floured baking sheet with this pastry – no need to roll it out, just press it out with your hands – and bake at Gas Mark 4, 350°F, 180°C until top is lightly set (about five to eight minutes).

Meanwhile whisk egg whites until stiff, whisk in granulated sugar, add almonds and stir over lowest possible heat in a thick saucepan until mixture is tinged a pale pink. Remove from heat, stir in the ⅓ oz of flour. Spread half-baked pastry with warmed jam and then with the warm almond mixture. Bake at Gas Mark 6, 400°F, 200°C until golden brown.

Cut into squares while still hot and set to cool on a rack. Carefully dip one side of each square into melted chocolate and set on waxed paper to dry.

OBSTSCHNITTEN

Fresh Fruit Slices

You'll find them in *patisseries* all over Austria – slices of soft, almost creamy sponge cake with whatever fruit happens to be in season slightly sunk into the cake and sitting under a cloud of vanilla-scented icing sugar. They are not to be confused with yeast-based fresh fruit cakes such as *Zwetschkenfleck* (see page 322) which are more robust. Ripe apricots and morello cherries are particularly good for this cake, though on consideration I'm also rather partial to peaches and greengages. There are a great number of slightly varying recipes for this type of cake, but I have never found one better than the version given to me by one of Austria's top *patissiers*. You will notice that two types of flour are used – he swore that this made all the difference and I have not had the courage to experiment otherwise.

8 oz (225 g) butter
8 oz (225 g) granulated
  sugar
5 eggs
5½ oz (150 g) strong plain
  flour
2½ oz (75 g) fine cake
  flour
grated rind of ½ lemon

1 teaspoon vanilla sugar
fresh fruit to cover
icing sugar sifted with a
  little vanilla sugar for
  the top
butter and flour for the
  cake tin

Preheat oven to Gas Mark 6, 400°F, 200°C. Sift together the two flours. Cream butter, vanilla sugar and sugar until light and fluffy. Gradually beat in the eggs, one by one. Fold in the flour and grated lemon rind.

Spread mixture over a buttered and floured baking sheet or roasting tin measuring approximately 14 × 11 inches. Cover top lightly with fresh fruit – halved apricots, stoned morello cherries, sliced peaches or halved greengages. Do not press the fruit into the cake mixture – it will sink a little of its own accord. Bake for thirty to thirty-five minutes. Dust whilst still warm with icing sugar sifted with vanilla sugar. Cut into slices when cold.

RIBISELSCHAUMSCHNITTEN

Redcurrant Slices with Soft Topping

3 scant oz (80 g) icing
  sugar
4 generous oz (120 g)
  butter
6½ oz (180 g) plain flour
1 egg yolk
1 teaspoon baking powder

1 lb (450 g) redcurrants
4 egg whites
5 generous oz (150 g)
  granulated sugar
butter and flour for the
  baking sheet

Sift together icing sugar, flour and baking powder. Cut butter into the dry ingredients and work to a stiff dough with the egg yolk. Line a buttered and floured baking sheet measuring about 13 × 9 inches (33 cm × 23 cm) with the pastry. Prick lightly with a fork and bake at Gas Mark 5, 375°F, 190°C for about twenty to twenty-five minutes.

Remove stems from redcurrants whilst pastry is baking. Whisk egg whites until stiff, whisk in half the sugar, fold in remaining sugar and redcurrants. Spread over pastry base, masking it completely. Bake at Gas Mark 9, 475°F, 240°C for a few minutes until the top is lightly coloured. Cut into slices with a hot knife – dip knife frequently into hot water and wipe dry quickly.

RIBISELSCHNITTEN I

Redcurrant Slices

For the pastry
6 oz (150 g) plain flour
2 oz (50 g) caster sugar
4 oz (100 g) butter
juice ½ lemon
1 teaspoon grated lemon
  rind
1 teaspoon vanilla sugar

For the filling
1 lb (450 g) redcurrants
½ oz (15 g) caster sugar

For the meringue
2 egg whites
4 oz (100 g) caster sugar

Sift flour into a bowl or onto pastry board and add the sugar and vanilla sugar. Cut butter into flour and sugar mixture. Add the lemon juice and grated lemon rind and work to a stiff dough.

Line a buttered and floured baking sheet measuring about 13 × 9 inches (33 cm × 23 cm) with the pastry. Prick lightly with a fork and chill for one hour. Bake at Gas Mark 5, 375°F, 190°C for twenty to twenty-five minutes, until light golden brown.

Remove stems from the redcurrants whilst pastry is baking. Take pastry from the oven, cover thickly with redcurrants and sprinkle with the sugar. Mask redcurrants completely with meringue made by whisking egg whites until stiff, whisking in half the sugar, then folding in remaining sugar. Bake at Gas Mark 1, 275°F, 140°C until meringue has set and is just lightly tinged with colour. (Keep the oven door open after removing the pastry to help lower the temperature.) Cut into slices when cold.

Ribiselschnitten II

For the pastry
4½ oz (125 g) plain
  flour
1½ oz (40 g) icing
  sugar
pinch of vanilla
  sugar
3 oz (85 g) butter
1 egg yolk
butter and flour for
  the baking sheet

Topping
redcurrant jam or jelly
2 egg yolks
2 oz (50 g) icing sugar
1 generous oz (30 g)
  ground almonds
1 tablespoon rum

Sift together flour, icing sugar and vanilla sugar. Rub butter into dry ingredients and work to a paste with the egg yolk. Chill for half an hour, then roll out to about ¼ inch (4 mm) thickness. Line a buttered and floured baking sheet with the pastry, prick lightly with a fork and bake at Gas Mark 6, 400°F, 200°C for four to five minutes.

Whisk together egg yolks with the icing sugar until thick and fluffy, then add rum and ground almonds. Spread redcurrant jam or jelly lightly over the pastry, then cover with the topping. Bake until golden brown. Leave to cool in the tin and cut into slices when cold.

ROSENKRAPFEN

Rose Cakes

Makes 9 – 10

5 oz (140 g) plain flour	1½ oz (40 g) butter
2 teaspoons vanilla sugar	1 egg white
pinch of salt	oil or lard for deep frying
2 egg yolks	vanilla sugar, redcurrant
1 dessertspoon double	or raspberry jam for
cream	topping
1 dessertspoon rum or brandy	

Sift together flour, salt and vanilla sugar. Sift again onto a pastry board. Make a well in the centre and add the egg yolks, cream and rum or brandy. Work to a stiff paste with the butter cut into small pieces. Cover with a cloth and leave for fifteen minutes.

Roll out as thinly as possible. Using three round pastry cutters (or glasses) graded in size, cut the dough into an equal number of rounds of each size. Place the two smaller rounds on top of the largest round, moistening the centre with a little egg white. Press down the centre of each 'rose' with a fingertip to make a small well. Make a few incisions round each 'rose' to mark the petals. Have ready a small pan of hot deep fat. Drop in the 'roses' separately, petal side down. Turn them over carefully when the petal side has browned, then fry on the other side. Drain on kitchen paper, dust with vanilla sugar and place a small blob of jam in the centre of each 'rose'.

SCHOKOLADESCHNITTEN

Chocolate Slices

3 oz (80 g) butter	butter and flour for the
3 oz (80 g) icing sugar	baking sheet
4 egg yolks	chocolate cream as
3 oz (80 g) grated	for *Dobos Torte*
chocolate	(see page 340) or
5 egg whites	*Panamatorte* (see
1 teaspoon grated lemon rind	page 357)
3 oz (80 g) fine	grated chocolate
breadcrumbs	

Cream butter with sugar. Add egg yolks gradually, as well as the grated chocolate. Whisk egg whites until stiff, fold into mixture alternately with the grated lemon rind and fine breadcrumbs. Spread about 1½ inches deep on a buttered and floured rectangular baking tin and bake at Gas Mark 5, 375°F, 190°C.

Carefully remove from tin and set to cool on a rack. Cut into slices when cold, cut through once and sandwich slices together with chocolate cream, spreading a little of the cream over top and sides as well. Sprinkle grated chocolate over the top.

TOPFENSCHNITTEN I

Curd Cheese Slices

½ lb (225 g) shortcrust pastry	1 teaspoon vanilla sugar
2 eggs	a little grated lemon rind and juice
2 oz (60 g) butter	1 tablespoon raisins
2 oz (60 g) caster or icing sugar	½ lb (225 g) morello cherries
9 oz (250 g) curd cheese	butter and flour for the baking sheet
1 oz (25 g) plain flour	

Roll out the pastry and line a buttered and floured baking sheet with it.

Separate eggs. Cream butter with half the sugar, beat in the yolks and the cheese. Add lemon juice and rind and the vanilla sugar. Whisk whites until stiff, whisk in remaining sugar. Fold whites into the cheese mixture, then add raisins and flour. Cover pastry with stoned morello cherries, then spread with the cheese mixture. Bake at Gas Mark 4, 350°F, 180°C for approximately one hour. Cut into slices when cold.

Topfenschnitten II

For the pastry	*Cream topping*
2 eggs	3½ oz (100 g) butter
2 oz (50 g) caster sugar	3½ oz (100 g) icing sugar
2 oz (50 g) ground almonds or walnuts	5½ oz (150 g) curd cheese
⅓ oz (10 g) plain flour	2 egg yolks
butter and flour for the baking sheet	grated lemon rind
	toasted ground almonds for sprinkling over top

Whisk together eggs and sugar over steam until thick, remove from heat and whisk until cool. Fold in ground almonds or walnuts and flour. Spread on a buttered and floured baking sheet and bake at Gas Mark 5, 375°F, 190°C until golden brown. Cut into slices and remove from baking sheet whilst still warm.

Cream butter and sugar for the topping, add the curd cheese and beat in the egg yolks. Finally beat in the grated lemon rind. Spread this cream thickly over the pastry slices and sprinkle toasted ground almonds over the top.

ZIGEUNERSCHNITTEN

Gipsy Slices

Known as *Rigo Jancsi* in Hungary, where the pastries are square rather than rectangular and the cream filling is spread even thicker – and thereby hangs a romantic culinary tale. Rigo Jancsi was the name of a gipsy violinist who won the heart of a princess (by marriage rather than by birth, but we'll skip over that) who left her princely husband for him. Apparently their first – and fateful – meeting took place in Paris, whereupon Paris *patissiers* created these luscious pastries in the violinist's honour, giving them his name. In Austria they are called, more discreetly, *Zigeunerschnitten* (gipsy slices), which merely hints at their origin; but the cream filling is quite officially referred to as *Pariser Creme* with due deference to the city whose *patissiers* created it.

Makes 15 – 20 slices

For the pastry
3½ oz (100 g) chocolate
1½ oz (40 g) butter
4 eggs
3½ oz (100 g) granulated
    sugar
4 generous oz (120 g)
    strong flour

Pariser Creme
4½ oz (120 g) chocolate
9 fluid oz (¼ l) double
    cream

Chocolate icing as for
    Sachertorte (page 365)

Preheat the oven to Gas Mark 6, 400°F, 190°C. Grate or break the chocolate into small pieces and put it in a warm place to melt.

Whisk eggs and sugar in a bowl over steam until thick and creamy. Remove from heat and whisk until cool. Fold in the flour and finally add the melted, but not hot chocolate into which the butter has been stirred. Spread about ½ inch (1 cm) deep on buttered and lightly floured greaseproof paper set on baking sheets, and bake for approximately ten minutes. Remove paper whilst the pastry is still hot. Cut into slices when cold.

To make the filling, break chocolate into small pieces, or grate it. Put into a small, heavy saucepan with the cream and heat gently, stirring constantly. Allow the mixture to boil up once, remove from heat immediately and pour into a bowl.

Allow to cool, stirring from time to time, then set to chill for at least thirty minutes.

Whisk cream very lightly, using a balloon whisk, not a rotary beater, until it will only just hold its shape. Chill again before use.

This is a very delicate cream – if chilled too much it may have got too stiff, but this does not matter; just allow it to 'come to' in a warm room for a little and then stir it to the right consistency. The real danger is in overbeating, hence the stipulation of a hand whisk rather than a rotary beater.

Cut through each pastry slice and sandwich together with a thick layer of the cream filling – which should be about twice the thickness of the pastry. Cover tops of pastry with chocolate icing.

HUSARENKRAPFERL

Hussars

Makes 18 – 20

5 oz (140 g) butter
2½ oz (70 g) icing sugar or caster sugar
1 egg yolk
grated lemon rind
6 oz (170 g) plain flour
egg for brushing over pastry
1 oz (30 g) blanched slivered almonds

about 3 tablespoons apricot or strawberry jam
vanilla sugar
butter and flour for baking tray

Cream butter and sugar until light and fluffy. Beat in the egg yolk and lemon rind and work in the flour. Pat into a round and chill for at least half an hour.

Take pieces of the mixture about the size of a walnut and roll into balls between your hands. Arrange well apart on buttered and floured baking trays. Make a dent in the centre of each pastry ball with the handle of a wooden cooking spoon – this will spread it out a little. Brush over the pastry with egg, or with the left-over egg white, and sprinkle with almonds. Bake at Gas Mark 5, 375°F, 190°C until golden brown.

Remove from baking sheet whilst still warm and put a small dab of jam in the centre of each. Dust with vanilla sugar.

ISCHLER KRAPFEN

Ischl Tartlets

Makes about 20 tartlets
For the pastry
5 oz (140 g) plain flour
2½ oz (70 g) icing sugar
2½ oz (70 g) ground
  walnuts, hazelnuts or
  unblanched almonds
5 oz (140 g) butter
butter and flour for the
  baking sheet

For the icing
4½ oz (120 g) plain
  chocolate
¾ oz (20 g) butter
¼ pint (150 ml) water
6 oz (160 g) caster sugar
raspberry or redcurrant
  jam or jelly
hazelnuts, halved
  almonds or walnuts for
  decoration

Sift together flour and icing sugar and add the ground nuts. Cut the butter into the dry ingredients and work to a smooth dough. Pat into a round and chill for at least thirty minutes.

Roll out the dough on a lightly floured surface to about ⅛ inch thickness and stamp into rounds, about 2 – 2½ inches diameter (5 – 6 cm). (Any offcuts of pastry can be gathered up, pressed together and rolled out again.) Bake on a buttered and floured baking sheet at Gas Mark 5, 375°F, 190°C for about eight minutes then cool on a rack.

When quite cold – preferably the next day – sandwich two and two together with raspberry or redcurrant jam or jelly, spreading a very thin layer of jam over the top as well. Do not cover the sides. Spread chocolate icing over the top and decorate with a hazelnut, halved walnut or almond.

For the chocolate icing break chocolate into small pieces, and set to melt either in a low oven or over steam. As soon as it has melted, remove from heat, allow to cool a little and stir in the butter. Dissolve sugar in water over low heat. Bring to boil and cook to 225°F, 108°C on a sugar thermometer – the soft ball stage. Leave to cool, then beat into softened chocolate and spread over top of tartlets.

KÖRBCHEN MIT SCHLAGOBERS

Tartlets with Whipped Cream

6 oz (150 g) plain flour
2 oz (50 g) ground
  almonds
2 oz (50 g) caster sugar
4 oz (100 g) butter
1 egg yolk

lightly sweetened whipped
  cream
a little strawberry jam
butter and flour for the
  baking tins

Mix together the dry ingredients. Cut butter into dry ingredients and quickly work to a paste with the egg yolk.

Line small buttered and floured patty tins with the paste. Chill for half an hour. Prick the paste with a fork and bake at Gas Mark 5, 375°F, 190°C until golden brown.

Carefully remove from tin and set on a rack to cool. Just before serving fill with lightly sweetened whipped cream and place a small blob of strawberry jam (or a preserved strawberry) in the centre.

LINZER PASTETEN

Almond Pastries

6 oz (170 g) plain flour
5 oz (140 g) icing sugar
5 oz (140 g) ground
  unblanched almonds
pinch each of powdered
  cinnamon and allspice
1 teaspoon grated lemon
  rind

5 oz (140 g) butter
4 hardboiled egg yolks
a little egg white
a little egg yolk
blanched, nibbed or
  slivered almonds
cranberry jam
butter and flour for the
  baking sheet

Butter and flour a baking sheet. Preheat the oven to Gas Mark 5, 375°F, 190°C.

Sift together flour and sugar. Add the ground almonds, cinnamon, allspice and lemon rind. Rub in the butter and the hardboiled egg yolks. (You can use the whites – chopped finely – for sprinkling over a crisp lettuce salad.) Roll out the pastry to about 1/4 inch thickness. Stamp into rounds about 2 inch in diameter. Gather up the offcuts and roll them between the palms of your hands to pencil slimness, then use them to form a small band round each pastry, sealing them down with a little egg white. Brush over the pastries with egg yolk and sprinkle rim with almonds. Bake until golden brown. Set to cool on a rack and fill the centres with cranberry jam.

MANDELKIPFERL

Almond Crescents

Topfenblätterteig (see
  page 296)
Filling
3 oz (90 g) ground
  almonds
2 egg whites

juice and rind of ½ lemon
1 oz (30 g) icing sugar
egg yolk for brushing over
  pastry

Roll out chilled pastry to ⅛ inch thickness. Cut into squares and then cut across diagonally into triangles.

Whisk egg whites until stiff, whisk in the sugar. Fold in ground almonds, lemon juice and grated lemon rind. Place a little of the filling at the widest end of each triangle and roll up pastry from that end. Form into crescents. Brush with egg yolk and bake at Gas Mark 6, 400°F, 200°C until golden brown (about twelve minutes).

MÜRBE SCHNITTEN

Pastry Slices

For the pastry
5½ oz (150 g) plain flour
1 teaspoon baking powder
3 oz (80 g) icing or caster
  sugar
1 egg
5½ oz (150 g) butter

Filling
3½ oz (100 g) ground
  walnuts, hazelnuts or
  almonds
3½ oz (100 g) icing sugar
2 tablespoons milk
1 teaspoon vanilla sugar
dash of rum
breadcrumbs

Sift together flour, sugar and baking powder. Add the egg and the butter and work to a smooth dough. Roll two-thirds of the dough into a rectangle about a quarter-inch thick. Set on a buttered and floured baking sheet, prick with a fork and bake for about eight minutes at Gas Mark 5, 375°F, 190°C.

Meanwhile mix together ground nuts, sugar, milk and a good dash of rum and, if necessary, some breadcrumbs. Roll remaining pastry into strips. Take half-baked pastry from the oven, spread carefully with the nut mixture and arrange uncooked pastry strips in a criss-cross pattern over the filling. Return pastry to oven to complete baking until golden brown on top. Cut into slices when cold and sprinkle thickly with vanilla sugar.

NUSS SCHIFFERL

Walnut Boats

For the pastry
2 oz (70 g) icing sugar
4 oz (140 g) butter
6 oz (210 g) plain flour

For the filling
2 oz (50 g) ground walnuts
　or hazelnuts
2 oz (50 g) icing sugar
dash of rum
2 tablespoons biscuit or
　cake crumbs
1 teaspoon vanilla sugar
1 teaspoon grated orange
　or lemon rind
milk to moisten
lemon water icing

Cut butter into sugar, add the flour and quickly work to a paste. Pat into a round and chill for half an hour.

Roll out pastry to about ⅛ inch thickness and line small oblong patty tins with it. Prick lightly with a fork and bake at Gas Mark 5, 375°F, 190°C until golden brown. Carefully remove from tins and set to cool on a rack.

For the filling, toast the crumbs lightly, then mix together all the ingredients for the filling with sufficient milk to make a stiff paste. Fill pastry shells, smooth over top with a knife dipped into hot water and cover with thin lemon water icing.

NUSS TORTLETTEN

Walnut Tartlets

A delicious way of using up left-over egg whites, particularly if they have been left to accumulate in a jug in the refrigerator, as mine often do, and you have forgotten how many egg whites there are, for this recipe gives egg white quantities in liquid measures! In case you are starting from scratch, 4 egg whites are about equal to ¼ pint (5 fluid oz/140 ml).

Makes about 20 small cakes
¼ pint (140 ml) egg whites
6 oz (170 g) caster sugar
1½ oz (45 g) plain flour
2½ oz (70 g) ground
　walnuts

butter and fine biscuit
　crumbs for baking sheet

Butter one or two baking sheets and dust with fine biscuit crumbs. Whisk egg whites with the sugar over steam until hot and very thick –

about the consistency of thick whipped cream. Remove from heat and
whisk mixture until cool. Fold ground walnuts into the mixture together
with the flour. Arrange mixture in neat spoonfuls on the prepared baking
sheet and bake at Gas Mark 2, 300°F, 150°C until pale golden brown –
about thirty minutes. Remove very carefully from the baking sheet and
set the cakes to cool on a rack.

They are very light and delicious just as they are, slightly moist inside
but likely to go soft unless stored in an airtight tin. If you want to
embellish them even further, sandwich together with the following
cream and set them in small paper cases for easier handling.

Chocolate butter cream
2½ oz (70 g) butter   1 egg yolk
2½ oz (70 g) icing sugar   a little vanilla sugar
2 oz (50 g) softened
   chocolate

Cream butter and sugar until light and fluffy, then beat in the yolk,
softened chocolate and vanilla sugar.

POLSTERZIPFEL

Cushion Corners

Called cushion corners because these little pastries puff up like plump,
downy cushions. Very easy to make, but they should be eaten as fresh
as possible since their keeping qualities are limited.

Makes about 18
Topfenblätterteig (see   egg for brushing over
   page 296)   pastry
jam for filling   vanilla sugar

Roll out pastry to ⅛ inch thickness, then cut into 2 inch (5 cm) squares,
using a zig-zag cutter if possible. Put a blob of jam in the centre of
each square, fold over and press down edges so that the pastry forms
a triangle. Brush with egg and bake at Gas Mark 6, 400°F, 190°C for
about eight to ten minutes, until golden brown. Sprinkle with vanilla
sugar whilst still hot.

STANITZL

Small crisp cornets filled with ice-cold whipped cream and raspberries
or strawberries – wild strawberries, for a truly exquisite result. There
are two versions of the pastry, the second one slightly more extravagant
than the first.

Makes 18 – 20 cornets
For the pastry, version I
2 eggs
³/₄ cup icing or caster
     sugar
³/₄ cup plain flour
butter and flour for the
     baking sheet

Version II
3 eggs and their weight in
     icing or caster sugar
weight of 2 eggs in plain
     flour
about 2 oz (50 g) ground
     walnuts, almonds or
     hazelnuts
butter and flour for the
     baking sheet

For the filling
whipped, slightly
     sweetened cream
raspberries, strawberries
     or wild strawberries

The method for both kinds of pastry is the same: whisk eggs with sugar until thick and creamy. Fold in the sifted flour (and ground nuts for the second version). Drop the mixture in spoonfuls onto a buttered and floured baking sheet, placing them well apart, and flatten a little with a palette knife. Bake at Gas Mark 5, 375°F, 190°C until pale brown.

Remove from baking sheet while still hot, using a palette knife or spatula, and quickly twist into cornets. The easiest way to do this – unless you have a cornet-shaped mould – is to twist the pastry round the handle of a wooden cooking spoon, then stack the cornets in a glass inside each other to stop them from unfolding. The pastry hardens as it cools. Fill with sweetened cream just before serving and pile the fruit on top of the cream at the opening.

TOPFENBLÄTTERTEIG

Flaky Pastry Made with Curd Cheese

¹/₄ lb (125 g) plain flour
¹/₄ lb (125 g) butter
¹/₄ lb (125 g) curd cheese

Sift flour onto pastry board. Cut butter into small pieces, crumble curd cheese into the flour and quickly work to a dough. Chill for at least half an hour before using. (An egg yolk may be added to this basic recipe.)

The pastry can be used for sweet as well as for savoury biscuits and pastries. It is very light and flaky, but the keeping qualities are limited and any biscuits or such should be eaten as soon as possible.

Good for making sausage rolls or cut into strips, brushed with egg white and sprinkled with coarse salt, paprika and caraway seeds and baked to serve with drinks. For sweet uses see *Polsterzipfel* and *Mandelkipferl*.

HASELNUSS BÄCKEREI

Small Hazelnut Meringues

Makes about 40
1 egg
4 oz (110 g) icing or caster
  sugar

4 oz (110 g) hazelnuts,
  ground

Separate egg. Whisk white until stiff, then whisk in the sugar. Add lightly beaten yolk and the ground hazelnuts.

Rinse your hands under cold water, and keeping them wet form mixture into small balls and set them on a baking sheet lined with lightly buttered and floured greaseproof paper. Bake at Gas Mark $\frac{1}{2} - 1$, $250 - 275°F$, $120 - 140°C$ until very lightly coloured and completely dry – they sound hollow when tapped gently. Leave to cool and store in an airtight tin.

A blanched hazelnut can be pressed into the centre of each meringue before baking by way of decoration.

KÄSEBÄCKEREI

Cheese Biscuits

$3\frac{1}{2}$ oz (100 g) plain flour
pinch of salt
paprika
2 generous oz (60 g)
  grated Parmesan cheese
$1\frac{1}{2}$ oz (40 g) ground
  almonds
2 generous oz (60 g) butter
egg white for brushing
  over pastry

butter and flour for baking
  sheet
grated Parmesan for
  sprinkling
anchovy butter or Liptauer
  cheese (optional)

Sift together flour, salt and paprika, then mix with other dry ingredients and work to a stiff paste with the butter. Roll out to $\frac{1}{8}$ inch thickness and cut into shapes with a biscuit cutter. Brush with egg white, sprinkle with grated Parmesan cheese and bake at Gas Mark 5, 375°F, 190°C until golden brown. Or sprinkle only half the biscuits with Parmesan cheese and, when cold, sandwich two and two together with anchovy butter or Liptauer cheese.

It seems only fair to add that my perfectionist Aunt Paula (of chocolate gateau fame) used only a scant 3 oz (80 g) flour 'for finer consistency'. Using slightly more flour makes for a firmer – and in her opinion less elegant – biscuit.

LEBZELT BÄCKEREI

Honey Biscuits

½ teaspoon bicarbonate of soda	pinch each of powdered cinnamon, cloves,
18 oz (500 g) plain flour	nutmeg and ginger
2 eggs	6 oz (170 g) honey
7 oz (200 g) icing sugar	

Sift together bicarbonate of soda and flour. Put sugar and eggs into a bowl and whisk until light and frothy. Add the warmed honey, spices and finally the flour. Mix well with a wooden spoon, pat into a round, cover and chill for three hours.

After that time knead a little, then roll out the dough to about ¼ inch thickness. Cut into shapes with a biscuit cutter. Brush with egg and bake for about seven minutes on a well-buttered and floured baking sheet at Gas Mark 6, 400°F, 200°C.

These biscuits harden slightly as they cool and soften again during storage – a small apple kept in the biscuit tin helps the softening process.

MOSERBOGEN

I cannot pretend to be the first to discover this speciality of the Sporthotel Moser at Bad Hofgastein – crisp orange-flavoured 'arcs' which I find greatly superior to Florentines – but I was certainly the first who dared ask for the recipe. I was not only given it, but also permission to publish it in the *Daily Telegraph* quite a few years ago. I do not know whether it was a direct result of this publicity, but when I called at the Moser recently, they had established a flourishing mail order business, sending fragile *Moserbogen* all over the world. I shudder to think in what state they arrive – except that a *Moserbogen* will still be delicious, even if crushed to smithereens . . .

3 oz (80 g) butter	7 oz (200 g) blanched almonds, cut into thin strips and dried in the oven
7 oz (200 g) icing sugar	
2 fluid oz (60 ml) fresh orange juice	
2 heaped teaspoons grated orange rind	1½ oz (40 g) plain flour butter and flour for the baking sheets

Preheat oven to Gas Mark 6½, 410°F, 210°C. Butter and lightly flour two large baking sheets.

Cream butter and sugar, beat in the orange juice and rind, then fold in the almonds and finally the flour. Set spoonfuls of this mixture – well apart – on the baking sheets, flatten a little with a palette knife. Bake until golden brown which is only a matter of minutes.

Butter and flour a large rolling-pin or a preserving jar. Lift each round carefully off the baking sheet with a palette knife or a spatula and drape over the rolling-pin or the preserving jar. Leave to cool and then lift off carefully.

All this may sound more complicated than it is – *Moserbogen* are not unlike brandy snaps in texture and respond to the same treatment: if you have left them too long they will harden before you have a chance to bend them into shape. Return them to a warm oven and they will be pliable once more. Store in an airtight tin when quite cold.

PARISER STANGERL

Parisian Biscuits

Makes about 24
For the biscuits
5 oz (140 g) icing sugar
5 oz (140 g) ground
  almonds
good pinch of ground
  cinnamon and cloves
1 – 2 egg whites

For the icing
3½ oz (100 g) icing sugar
1 egg white
a little lemon juice
butter and flour for the
  baking sheet

Mix together sugar, ground almonds and spices. Work in sufficient egg white to make a very stiff paste. Roll out to about ⅛ inch thickness on a lightly floured surface and cut into strips about 2½ inches long and ¾ inch wide (6 cm × 2 cm).

To make the icing, beat egg white and a little lemon juice into the icing sugar to make a very stiff paste (if necessary add a little more sugar). Spread the icing over the uncooked slices, then set them on a lightly buttered and floured baking sheet and put them in a very cool oven or in a warming drawer for about one hour to dry (the lowest setting in the oven, with the door slightly ajar), then bake at Gas Mark 1 – 2, 275° – 300°F, 140° – 150°C for about thirty minutes, until the icing is lightly tinged with colour.

My grandmother always put a very thin layer of apricot jam on the slices, left them to dry and then spread them with the icing. She would also set them on rice paper because it made the handling easier.

SCHINKENBÄCKEREI

Ham Biscuits

11 oz (300 g) plain flour	about 4 oz (110 g) finely
pinch of salt	chopped ham
7 oz (200 g) butter	caraway seeds
2 hardboiled egg yolks	coarse salt
lightly beaten egg	finely grated Parmesan
2 – 3 fluid oz (¹⁄₁₆ l) double	cheese
cream	

Sift together flour with a pinch of salt. Crumble butter into flour, add the hardboiled yolks and quickly work to a paste with the cream. Pat into a round and chill for one hour.

Roll out to ⅛ inch thickness, brush with lightly beaten egg and sprinkle with chopped ham. Fold sides to middle, fold over, roll out pastry as before. Brush again with egg, sprinkle again with chopped ham, fold sides to middle, fold over and roll out. Leave to rest for twenty minutes. Roll out to ⅛ inch thickness again and brush with egg. Sprinkle with coarse salt and caraway seeds and leave for one to two hours. Cut into strips or shapes and sprinkle with finely grated Parmesan cheese. Bake at Gas Mark 6, 400°F, 200°C until golden brown.

Parmesan cheese may be used instead of the chopped ham, or you can use chopped ham for the first sprinkling and Parmesan cheese for the second.

SCHOKOLADE BUSSERL

Chocolate Kisses

5 oz (140 g) blanched	3 oz (85 g) softened
almonds	chocolate
2 egg whites	rice paper
2½ oz (70 g) icing sugar	

Cut almonds into strips. Whip egg whites until stiff, fold in half the icing sugar, whisk again until smooth. Fold in remaining sugar, softened chocolate (which must not be hot) and almonds. Put spoonfuls onto rounds of rice paper, leaving room for them to spread. Dry in very slow oven at Gas Mark 1, 275°F, 140°C until set.

STANGERL

I have always had a slight suspicion that these were an easier version of *Pariser Stangerl* invented by my very practical aunt, though this was persistently denied. There's no doubt about it, however, that they are far less tricky to make, though setting them on rice paper for baking is still a good idea.

For the biscuits
7½ oz (210 g) icing sugar
7½ oz (210 g) ground
  walnuts
1 egg
a little lemon juice
1 generous oz (35 g)
  grated chocolate
butter and flour for the
  baking sheet

For the icing
4 oz (110 g) icing sugar
1 egg white

Mix together sugar and ground walnuts. Work to a stiff paste with the egg, a little lemon juice and grated chocolate. Roll out on a lightly floured board and cut into strips. Set on a buttered and floured baking sheet and bake at Gas Mark 5, 375°F, 190°C until golden brown – about fifteen minutes. Set on a rack to cool.

Beat icing sugar into egg white to make a stiff paste and spread over biscuits. Leave to dry.

TEEBÄCKEREI I

Biscuits

6 oz (150 g) plain flour
6 oz (150 g) icing sugar
6 oz (150 g) ground
  unblanched almonds
4 oz (100 g) butter
1 oz (25 g) grated
  chocolate

1 egg or 2 egg yolks
pinch of cinnamon and
  nutmeg
egg white for brushing
  over pastry
ground almonds for
  sprinkling over pastry

Mix together the dry ingredients including the spices. Cut butter into small pieces and crumble into dry ingredients. Work to a stiff dough with the egg. Roll out on a floured board to ⅛ inch thickness and cut into shapes with a biscuit cutter. Set on a buttered and floured baking sheet, brush with egg white and sprinkle with ground almonds. Bake at Gas Mark 5, 375°F, 190°C until nicely browned.

Teebäckerei II

10 oz (280 g) plain flour	1 teaspoon baking powder
2½ oz (70 g) butter	3 tablespoons double or sour cream
3½ oz (100 g) icing sugar	
1 egg	1 egg

Sift together the dry ingredients, crumble butter into the mixture and work to a smooth dough with the egg and cream (or sour cream). Pat into a round, cover and leave in a cool place overnight. Roll out on a floured pastry board and cut into shapes with a biscuit cutter. Bake on a buttered and floured baking sheet at Gas Mark 5, 375°F, 190°C until golden brown.

VANILLEKIPFERL

Vanilla Crescents

Recipes for *Vanillekipferl* are abundant throughout Austria and my family was no exception – I have got at least a dozen different versions. My mother's and my favourite aunt's seem to have been the most popular, appearing time and again in handwritten cookery books belonging to other members of my family, with mother's or aunt's name scrupulously noted each time. I have never been able to decide which I prefer and I find it only fair to give both, the method being the same for either recipe.

Makes about 36

Mother's recipe	*Favourite aunt's recipe*
5½ oz (150 g) butter	7½ oz (210 g) butter
5½ oz (150 g) unblanched ground almonds	2½ oz (70 g) unblanched ground almonds
5½ oz (150 g) plain flour	10 oz (280 g) plain flour
5½ oz (150 g) icing sugar	5 oz (140 g) icing sugar with 1 teaspoon vanilla sugar
2 egg yolks	
4 oz (110 g) icing sugar sifted with 1 tablespoon vanilla sugar	1 egg yolk (optional)
	4 oz (110 g) icing sugar sifted with 1 tablespoon vanilla sugar
butter and flour for the baking sheet	butter and flour for the baking sheet

Mix together the dry ingredients, then crumble the butter into them. Add egg yolks and work quickly to a smooth dough. Cover and set aside in a cool place for at least half an hour.

Take small pieces of the dough and roll them between your hands into lengths of about 2½ inches (6 cm). Bend into crescents and set them on a buttered and floured baking sheet and flatten them slightly. Bake at Gas Mark 5, 375°F, 190°C until deep golden brown. Lift crescents carefully off the baking sheet and whilst still hot roll them in the icing sugar sifted with vanilla sugar. Gently shake off any surplus sugar and leave to cool.

WITWENKÜSSE

Widow's Kisses

You can use almonds or hazelnuts instead of walnuts, or a mixture of all three. Almonds should be used unblanched, but hazelnuts are best toasted lightly in the oven first and the skins rubbed off before grinding.

Makes 2 – 3 dozen
2 egg whites
2½ oz (70 g) icing sugar
2½ oz (70 g) chopped
   walnuts
2½ oz (70 g) chopped
   candied peel
rice paper

Whisk egg whites and sugar in a bowl set over a saucepan half filled with simmering water until very thick. Remove from heat and whisk until cold. Fold in chopped walnuts and the candied peel. Cover a baking tray with rice paper and place teaspoonfuls of the mixture on the rice paper, well apart. Bake at Gas Mark ½, 250°F, 120°C for about 1½ – 2 hours, until very lightly browned and dry.

ZAUNERSTOLLEN

These should really be made with *Zauner Oblatten* – wafers which contain sugar and nuts made by the House of Zauner at Bad Ischl. Layered and folded ice cream wafers can be used, provided they are really dry and crisp.

¼ pint (⅛ l) double cream
3½ oz (100 g) plain
   chocolate, grated
3½ oz (100 g) hazelnuts
3½ oz (100 g) ice cream
   wafers
chocolate icing as for
   Sachertorte (page 365)

Place hazelnuts on a baking sheet and put them in a hot oven for a few minutes until the skins come away easily. Rub off their skins in a clean kitchen towel or between sheets of kitchen paper. Grind the nuts.
   Put grated chocolate into a saucepan together with the cream and

heat gently, stirring constantly. Bring to boil, remove from heat and leave to cool. Add hazelnuts and crumbled ice cream wafers.

Pour into a loaf tin lined with buttered greaseproof paper and leave in a cool place for two days. Turn out of the tin, remove paper and cover with chocolate icing. Leave icing to set, then cut into slices with a sharp knife frequently dipped into hot water and shaken dry.

ZIMTSTERNE

Cinnamon Stars

9 oz (250 g) icing sugar
¼ oz (6 g) cinnamon
9 oz (250 g) ground
  almonds
3 tablespoons water
about ½ egg white
icing sugar for the pastry
  board

butter and icing sugar for
  the baking sheet
3½ oz (100 g) icing sugar
  and a little lemon juice
  for the icing

Sift together sugar and cinnamon. Add ground almonds and mix together. Make a little well in the centre, add water and about ½ egg white and mix to a smooth dough. Roll out on a sugared – not floured – pastry board to ¼ inch thickness and cut into stars with a pastry cutter. Set on floured and sugared baking sheet and dry at lowest possible oven heat, then bake at Gas Mark 2, 300°F, 150°C until golden brown. Set to cool on a rack. Mix icing sugar to a smooth paste with lemon juice and spread over biscuits when cold. Leave to dry.

CAKES AND PASTRIES
WITH YEAST

CAKES AND PASTRIES WITH YEAST

YEAST

There is nothing complicated about cooking with yeast, and something infinitely comforting about shutting oneself in a cosy kitchen and causing the delicious smell of freshly baked pastries to scent the whole house.

Recipes vary, but the fundamentals remain the same: a warm, slightly steamy kitchen as free from draughts as possible; a comfortably warm place for the dough to rise in (yeast dies if the heat is too great – if you haven't got a good place for it you can set the bowl over steam); and the necessity to 'prove' the yeast. To do this you mix it with a little sugar, flour and tepid milk and put it in a warm place, thus proving that it is still 'live' – it will come up in a froth of small bubbles if it is, but if it isn't you haven't wasted any other ingredients – and converting it to a form which is easily distributed through the dough. I always use fresh yeast, available from most bakers.

Yeast dough is quite tough, though it feels very soft to the touch. It does not require special handling, but is grateful for being worked on a wooden pastry board or table, and it does not take too kindly to cold surfaces or utensils.

Although the quantities of milk are stated in the recipes, these may vary occasionally, according to the nature of the flour.

BUCHTELN

Small Yeast Buns

1 oz (25 g) fresh yeast	2 egg yolks
2 oz (60 g) caster sugar	2 eggs
18 oz (500 g) strong plain flour	grated rind of ½ lemon
	apricot jam or *Powidl*
pinch of salt	melted butter for brushing
9 fluid oz (¼ l) tepid milk	over pastry
3 oz (80 g) melted butter	vanilla sugar

Cream yeast with a teaspoon of the sugar, gradually add the milk and sprinkle with a teaspoon of the flour. Set in a warm place to prove.

Sift remaining flour with salt into a warmed bowl. Whisk together egg yolks, eggs and sugar. Stir into the flour and add yeast as soon as it starts to bubble. Mix in the melted but not hot butter and beat with a wooden spoon or work with the dough hook of an electric mixer until the dough leaves sides of the bowl clean and 'blisters' lightly. Add the grated lemon rind. Cover bowl with a cloth and leave to rise in a warm place until almost doubled in bulk.

Dust a pastry board with flour, work the dough lightly and then roll it out to about the thickness of a finger and cut it into squares measuring about $2\frac{1}{2} \times 2\frac{1}{2}$ inches (6 × 6 cm). Put a teaspoon of apricot jam or *Powidl* (the latter thinned down with a little rum) in the centre of each square. Pick up the four corners of each square and pinch them together well so that the jam is completely enclosed. Brush each bun with melted butter and pack them next to each other in a buttered and floured roasting tin. The buns should just touch each other and should sit on their pinched-together edges. Brush a little melted butter over their tops, cover tin with a cloth and set to rise in a warm place for about three quarters of an hour. Bake at Gas Mark 5, 375°F, 190°C for thirty to thirty-five minutes.

Remove from cake tin and leave to cool on a rack or hair sieve. Separate buns – they will come apart quite easily – and sprinkle liberally with vanilla sugar. Best eaten as freshly baked as possible – slightly indigestible, but delicious!

FASCHINGSKRAPFEN

Carnival Doughnuts

Faschingskrapfen are strictly seasonal – the traditional Carnival season starting on Twelfth Night and lasting until Ash Wednesday (officially Carnival starts in November), though they usually make their first appearance on New Year's Day. In the very old days *Faschingskrapfen* were apparently confined to the last four days of Carnival, which was just as well, for in those days a *Krapfen* broken in half and offered to a girl amounted to a proposal of marriage. During the 1815 Carnival season ten million *Krapfen* were eaten in Vienna alone – I wonder how many proposals were made and accepted?

At one time the story went round that *Faschingskrapfen* were invented by a furious cook called Cilli who threw a lump of dough at her husband in a fit of temper. Her aim was not exactly accurate – the dough landed in a nearby vat of hot fat where it blew up to feather lightness. A pretty story, but unlikely (though *Faschingskrapfen* were apparently known as *Cilli Krapfen* at one time) because the distinctive white band which runs round the middle of every self-respecting *Faschingskrapfen* can only be achieved by cutting them out with a pastry cutter.

You will often find two separate platters of *Faschingskrapfen* at bakers' and confectioners' shops, one of freshly fried doughnuts, and the other honestly marked 'yesterday's *Krapfen*', sold at a reduced price: the hallmark of a good and honest baker, and a respectable *Faschingskrapfen*.

As well as flaunting that white band round their middles, respectable *Faschingskrapfen* should also be deep golden brown, nicely rounded and rather well-proportioned. To achieve this, here are my own special hints – but it might be as well to say at this point that many a *Krapfen* which lacked one or more of the above qualifications has been devoured with prodigious speed in my kitchen!

1) Have everything nicely warmed – flour, mixing bowl, pastry board, hands etc, and be careful to shut out all draughts. This is more important with doughnuts than with any other type of yeast pastry.
2) You may prefer to let the dough rise once only, when the *Krapfen* are already cut out, rather than letting it rise twice, before rolling out and then again when the doughnuts have been stamped into rounds. Personally I prefer the latter method, which gives a finer texture. It is of course a matter of personal preference, but if you decide to let the *Krapfen* rise only once you must allow more time for this.
3) Do not expect the dough to be too firm – it should be very soft and only just manageable. Press it out with your knuckles or roll it out very gently and you will at the same time dispel any small air bubbles which would swell during the frying and spoil the appearance of the finished product. Some cooks even advise a few smart slaps with the hand against the dough – for which I have so far lacked the courage, but it sounds reasonable enough.
4) Whether rolling out the dough or pressing it out with your knuckles, lift the dough very carefully from time to time so that it 'runs' towards the centre – this gives a better shape to the finished product.
5) Whenever you handle the doughnuts or the dough, turn them upside down, e.g. when you set the doughnuts on the tray to rise, when you put them into the hot fat etc.
6) Brush off all flour before putting doughnuts into the fat.
7) Do not cut the doughnuts too small – about 2½ inches (6 cm) in diameter is best.
8) In Austria one can buy special *Krapfenschmalz* in which to fry the doughnuts. Pure lard – the emphasis is on pure – is excellent, but it browns the *Krapfen* too fast and a mixture of pure lard and oil is probably best. A small piece of beeswax added to the fat greatly improves the appearance of the *Krapfen*.
9) The doughnuts should literally 'swim' in the fat which means that not only must the fat be deep enough (about 2½ inches) but that the *Krapfen* must have risen sufficiently so that they are light enough to float.
10) Temperature of the fat must be right: 315° – 325°F, 155° – 160°C.
11) Fry the doughnuts on one side in a covered frying pan, turn them over and fry on the other side without a lid.

3 scant fluid oz (80 ml)
  double cream
8 oz (225 g) strong plain
  flour
1/2 oz (15 g) fresh yeast
1 teaspoon sugar
2 tablespoon tepid milk
1 dessertspoon rum
1 teaspoon grated orange
  or lemon rind
1 tablespoon orange juice

1 oz (25 g) icing sugar
pinch of salt
3 egg yolks
2 oz (50 g) melted butter
apricot jam
fat for frying
icing sugar sifted with
  vanilla sugar for
  sprinkling

Cream yeast with the teaspoon of sugar, add the tepid milk, sprinkle in a teaspoon of the flour and set to prove in a warm place.

Whisk together egg yolks and icing sugar, gradually add the cream, orange juice and rind, rum and a pinch of salt. Fold in the flour, add the yeast when it has started to bubble, and finally the melted butter. Beat well with a wooden spoon or use the dough hook of an electric mixer, until the dough leaves the sides of the bowl clean and starts to blister. Cover with a cloth and leave in a warm place until about doubled in bulk.

Place dough on a lightly floured pastry board, work very lightly so that it is perfectly smooth, then roll out carefully with a rolling pin or press out with your knuckles to about 1/8 inch thickness. Mark half the dough into rounds with a cutter or with a glass measuring just over 2 1/2 inches (6 cm) in diameter, cut remaining dough into rounds of the same size. Place a little apricot jam into the centre of the marked rounds, cover with the cut-out rounds, placing them upside down (i.e. side that was uppermost on the pastry board now covers the jam). Press down the edges and with a slightly smaller circular cutter stamp into rounds. Set on a tray (or baking sheet) covered with a clean cloth sprinkled with flour. Invert a warmed cloth over them and leave to rise in a warm place.

Use left-over dough in the same way, adding a little milk if it has become too dry. Touch doughnuts very lightly with your fingers to test and when they feel 'downy' they are ready for frying (they should have increased by about a third in volume). Test temperature of the fat by sprinkling in a drop of water – if it sizzles, the fat is of the right temperature (the dampened handle of a wooden cooking spoon dipped into the fat is another good test, or if you want to be methodical use a thermometer).

Put the doughnuts upside down into the hot fat. Cover frying pan with a lid and fry doughnuts until one side is golden brown. Turn doughnuts over onto the other side with the handle of a wooden cooking spoon (sometimes they conveniently turn over by themselves when one side is fried) and finish frying on the other side with the lid off. Drain on kitchen paper and dust with icing sugar sifted with vanilla sugar.

FOCHAZ

The traditional Easter bread of the Tyrol, very slightly sweetened, to be eaten with the equally traditional Easter ham. *Fochaz* has its culinary cousins in most Austrian provinces, though the Carinthian *Fochanzn* is more like the Tyrolean *Zelten*. Just to be contrary, the Carinthian Easter bread – almost identical to *Fochaz* – is called *Woazenes*.

Makes 2 – 3 rounds of bread

18 fluid oz (500 ml) milk
7 oz (200 g) butter
1½ oz (40 g) fresh yeast
2 oz (50 g) caster sugar
2 teaspoons salt
2 lb 11 oz (1200 g) strong
   flour
1 teaspoon aniseed

2 eggs
butter and flour for the
   baking sheets

Heat the milk until lukewarm. Set the butter to melt in a warm place – put it in a small bowl and stand the bowl in hot water. Cream the yeast with a teaspoon each of sugar and flour. Add about a quarter of the milk and set to prove in a warm place.

Sift remaining flour, sugar and salt into a mixing bowl. When the yeast starts to bubble, stir it into the flour, then work in remaining milk, eggs and about half the aniseed. Finally work in the softened butter. Knead well until the dough is shiny and begins to blister. Divide dough into two or three equal portions and shape into rounds. Place the rounds on buttered and floured baking sheets. Flatten the tops lightly. Brush with warm water and sprinkle with remaining aniseed. Set to rise in a warm place until almost doubled in bulk. Bake at Gas Mark 7, 425°F, 220°C for twenty-five to thirty minutes.

GIBANZEN

Cheescakes Made with Yeast

The pastry used for *Zwetschkenfleck* (see page 322) is also suitable, but I prefer the more moist cake given by the following recipe.

Makes two cakes

For the dough	For the topping
4 oz (120 g) butter	1 lb (450 g) curd cheese
13 fluid oz (375 ml) lukewarm milk	6½ oz (180 g) caster sugar
½ oz (12 g) fresh yeast	12 fluid oz (330 ml) double or sour cream
1½ oz (40 g) caster sugar	1 egg
9 oz (250 g) strong flour	1 tablespoon vanilla sugar
1 tablespoon vanilla sugar	about 2 oz (50 g) granulated sugar
pinch of salt	
½ teaspoon grated lemon rind	
2 egg yolks	

Preheat the oven to Gas Mark 7, 425°F, 220°C. Set the butter in a warm place to melt. Cream yeast with a heaped teaspoon of the sugar in a cup, stir in enough of the milk to fill the cup to about two-thirds and sprinkle a teaspoonful of the flour over the top. Set in a warm place to prove.

Sift flour, salt, remaining sugar and vanilla sugar into a bowl and add the lemon rind. When the yeast has risen to the top of the cup add it to the flour, together with the remaining milk and the egg yolks. Beat well to blend – the dough will be very soft – then beat in the melted butter which should be barely warm to the touch. If using an electric blender do not use the dough hook attachment, but the egg whisk. Beat until the mixture begins to throw bubbles. Cover with a cloth and set to rise in a warm place.

Meanwhile prepare the topping. Cream the cheese with the sugar, gradually beat in three-quarters of the cream, the egg and the vanilla sugar. Cover and set aside.

When the dough has almost doubled in size – after about forty-five minutes – beat again lightly, then pour into two buttered and floured 9 or 10 inch cake tins. Cover and set to rise again in a warm place. After thirty minutes divide the topping equally between the two cake tins. As the dough is very soft – almost the consistency of a batter – you will find it difficult to spread the topping, but don't panic. Just divide it over the surface. It will sink to the bottom of the cake tin almost immediately, with the dough merrily bubbling over the top, and this is perfectly in order. Bake for thirty-five to forty minutes by which time the cakes will not be quite baked, but a nice golden brown on top. Quickly pour remaining cream over the top of each cake (if double cream is used, a little lemon juice may be added) and sprinkle with granulated sugar, then lower the oven heat to Gas Mark 6, 400°F, 200°C to complete baking. Total baking time about fifty minutes.

GUGLHUPF (for recipes see pages 268 and 273)

Guglhupf is the centrepiece of every respectable *Jause*, that rich afternoon meal which may well include a variety of delicately dressed open sandwiches and an elaborate gateau or two. It is also very much part of late and leisurely Sunday breakfasts, and a favourite birthday cake – sometimes with a small bunch of flowers in the centre.

There are many variations on the *Guglhupf* theme: *Sacherguglhupf* (named after the house of Sacher), which has a thin chocolate icing; *Schokoladeguglhupf*, which is marbled (melted chocolate is added to half the dough); the rather elaborate *Patzerlguglhupf* (see page 316); and a friend's uncle had a *Guglhupf* especially created for him and named after him, which was laced with tiny slivers of spun sugar. When staying at his summer residence at Bad Ischl, the Emperor Franz Josef would walk, at an ungodly hour, over to the villa of his friend and confidante Frau Katharina Schratt to breakfast on a freshly baked *Guglhupf*, prepared, according to legend, with her own fair hands (according to the famous Patisserie Zauner at Bad Ischl, they always made an 'understudy' just in case Frau Schratt's *Guglhupf* failed to rise to the occasion).

Even when it comes to just an 'ordinary' *Guglhupf*, variations abound. There is what could be called the 'standard' *Guglhupf* recipe, though I doubt whether it is the same in any two families; there is what my family called French *Guglhupf*; and for a 'simple and plain' *Guglhupf* which is anything but that, there's *Brünner Guglhupf* made according to an old family recipe (I have never found out whether it was the recipe or the cook which came from the town now known as Brno – known also as the cradle of good yeast cookery).

A special *Guglhupf* mould is essential, since one of the joys of a good *Guglhupf* is the almonds embedded in the fluted edges. The best *Guglhupf* moulds are earthenware ones – redolent after years of use with the scent of vanilla and almonds.

Brünner Guglhupf

Quantities for a Guglhupf *mould holding 2 litres*

6 oz (160 g) butter	1 tablespoon dark rum
2 oz (60 g) blanched slivered almonds	1 teaspoon finely grated lemon rind
4 oz (100 g) icing sugar	4½ fluid oz (125 ml) double cream
1 tablespoon vanilla sugar	
4 egg yolks	9 oz (250 g) strong flour

$^3/_4$ oz (20 g) fresh yeast	icing sugar sifted with
2 oz (50 g) raisins or	half the vanilla sugar
sultanas	for dusting
2 egg whites	

Preheat oven to Gas Mark 5, 375°F, 190°C. Cream the butter until light and fluffy, then use a little of the butter to coat the inside of the *Guglhupf* mould, especially around the centre funnel. Sprinkle with the slivered almonds and then dust the mould with a little flour. Heat the cream to lukewarm – this is best done by standing the cream in a small jug in a saucepan of hot water.

Cream the yeast with a teaspoon of the icing sugar, add about half the lukewarm cream and a teaspoon of the flour and set in a warm place to prove. Sift flour into a bowl and set it in a warm place. Cream remaining sugar and half the vanilla sugar into the butter, then beat in the egg yolks one by one, then the rum and the grated lemon rind.

When the yeast has started to bubble, add remaining cream to yeast mixture. Beat flour into butter mixture, then add yeast mixture. Beat the dough – which is fairly soft – really well, either with a wooden spoon, your hand or the dough hook of an electric mixer. It should be smooth, soft and begin to come away clean from the sides of the bowl. Add sultanas or raisins. Whisk egg whites until stiff, then fold into the mixture. Distribute mixture evenly in the mould – it should fill it to about two to three fingers from the top.

Cover top of mould lightly with a cloth and set in a warm place to rise until it reaches the width of a finger from the top of the mould. This takes between $1 - 1^1/_4$ hours. Put into preheated oven and after thirty minutes lower heat to Gas Mark 4, 350°F, 180°C.

Total baking time is about fifty minutes and if the top appears to have browned too quickly, cover it with lightly buttered paper towards the end of the baking time. If the mixture around the centre funnel shows signs of 'closing the gap' (it shouldn't, but this has been known to happen) put a cone of buttered paper inside the funnel to prevent this. Turn the *Guglhupf* onto a rack to cool and sprinkle with icing sugar sifted with remaining vanilla sugar.

Guglhupf aus Germteig I

Guglhupf Made with Yeast Dough

$^2/_3$ oz (20 g) fresh yeast	2 teaspoons vanilla sugar
4 oz (110 g) caster sugar	grated lemon rind
1 lb (450 g) plain strong	2 oz (50 g) slivered
flour	almonds for the cake tin
9 fluid oz (250 ml) tepid milk	butter and flour for the
6 oz (160 g) butter	cake tin
3 egg yolks	icing sugar scented with
2 oz (50 g) raisins	vanilla for sprinkling

Preheat oven to Gas Mark 7, 425°F, 220°C. Cream yeast with a teaspoon of the sugar, add about three-quarters of a cupful of tepid milk and a teaspoon of the flour and set in a warm place to prove. Butter the *Guglhupf* mould well, sprinkle with slivered almonds and dust lightly with flour (ground almonds instead of flour are even better).

Cream butter and remaining sugar and vanilla sugar, then gradually beat in the egg yolks. Add a little of the flour, then the proven yeast and the remainder of the flour alternately with the milk. Beat well with a wooden spoon until the dough leaves the sides of the bowl and the spoon clean. Add raisins and grated lemon rind.

Arrange dough in the *Guglhupf* mould, which it should fill to three-quarters. Cover with a cloth and set in a warm place to rise until the dough comes to within an inch of the rim of the mould. Put the cake into preheated oven, after about six minutes lower heat to Gas Mark 6, 400°C, 200°C, and a little later to Gas Mark 4½, 360°F, 185°C. Cover top of cake with buttered greaseproof paper if it browns too quickly during baking. When baked, turn carefully out of the mould onto a rack, leave to cool a little, then sprinkle thickly with icing sugar scented with vanilla.

Guglhupf aus Germteig II

In Vienna this is sometimes called 'French *Guglhupf*', and the method is slightly quicker.

9 oz (250 g) strong plain flour
½ oz (15 g) fresh yeast
2 tablespoons caster sugar
½ cup tepid milk
4 oz (110 g) butter
3 eggs
½ cup raisins

grated lemon rind
butter and flour for the *Guglhupf* mould
about 2 oz (50 g) slivered almonds for the mould
icing sugar scented with vanilla for sprinkling

Preheat oven to Gas Mark 7, 425°F, 220°C. Sift the flour into a warmed bowl. Cream yeast with a teaspoon of the sugar, add the tepid milk. Make a well in the centre of the flour and pour in the yeast mixture. Sprinkle a little of the flour over the top, cover bowl with a cloth and set in a warm place to prove.

Butter a *Guglhupf* mould, sprinkle with slivered almonds and dust with flour (or ground almonds). Set butter in a warm place. When the yeast mixture begins to bubble, mix yeast into remainder of flour, add remaining sugar and lightly beaten eggs. Beat mixture well with a wooden spoon – or use the dough hook of an electric mixer until it leaves spoon and sides of bowl clean. Stir in the raisins and grated lemon rind.

Arrange mixture in prepared cake mould which should be about two-thirds full. Cover mould with a cloth and set in a warm place to rise. When the mixture has risen to within an inch of the top of the cake tin, put the cake into the preheated oven, after five minutes turn down the heat to Gas Mark 5, 375°F, 190°C and later to Gas Mark 4½, 360°F, 185°C, without opening the oven door.

Bake for about forty minutes in all – you may have to cover the top of the cake with buttered greaseproof paper towards the end in case it browns too quickly. Carefully remove cake from mould and set on a rack. Dust with icing sugar scented with vanilla whilst still warm.

Patzerlguglhupf

Patzerl means 'tiny portion' and *Patzerlguglhupf* is 'constructed' with lots of *Patzerln*, containing three different kinds of filling which give a marbled effect when the *Guglhupf* is cut. There are quite a few variations on that theme, but my favourite is the one created by Austria's original Radio Chef, the late Franz Ruhm, especially for Otto Stradal's *So kocht nur eine Wienerin* (Forum Verlag).

For the dough
1 generous oz (30 g) fresh
    yeast
1 teaspoon caster sugar
about 9 fluid oz (250 ml)
    lukewarm milk
3½ oz (100 g) plain flour
3½ oz (100 g) melted
    butter
3 egg yolks
1 teaspoon grated lemon
    rind
salt
1 tablespoon rum
2½ oz (70 g) icing sugar
18 oz (500 g) sifted plain
    flour
vanilla sugar sifted with
    icing sugar for dusting
butter and flour for the
    cake tin

Filling 1
3½ oz (100 g) curd cheese
1 teaspoon sugar
1 egg yolk
1 generous oz (30 g)
    raisins
little grated lemon rind

Filling 2
3½ oz (100 g) ground
    poppyseeds or ground
    walnuts
1 tablespoon fine
    breadcrumbs
cinnamon
dash of rum
a little hot milk
about 1 tablespoon icing
    sugar
vanilla sugar

Filling 3
2 heaped tablespoons
    Powidl (see page 2)
cinnamon
dash of rum
sugar

Preheat the oven to Gas Mark 4, 350°F, 180°C. Prepare the fillings and set aside: sieve the curd cheese if necessary, then beat in sugar and egg yolk. Add lemon rind and raisins. Mix together poppyseeds (or walnuts), breadcrumbs, cinnamon, rum and enough hot milk to give a thick paste (the original recipe does not add sugar to this filling, but I like to add a scant tablespoon of icing sugar and a pinch of vanilla sugar). Mix *Powidl* with cinnamon, a dash of rum and about two teaspoons of icing sugar.

Cream yeast with caster sugar, add 4½ oz (125 ml) of the lukewarm milk and the 3½ oz (100 g) flour, dust with a little extra flour and cover with a cloth. Set in a warm place to prove.

Butter and flour a large *Guglhupf* mould. Sift the 18 oz (1 lb) flour into a warmed bowl with a pinch of salt and the icing sugar, add the proved yeast, egg yolks, melted but not hot butter, lemon rind, rum and enough lukewarm milk (about 4½ fluid oz/125 ml, but this depends on the flour) to give a smooth, medium-firm dough. Beat well, either by hand or with the dough hook attachment of an electric beater, until the dough is quite smooth and leaves the sides of the bowl clean.

Dust pastry board with flour, tip the dough onto the board and press out lightly with your hands, then cut into twenty-four or thirty equal parts. The number does not matter as long as it can be divided by three. Flatten each piece of dough with your hands, put a blob of filling on it and close dough firmly over the top. Divide the fillings so that you have an equal number of little 'parcels' for each filling. Set the little parcels in the prepared *Guglhupf* mould, alternating the fillings, to within the width of two fingers from the top of the mould. Cover with a cloth and set in a warm place to rise to within the width of a finger from the top – about one hour.

Bake *Guglhupf*, leaving the oven door very slightly ajar for the first ten minutes. After that time close the oven door to complete baking – about sixty to seventy minutes in all. Carefully turn the *Guglhupf* onto a hair sieve or a rack, dust with vanilla sugar whilst still warm, then dust with icing sugar when cold.

KÄRNTNER REINLING

Carinthian Yeast Cake

There are a great many versions of this cake, but only one really authentic book on Carinthian cooking, *Kärntner Kochbüchl* by Lia Miklau. This is her recipe and she suggests that dried pears, grated very finely, could also be included in the filling. Dried cranberries are often used instead of raisins.

The name *Reinling* stems from *Rein* (saucepan), and traditionally *Reinling* was baked in a large, short-handled saucepan (some Austrian saucepans have loops instead of handles). Nowadays it is often baked in a *Guglhupf* mould. This is not traditional, since a proper *Reinling* does not have a centre funnel. A *Hochzeit Reinling* (Wedding Cake *Reinling*), on the other hand, does have such a hollow, which will hold flowers. Wedding Cake *Reinlings* are usually filled with chopped walnuts and honey as well as with the usual ingredients, and are decorated with ribbons as well as with flowers – and 'when fed to horses it makes them fiery', says Lia Miklau. Now, there's a thought . . .

1½ oz (40 g) fresh yeast
1½ oz (40 g) caster sugar
18 – 27 fluid oz
   (500 – 750 ml) lukewarm
   milk
2¼ lb (1 kg) plain strong
   flour
pinch of salt
2 eggs
1 egg yolk
4 oz (100 g) softened
   butter

7 oz (200 g) raisins or
   sultanas
ground cinnamon
about 2 tablespoons sugar
butter and flour for the
   baking dish

The best dish in which to bake a *Reinling* is a heavy iron or earthenware roasting dish, not a cake tin.

Cream yeast with 1 teaspoon of the sugar, add about a cupful of the milk and set to prove in a warm place.

Sift flour, salt and remaining sugar into a bowl and beat in proven yeast mixture. Gradually add the eggs, egg yolk, milk and softened butter. Work the dough well, with a wooden spoon or your hands, or the dough hook attachment of an electric beater, until it is smooth and beginning to blister. The dough should be of a fairly soft consistency. Cover with a cloth and leave to rise until doubled in bulk. Lia Miklau is quite emphatic about the temperature at which this should take place – between 18° – 20°C – and it will take about an hour to double in bulk.

Knead again briefly, then roll out the dough to the thickness of a finger. Sprinkle with raisins, cinnamon and sugar (plus finely grated dried pears for authencity). Roll up the dough from the long side and place in a buttered and floured large, round baking dish in a loose, snail-like coil. Set aside in a warm place for about forty minutes or until well risen. Bake at Gas Mark 4, 350°F, 180°C for about an hour, lowering heat towards end of baking time if necessary.

Leave to cool in the baking dish, but loosen sides and bottom of the cake as soon as the cake is taken out of the oven. Real *Reinling* should be crisp on top and fairly substantial inside, 'not light and fluffy', says Lia Miklau: 'You want to be sure you're eating something, don't you?'

SCHINKENKIPFERL

Ham Crescents

Particularly delicious if served warm – preferably freshly baked.

5 oz (140 g) butter
5 oz (140 g) lean ham
1 tablespoon double or
   sour cream
salt and pepper
nutmeg
10 oz (280 g) strong flour
pinch of salt
3/4 oz (20 g) fresh yeast
2 oz (55 g) melted, but not
   hot butter

1 teaspoon caster sugar
6 fluid oz (170 ml)
   lukewarm milk
2 egg yolks
butter and flour for the
   baking sheet
beaten egg for brushing
   over pastry

Put the butter and coarsely cut ham into a food processor and blend to
a paste. Spread a little on a piece of bread to taste and then season with
salt, pepper and nutmeg (since the saltiness of ham varies considerably,
tasting is essential). Transfer the ham mixture onto a sheet of kitchen
foil and shape into a brick, using a spatula or palette knife. Wrap in foil
and chill until firm.

Cream yeast with sugar, add lukewarm milk and a teaspoon of the
flour. Set in a warm place to prove. Place the 2 oz (55 g) butter in a
cup and stand it in hot water to allow it to melt. Sift remaining flour
with salt, make a well in the centre and drop in the egg yolks. When
the yeast begins to bubble add it to the flour, mix well and stir in the
melted butter. Work the dough until it is very smooth – with dough
hook attachment of an electric mixer if possible, since the mixture is
very soft at this stage. Shape dough into a ball, sprinkle with a little
flour, cover with a cloth and leave for half an hour.

Roll out the dough on a floured pastry board to about three times
the size of the ham/butter brick – the dough should be slightly thicker
towards the centre. Place the chilled brick in the centre, fold sides of
dough over the brick and beat well with a rolling pin. Roll out pastry
to a strip, fold sides to middle, then fold pastry in half – rather like
closing a book. Cover pastry with a cloth and leave in a cool place for
half an hour.

Repeat rolling and folding process, first folding pastry into three
parts, rolling it out, then folding it into four parts and finally folding
it over again. Leave dough for fifteen minutes after final folding, then
roll out to about 1/8 inch thickness. Cut into squares and the squares
into triangles (using a zig-zag cutter gives a nice finish). Roll up each
triangle, starting at the widest edge and shape into crescents. Set the
crescents on a buttered and floured baking sheet and leave in a warm

place for about twenty minutes. Brush with beaten egg yolk and bake at Gas Mark 6, 400°F, 200°C for about twenty minutes.

STREUSELKUCHEN

One of the best 'plain' cakes to have with coffee.

For the cake
9 oz (250 g) plain strong
   flour
½ oz (15 g) fresh yeast
2 heaped tablespoons
   caster sugar
5 fluid oz (140 ml) tepid
   milk
4 egg yolks
2 oz (60 g) melted butter
butter and flour for the
   baking dish

For the topping
5 oz (140 g) plain flour
3 oz (80 g) caster or
   granulated sugar
1 tablespoon vanilla sugar
5 oz (140 g) butter
1 teaspoon grated lemon
   rind
1 teaspoon powdered
   cinnamon
2 oz (60 g) ground
   almonds

Sift the flour into a warmed bowl and make a little well in the centre. Cream the yeast with a teaspoon of the sugar, stir in the tepid milk and set aside to prove.

As soon as the yeast starts to bubble, pour it into the centre of the flour. Add the remaining sugar, the egg yolks and the butter. Beat well until the dough is smooth and shiny and begins to blister, using a wooden spoon or the dough hook of an electric mixer. Pat the dough into a ball, cover top of the bowl with a cloth and set the dough in a warm place until it has doubled in bulk – depending on the warmth of the kitchen this will take about one hour.

Meanwhile butter and flour a deep baking dish – I use a roasting tin measuring about 11 × 13 inches. Rub together all the ingredients for the topping until they are the consistency of rather coarse breadcrumbs.

Knead the dough again briefly, then put it into the centre of the baking tin. Press it out with your knuckles until it covers the the bottom of the tin. Sprinkle the topping over the dough, cover the tin lightly with a clean cloth and set it in a warm place until the dough has once more doubled in bulk – about forty-five to sixty minutes. Preheat the oven to Gas Mark 5, 375°F, 190°C. Bake for about forty minutes.

The top may be dusted with a little more icing sugar after the cake has cooled, but don't overdo it – one of the charms of this particular cake is that it is not too sweet.

ZELTEN

The traditional Christmas cake of the Tyrol for which there are almost as many recipes as there are women still baking their own *Zelten*.

Zelten improve greatly with keeping and should be made at least two
to three weeks before Christmas. (*Sankt Sebastian, schneid den letzten
Zelten an* is an old saying, meaning that the end of January is the date
for slicing into your last *Zelten*.) In the Tyrol the dough with which
the fruit is mixed is usually bought at the bakers, which does of course
simplify matters; but the method given here is one which gives the
nearest possible results, bearing in mind that bakers' dough is usually
made with sourdough leavening. (Some cooks wrap the *Zelten* in very
thin flour and water paste before baking. The ends are secured firmly,
the paste is pricked all over with a thin needle and the *Zelten* are left to
rise before baking.)

Fruit mixture
2¼ lb (1 kg) dried figs
18 oz (½ kg) sultanas
18 oz (½ kg) almonds
4 oz (125 g) pine nuts
4 oz (125 g) candied lemon
 peel
4 oz (125 g) candied mixed
 peel
9 oz (250 g) dates
4 oz (125 g) hazelnuts
4 oz (125 g) walnuts
4 oz (125 g) raisins
cinnamon
powdered cloves
juice of 1 – 2 oranges
18 fluid oz (½ litre) dark
 rum
9 fluid oz (¼ litre) brandy
 or Weinbrand
1 – 2 tablespoons sugar
halved walnuts or
 blanched whole almonds
 and glacé fruit for
 decoration
sugar solution or honey
 dissolved in water for
 brushing over pastry

For the dough
1¾ lb (800 g) rye flour
18 fluid oz (½ litre) water
½ oz (15 g) salt
1½ oz (40 g) fresh yeast

To prepare the fruit, wash raisins and sultanas and dry them. Remove
stones from dates. Chop raisins, dates and sultanas. Do not blanch the
almonds, just chop them coarsely, also hazelnuts, walnuts, peel and pine
nuts. Cut the figs into slivers.

Put all the fruit into a large bowl, add the cinnamon and cloves and
a little sugar. Add rum, brandy and orange juice and stir everything
until well blended. Leave to stand for twelve hours in a cold room
or larder.

To prepare the dough, sift flour and salt into a bowl, make a well
in the centre. Crumble yeast into the centre. Heat the water to tepid,

add a fifth of the water to the yeast and mix to a smooth paste. Set to prove in a warm place.

At first the yeast will start to bubble and rise, then it will collapse slightly – at which point you add another 2 fluid oz (50 ml) of the water and draw in enough of the flour to make a smooth paste. Leave to rise and collapse again, then mix in another 2 fluid oz (50 ml) of the water and repeat procedure. Finally add the remaining water, reheated to tepid if necessary, and work everything to a smooth dough. Cover with a cloth and leave to rise in a warm place until almost doubled in bulk.

Work together fruit and dough until well blended. Shape into oblongs about 18 – 20 cm long and about 4 – 5 cm thick. Set on a buttered baking sheet and decorate top with glacé fruit, almonds or walnuts.

Leave the *Zelten* to rise for twenty to thirty minutes, then brush with a light sugar solution or with water in which a little honey has been dissolved. Bake at Gas Mark 7, 425°F, 220°C for ten minutes, then lower heat to Gas Mark 4, 350°F, 180°C to complete baking. Total baking time will be about 1 hour.

Remove *Zelten* from baking sheet and cool on a rack. Wrap well before storing.

ZWETSCHKENFLECK

Yeast Cake Made with Fresh Plums

Makes two cakes

For the dough
1/4 pint (125 ml) milk
3/4 oz (20 g) fresh yeast
2 oz (60 g) caster sugar
11 oz (300 g) strong flour
pinch of salt
3 oz (80 g) butter
2 teaspoons vanilla sugar
2 eggs
grated lemon rind
butter and flour for the
   baking sheets

For the topping
1 1/2 lbs (650 g) plums
2 tablespoons caster sugar
ground cloves
nutmeg
cinnamon
vanilla sugar

Heat the milk to lukewarm. Cream yeast with a teaspoon of the sugar in a cup, fill to about two thirds with lukewarm milk and sprinkle with a teaspoon of the flour. Set in a warm place to prove. Sift remaining flour, salt, vanilla sugar and sugar into a bowl. Set the butter to soften in a warm place.

When the yeast starts to bubble, add it to the flour, work in the remaining milk, eggs, lemon rind and finally the softened butter. Beat well with a wooden spoon, or use the dough hook attachment of an electric mixer – or simply your hand – until the dough is smooth and shiny and starts to blister. Cover with a cloth and set to rise in a warm place until nearly doubled in size – about fifty minutes.

Knead the risen dough lightly and divide into two equal parts. Butter and lightly flour two baking sheets measuring approximately 8 × 11 inches and press out the dough over the surface of each baking sheet – the easiest way of doing this is using your hands previously dipped into warm water.

Halve the plums and remove the stones. Cover dough with halved plums, dust very lightly with sugar, cinnamon, cloves and nutmeg. Leave to rise for about thirty minutes, then bake at Gas Mark 7, 400°F, 200°C for about forty minutes. Dust with vanilla sugar whilst still warm.

Incidentally, it does not matter whether the plums are put on top of the dough before or during the dough's second rising or even if they are placed on top just before the baking sheets are put into the oven. The only difference will be the amount of juice from the plums – and this in turn depends on the type of plums used. The best plums for this cake are the small blue ones – rather like large damsons – which are called *Zwetschken* in Austria and sometimes sold under this name in England (with variable spelling!).

GERMBUTTERTEIG I

Puff Pastry Made with Yeast

8 oz (225 g) strong flour	½ oz (15 g) caster sugar
4 oz (110 g) butter	1 egg yolk
about ½ cup milk	salt
1 scant oz (25 g) fresh yeast	

Sift flour with a pinch of salt and divide into two equal parts. Cut butter into half the flour, knead just a little, shape into a brick and chill.

Cream yeast with sugar, add lukewarm milk and a teaspoon of the remaining flour and set to prove in a warm place. Sift remaining flour into a warmed bowl, make a little well in the centre and drop in the egg yolk. When the yeast starts to bubble, add to the flour and egg and knead to a smooth dough. A little more lukewarm milk may have to be added – this depends entirely on the size of the egg yolk and the quality of the flour. Pat yeast dough into a round, cover with a cloth and set to rise in a warm place for about fifteen minutes.

When the dough has risen place it onto a floured board and roll into an oblong about three times the size of the chilled butter brick. Place butter brick in the centre and fold the yeast dough over it. Beat with a rolling pin from the centre outwards, then roll out to the original size. Fold the dough in three again, give a half turn, then roll out again. Repeat the folding and rolling twice more, then place pastry in a cool place for at least half an hour before use.

Germbutterteig II

12 oz (340 g) strong flour	1 teaspoon caster sugar
8 oz (230 g) butter	6 fluid oz (170 ml) milk
3/4 oz (20 g) fresh yeast	2 large egg yolks

Cut 6 oz (170 g) butter into 2 oz (60 g) flour, shape into a brick and chill.

Cream yeast with sugar, add lukewarm milk and 1 teaspoon of the flour and set in a warm place to prove. Put remaining butter into a small bowl and stand the bowl in a saucepan (or larger bowl) with hot water for the butter to melt.

Sift remaining flour with salt, make a well in the centre and drop in the egg yolks. When the yeast begins to bubble, add it to the flour, mix well and stir in the melted, but not hot butter. Knead until the dough is very smooth. Shape dough into a ball, sprinkle with a little flour, cover with a cloth and leave for a quarter of an hour, then knead again until smooth. Roll out the dough on a floured pastry board to about three times the size of the butter brick – the dough should be slightly thicker towards the centre. Place the chilled butter brick in the centre, fold sides of dough over the butter brick and beat well with a rolling pin. Roll out pastry to a strip, fold sides to middle, then fold pastry in half – rather like closing a book. Cover pastry with a cloth and leave in a cool place for half an hour.

Repeat rolling and folding process – first folding pastry into three parts, rolling it out, then folding it into four parts and finally folding it over again. Leave dough for at least fifteen minutes – longer if possible – in a cool place, then use as required.

GRAMMELPOGATSCHERL

Do not try to pronounce the name for these rather sturdy and particularly delicious savoury biscuits, the main ingredient of which are *Grammeln* – the small bits of crackling which remain in the pan after rendering down pork or goose fat. *Grammelpogatscherln* are at their very best whilst still warm from the oven, and they are sometimes available at a truly notable Heurigen such as the Streiterhof in Baden near Vienna, where I was given this recipe.

12 oz (330 g) strong flour	6 oz (165 g) *Grammeln*
1 flat teaspoon salt	(see above)
1 oz (30 g) fresh yeast	caraway seeds
pinch of sugar	1 lightly beaten egg or egg
2 tablespoons milk	yolk for brushing over
1 egg	pastry
about 6 fluid oz (170 ml)	fat and flour for the
sour cream	baking sheet

Sift flour with salt onto a pastry board and make a well in the centre. Cream yeast with a pinch of sugar, stir in the tepid milk and sprinkle with a teaspoon of the flour. Set in a warm place to prove. Mince the *Grammeln* or chop them finely. Mix with the flour.

When the yeast has risen, pour it into the centre of the flour mixture. Add egg and enough sour cream to give a medium-firm dough. Put the dough into a warmed bowl, cover and leave to rise in a warm place until doubled in bulk. Knead briefly, then roll out to about ½ inch (1 cm) thickness on a floured pastry board. Stamp into rounds of 1¼ – 1½ inches (3 – 4 cm) diameter. Mark with a criss-cross pattern with the back of a knife. Brush lightly with beaten egg and sprinkle with caraway seeds.

Set the rounds on a greased and floured baking sheet and allow to rise again in a warm place for about half an hour. Bake at Gas Mark 4, 350°F, 180°C for fifteen to twenty minutes.

HASELNUSS ROLLEN

Hazelnut Rolls

Makes about 25 rolls

puff pastry made with yeast I (see page 323)	1 egg white
	cinnamon
5 oz (140 g) ground hazelnuts	grated lemon rind
1 dessertspoon honey	egg for brushing over pastry
1 tablespoon caster or icing sugar	butter and flour for baking sheet
½ oz (15 g) grated plain chocolate	

Set aside about a tablespoon of ground hazelnuts for sprinkling over the rolls. Put all the other ingredients for the filling into a bowl and mix to a fairly stiff paste. If it appears too dry – meaning that the egg white was rather small – add a little more honey to bind.

Preheat the oven to Gas Mark 6, 400°F, 200°C. Roll out the dough to about ⅛ inch thickness, cut into 2 or 2½ inch squares. Place a little of the filling down the centre of each square, brush the edges with a little egg, fold over the dough and press down to seal. Put the small rolls on a buttered and floured baking sheet and set them in a warm place to rise for about twenty minutes. Brush the rolls lightly with beaten egg, sprinkle with ground hazelnuts and bake until golden brown – about twenty to twenty-five minutes.

KNIAKIACHL

Deep Fried Pastry Circles

Delicious rounds of yeast pastry, crisply fried. Sometimes they are eaten as an accompaniment to meat, filled with *Sauerkraut* or spiced cabbage; at other times they may be dusted with sugar and the centre filled with jam. Either way they must be thinner in the centre than round the rim – the story goes that in the old days each round of pastry was stretched over the knee of the cook, hence the name, which means 'knee pastry'. Their equivalent can be found in other parts of Austria as well, usually called *Bauernkrapfen* (farmers' buns) or *Ziehkrapfen* (pulled buns). The name *Kniakiachl* occurs only in the Tyrol . . . and I ask natives of the Tyrol to forgive me for my spelling of the name, since I could not find two who agreed on it!

¼ pint (125 ml) milk
1 oz (25 g) fresh yeast
4 oz (100 g) caster sugar
1 lb (500 g) strong flour
pinch of salt
2 eggs
1 egg yolk

1 tablespoon rum
4 oz (100 g) melted butter
lard or oil for deep frying

Heat the milk to lukewarm. Cream yeast with 1 teaspoon of the sugar and 1 teaspoon of the flour. Add about half the milk and set aside in a warm place to prove.

Sift remaining flour, salt and sugar into a bowl and make a well in the centre. Add the yeast mixture as soon as it has started to bubble and work in the eggs, egg yolk, rum and the remaining milk. Finally beat in the melted butter. Beat well with a wooden spoon or by hand, or use the dough hook of an electric mixer, until the dough is smooth, shiny and begins to blister. Cover with a cloth and set aside in a warm place until almost doubled in bulk. Knead again briefly and then divide the dough into twenty to twenty-five portions and shape into rounds. Cover lightly and leave to rise again for about half an hour. Stretch each portion so that it is thinner in the centre with a rather thick rim. Drop – upside down – into deep hot fat and fry on both sides. Total frying time about four minutes. Drain on kitchen paper.

KRANZKUCHEN

Ring Cake

puff pastry made with
  yeast II (see page 324)
1 tablespoon melted butter
1 oz (30 g) ground or
  chopped almonds
  (unblanched)
½ cup raisins
1 oz (30 g) grated
  chocolate

1 tablespoon cake or
  biscuit crumbs
rum
icing sugar
cinnamon
egg for brushing over
  pastry

Preheat oven to Gas Mark 5, 375°F, 190°C. Roll out pastry into a rectangular piece, about ⅛ inch thick.

Mix together ground or chopped almonds, raisins, grated chocolate, crumbs and about a tablespoon of sugar. Sprinkle over pastry, then sprinkle with rum, a little cinnamon and finally the melted butter. Roll up as for Swiss roll. Placing the folded edge underneath, twist into a round and set in a buttered and floured cake tin. Secure ends well so that the filling stays sealed in during baking. Make a few incisions along the top. Cover with a cloth and set in a warm place to rise.

When risen to about twice its original size – after about forty minutes – brush with egg, bake until deep golden brown, lowering the heat to Gas Mark 4, 350°F, 180°C after twenty-five minutes. Remove from oven, leave to cool in the cake tin for a little, then turn carefully onto a rack. Stir a little rum into some icing sugar and spread over the top of the cake while it is still warm, but not hot.

MOHNSTRUDEL

Poppyseed Strudel

For the pastry
14 oz (400 g) strong flour
pinch of salt
1 oz (25 g) fresh yeast
2½ oz (70 g) caster sugar
7 fluid oz (190 ml) tepid
  milk
3½ oz (100 g) melted
  butter
2 eggs
1 teaspoon grated lemon
  rind
butter and flour for the
  baking sheet
lightly beaten egg for
  brushing over pastry

For the filling
9 oz (250 g) ground
  poppyseeds
9 fluid oz (¼ l) milk
1 teaspoon grated lemon
  rind
pinch of cinnamon
3½ oz (100 g) caster sugar
1 oz (25 g) raisins
2 oz (60 g) butter

Cream yeast and a teaspoon of the sugar, add half the tepid milk and sprinkle with a teaspoon of the flour. Set in a warm place to prove.

Sift flour and salt into a warmed mixing bowl. Make a well in the centre of the flour, add grated lemon rind, eggs, remaining milk, melted, but not hot butter and the proven yeast. Beat well with a wooden spoon or work with the dough hook attachment of an electric mixer until the dough leaves the sides of the bowl clean. Sprinkle with a little flour, cover bowl with a cloth and leave the dough to rise in a warm place until nearly doubled in bulk – about one hour.

For the filling cook ground poppyseeds in milk until thick. Add butter and sugar and remove from heat. Stir well, adding grated lemon rind and a sprinkling of cinnamon. Stir in the raisins. Cool before using.

Tip dough onto a floured pastry board, knead very lightly so that it is perfectly smooth and roll out to about ⅛ inch thickness. Spread with filling and roll up as for Swiss roll. Set on a buttered and floured baking sheet, bending the pastry into a horseshoe shape. Leave to rise in a warm place for half an hour, brush with lightly beaten egg and bake at Gas Mark 5, 375°F, 190°C for about fifty to sixty minutes.

NUSSKRANZ

Hazelnut or Walnut Ring

puff pastry made with
   yeast II (see page 324)
butter and flour for the
   cake tin
egg for brushing over
   pastry

Icing
4 oz (110 g) icing sugar
a little rum, preferably
   white

Filling
6 oz (170 g) hazelnuts or
   walnuts
1 tablespoon honey
1 tablespoon icing sugar
1 teaspoon vanilla sugar
1 generous oz (30 g)
   grated chocolate
nutmeg
1 – 2 egg whites

First prepare the filling: set the hazelnuts on a baking sheet and put them into a hot oven (Gas Mark 7, 425°F, 220°C) until browned and the skins come away easily. Put the hazelnuts between sheets of kitchen paper and rub off the skins. Grind the hazelnuts and put them into a bowl. (If using walnuts, just grind them – browning is not necessary.) Add the honey, icing sugar, vanilla sugar, chocolate and nutmeg and work in enough egg whites to form a thick paste. Cover and set aside.

Preheat oven to Gas Mark 5, 375°F, 190°C. Roll out the yeast pastry to a rectangle about ⅛ inch (3 mm) thick. Cut into three strips, using a fluted pastry wheel if possible. Divide the filling into three and place down the centre of each strip. Fold over one side of the pastry, brush with a little beaten egg, then fold over the other side. Pull each roll gently to stretch it a little, then plait the three rolls very loosely. Twist into a ring with the fold uppermost and set in a buttered and floured 10 inch (25 cm) spring-clip cake tin. Cover with a cloth and leave to rise in a warm place for about forty minutes.

Brush carefully with beaten egg and bake in preheated oven for fifteen minutes, then lower the heat to Gas Mark 4, 350°F, 180°C for a further twenty-five to thirty minutes.

Leave the cake to cool in the tin while you make the icing: sift the icing sugar and stir in enough rum to make a thick paste. Carefully remove the cake from the tin and set it on a rack or a hair sieve. Dribble the icing over it with a teaspoon (do not spread it) and leave to set.

NUSSPOTITZE

Rich Yeast Cake Filled with Walnuts

A close relation of the Carinthian *Reinling, Potitze* originated in Slovenia and the name stems from *potica* (cake) and *potivi* (to wrap over). It is claimed as their very own by the people of Styria and can therefore be described as a truly Austrian cake! The shape varies slightly according to region – as a rule the dough is rolled out into a rectangular shape, filled and then rolled from both sides to the middle and baked in a rectangular tin. In some cases the dough is just rolled up after filling – rather like a Swiss roll – and baked in a savarin or ordinary cake tin; and when it has found its way to Vienna it is sometimes even baked in a *Guglhupf* mould.

For the pastry
1 oz (25 g) fresh yeast
2½ oz (70 g) caster sugar
¼ pint (125 ml) tepid milk
10 oz (280 g) strong flour
5 oz (140 g) butter
3 egg yolks
grated lemon rind
butter and flour for the
    baking tin

For the filling
1 lb (450 g) ground
    walnuts
6 oz (160 g) caster sugar
¼ pint (125 ml) rum
⅜ pint (190 ml) honey
2 tablespoons raisins
a little grated lemon rind
lemon juice
cinnamon
2½ fluid oz (65 ml) double
    cream

Butter and flour a rectangular cake tin. Cream yeast with a little of the sugar, add tepid milk. Add a teaspoon of the flour and set to prove in a warm place.

Cream butter with remaining sugar, add the yolks one by one. Add sifted flour, lemon rind and yeast mixture. Beat well with a wooden spoon or the dough hook attachment of the electric mixer until the dough comes away clean from the sides of the bowl. Sprinkle pastry board with flour, roll out the dough to about the thickness of a finger. Cover with the filling and roll the dough from both sides to the middle. Carefully lift the cake into the prepared tin, cover with a cloth and leave in a warm place until doubled in size – about forty minutes. Bake at Gas Mark 5, 375°F, 190°C for about an hour.

For the filling put all the ingredients, except honey and rum, into a bowl. Heat the honey and stir into the ingredients in the bowl, then stir in the rum.

Sometimes the dough is divided into two parts, each rolled out, filled and rolled up separately, then set side by side in the tin, folds uppermost.

NUSS ROULADE

Walnut Roulade

For the pastry
1 oz (30 g) fresh yeast
1 teaspoon caster sugar
2 tablespoons lukewarm
  milk
6 oz (180 g) strong flour
6 oz (180 g) butter
3 egg yolks
butter and flour for the
  baking sheet

For the filling
3 egg whites
6 oz (180 g) icing sugar
6 oz (180 g) ground
  walnuts
1 teaspoon vanilla sugar

Cream the yeast with the sugar in a cup, then stir in the lukewarm milk. Sprinkle a teaspoon of the flour over the top and set to prove in a warm place.

Sift the remaining flour into a bowl or onto a pastry board, cut the butter into the flour and then crumble it with your fingers until the mixture has the consistency of fine breadcrumbs. Make a well in the centre, add the yeast mixture and the lightly beaten egg yolks and work quickly to a paste. Pat into a round, dust with flour and place in the refrigerator for one to two hours, either slipped into a plastic bag or wrapped lightly in a floured cloth – the dough will be fairly soft.

Butter and flour a baking sheet. Preheat the oven to Gas Mark 7, 425°F, 220°C. Roll out the pastry into a rectangle about 1/4 inch thick, measuring approximately 14 × 10 inches. Whisk the egg whites until stiff, gradually whisk in the sugar and the vanilla sugar, then fold in the ground walnuts. Spread this mixture over the pastry to within about 1/2 inch of the edges, then roll up the pastry lightly – rather like a Swiss roll. Set pastry, 'seam' underneath, on the buttered and floured baking sheet and place in the preheated oven. Bake for the first ten minutes leaving the oven door slightly open, then close the door gently and lower the heat to Gas Mark 4, 350°F, 180°C and bake for a further twenty-five to thirty minutes. Set to cool on a rack and serve sliced.

NUSS STRUDEL

Walnut Strudel

Pastry as for *Mohnstrudel*
  (see page 327)
Filling

7 oz (200 g) ground walnuts	1 teaspoon grated lemon rind
3 oz (85 g) cake or biscuit crumbs	pinch each of allspice and cinnamon
2 oz (50 g) caster sugar	1 teaspoon vanilla sugar
2 tablespoons butter	1 – 2 oz (25 – 50 g) raisins
¼ pint (⅛ l) milk	(optional)
good dash of rum	

Prepare in exactly the same way as *Mohnstrudel*. For the filling dissolve sugar and butter in milk, bring to boil and pour over walnuts and crumbs. Mix well, add rum, grated lemon rind, vanilla sugar, cinnamon, allspice and raisins. Leave to cool before using.

As a variation – and for a rather more luxurious filling – replace the cake or biscuit crumbs with ground hazelnuts and add a tablespoon honey.

PRESSBURGER BEUGELN

Walnut and Poppyseed Crescents

Small crescents with a filling of either ground walnuts or ground poppyseeds and spices – the ones filled with walnuts are slender and slightly pointed, the poppyseed ones rather broad so that you can tell the filling by their outer appearance. *Pressburger Beugeln* are also known for the shiny, marbled effect of the pastry. Whether they really originated in Pressburg – now Bratislava, formerly Poszony – is not quite certain, but it was always maintained that the best ones were to be found in the pastry shops of that town – though they are in fact available throughout Austria and I recently had a particularly delectable one in Budapest.

There are a great number of variations concerning the fillings – grated honeycake can be used instead of the biscuit or cake crumbs in the walnut filling, or can replace some of the poppyseeds. Honey is sometimes used instead of, or in addition to, the sugar, and raisins or strips of candied peel are often added to either filling.

Makes 16 – 18 crescents
For the pastry
8 oz (225 g) strong flour
pinch of salt
1 oz (25 g) icing sugar
4 oz (110 g) butter
½ oz (10 g) fresh yeast
4 tablespoons milk
1 egg for glazing

Walnut filling
4 oz (100 g) ground
  walnuts
2½ oz (70 g) biscuit or
  cake crumbs
2 oz (60 g) caster sugar
pinch each of cinnamon,
  nutmeg and cloves
1 teaspoon vanilla sugar
1 tablespoon dark rum
4 tablespoons water
grated lemon rind

Poppyseed filling
6 oz (160 g) ground
  poppyseeds
3 oz (80 g) caster sugar
1 teaspoon vanilla sugar
6 tablespoons water
pinch of cinnamon
grated lemon rind
1 tablespoon dark rum

For the pastry sift together flour, salt and sugar. Dissolve yeast in milk – it is not necessary to warm the milk first, in fact it is better to use milk at room temperature. Cut the butter into the flour, add milk gradually and mix to a smooth dough. Cover with a cloth and leave in a cool place for about twenty minutes.

For the walnut filling dissolve the sugar in the water and bring to boil. Mix together walnuts and crumbs, add lemon rind, rum, vanilla sugar and spices. Chill well before using. The filling should be quite stiff and more crumbs or walnuts may be added if necessary.

To make the poppyseed filling, dissolve sugar in water and bring to boil. Pour over poppyseeds, add remaining ingredients and chill before use.

Knead dough lightly, divide into two parts and shape each part into a roll. Divide each roll into eight or nine equal portions and flatten each portion into an oval by hand or with a rolling pin.

Place a little of either filling in the centre of each oval, fold over pastry and press together edges. Shape into crescents and set them on a buttered and floured baking sheet so that the fold is underneath. Separate eggs. Brush over top of crescents with egg yolk and set them in a cool place for the egg yolk to dry, then brush with egg white. Bake at Gas Mark 5, 375°F, 190°C for about twenty minutes until golden brown, lowering the heat towards the end of the baking time if necessary. Remove carefully from baking sheet and set on a rack to cool.

SCHNECKEN

'Snails'

Germbutterteig I (puff
  pastry made with yeast
  – see page 323)

Filling   *Icing*
1 oz (30 g) raisins   3 oz (90 g) icing sugar
1½ oz (45 g) ground   a little rum
  walnuts
1½ oz (45 g) icing sugar
generous oz (35 g) grated
  plain chocolate
1 oz (30 g) melted butter
butter and flour for baking
  sheet

Roll out the pastry into a rectangle about ³/₄ inch thick. Mix together
the dry ingredients for the filling and sprinkle over pastry, then sprinkle
with melted butter. Roll up as for Swiss roll. Cut into slices about ½
inch thick. Place cut side down on a buttered and floured baking sheet,
tucking the little flap of pastry where it was folded over underneath
each piece. Cover lightly with a cloth and leave to rise in a warm place
for about thirty-five minutes.

Brush with beaten egg and bake at Gas Mark 5½, 390°F, 195°C until
golden brown. Carefully remove to a rack.

Stir enough rum into the icing sugar to make a stiff paste and dribble
this over the pastries while they are still warm but not hot.

TOPFENGOLATSCHEN

Yeast Pastries with Curd Cheese Filling

Germbutterteig I (puff
  pastry made with yeast
  – see page 323)
Filling
½ lb (225 g) curd cheese   egg for brushing over
3 oz (90 g) caster sugar   pastry
2 egg yolks   butter and flour for the
a little double cream   baking sheet
1 teaspoon grated lemon   icing sugar sifted with
  rind   vanilla sugar for
1 generous oz (30 g)   sprinkling over pastry
  raisins

Sieve the cheese if necessary to get rid of lumps. Cream cheese with
the sugar, then add the egg yolks, raisins, grated lemon rind and enough
cream to give a fairly thick consistency.

Roll out the pastry to about ⅛ inch thickness. Cut into squares and place a spoonful of the filling in the centre of each square. Fold the four corners of each square to the middle so that the filling is completely encased. Seal centre with a small round of pastry (use pastry trimmings for this). Place pastries on buttered and floured baking sheet and set to rise in a warm place. When well risen brush over with egg and bake at Gas Mark 5½, 390°F, 195°C until golden brown. Sprinkle whilst still warm with icing sugar sifted with vanilla sugar.

GATEAUX AND ICINGS

GATEAUX AND ICINGS

There is no real translation for *Torte* and for want of a better word I have referred to the recipes in the following chapter (which also includes roulades) as gateaux. That they stand in a group all by themselves no one will dispute. Most significant perhaps is their pristine look with the absence of all superfluous trimmings. A smoothly spread top, a modest sprinkling of grated chocolate or nuts, a preserved cherry or two – that is all. Occasionally, though rarely, they are topped with a small swirl of the filling, as if that amount had been left over and couldn't bear to be wasted.

Some *Torten* are filled and iced, others iced only. Sometimes the filling spreads over the top and sides of the gateau, or the top may just be dusted with icing sugar.

Use a spring-clip cake tin so that the cake slides out easily. Do not expect the cake to rise too much during baking – it will be handsome rather than high. Cool the cake on a hair sieve or a rack, upside down. This is important, for the cake should also be iced that way: the absolutely flat part which touched the baking tin uppermost. If the cake has risen too much during baking, trim it a little so that it stands straight.

ALPENBUTTERTORTE

My favourite birthday cake – the original was always decorated with morello cherries preserved in sugar (one cherry for each year, instead of candles). Halved walnuts or glacé cherries spiked with strips of angelica would make a reasonable, though – at least in my opinion – not quite adequate alternative.

For the cake
3 egg yolks
4 eggs
5 oz (140 g) icing sugar
4½ oz (120 g) plain flour
butter and flour for the
    cake tin

For the filling
¼ pint (150 ml) double
    cream
3 egg yolks
½ teaspoon cornflour
2 teaspoons vanilla sugar
5 oz (140 g) butter
1 generous oz (30 g) icing
    sugar

For the icing
3 tablespoons apricot jam
about 8 oz (230 g) icing
    sugar
strong black coffee
glacé cherries or halved
    walnuts, angelica for
    decoration

Butter and flour a 9½ inch (24 cm) cake tin. Preheat oven to Gas Mark 4, 350°F, 180°C. Whisk together egg yolks and eggs, add sifted icing sugar and whisk until the mixture is very thick and pale yellow. Lightly fold in the sifted flour. Bake for about forty to forty-five minutes, until golden brown and firm. Turn out onto a rack or a hair sieve and leave to cool.

For the filling blend together cream, egg yolks and cornflour and whisk over steam until thick. Remove from heat, stir until cool. Cream butter, sugar and vanilla sugar, add the cream mixture by the teaspoonful, beating well after each addition.

Cut through the cake twice and sandwich together the layers with the cream filling. Spread sieved warmed apricot jam over top and sides of the cake and leave to dry.

Sift the icing sugar into a bowl and stir in enough strong black coffee to give a thick paste. Spread over top and sides of the cake and leave to set. Decorate with halved walnuts or glacé cherries and angelica.

ANATOLTORTE

Anatol is the hero of a cycle of plays by Arthur Schnitzler – some of which feature the famous 'Sweet Viennese girl'.

'What is she like?' Anatol is asked.

'She is not particularly clever and she is not even very beautiful. But she has the soft charm of an evening in spring, the bearing of an enchanted princess and the spirit of a woman who knows how to love,' is Anatol's answer. 'And' – he should have added – 'she lives almost exclusively on chocolate gateau and marrons glacés' (in *Abschiedssouper* she even pockets a few by way of souvenir).

No doubt the cake was created to mark some occasion – possibly a First Night celebration – though not, it seems, by Mrs Arthur Schnitzler, as I'd always been led to believe because 'mother could not cook at all' said her son, Professor Heinrich Schnitzler. He shook his head sadly: 'No, not at all'. But whoever first made this cake, it is delicious.

For the cake	For the cream
5 eggs	3 tablespoons double cream
5 oz (140 g) butter	3 egg yolks
5 oz (140 g) icing sugar	3½ oz (100 g) caster or
8 oz (210 g) cooked sieved	icing sugar
chestnuts	1 dessertspoon vanilla sugar
1 oz (25 g) grated plain	2 oz (50 g) softened
chocolate	chocolate
	4½ oz (120 g) butter
	marrons glacés for
	decoration

Separate eggs. Cream butter and sugar until thick and fluffy, beat in the yolks one by one, followed by the sieved chestnuts and the grated chocolate. Whisk egg whites until stiff, then fold into the mixture. Bake in a lined and buttered 9 or 10 inch (23 cm or 25 cm) cake tin at Gas Mark 3, 325°F, 160°C for fifty to sixty minutes until firm. Cool on a rack or hair sieve.

For the cream whisk together egg yolks, sugar, cream and vanilla sugar over steam until thick. Cream butter until fluffy, then beat in the cooled egg cream gradually, and the melted but not hot chocolate.

Cut through the cake once, fill with about two thirds of the cream and spread remaining cream over top and sides. Decorate with marrons glacés.

BISKOTTENTORTE

This requires no baking. It was always a favourite cake for guests, expected or unexpected, though it is infinitely better if left overnight in the refrigerator. Sizes of boudoir biscuits vary considerably. The Italian ones sold in this country are usually closer to the Austrian in proportion.

6 oz (160 g) unblanched
   almonds, hazelnuts, or
   walnuts, or a mixture of
   all three
about 1 pint (scant ½ litre)
   milk
6 oz (160 g) butter
6 oz (160 g) icing sugar
2 teaspoons vanilla sugar
4 egg yolks
good dash of rum
about 36 large boudoir
   biscuits

For decoration
scant ½ pint (¼ l) double
   cream
1 scant tablespoon icing
   sugar
2 teaspoons vanilla sugar
2 tablespoons ground
   walnuts, hazelnuts or
   almonds (see recipe)

Put the nuts on a baking sheet and toast them slightly in the oven (Gas Mark 6, 400°F, 200°C). If using hazelnuts, rub off the skins with a paper towel. Grind the nuts and set aside 2 tablespoons for decoration.

Heat ¾ cup of the milk and pour over remaining ground nuts. Leave to cool. Butter a 9½ inch (24 cm) spring-clip cake tin. Cream butter and sugar, beat in vanilla sugar, then add egg yolks separately with the cooled nuts.

Put remaining milk into a soup plate or shallow bowl and add a good dash of rum. Dip the boudoir biscuits, one by one, into the milk and line the bottom of the cake tin with them, trimming them to size where necessary. (They must be dipped as they are needed, not all at once, which would make them too wet and soggy.) Spread half the cream over the biscuits and then arrange another layer of dipped boudoir biscuits. Spread with remaining cream and finish off with a layer of dipped boudoir biscuits.

Cover cake with a buttered plate – or bottom of a smaller cake tin – which just fits inside the cake tin, and place a weight on top. Chill well preferably overnight.

Slide out the cake very carefully. Whisk cream then whisk in sugar and vanilla sugar. Either mask the whole cake with whipped cream and sprinkle with remaining ground nuts, or cut some additional sponge fingers to the height of the cake, stick them right round the cake, tie with ribbon and pile the whipped cream in the centre, then sprinkle with the toasted nuts.

BURGENLÄNDISCHE MOHNTORTE

Poppyseed Gateau

Café Sommer at Mörbisch is a magical place, particularly during the time of the Summer Lakeside Festival when it stays open well into the early hours of the morning, by which time the butcher across the road starts opening his doors, ready to serve hot Goulash soup to late revellers. One of Café Sommer's specialities is this particular poppyseed gateau which they serve warm, covered with hot chocolate sauce – more of a pudding than a cake. At other places in the Burgenland it is served as a cake, adorned merely with a sprinkling of icing sugar.

4½ oz (120 g) butter	4½ oz (120 g) ground
4½ oz (120 g) icing sugar	poppyseeds
3 eggs	butter and flour for the
dash of rum	cake tin

Cream butter and sugar until very light and fluffy. Separate eggs. Beat yolks into creamed butter, beating well after each addition. Add ground poppyseeds and rum. Whisk whites until stiff, fold in carefully. Bake at Gas Mark 4, 350°F, 180°C for about fifty minutes. Carefully remove from cake tin and set to cool on a rack or hair sieve.

DOBOS TORTE

You will seldom find an Austrian *patisserie* where *Dobos Torte* does not take pride of place in the display. Yet its origin is strictly Hungarian – albeit before the end of the Austro-Hungarian Monarchy. Created in 1887 in Budapest, by Josef Dobos, an almost legendary figure who generously allowed the recipe to be published in later years, it is a truly luscious layer cake in which the thickness of the cream filling should about equal that of the pastry.

There is no difficulty in preparing the cake layers or the chocolate cream filling, but the caramel sugar top can be slightly tricky. You may find it easier to aim at *Dobos Schnitten* (Dobos slices), or a square cake, for your first attempt, and 'graduate' to the round gateau. I must confess that I have never seen the original recipe (published in 1906 I believe), but this particular recipe of mine makes an absolutely authentic *Dobos Torte* and for all I know it *is* taken from the original – it has certainly been around my family long enough to qualify.

For 1 round gateau or 12–14 slices of 5–6 layers

For the cake	*For the filling*
4½ oz (120 g) plain flour	5½ oz (150 g) butter
6 eggs	4½ oz (120 g) icing sugar
5 oz (140 g) icing sugar	1 dessertspoon vanilla
1 teaspoon vanilla sugar	sugar
butter and flour for the	2 generous oz (60 g) plain
baking paper for cake	chocolate
tins	1 egg

For the caramel top
5½ oz (150g) caster sugar
small knob of butter
about 2 tablespoons water
melted butter for the
pastry board

To make the gateau – unless you have six identical spring-clip cake tins – trace out five or six identical rounds on sheets of greaseproof paper or baking parchment, and set on larger baking sheets.

Preheat the oven to Gas Mark 7, 425°F, 220°C. Sift the flour twice. Separate eggs. Whisk yolks with half the icing sugar until very thick and creamy. Whisk whites until stiff, fold in remaining sugar and vanilla sugar and whisk again until smooth and glossy. Fold egg whites into yolks, alternately with the sifted flour. Spread evenly to the depth of ½ an inch (1 cm) over the prepared cake tins, or over the rounds drawn on baking paper (or, if you are making Dobos slices or a rectangular cake, over baking sheets covered with buttered and floured greaseproof paper or baking parchment).

Bake until golden brown – about eight to ten minutes. Remove paper carefully and set the pastry to cool. When quite cold place pastry between sheets of waxed or greaseproof paper, cover with a board and weigh down a little.

For the filling break the chocolate into small pieces and set to melt in a warm place. Cream butter and icing sugar until fluffy, beat in the vanilla sugar, then beat in the softened but not hot chocolate and finally the egg.

There is also a lighter, though slightly more complicated filling which is made as follows

Dobos filling II

2½ fluid oz (65 ml) milk	⅓ oz (20 g) cornflour
1 egg yolk	5½ oz (150 g) butter
1½ oz (40 g) icing sugar	5½ oz (150 g) icing sugar
1 dessertspoon vanilla sugar	2 oz (50 g) plain chocolate

Blend together milk, egg yolk, icing and vanilla sugar and the cornflour and whisk over steam – or in a double boiler – until thick. Set aside to cool, stirring from time to time. Break chocolate into small pieces and set to melt in a warm place. Cream butter and sugar, beat in the softened chocolate and then gradually beat in the cold egg/milk cream.

Having prepared the pastry and the chocolate filling, select and put aside the best-looking of the pastry sheets for the top. Sandwich together the other pastry layers with the chocolate cream, spreading it over top and sides of the cake as well.

Place the pastry piece for the top on a board – or preferably a marble slab – spread lightly with melted butter. Put the sugar in a small heavy pan, together with the water and set over low heat for the sugar to dissolve. Stir in a small knob of butter. When the sugar has dissolved increase the heat and cook sugar until it is pale golden brown. Remove from heat, cool for a little – a question of seconds rather than minutes – then spread quickly over the pastry sheet. Mark into portions with a knife dipped frequently into hot water and run quickly over butter. Put this caramelized layer on top of the cake. If the sugar hardens too quickly for you to finish marking it, place the layer into a warm oven for a few seconds and the sugar will soften again.

DÖZY TORTE

6 eggs	butter and flour for the cake tin
6½ oz (180 g) plain or bitter chocolate	grated chocolate
6½ oz (180 g) butter	
6½ oz (180 g) icing sugar	
dash of rum	

Butter and flour a 10 inch (25 cm) spring-clip cake tin. Preheat the oven to Gas Mark 1, 275°F, 140°C.

Separate eggs. Break the chocolate into small pieces and set to melt in a warm place. Cream butter and sugar until very light and fluffy, then beat in the egg yolks gradually, beating well after each addition. Beat in the melted but not hot chocolate and the rum.

Whisk whites until stiff and fold into the mixture.

Put a third of the mixture into the prepared cake tin and bake for
thirty-five minutes – the cake will still be a little moist inside.

Carefully remove the spring-clip from the tin, but leave the cake to
sit on the base. Set to cool and then spread remaining mixture on top
and sides of the cake. Sprinkle with grated chocolate. Do not attempt
to remove the cake from the base – just set it on a larger plate or dish
and serve it from there.

GRIESSTORTE

Semolina Cake

3 eggs	2 oz (50 g) semolina
3½ oz (100 g) icing sugar	butter and ground
1¼ oz (35 g) ground	almonds for the cake tin
almonds	apricot jam
grated rind of ½ lemon	lemon water icing (see
1 teaspoon lemon juice	page 375)

Separate eggs. Add lemon juice to yolks and whisk with icing sugar
until thick. Whisk whites until stiff. Fold whites into yolk mixture,
alternately with ground almonds and semolina. Finally fold in grated
lemon rind.

Bake in well-buttered cake tin, sprinkled with ground almonds, at
Gas Mark 4½, 360°F, 185°C. Carefully remove from cake tin and leave
to cool on a rack or on a hair sieve. Cover with warmed jam and leave
to dry, then cover with thin lemon water icing.

HASELNUSS SCHAUMTORTE

Hazelnut Cream Gateau

Another luscious confection for which dieting is only too readily
forgotten. If the quantities seem too extravagant, halve them and you
will still have a memorable – albeit smaller – gateau.

For the cake
4 oz (110 g) ground
  hazelnuts
2 oz (50 g) butter
8 eggs
4 oz (110 g) icing sugar
2 teaspoons vanilla sugar
2½ oz (70 g) plain flour
butter and flour (or
  ground hazelnuts) for the
  cake tin
hazelnuts or grated
  chocolate for decoration

For the filling
½ pint (280 ml) double
  cream
2 tablespoons icing sugar
1 teaspoon vanilla sugar
about 1½ oz (40 g) ground
  hazelnuts

Preheat the oven to Gas Mark 5, 375°F, 190°C. Put 6 oz (170 g) hazelnuts on a baking sheet and brown them in the oven until lightly coloured and the skins rub off easily. Put the hazelnuts into a clean cloth or between sheets of kitchen paper and rub off the skins. Grind the hazelnuts and weigh out the 4 oz (110 g) required for the cake. Butter and flour (or sprinkle with ground hazelnuts) two 8 or 9 inch spring-clip cake tins (24 cm or 26 cm). Set the butter to melt in a warm place – a cup standing in hot water is the easiest way of doing this. Separate eggs. Set aside two flat tablespoons of the sugar.

Whisk yolks with remaining sugar until very thick and creamy. Whisk whites until stiff. Whisk in the reserved two tablespoons sugar and vanilla sugar. Fold whites into yolks, alternately with ground hazelnuts and flour.

Finally add the melted but not hot butter.

Bake in two separate layers until pale golden brown – about twenty-five minutes. Remove very carefully from the cake tins and set to cool on a rack.

For the filling whisk the cream until stiff, then fold in sugar, vanilla sugar and remaining ground hazelnuts. Sandwich the two layers together with the cream, reserving a little for spreading over top and sides of the cake. Decorate top with ground or whole hazelnuts or sprinkle with a little grated chocolate. Fresh raspberries added to the whipped cream filling make this cake even more delicious.

HIMBEERTORTE MIT WINDMASSE

Raspberry Meringue Tart in Marzipan Pastry

A good brand of shop-bought marzipan will do very well for this recipe.

3½ oz (100 g) marzipan	about 1 lb (450 g)
3½ oz (100 g) butter	raspberries
5 oz (140 g) plain flour	butter and flour for the
1 egg yolk	cake tin
3 egg whites	egg for brushing over
5½ oz (150 g) caster sugar	pastry

Preheat the oven to Gas Mark 4, 350°F, 180°C. Put the marzipan in the refrigerator to chill and harden. Rub the butter into the flour, then coarsely grate the marzipan into the mixture. Quickly work in the egg yolk, handling the mixture as little as possible.

Butter and flour a 10 inch spring-clip cake tin or flan case. Press out the pastry to line bottom and sides of the tin – no need to roll out the pastry, just gently press it out with your fingers – then prick it all over with a fork and chill for thirty minutes. Brush over pastry with lightly beaten egg or egg white and bake for about twenty-five to thirty minutes, until golden brown. Take out of the oven, but leave in the tin to cool.

Reduce oven heat to Gas Mark 1, 275°F, 140°C. Whisk egg whites until stiff, then whisk in the sugar gradually. Spread raspberries over cooled pastry base and mask completely with the meringue mixture. Bake until the top is just lightly tinged with colour.

HOFRATSTORTE

Court Counsellor's Gateau

Hofrat – Counsellor to the Imperial Court – was a title conferred by the Emperor. Austria has now been a republic for some considerable time, but every year the President of that republic bestows the title of Hofrat on worthy citizens. There are subtle differences, such as *vortragender Hofrat* (presenting or reciting Hofrat – though it is not quite clear what or to whom anything is being presented or recited) and *wirklicher und geheimer Hofrat* (real and confidential Court Counsellor), but the recipe for the gateau created in honour of the title has remained unchanged throughout the decades.

For the cake
7½ oz (210 g) butter
7½ oz (210 g) icing sugar
2 eggs
3 egg yolks
grated rind of ½ lemon
7½ oz (210 g) ground
  unblanched almonds
2 oz (50 g) biscuit crumbs
3½ oz (100 g) redcurrant
  jam or jelly
2 *Oblaten* (see *Note*)
butter and flour for the
  cake tin

For the icing
2 tablespoons redcurrant
  jam or jelly
8 oz (225 g) icing sugar
dash of lemon juice
1 egg white

Note: *Oblaten* – thin round wafers – are sold as such in some good delicatessen. Sometimes they are called *Karlsbader Oblaten*, or *Oblati*, depending on their country of origin. If not available, use ice cream wafers, laying them side by side and trimming the edges.

Cream butter and sugar until light and fluffy, then beat in eggs and egg yolks gradually. Beat in grated lemon rind, almonds and biscuit crumbs. Spread half the mixture into a buttered and floured cake tin – a 9-inch tin is best, but you may have to use a slightly different size according to the *Oblaten*. Cover mixture with one of the *Oblaten*, spread with redcurrant jam or jelly, gently put the second *Oblate* on top and cover with the remainder of the cake mixture. Bake at Gas Mark 5, 375°F, 190°C for about forty-five to fifty minutes. Leave to cool on a rack or on a sieve, then cover with warmed redcurrant jam or jelly. Leave to dry.

Sift the icing sugar, beat in enough of the egg white to give a very stiff paste, then beat in a dash of lemon juice. Cover top and sides of the cake with the icing and leave to dry.

IGEL

'Hedgehogs'

14–16 small sponge cake rounds, measuring about 2 inches in diameter and 1½ inches high	6 tablespoons very strong black coffee
a little Drambuie or Cointreau	toasted almond slivers
5 generous oz (150 g) butter	
3 tablespoons icing sugar	
3 egg yolks	

Set the sponge cakes on a flat dish, sprinkle with liqueur and put in a cold place. Cream butter and sugar, beat in the egg yolks one by one and then, gradually and almost drop by drop, add the black coffee. Pile a little of this cream on top of each sponge round, smooth it over with a palette knife so that it is a little higher in the centre and spike with slivers of toasted almonds.

The same mixture can also be used to make one large 'hedgehog', using square or rectangular sponge cakes which are arranged crossways on a serving dish, layered with the butter cream. Smooth over the top with the butter cream, chill well and spike with almonds before serving.

KAFFEECREMETORTE

Coffee Cream Gateau

For the cake	For the filling
2½ oz (70 g) hazelnuts	4 oz (110 g) butter
3 egg whites	4 oz (110 g) icing sugar
5 oz (140 g) icing sugar	3 egg yolks
2½ oz (70 g) ground almonds	4 tablespoons strong black coffee
butter and flour for the cake tins	

Place the hazelnuts on a baking sheet and put them in a hot oven (Gas Mark 6, 400°F, 200°C) for a few minutes, until the skins rub off easily.

Remove skins by putting the hazelnuts in a tea towel or between sheets of kitchen paper and rubbing gently until all the skins come away. Grind the hazelnuts, then mix with ground almonds. Turn down the oven heat to Gas Mark 5, 375°F, 190°C.

Whisk egg whites until stiff, whisk in half the sugar, then fold in remaining sugar, alternately with hazelnut and almond mixture. Bake in two separate buttered and floured 9 inch cake tins until golden brown – about fifteen to twenty minutes. (The mixture is rather delicate and stiffens quickly as it cools – in order to avoid crumbling or breakage, use a spring-clip cake tin and handle carefully.) Remove cakes from tins and set on a rack or hair sieve to cool.

For the cream filling whisk egg yolks with coffee and sugar over steam until thick. Remove from heat and whisk until cool – set the basin over a bowl of ice to accelerate this process. Cream butter and add the coffee mixture by the spoonful. Sandwich the two cake halves together with this cream, spreading some over top and sides as well.

KAFFEE ZIEGEL

Coffee 'Brick'

Since the size of boudoir biscuits varies considerably, it is impossible to give the exact number required – simply aim for a square-shaped gateau.

boudoir biscuits	5 fluid oz (140 ml) single
5 oz (140 g) butter	cream
5 oz (140 g) icing sugar	dash of rum
3 – 4 egg yolks	whipped cream and finely
1 teaspoon vanilla sugar	ground coffee beans for
3 tablespoons strong black	decoration
coffee	

Cream together butter and icing sugar until very light and fluffy. Gradually beat in the egg yolks, vanilla sugar and 2 tablespoons of the coffee.

Tip the single cream into a soup plate and add the remaining coffee and a dash of rum. Pull some of the boudoir biscuits quickly through the cream – one by one so that they do not get soggy – and arrange them side by side on a dish so that they form a square. Spread a little of the butter cream over them, then cover with more boudoir biscuits which have also been pulled through the coffee/cream mixture, laying them at right angles across the first layer. Continue until all the butter cream has been used up. Cover the resulting 'brick' lightly with foil and set it to chill overnight in a cool place (preferably not in a refrigerator).

Just before serving, mask the gateau with whipped, lightly sweetened cream and sprinkle with very finely ground coffee beans.

KASTANIENTORTE I

Chestnut Gateau (without Baking)

For the base
1 lb (450 g) chestnuts
2½ oz (70 g) butter
3½ oz (100 g) icing sugar
1 teaspoon vanilla sugar
a good dash of rum

For the topping
3½ oz (100 g) bitter
   chocolate
1 oz (30 g) butter

There are easier ways of preparing the chestnuts than the one I am advocating – like slitting the chestnuts across and putting them first into a hot oven – but they do not work quite as well for this particular recipe. Canned chestnuts or tinned chestnut purée are not suitable either, the former having absorbed too much water and the latter being too soft. To get the right consistency for this particular recipe the chestnuts should be boiled whole and without previously slitting the skins.

Put the chestnuts into a large saucepan, cover with plenty of cold water, bring to the boil and cook until the chestnuts are soft. This usually takes about thirty to forty minutes, depending on size and you will simply have to test them to see if they are done. Just fish out one of the chestnuts with a slotted spoon and plunge a sharp pointed knife through the hard outer skin. If it goes smoothly through the chestnut flesh, they are done. Keep the water simmering gently as you fish out two or three chestnuts at a time and peel off the skins, then push the chestnuts through a sieve or a potato ricer while they are still hot. Proceed until all the chestnuts have been peeled and sieved (do not use a food processor: it does not work as well as sieving or using a potato ricer).

Cream together butter and sugar until light and fluffy, beat in the vanilla sugar and the rum and then mix in the sieved chestnuts – it may at first seem quite a lot of chestnuts for the amount of butter, but it will all work into a rather smooth paste. Line a 7-inch spring-clip cake tin with greaseproof paper. Press the chestnut mixture into the tin, level the top and cover with a plate which should just fit the inside of the tin. Place a weight on top and chill overnight.

The next day lift out the cake and peel off the greaseproof paper. Set the cake on a plate and prepare the topping. Break the chocolate into small pieces, put them into a bowl and set to melt over steam or in a warm oven. Soften the butter a little, then beat the butter into the melted but not hot chocolate. Smooth over the cake and leave to set. Serve cut into thin slices – with sweetened whipped cream if you like, though it is excellent just on its own.

Kastanientorte II

Chestnut Gateau (Baked)

6 eggs
5 oz (140 g) icing sugar
5 oz (140 g) cooked sieved
    chestnuts
2 oz (50 g) breadcrumbs
butter and flour for the
    cake tin

Filling
9 fluid oz (¼ l) double
    cream
2 tablespoons icing sugar
4 oz (110 g) cooked sieved
    chestnuts

Separate eggs. Whisk yolks with sugar until thick and creamy. Whisk whites until stiff. Add chestnuts to yolk mixture, fold in whisked whites and breadcrumbs. Bake at Gas Mark 4, 350°F, 180°C in a buttered and floured spring-clip cake tin for about forty minutes. Carefully remove from cake tin and cool on a rack or hair sieve. When the cake is quite cold – preferably the next day – cut through once and sandwich the two halves together with the filling, spreading a little over top and sides as well.

For the filling whisk cream until stiff with sugar, then fold in the sieved chestnuts.

For an even more luscious cake use all the filling for the cake, spread warmed apricot jam over top and sides and then cover with chocolate icing as for *Sachertorte* (see page 365).

Yet another version is to fill the gateau with sweetened whipped cream and spread a little of the whipped cream over top and sides. Cover top of the cake with sieved chestnuts – simply sieve them or push them straight through a potato ricer onto the cake.

LINZERTORTE

Some years ago I was credibly told that Linzertorte was not named after the town of Linz, but after Linzer, chef to the Archduke Charles, victor over Napoleon at Aspern, and that the cake was created to please the many children of the Archduke 'with lots of almonds and nuts'. A pretty story, but alas, soon disproved. An elaborate – and possibly also the first – illustration for *der geflochtne Lintzer Dorten* appears in Conrad Hagger's *Neues Saltzburgisches Koch-Buch* published in 1718, long before the Archduke was born!

There are of course many versions of this very popular recipe which is a rich jam tart rather than a gateau. *Das kleine Linzer Kochbuch*, containing more than 300 *sehr guter und wohl geprüfter Kochregeln* collected by 'several famous female cooks', gives in the 1841 edition a very simple recipe consisting of half a pound each of blanched almonds (pounded to the consistency of semolina), butter, flour and sugar, plus the juice and grated rind of a lemon and 4 egg yolks. Maria Anna Neudecker lists the same quantities, but uses 6 egg yolks as well as the yolks of 6 hardboiled eggs, and flavours the *Linzertorte* with cinnamon (half a pound in those days – I am told – amounted to 560 g), and the fresh fruit in her recipe is morello cherries or redcurrants. Recipes for *Linzertorte* abound. You can choose from *Linzertorte weiss* (made either with or without blanched almonds) or *Linzertorte braun* (in which almonds or nuts play a prominent part) and then there is *gerührte Linzertorte* (see page 351), where the butter is creamed before the dry ingredients are added rather than crumbling the butter into them. Any recipe as old as *Linzertorte* is bound to get altered – and I confess a contribution to this rule: the addition of nutmeg is strictly my own, and not found in any other variation. I think it is an improvement, but you may care to experiment with a small pinch of allspice instead. There is also a fair amount of controversy over the type of jam to be used. Most recipes specify redcurrant jam, others say apricot, whilst the clever ones just murmur 'jam'. I think they are all misguided: raspberry jam is best!

5 oz (140 g) caster sugar	5 oz (140 g) butter
5 oz (140 g) plain flour	3 egg yolks
5 oz (140 g) unblanched almonds	raspberry jam
good pinch each of powdered cinnamon, cloves and nutmeg	vanilla sugar
	butter and flour for the flan case

Mix together all dry ingredients. Cut butter into small pieces, then crumble them into the dry ingredients. Add egg yolks and lemon juice and quickly work to a dough. Pat into a round and chill for about half an hour.

    Line bottom and sides of a buttered and floured flan case measuring 9 or 10 inches in diameter with two-thirds of the pastry. There is no need to roll out the pastry with a rolling pin – just press it into shape with your hands. Prick lightly over the pastry with a fork – this is not strictly necessary, but it will prevent it from rising in the wrong places. Roll out remaining pastry between your hands. Spread pastry base with jam, arrange the slightly flattened pastry strips in a lattice pattern over the top and place a strip around the edge. Bake at Gas Mark 4, 350°F, 180°C for about forty to fifty minutes.

    Dust with vanilla sugar whilst still warm. If you like the pastry to be very crisp, you may brush over the top with lightly beaten egg, but this is slightly tricky because you will have to avoid getting egg on the jam filling. Personally I don't think it is necessary.

Gerührte Weisse Linzertorte

Linzertorte (creamed version)

This recipe, which I found in the hand-writing of one of my favourite and most revered cooks, was marked *wirkliche echte Linzertorte* (genuine real *Linzertorte*). It is irresistible!

6 oz (170 g) butter	1 teaspoon grated lemon
3 oz (90 g) caster sugar	rind
1 egg	jam
2 generous oz (60 g)	butter and flour for the
ground almonds or	cake tin
hazelnuts	rice paper
7 oz (200 g) plain flour	

Cream butter and sugar and beat in the egg. Beat in flour, almonds (or hazelnuts) and grated lemon rind. Spread half the mixture in a buttered and floured cake tin. Cover with a round of rice paper cut to fit and spread with jam to within three-quarters of an inch of the edge. With the help of a piping bag, pipe the remaining mixture round the edge and in a criss-cross pattern over the jam. Bake at Gas Mark 4½, 360°F, 185°C for about forty-five minutes. Dust with icing sugar when cold.

MANDELTORTE

Almond Gateau

4 eggs	*For the filling*
5 oz (140 g) icing sugar	5 fluid oz (125 ml) double
grated rind of 1 orange	cream
2 oz (55 g) ground boudoir	4 egg yolks
biscuits	1 teaspoon vanilla sugar
5 oz (140 g) ground	3½ oz (100 g) butter
almonds	2½ oz (70 g) icing sugar
juice of 1½ oranges	ground almonds for
butter and ground	sprinkling over top
almonds for the cake tin	

Separate eggs. Whisk yolks with icing sugar until thick and fluffy. Fold in grated orange rind, then add the orange juice and whisk again to blend. Whisk whites until stiff and fold into mixture, alternately with the biscuit crumbs and ground almonds. Bake in a buttered cake tin sprinkled with ground almonds at Gas Mark 4, 350°F, 180°C for about fifty minutes. Carefully turn out of cake tin and set to cool on a rack or a hair sieve.

To make the cream filling whisk cream with egg yolks and vanilla sugar over steam until thick. Remove from heat and whisk until cold. Set to chill. Cream butter and sugar and gradually add the egg cream.

When cake is cold, cut through once or twice and fill with the butter cream, spreading a little over top and sides as well. Sprinkle with ground almonds.

MOHNTORTE

Poppyseed Gateau

5 eggs	dash of rum
5 oz (140 g) butter	butter and flour for the
6½ oz (180 g) icing sugar	cake tin
6½ oz (180 g) freshly	2 tablespoons redcurrant
ground poppyseeds	jelly
3½ oz (100 g) ground	chocolate icing as for
almonds	*Sachertorte* (see page
1 teaspoon lemon juice	365)
pinch of cinnamon	

Separate eggs. Cream butter and sugar until light and fluffy. Add yolks gradually, beating well after each addition. Stir in the ground poppyseeds and add lemon juice, cinnamon and rum. Whisk whites until stiff and fold into the mixture, alternately with the ground almonds. Bake in a buttered and floured cake tin at Gas Mark 3½ – 4, 340° – 350°F, 170° – 180°C for approximately one hour. Cool on a rack and when quite cold – preferably the next day – cover with warmed redcurrant jelly, leave to dry and then spread with chocolate icing.

MÜRBE TORTE I

6½ oz (180 g) butter	butter and flour for the
4 oz (110 g) ground	baking sheet
hazelnuts	Cream filling as for
4 oz (110 g) icing or caster	*Nusstorte* (see page 354)
sugar	or *Panamatorte* (see
7½ oz (210 g) plain flour	page 357)
1 teaspoon vanilla sugar	
1 teaspoon baking powder	

Sift together flour and baking powder, sift again, then add the icing sugar and vanilla sugar. Cut butter into dry ingredients, add hazelnuts and quickly work to a dough. Divide into three equal parts and press or roll into rounds. Set the rounds on buttered and floured baking sheets, prick lightly with a fork and bake at Gas Mark 5, 375°F, 190°C until golden brown. Carefully remove from tin and set to cool on a rack. When quite cold sandwich together with cream filling as for *Nusstorte* or *Panamatorte*.

Mürbe Torte II

5 oz (140 g) plain flour	jam for filling
2 oz (50 g) icing sugar	icing sugar sifted with
2 hardboiled egg yolks	vanilla sugar
grated rind of ½ lemon	
5 oz (140 g) butter	
butter and flour for the	
baking sheet	

Sift together flour and icing sugar. Mix with crumbled egg yolks and lemon rind, then cut the butter into the dry ingredients. Quickly work to a dough and chill for half an hour. Divide dough into two equal parts, roll or press out into rounds and set on a buttered and floured baking sheet. Prick with a fork and bake at Gas Mark 5, 375°F, 190°C until golden brown. Set on a rack to cool and when quite cold sandwich together with jam. Dust top with icing sugar sifted with vanilla sugar.

NUSSCREMETORTE

Walnut Gateau

For the cake	*For the icing*
6 eggs	2 tablespoons redcurrant
5 oz (140 g) icing sugar	jelly
2 scant oz (45 g) fine	7 oz (200 g) icing sugar
breadcrumbs	lemon juice or rum
5 oz (140 g) ground	walnut halves
walnuts	
2 tablespoons rum	
butter and ground walnuts	
for the cake tin	

For the filling
4 fluid oz (100 ml) double
  cream
2 oz (50 g) icing sugar
2½ oz (70 g) ground
  walnuts
3 eggs yolks
1 tablespoon rum

Preheat the oven to Gas Mark 5, 375°F, 190°C. Butter a 9-inch (23 cm) spring-clip cake tin and dust with ground walnuts.

Separate eggs. Moisten breadcrumbs with the rum. Whisk yolks with the sugar until thick and creamy. Beat in the softened breadcrumbs. Whisk whites until stiff. Fold whipped whites into yolks alternately with the ground walnuts. Bake for forty to fifty minutes.

Cool upside down on a rack or a hair sieve. When cold – preferably the next day – cut through once or twice and fill with the following cream.

Put cream, sugar and ground walnuts into a thick saucepan. Heat gently, stirring constantly, until thick. Remove from heat, leave to cool a little, then pour into the top of a double boiler or into a bowl set over a saucepan half-filled with simmering water, and beat in egg yolks one by one. Cook carefully until thick, then add the rum. Remove from heat, stir from time to time while cream cools.

After the cake has been filled, warm the redcurrant jelly and spread over top and sides of the cake. Leave to dry.

To make the icing, sift the sugar into a bowl and stir in enough rum or lemon juice to give a fairly thick paste. Spread over top and sides of the cake. Decorate with halved walnuts. For a special touch, dip the walnut halves into hot caramelized sugar first and leave to dry on a buttered baking sheet or foil.

NUSSTORTE

Walnut Layer Cake

For the cake
7½ oz (210 g) plain flour
5 oz (140 g) caster or icing
  sugar
5 oz (140 g) ground
  walnuts
5 oz (140 g) butter
butter and flour for baking
  sheets

For the filling
½ pint (275 ml) double
  cream
1 lightly heaped
  tablespoon icing sugar
1 flat teaspoon vanilla
  sugar
sifted icing sugar for the
  top

Mix together flour, sugar and ground walnuts. Cut butter into dry ingredients and work to a smooth paste. Divide mixture into four equal-sized pieces. Roll out each piece into a round or square – the shape does not really matter, as long as the pieces are all of the same size (I use the bottom of a spring-clip cake tin as a guide). Bake the pastry on well-buttered and floured baking sheets at Gas Mark 5, 375°F, 190°C until deep golden brown – about twelve to fifteen minutes.

As soon as the pastry comes out of the oven, loosen it carefully with a spatula or a palette knife. When the rounds or squares have cooled a little, set them on a rack to cool completely. (This is the only slightly tricky part of the operation as the pastry is rather fragile and has to be handled carefully.)

Whisk cream with icing sugar and vanilla sugar until just stiff. Spread a third of the whipped cream over a pastry round or square, top with another, spread again with cream and so on, leaving top pastry bare. Chill gateau overnight. Dust the top lightly with icing sugar before serving.

OBSTROULADE

Fruit Roulade

This was the speciality of Ilse Dobrowa at a small inn called Zum Brauhaus at Göstling an der Ybbs, in the depths of Lower Austria. The preferred filling – somewhat surprisingly – consisted of bananas moistened with rum, wrapped in whipped cream, which goes well with the nutty flavour of the pastry. The Dobrowas have long since departed from Göstling and with them probably the house speciality, but the original recipe is quite easy to follow – except that I prefer strawberries or raspberries (sprinkled with Kirsch or Framboise respectively) to say nothing of wild strawberries!

4 eggs	a little rum
3 oz (80 g) icing or caster sugar	10 fluid oz (275 ml) double cream
1 generous oz (30 g) plain flour	1 flat teaspoon vanilla sugar
1 generous oz (30 g) ground walnuts	butter and flour for the baking sheet
1–2 bananas (or other fruit)	

Line a baking sheet measuring approximately 12 × 8 inches (30.5 × 20 cm) with baking parchment or buttered greaseproof paper, dusted lightly with flour. Preheat oven to Gas Mark 5, 375°F, 190°C.

Whisk together eggs and sugar until very thick and creamy. Lightly fold in the flour and ground walnuts. Spread the mixture over the baking sheet and bake for about twenty minutes.

Sprinkle a sheet of clean kitchen paper with flour and turn the pastry onto this. Peel off the paper whilst the pastry is still hot. Lightly roll up the pastry – it is more a case of folding over than rolling up – and leave to cool. Slice the bananas thinly and sprinkle with rum. Whisk cream until stiff and add the vanilla sugar.

When the pastry has cooled, trim off the edges if necessary, brush off excess flour and spread with the whipped cream. Arrange the banana slices on top and fold up very lightly. Do not roll up as for Swiss roll, just fold the pastry over so that the cream filling is in the centre. Wrap the roll in kitchen foil, folded side down, and chill for at least one hour before slicing.

You could save a little of the whipped cream for spreading over the top, but I find that a light dusting of icing sugar is all that is needed.

ORANGENTORTE

Orange Gateau

A very light, elegant gateau which may be filled and decorated in various ways.

5 eggs	1 oz (30 g) fine
juice and finely grated	breadcrumbs
rind of 1 orange	butter and ground
juice of ½ lemon	almonds for cake tin
5 oz (140 g) icing sugar	
5 oz (140 g) ground	
almonds	

Butter a 9 inch spring-clip cake tin and dust lightly with flour or ground almonds. Separate eggs. Whisk together yolks, lemon juice, orange juice, and all but 1 tablespoon of the sugar until very thick and creamy. This may look impossible at first but it can be done, unless you have used a particularly juicy orange, in which case add a little extra sugar – no more than a flat tablespoon – to the yolk mixture, and also use an extra egg white later on in the procedure.

Whisk whites until stiff, whisk in the tablespoon of sugar previously set aside and fold whites into yolks, alternately with ground almonds, grated orange rind and the breadcrumbs. Bake at Gas Mark 5, 375°F, 190°C for about forty minutes. Remove cake carefully from tin and set to cool on a rack or a sieve.

The decoration of the cake is a matter of choice – it is delicious with just a dusting of icing sugar sprinkled over the flat top. Alternately, spread it with warmed apricot jam, leave to dry and then cover with orange water icing (add enough strained juice to 7 oz (200 g) icing sugar to make a stiff paste) and spread it over the cake. Using the juice of a blood orange gives a splendid effect and further embellishments could be orange segments dipped into sugar cooked to 'small crack' stage. For special occasions cut through the cake before icing and fill with sweetened whipped cream to which some very finely grated orange rind and a dash of Cointreau have been added, then glaze with apricot jam and cover with orange icing as before.

PANAMATORTE

This is the gateau in its full glory such as would be prepared for great family gatherings. For a smaller, but no less delicious cake, use three eggs and halve all the other quantities and cut through the cake only once.

For the cake
7 eggs
5 oz (150 g) icing sugar
5 oz (150 g) unblanched
   ground almonds
4 oz (100 g) grated
   chocolate
butter and ground
   almonds for the cake tin
2 oz (50 g) toasted ground
   or coarsely chopped
   almonds

For the filling
5 oz (150 g) butter
5 oz (150 g) icing sugar
1 teaspoon vanilla sugar
2 eggs
2 generous oz (60 g)
   softened chocolate

Separate eggs. Mix grated chocolate with ground almonds. Whisk yolks with about two-thirds of the sugar until thick and creamy. Whisk whites until stiff, fold in remaining sugar and whisk again until smooth. Fold whites into yolks, alternately with the chocolate/almond mixture. Bake in a 10 inch (25 cm) spring-clip cake tin, buttered and dusted with ground almonds at Gas Mark 4, 350°F, 180°C for about one hour.

Carefully remove from cake tin and set to cool on a rack or hair sieve. When cold cut through the cake twice and fill with two-thirds of the cream, spreading remaining cream over top and sides. Sprinkle top and sides with toasted ground or coarsely chopped almonds.

For the cream filling, cream butter and sugar, beat in vanilla sugar, eggs and softened chocolate. Cream the mixture really well – it should be quite thick and fluffy.

PAULINENTORTE

My favourite aunt's favourite chocolate cake – created by and duly named after her – in its full extravagant glory. Halve the quantities for a smaller, but no less luxurious cake.

6 eggs
2 oz (50 g) fine
   breadcrumbs
dash of rum
2½ oz (70 g) ground
   unblanched almonds
3½ oz (100 g) grated
   chocolate

5 oz (140 g) icing sugar
juice and grated rind of
   ½ lemon
butter and flour for the
   cake tin

Separate eggs. Place breadcrumbs into a bowl, moisten with rum. Sprinkle ground almonds and grated chocolate over the top. Whisk yolks with sugar until thick and creamy, add lemon juice and rind. Whisk whites until stiff and fold into yolks, alternately with breadcrumbs, almonds etc. Bake in a buttered and floured cake tin at Gas Mark 4½, 360°F, 185°C for about fifty minutes. Cover with chocolate icing as for *Sachertorte* (see page 365).

PUNSCHTORTE

Punch Gateau

For the cake
1½ oz (40 g) butter
8 eggs
5½ oz (160 g) icing sugar
5½ oz (160 g) sifted plain
   flour
butter and flour for the
   cake tin

For the filling
5 generous oz (150 g)
   lump sugar
1 orange
1 lemon
scant ¼ pint (⅛ l) water
3 tablespoons rum
2 – 3 tablespoons apricot
   jam

For the icing
apricot jam
about 9 oz (250 g) icing
   sugar
white rum
water
a few drops pink food
   colouring

Butter and flour a 9 or 10 inch spring-clip cake tin. Preheat oven to Gas Mark 4–5, 350°–375°F, 180°–190°C. Put the butter into a small bowl or cup and leave to melt by standing it in hot water.

Whisk eggs with icing sugar over steam until thick, remove from heat and whisk until cool. Gently fold in the sifted flour and melted but not hot butter. Bake for about fifty minutes. Turn out carefully and set to cool on a wire rack or a hair sieve.

The next day cut the cake into three layers – the centre layer should be slightly thicker than the other two. Cut the centre layer into cubes and put them into a bowl. Rub the sugar lumps over the orange to impart flavour, then put the sugar into a small saucepan, together with the juice of the lemon and the orange. Add a scant ¼ pint (⅛ l) water. Stir over low heat until sugar has dissolved, bring to boil, then stir in rum and 2 – 3 tablespoons apricot jam. Blend well and pour hot over cubed cake pieces and mix well.

Sandwich together the two remaining cake layers with this mixture, press down and leave to cool. You can put a board on top to ensure that the cake will be absolutely even, but this is not really necessary. Spread top and sides of cake with warmed apricot jam. Blend icing sugar to a thick paste with water, rum and a few drops of pink food colouring and spread over cake. Leave to dry.

Anyone in Vienna will tell you that this gateau should really have a fondant icing which is quite cumbersome to make – I find that water icing, which is far less trouble, works almost equally well.

The same mixture and procedure is sometimes used to make small, individual cakes – about 2 – 3 inches in diameter – which are called *Punschkrapferl*.

REHRÜCKEN

'Saddle of Venison' Gateau

This is simply a good chocolate cake baked in a special oblong and ridged cake tin, then covered with chocolate icing and spiked with strips of blanched almonds to imitate the larding of a saddle of venison (the literal translation of *Rehrücken*). The ridges on the tin denote the slices into which the cake is cut later on and there is also a long dent running down the centre which, after the cake has been iced, is sometimes studded with glacé cherries or filled with redcurrant jelly to denote the 'backbone'. Occasionally the cake is cut through lengthways and filled with a chocolate butter cream, but mostly it is just served with a good helping of sweetened whipped cream. The recipe quoted below gives a rich, lightly spiced *Rehrücken*, but any good chocolate cake mixture can be used including the recipe for *Sachertorte*, when the cake becomes known as *Sacher Rehrücken*.

5 eggs	pinch each of powdered
5 oz (140 g) butter	cloves and cinnamon
5 oz (140 g) icing sugar	butter and flour for the
5 oz (140 g) softened	cake tin
chocolate	redcurrant jelly
5 oz (140 g) ground	chocolate icing (see page
unblanched almonds	365)
1½ oz (40 g) fine	blanched almonds cut into
breadcrumbs moistened	strips
with rum	
½ oz (15 g) finely chopped	
mixed peel	

Separate eggs. Cream butter and sugar until light and fluffy. Add yolks gradually, then beat in the softened but not hot chocolate. Whisk whites until stiff and fold into the mixture, alternately with the ground unblanched almonds. Finally add moistened breadcrumbs, cinnamon, cloves and the mixed peel. Bake at Gas Mark 4½, 360°F, 185°C for about fifty minutes. Test before removing from oven and carefully invert onto a rack.

Leave to cool, then spread with warmed redcurrant jelly, leave to dry and then cover with chocolate icing and stud with strips of blanched almonds.

The above is an old family recipe, obviously approved by various discriminating members of my family, for I found it 'starred' in several hand-written cookery books as being the best of its kind. Only quite recently I chanced across the recipe for *Rehrücken* by the venerable Katharina Prato which runs as follows:

6 eggs	2½ oz (70 g) breadcrumbs
5 oz (140 g) butter	moistened with rum
5 oz (140 g) icing sugar	5 oz (140 g) ground
a little grated lemon rind	blanched almonds
5 oz (140 g) chocolate (of	
which an unspecified	
proportion is used for	
the icing)	

I'd like to think that my various grand-aunts, aunts and my grandmother could be discussing with Katharina Prato the merits of their only slightly differing recipes in some well-deserved culinary heaven.

RIBISELSCHAUMTORTE

Redcurrant Meringue Gateau

For the pastry
5 oz (130 g) plain flour
1 oz (20 g) ground walnuts
  or hazelnuts
4 oz (100 g) butter
2 oz (50 g) caster or icing
  sugar
1 teaspoon vanilla sugar
little grated lemon rind
  and juice
2 egg yolks
butter and flour for the
  baking tin

For the meringue
2 egg whites
4 oz (110 g) caster sugar
1 lb (450 g) redcurrants
1 – 2 tablespoons icing
  sugar

Sift flour, add sugar, vanilla sugar and ground walnuts or hazelnuts. Cut butter into dry ingredients, add lemon rind and juice and quickly work to a dough with the egg yolks. Pat into a round and leave in a cool place for one hour.

Roll out – or press out with your knuckles – to line a 10 inch (25 cm) buttered and floured flan case with a loose bottom and prick lightly with a fork. Bake at Gas Mark 5, 375°F, 190°C for twenty to twenty-five minutes, until just golden brown. Take out of the oven.

Lower the oven heat to Gas Mark 1, 275°F, 140°C (leave the oven door open to reduce the heat more quickly). Cover top of pastry thickly with redcurrants, having removed the stems. Sprinkle with icing sugar whilst the pastry is still hot. (It is best to free the currants of their stems at the very last minute as too much juice collects otherwise.) Whisk egg whites until very stiff, whisk in half the caster sugar, then fold in remainder. Pile on top of redcurrants, masking them completely. Bake until top of the meringue is barely tinged with colour and sounds hollow. Carefully remove flan ring, leaving cake to cool on its original base.

ROULADE: HASELNUSS

Hazelnut Roulade

For the pastry
4½ oz (130 g) hazelnuts
3 eggs
3½ oz (100 g) icing sugar
butter and flour for the
    baking sheet

For the filling
5 fluid oz (140 ml) double
    cream
2 oz (50 g) grated plain
    chocolate
1 dessertspoon vanilla
    sugar
icing sugar for the top

Preheat oven to Gas Mark 5, 375°F, 190°C. Line a baking sheet measuring about 10 × 12 inches with buttered and floured greaseproof paper or baking parchment.

Put the hazelnuts on a heatproof plate or baking sheet and brown them in the oven until the skins rub off easily, best done by rolling the hazelnuts between kitchen paper. Grind the hazelnuts.

Separate eggs. Whisk together yolks and sugar until thick and creamy. Whisk whites until stiff and fold into the yolks, alternately with the ground hazelnuts. Spread over the prepared baking sheet and bake until nicely browned and slightly firm to the touch – about ten to twelve minutes. Turn onto lightly floured greaseproof paper and peel off the backing. Trim any untidy edges and roll up the pastry very lightly.

Whisk the cream and vanilla sugar until thick, fold in grated chocolate. Carefully unroll the pastry, brush off any flour and spread with the cream mixture. Roll up the pastry very lightly and dust top with icing sugar.

ROULADE: KATI'S

Another one of Kati's (see *Kati Torte*) masterpieces. One day when Kati was rather upset – like all the best cooks she had a fierce temper to match her talents – we tried to pacify her by giving extra praise to her roulade. Kati was not to be won over that easily. 'Ah, but the recipe for this roulade' – at this she lifted her head and looked straight at my mother-in-law – 'comes from a family where they really appreciated fine cooking.'

For the pastry
4 eggs
2 rounded teaspoons
   potato flour
2 rounded teaspoons plain
   flour
9 fluid oz (¼ litre) milk
pinch of sugar
1 oz (25 g) butter
butter and flour for the
   baking sheet

For the filling
1 teaspoon powdered
   gelatine
2 – 3 teaspoons hot water
3 egg yolks
2 tablespoons caster sugar
2 teaspoons vanilla sugar
good dash of rum
scant ½ pint (¼ l) double
   cream

For the sauce
5 fluid oz (⅛ l) double or
   single cream
slightly sweetened
   strawberry purée (see
   note)

Line a baking sheet measuring about 11 × 12½ inches with baking parchment or buttered and floured greaseproof paper. Preheat oven to Gas Mark 5, 375°F, 190°C. Separate eggs. Sift together potato flour and plain flour. Heat the milk.

Melt the butter in a small saucepan, stir in the sugar and the flour. Blend well, then add heated milk gradually. Stirring constantly, cook over gentle heat until the mixture begins to leave the sides of the pan clean. Remove from heat, beat in the egg yolks one by one. Whisk egg whites until stiff and fold into the mixture when it has cooled completely. Spread onto the prepared baking sheet and bake until golden brown – about twenty-five minutes. Turn onto a lightly floured sheet of paper or foil and remove lining paper. Roll pastry very lightly over fresh paper or foil sprinkled with flour. Set aside to cool.

At this point honesty compels me to say that Kati's instructions differ from mine – she insisted that the pastry should be made like choux pastry, i.e. dissolve butter with a pinch of sugar in milk, bring to boil and then tip in the flour all at once. Work with a spoon until thick, remove from heat and then beat in the egg yolks. Try as I may, I have never managed to do this successfully: there are invariably lumps. Of course the quantity of flour is minute and it may be that the difference in humidity caused the failures, but rather than using a larger quantity of flour which could spoil the recipe, I now follow the method given above, and so far no-one has spotted the difference.

For the filling dissolve gelatine: put in a cup, add the hot water and stand the cup in a small pan containing hot water. Stir until the liquid is quite clear. Whisk egg yolks with caster sugar over steam until thick. Remove from heat, add the dissolved gelatine and whisk until cool, adding a good dash of rum at the same time. Whisk cream until thick, whisk in vanilla sugar (reserve enough to spread thinly over finished roulade), fold remaining whipped cream into cooled egg mixture. Chill a little before use.

Brush any adhering flour from the pastry, then spread the cream filling thickly down the centre of the pastry and fold over very lightly. Do not roll as for Swiss roll. Place on an oblong or rectangular serving dish with the folded side underneath. Spread reserved whipped cream over the top of the roulade. Chill before serving and cut into slices.

Kati always served very lightly sweetened strawberry purée folded into whipped cream separately. I find that wild strawberry jam (or Little Scarlet) thinned down with cream and chilled, makes an excellent short cut to this.

ROULADE: SCHOKOLADE

Chocolate Roulades

Chocolate roulades were favourites in my family and there was fierce competition as to who had the best recipe. Even now I can't decide, so I have given all three. *

Schokolade Roulade I (mit braunen Mandeln)
Chocolate roulade (with brown almonds)

For the pastry
2 oz (60 g) plain chocolate
3 eggs
2 oz (60 g) caster or icing sugar
1 generous oz (30 g) unblanched ground almonds

For the filling
9 fluid oz (250 ml) double cream
1 heaped tablespoon icing sugar
2 teaspoons vanilla sugar

Break chocolate into small pieces and put in a warm place to soften. Separate eggs. Whisk yolks with sugar until thick and creamy, add softened but not hot chocolate. Whisk whites until stiff and fold into mixture. Finally fold in ground almonds.

Line a baking sheet with baking parchment or buttered and lightly floured greaseproof paper and spread mixture over it. Bake at Gas Mark 5, 375°F, 190°C for about ten minutes – until lightly firm to the touch. Turn out onto a floured surface and peel off baking paper. Roll up lightly over paper. Unroll when cold, trim edges if necessary, brush off flour and spread pastry with whipped cream sweetened with sugar and vanilla sugar. Roll up pastry and dust top with a little icing sugar. Serve cut into thick slices.

Schokolade Roulade II

7 eggs
3½ oz (100 g) icing sugar
3½ oz (100 g) softened
  plain chocolate
2 oz (50 g) ground
  almonds

butter and flour (or
  ground almonds) for the
  baking tin
sweetened whipped cream
  for filling

Separate eggs. Whisk yolks and sugar until thick and creamy, then stir in the softened chocolate. Whisk whites until stiff. Fold whites into yolk mixture, alternately with the ground almonds. Line a baking sheet with foil or baking paper, brush with softened butter and sprinkle lightly with flour or ground almonds. Spread the mixture over the baking sheet and bake at Gas Mark 5, 375°F, 190°C for about twenty-five minutes.

Sprinkle a piece of baking paper very lightly with ground almonds and place the pastry on top. Carefully remove baking paper or foil and roll up the pastry very lightly. Leave to cool, unroll pastry and trim edges if necessary. Spread with sweetened whipped cream and roll up pastry again. Cut into thick slices for serving.

Schokolade Roulade III

For the pastry
6 egg yolks
5 lightly heaped
  tablespoons caster or
  icing sugar
4 lightly heaped
  tablespoons
  unsweetened cocoa
  powder
3 egg whites
butter and flour for the
  baking sheet

Filling as for *Schokolade
  Roulade I*

Preheat oven to Gas Mark 5, 375°F, 190°C. Line a baking sheet measuring approximately 12 × 8 inches with baking parchment or buttered and floured greaseproof paper.

Whisk together egg yolks and sugar until thick and creamy and almost white in colour. Fold in 3 tablespoons of the cocoa. Whisk whites until stiff and fold into the mixture, alternately with the remaining cocoa.

Spread the mixture over the prepared baking sheet and bake for about ten minutes – until the top is slightly firm to the touch. Wring out a tea towel in cold water and spread it over the kitchen table (or dust the table lightly with flour), turn out the pastry very carefully, then peel off the paper. Roll up the pastry in the tea towel (or in kitchen paper dusted very lightly with flour) and allow to cool.

Unroll carefully, brush off any flour and spread whipped cream over the pastry, then roll up lightly. Cut into thick slices for serving.

SACHERTORTE

Following the *Tortenkrieg* (war of the cakes) between Demel and Sacher which went on for years, it has now been established that Sacher's is the one and only real *Sachertorte*. Sacher, and Sacher alone, has the right to affix the hallmark (in finest chocolate) upon this cake. (When the results of the court case were made known, one of the stalwart waitresses at Demel's swore that the proprietor of Sacher's would 'go to hell for this, to be boiled in hot chocolate'.) They'll never stop talking about *Sachertorte* in Vienna though – about how the real secret of Sacher's *Torte*, as against the one made at Demel's according to the original recipe sold to them by Eduard Sacher, lies not in the recipe but in the chocolate, which is made especially for Sacher (the venerable Frau Olga Hess, doyenne of Austrian food writers, firmly believed this to be the case). And of course there's hardly a Viennese cook worthy of her name who does not claim that *her* recipe for *Sachertorte* (passed down from grandmother if not great-grandmother) is the only authentic one. I make no such claim – though of course my grandmother once told me . . . and scores of 'real and genuine' *Sachertorte* recipes have since passed through my hands, including one in Frau Anna Sacher's own handwriting (it was, after all, her father-in-law who invented *Sachertorte*, but she was once heard to exclaim 'personally, I find it rather dry', which is possibly the reason why *Sachertorte* is served with sweetened whipped cream – upon request).

Having said all this, I still stick to my own family's recipe for *Sachertorte* – but if I had to restrict my repertoire to just one chocolate gateau, I would choose Kati's (see page 369).

For the cake	Icing
5 oz (150 g) plain chocolate	4½ oz (120 g) plain or bitter chocolate
1 tablespoon water	4½ oz (120 g) caster sugar
6 eggs	3 fluid oz (75 ml) water
5 oz (150 g) butter	1 – 2 drops olive oil
5 oz (150 g) icing sugar	
1 tablespoon rum or Madeira	
2 teaspoons vanilla sugar	
4 generous oz (120 g) plain flour	
3 tablespoons apricot jam	
butter and flour for the cake tin	

Break the chocolate into small pieces, add a tablespoon water and set in a warm place to melt. Preheat oven to Gas Mark 4, 350°F, 180°C. Separate eggs. Sift the flour twice.

Cream butter and 4 oz (110 g) of the sugar until light and fluffy, beat in the egg yolks, one by one. When the chocolate has softened, add rum or Madeira and stir, then beat the melted but not hot chocolate into the butter mixture. Whisk whites until stiff, then whisk in the remaining sugar and vanilla sugar. Fold whites into the butter mixture, alternately with the flour.

Bake in a buttered and floured 9 or 10 inch spring-clip cake tin for fifty to sixty minutes. Remove carefully from the cake tin and set on a rack or a hair sieve to cool. It is best to leave the cake for twenty-four hours before covering it with icing.

Warm the apricot jam, sieve it and spread it over top and sides of the cake while the jam is still warm. Leave to dry a little before covering with chocolate icing.

To make the icing break the chocolate into small pieces, put them to melt in a warm place. Dissolve sugar in water and cook to 'small thread' stage. Remove from heat and leave to cool a little. Stir lukewarm sugar solution into melted chocolate and add 1 – 2 drops olive oil. Spread quickly over cake while still warm, using a palette knife dipped frequently into hot water and shaken dry.

SALZBURGER MOHNTORTE

Salzburg Poppyseed Cake

For the cake
7 eggs
7 oz (200 g) butter
12 oz (350 g) icing sugar
1 teaspoon grated lemon rind
1 tablespoon vanilla sugar
12 oz (350 g) ground poppyseeds
6 oz (175 g) toasted ground hazelnuts
3 oz (90 g) raisins
3 oz (90 g) candied peel
1 teaspoon cornflour
pinch of cinnamon
dash of rum
butter and flour for the cake tin

For the icing
about 2 tablespoons apricot jam
12 oz (340 g) icing sugar
lemon juice

Butter and flour an 11 inch (27.5 cm) cake tin. Preheat the oven to Gas Mark 4, 350°F, 180°C. Separate eggs. Cream the butter with half the icing sugar, beat in grated lemon rind and vanilla sugar, then beat in yolks, one by one. Whisk whites until stiff, whisk in remaining sugar. Fold whites into butter mixture, then carefully fold in the poppyseeds, ground hazelnuts and the remaining ingredients. Pile into the prepared cake tin and bake for fifty to sixty minutes.

Cool slightly, then set to cool on a rack. Turn upside down for icing which is best done on the following day. Warm the apricot jam and cover top and sides of the cake. Leave to dry. Blend the icing sugar with enough lemon juice to give a thick paste. Cover top and sides of the cake with this, spreading it with a hot knife. Leave to dry.

SCHNEETORTE

Meringue Gateau

For the cake
6 egg whites
5½ oz (150 g) caster sugar
5½ oz (150 g) ground walnuts
1 generous oz (30 g) grated plain chocolate
1½ oz (40 g) finely chopped mixed peel
5 finely ground coffee beans

For the filling
redcurrant jam
5 fluid oz (125 ml) double cream
2 oz (50 g) softened chocolate

Whisk the egg whites until stiff, then whisk in the sugar. Fold in the grated chocolate, walnuts, mixed peel and ground coffee beans. Divide mixture between two lightly buttered and floured shallow cake tins, or draw equal circles on baking parchment and set them on a baking sheet, then divide the mixture between the two circles, smoothing it out with a palette knife. Bake at Gas Mark 1, 275°F, 140°C until dry – they will sound hollow when lightly tapped. Carefully remove paper and set the rounds to cool on a rack.

When cold sandwich the two halves together with redcurrant jam. Stir softened but not hot chocolate into whipped cream and spread over top and sides of the cake.

SCHOKOLADE-BLÄTTERTORTE

Layered Chocolate Gateau

3½ oz (100 g) butter
4½ oz (120 g) plain flour
2 oz (50 g) grated plain chocolate
1 tablespoon icing or caster sugar

pinch of cinnamon
apricot jam for filling
icing sugar
butter and flour for the baking sheets

Sift flour on a pastry board. Mix with grated chocolate, sugar and cinnamon. Crumble butter into dry ingredients and work to a paste. Divide into three and press or roll out into three equal-sized rounds or squares. Set on buttered and floured baking sheets and chill for half an hour. Bake at Gas Mark 5, 375°F, 190°C until golden brown. Carefully remove from tins and set to cool on racks. When cold sandwich together with apricot jam and dust the top with icing sugar.

SCHOKOLADECREMETORTE

Chocolate Cream Gateau

An incredibly luscious, yet light chocolate cream gateau. The recipe, passed to me on paper yellowed with age, was headed Kugler-Gerbaud – one of the best *patisseries* in the world, in Budapest.

For the cake	For the filling
6 eggs	2 oz (60 g) unblanched
3½ oz (100 g) plain or	almonds
bitter chocolate	5 oz (140 g) plain or bitter
3 tablespoons water	chocolate
2 oz (60 g) butter	4 tablespoons water
5 oz (140 g) icing sugar	1 tablespoon icing sugar
1 teaspoon vanilla sugar	5 oz (140 g) butter
5 oz (140 g) ground	1 heaped teaspoon vanilla
unblanched almonds	sugar
butter and flour for the	2 egg yolks
cake tin	

Preheat the oven to Gas Mark 4½, 360°F, 185°C. Butter and flour a 10-inch spring-clip cake tin.

Separate five of the eggs. Break the chocolate into small pieces and put them into a small, thick saucepan with the water. Stir over a low heat until the chocolate has melted. Remove the pan from the heat and leave to cool.

Cream together butter, sugar and vanilla sugar until very light and fluffy, then beat in the five egg yolks, one by one, beating well after each addition. Stir in the cooled chocolate and the sixth egg. Whisk the five egg whites until stiff, fold into the mixture, alternately with the ground almonds. Put the mixture into the prepared cake tin and bake for fifty to sixty minutes. Test the cake before taking it out of the oven and leave it to cool a little in the tin before turning out. Set to cool completely on a rack or a hair sieve.

For the filling, put the almonds on a baking sheet and set them to brown lightly in the oven. The oven temperature does not matter greatly, as long as you watch the almonds and do not let them burn. Grind the almonds. Break the chocolate into small pieces, put them in a thick saucepan, add the water and the icing sugar and stir over a low heat until the chocolate has dissolved completely. Cook very gently until the mixture has thickened slightly, then remove it from the heat and leave to cool. Cream butter with the vanilla sugar until light and fluffy, then beat in the cooled chocolate and the egg yolks. Finally stir in the ground toasted almonds.

Cut through the cake once and fill it with half the chocolate cream. Spread remaining cream over top and sides. You can also reserve some of the ground almonds and sprinkle them over the top and sides of the cake – it does not alter the taste, only the appearance.

SCHOKOLADETORTE

Chocolate Cake (using egg whites only)

6½ oz (180 g) plain chocolate	6½ oz (180 g) plain flour
7½ oz (210 g) butter	7½ oz (210 g) icing sugar
7 egg whites	butter and sugar for the cake tin

Preheat the oven at Gas Mark 4, 350°F, 180°C. Butter and flour a 9 or 10 inch cake tin. Break the chocolate into small pieces and put them in a bowl to melt – either in the oven or over steam. Remove chocolate from heat as soon as it has melted and keep warm.

Cream the butter until fluffy, then beat in the melted but barely warm chocolate. Whisk the egg whites until stiff, then whisk in the sifted icing sugar. Fold whites into butter and chocolate mixture, alternately with the sifted flour. Bake for about one hour – test before removing from oven. Carefully remove cake from the tin and set it to cool on a rack or a hair sieve.

It is a very good light cake in its own right, but for a little festive touch, cut it through once or twice, moisten each layer with a little Curaçao, then sandwich the layers together with apricot jam and/or sweetened whipped cream and cover with whipped cream or chocolate icing.

SCHOKOLADETORTE: KATI'S

Kati's Chocolate Gateau

For over fifty years Kati was my mother-in-law's cook in Vienna, and for over fifty years no family celebration was complete without her special chocolate gateau. She always shut the door firmly on anyone daring to come near 'her' kitchen before she would even start to break up the chocolate, so I am honoured indeed to be the only member of the family to whom she has entrusted the recipe for this marvellous gateau. Please treat it with the respect it deserves!

5½ oz (150 g) plain or
  bitter chocolate
dash of rum
3½ oz (100 g) butter
5½ oz (150 g) icing sugar
1 flat teaspoon vanilla
  sugar
4 eggs
5½ oz (150 g) ground
  walnuts

butter and flour (or
  ground walnuts) for the
  cake tin
2 heaped tablespoons
  apricot jam
chocolate icing as for
  Sachertorte (see page
  365)

Butter and flour (or dust with ground walnuts) a 9 or 10 inch (23 or 25.5 cm) spring-clip cake tin. Preheat oven to Gas Mark 4½, 360°F, 185°C.

Break the chocolate into small pieces, add a dash of rum and put in a warm place for the chocolate to melt. Cream butter and icing sugar until very light and fluffy. Beat in the vanilla sugar. Separate eggs. Beat the yolks into the creamed butter, one by one, then beat in the softened but not hot chocolate. Whisk whites until stiff and fold into the mixture, alternately with the ground walnuts.

Bake for about fifty to sixty minutes. Test carefully before removing from oven. Leave to cool for a little while in the tin, then remove carefully and set on a rack or hair sieve to cool completely. Like all Austrian gateaux, it is iced upside down, the absolutely flat bottom of the cake becoming the top.

Spread top and sides of the cake with warmed, sieved apricot jam and leave to dry, then cover with chocolate icing as for *Sachertorte*.

SCHOKOLADETORTE MIT MANDELN I

Chocolate Gateau with Almonds

2½ oz (70 g) chocolate
5 oz (140 g) icing sugar
2½ oz (70 g) finely ground
  blanched almonds
3½ oz (100 g) butter

4 eggs
1½ oz (40 g) plain flour
a little grated lemon rind
chocolate icing (see page
  365)

Break chocolate into small pieces and put in a warm place to melt. Sift together ground almonds with half the sugar and lemon rind. Cream butter and remaining sugar until thick and fluffy. Separate eggs. Beat egg yolks into creamed butter gradually. Whisk whites until stiff, fold into creamed butter alternately with almond/sugar mixture and flour. Bake for about forty-five minutes at Gas Mark 4½, 360°F, 185°C. Cover with warmed jam and chocolate icing when cold, preferably the next day.

Schokoladetorte mit Mandeln II

3 eggs
2½ oz (70 g) icing
 sugar
2½ oz (70 g) grated
 chocolate
2½ oz (70 g)
 unblanched ground
 almonds

butter and flour for
 the cake tin
apricot or raspberry
 jam
chocolate icing (see
 page 365)

Separate eggs. Whisk yolks with about two-thirds of the sugar until thick and creamy. Whisk whites until stiff, then whisk in remaining sugar. Fold whites into yolks, alternately with the ground almonds and grated chocolate. Bake in a buttered and floured cake tin at Gas Mark 4½, 360°F, 185°C for about thirty-five minutes. Cool on a rack or hair sieve. Cover with warmed apricot or raspberry jam, leave to dry and then cover with chocolate icing.

TOPFENTORTE

Curd Cheese Gateau

For the pastry
4 oz (105 g) plain flour
2½ oz (70 g) butter
1½ oz (40 g) icing sugar
1 egg yolk
butter and flour for the
 cake tin

Topping
9 oz (250 g) curd cheese
2 egg yolks
1 teaspoon vanilla sugar
2 oz (50 g) icing sugar
3 egg whites
1½ oz (40 g) caster sugar
2 tablespoons slivered
 almonds

Sift flour with the icing sugar, then work to a paste with the butter and the egg yolk. Butter and flour a spring-clip cake tin and line bottom with the pastry. Bake at Gas Mark 5, 375°F, 190°C until light golden brown – about ten minutes.

Whisk together egg yolks and icing sugar, beat in the cheese and vanilla sugar. Spread lightly over the cooled pastry. Whisk egg whites until stiff, whisk in the caster sugar. Pile mixture on top of the cheese mixture, sprinkle with the almonds and bake for another ten minutes.

TRAUNKIRCHNER TORTE

For the cake
4½ oz (120 g) hazelnuts
4½ oz (120 g) caster sugar
7 oz (200 g) plain flour
6 oz (165 g) butter
butter and flour for the
    baking sheets
icing sugar

For the filling
8 oz (225 g) raspberries or
    wild strawberries
8 oz (225 g) icing sugar
1 scant teaspoon powdered
    gelatine
½ pint (280 ml) double
    cream

Put the hazelnuts on a baking sheet and toast them in the oven at Gas Mark 6, 400°F, 200°C until the skins rub off easily by rolling them between sheets of kitchen paper, then grind the hazelnuts. Mix together ground hazelnuts, sugar and flour and rub in the butter. Work to a smooth dough, pat into a round and chill for about thirty minutes.

Divide the dough into three equal portions. Roll or press out each portion into a round of approximately 9 inches (23 cm) in diameter. Set the rounds on buttered and floured baking sheets and prick with a fork to prevent uneven rising. Bake at Gas Mark 5, 375°F, 190°C for about twenty-five minutes, until golden brown. Remove carefully and set to cool on a rack.

Sprinkle the fruit with sugar and leave to stand for about fifteen minutes. Purée the fruit in a blender or food processor and if using raspberries sieve the purée to get rid of the pips. Dissolve gelatine in 3 – 4 tablespoons hot water, cool and stir into the fruit purée. Whisk the cream until thick and fold into the fruit. Chill thoroughly.

Trim the pastry rounds if necessary and sandwich together with the fruit filling just as it is on the point of setting. Dust over the top with sifted icing sugar and serve as soon as possible after assembling.

This version of *Traunkirchner Torte* – though an old family recipe – would probably be frowned upon in Traunkirchen, an enchanting small town in the Salzkammergut, where the pastry rounds are more traditionally sandwiched together with a filling made by whisking 4 egg whites until stiff, whisking in 4 tablespoons icing sugar and then folding in 4 tablespoons good fruit preserve or purée. The cake is then kept in a cool place for a day or two and immediately before serving the top is decorated with whipped cream.

TRÜFFEL TORTE

Truffle Gateau

For the cake
3 eggs
4½ oz (125 g) butter
4½ oz (125 g) icing sugar
3½ oz (100 g) grated plain
  chocolate
5½ oz (150 g) plain flour
1 teaspoon baking powder
4½ fluid oz (125 ml) cold
  milk
butter and flour for the
  cake tin

For the filling
9 oz (250 g) plain
  chocolate
9 fluid oz (250 ml) double
  cream
3½ oz (100 g) butter
a little unsweetened cocoa
  powder

Preheat the oven to Gas Mark 5, 375°F, 190°C. Butter and flour a 9 or 10 inch spring-clip cake tin (in case of the latter you will get a shallower cake, but as it is a very rich cake you may find this preferable).

Separate eggs. Cream butter and sugar until very light and fluffy, then beat in the egg yolks, one by one. Gradually add the finely grated chocolate and then the flour sifted together with the baking powder, alternately with the milk. Whisk egg whites until stiff and fold very carefully into the mixture. Bake for fifty to sixty minutes and test before removing cake from oven. Carefully remove cake from tin and cool on a rack or hair sieve. Leave overnight before filling.

For the filling, grate the chocolate or break into small pieces. Put the cream, chocolate and the butter into a small, thick saucepan and heat very gently over low heat, stirring all the time, until the chocolate has melted. As soon as this happens, remove saucepan from the heat and pour the mixture into a bowl to cool. Do not stir the mixture until cool. When the mixture is quite cold – you can accelerate this by standing the bowl on crushed ice – whisk it until it will stand up in soft peaks (the colour of the chocolate will change as you whisk – it will get much lighter – and this is exactly as it should be). Cut through the cake once or twice (if you have used a 9 inch tin) and sandwich together with the chocolate cream, spreading a little over top and sides of the cake as well. Dust over top and sides with unsweetened cocoa powder and keep the cake in a cool place before serving.

WARME KAFFEETORTE

Warm Coffee Gateau

For the base
5 oz (140 g) plain flour
1 generous oz (30 g) icing
  sugar
1 generous oz (30 g)
  ground almonds
5 oz (140 g) butter
butter and flour for the
  cake tin

Topping
4½ fluid oz (⅛ l) strong
  black coffee
10 oz (280g) caster sugar
3 eggs

Sift together icing sugar and flour. Add ground almonds. Cut butter into the dry ingredients and work quickly to a dough. Roll out or press out with your knuckles to line bottom and sides of a buttered and floured 10 inch (25 cm) flan ring with a removable bottom. Chill for half an hour, prick base lightly with a fork, then bake at Gas Mark 5, 375°F, 190°C until golden brown. Leave to cool slightly.

Meanwhile prepare the topping. Separate eggs. Dissolve half the sugar in the coffee over low heat, bring to boil and then leave to cool. Whisk egg yolks with remaining sugar until thick, whisk in the sweetened coffee. Whisk egg whites until stiff and fold into the mixture. Pile the mixture into the pastry shell and bake at Gas Mark 9, 475°F, 240°C for about five minutes, until just set. Serve warm.

WIENER TOPFENTORTE

Viennese Curd Cheese Gateau

4 eggs
4½ oz (120 g) icing sugar
4½ oz (120 g) butter
4½ oz (120 g) ground
  walnuts or ground
  unblanched almonds

4½ oz (120 g) curd cheese
1 tablespoon vanilla sugar
grated rind of ½ lemon
butter and fine
  breadcrumbs for the tin

Separate eggs. Cream butter and sugar until light and fluffy, then beat in the yolks gradually. Add the cheese – sieved first if necessary – and walnuts (or almonds), vanilla sugar and grated lemon rind. Whisk egg whites until stiff and fold into the mixture. Bake at Gas Mark 4, 350°F, 180°C in a 9 or 10 inch buttered and breadcrumbed cake tin for about three quarters of an hour.

ICINGS FOR GATEAUX

(For chocolate icing see *Sachertorte*, page 365)

With the exception of *Dobos Torte*, top and sides of all iced cakes and gateaux (and most pastries as well) should be spread with warm jam before the icing is applied. In Austria this procedure is called *aprikotieren*, since apricot jam is used more often than not, though in fact any smooth jam can be used. I have always found redcurrant jelly excellent for this purpose – and the flavour of raspberries goes particularly well with some gateaux.

Water Icing is the simplest of all icings – the water being frequently replaced by lemon juice, rum or coffee. Sieve the icing sugar and add a very little warm water. Do not stir and leave it to stand for about ten minutes, then stir in the required flavouring (orange juice, lemon juice, liqueur, coffee, rum etc.). Add a little more sugar or liquid to obtain a smooth thick paste which is then spread over the cake.

An even simpler version is to stir the liquid into the sieved sugar, with or without any water added, depending on the strength of the flavour. This type of icing is best for pastries and small cakes, but can also be used quite successfully for gateaux. Quantities vary according to the size of cake to be covered – and also according to the dryness of the sugar; but for a 9 or 10 inch cake, 9 – 12 oz (250 – 340 g) should serve as a rough guide.

Fondant Icing is a different matter altogether. It is best to make a quantity of fondant to store and use as required. For this the sugar has to be cooked to 'medium blow' stage, which is about 235°C on the sugar thermometer. To test, dip a small wire loop (I use the rounded end of a thin skewer) into the hot sugar solution, hold it up, blow on it, and medium-sized bubbles should fly off.

Dissolve 1 lb (500 g) lump or granulated sugar in ¼ pint (⅛ l) water, together with 1 teaspoon glucose and a teaspoon vinegar. Brush inside of saucepan with a pastry brush previously dipped into cold water, skim off any impurities which rise to the top. As soon as all the sugar has dissolved, increase the heat and bring solution to boil – do not stir. Test as described before and as soon as the 'medium-blow' stage is reached, remove saucepan from heat. Pour sugar onto a marble slab, previously sprinkled with water, sprinkling a little cold water over top of sugar as well. Or simply plunge the saucepan with the sugar solution into a bowl of cold water and sprinkle cold water over the top. Leave to cool without touching, and then work the sugar solution with a spatula or a spoon until white and firm. Knead a little with your hands until fondant becomes pliable. Store in a jar covered with a damp cloth.

To use fondant: warm a sufficient quantity of icing, stirring gently. This is best done in a bowl over steam as the fondant must not get hot. Add required flavouring and, if necessary, a little warm water, or sugar solution.

BY WAY OF A SUMMARY
(*from* Der Phäake *by Josef Weinheber*)
By permission of Hoffmann & Campe Verlag, Hamburg

Ich hab sonst nix, drum hab ich gern
ein gutes Papperl, liebe Herrn:
Zum Gabelfruehstueck goenn ich mir
ein Tellerfleisch, ein Kruegerl Bier,
schieb an und ab ein Gollasch ein,
(kann freilich auch ein Bruckfleisch sein),
ein saftiges Beinfleisch, nicht zu fett,
sonst hat man zu Mittag sein Gfrett.
Dann mach ich—es is eh nicht lang
mehr auf Mittag—mein' Gesundheitsgang,
geh uebern Grabn, den Kohlmarkt aus
ins Michaeler Bierwirtshaus.
Ein Huehnersupperl, tadellos,
ein Beefsteak in Madeirasoss,
ein Schweinspoerkelt, ein Rehragout,
Omletts mit Chamgignon dazu,
hernach ein bisserl Kipfelkoch
und allenfalls ein Torterl noch,
zwei Seidel Goess—zum Trinken mag
ich nicht viel nehmen zu Mittag—
ein Flascherl Gumpolds, nicht zu kalt,
und drei, vier Glaserl Wermuth halt.
Damit ichs recht verdauen kann,
zuend ich mir ein Trabukerl an
und lehn mich z'rueck und schau in d' Hoeh,
bevor ich auf mein' Schwarzen geh.
Wann ich dann heimkomm, will ich Ruh,
weil ich ein Randerl schlafen tu,
damit ich mich, von zwei, bis vier,
die Decken ueber, rekreier'.
Zur Jausen geh ich in die Stadt
und schau, wer schoene Stelzen hat,
ein kaltes Ganserl, jung und frisch,
ein Alzerl Kaes, ein Stueckl Fisch,
weil ich so frueh am Nachmittag
nicht schon was Warmes essen mag.
Am Abend, muss ich Ihnen sagn,
ess ich gern leicht, wegn meinen Magn,
Hirn in Aspik, Kalbsfrikassee,
ein kleines Zuengerl mit Pueree,
Faschierts und hin und wieder wohl
zum Selchfleisch Kraut, zum Rumpsteak Kohl,
erst spaeter dann, bein Wein zur Not,
ein nett garniertes Butterbrot.
Glaubn S' nicht, ich koennt ein Fresser wern,
ich hab sonst nix, drum leb ich gern. . . .

... Since I've nought else, I can enjoy
My victuals all the more my boy:
Elevenses—I don't deny
Myself some meat and beer, and why,
Occasionally, not include
A Goulash? (*Bruckfleisch* too is good),
And juicy beef, though not too greasy
Lest midday find one feeling queasy.
Then for a stroll, a turn or two,
Across the City Ditch, and through
The Kohlmarkt—that's enough if I'm
To reach the Bierwirtshaus in time.
A chicken soup awaits me there—
A soup beyond reproach—a rare
Prime beefsteak in Madeira sauce,
A Goulash (evergreen resource!)
A savoury ragout of venison
A mushroom omelette, and the benison
Of luscious *Kipfelkoch* to follow,
Then *gateau* . . . and I feel less hollow.
Two pints of beer—I do not ask
A lot to drink at lunch—a flask
Of vintage Gumpolds, not too cold,
And vermouths, three or four all told.
Then, in the cause of good digestion,
A long cigar's the best suggestion.
A lean well back and scan the ceiling,
My coffee comes (and a nice full feeling).
So home—and there I must have peace,
From worldly cares to seek surcease
From two till four, and, stretched my length
Beneath the bedclothes, gather strength.
For tea I saunter into town
And scan the menus up and down
For knuckle end of pork—a dish
I'm partial to—a scrap of fish,
Cold gosling and a bite of cheese.
I'm really quite content with these,
For gourmets rigorously exclude,
So early, any *heating* food.
Dinner's upon us! Now I make
A *light* meal, for my stomach's sake.
Some brains in aspic, fricassée
Of veal, and tongue suffice for me . . .
And meat loaf. . . . Or I might enjoy
Smoked pork and cabbage, or would toy
With rumpsteak and a nice savoy,
And only later, 'pon my soul,
Take with the wine a garnished roll.
And now I think you will see why
Good food admits no other tie:
Because I've nothing else, you see
Life looks uncommon good to me. . . .

(*Translated from the Viennese by John Trench*)

BIBLIOGRAPHY

Beer, Gretel *Austrian Cooking*, André Deutsch, London 1954
Berzeviczy-Pallavicini, Federico von *Die k. & k. Hofzuckerbäckerei*, Wilhelm
 Goldmann Verlag, Munich 1982
Beutel, F. J. *Die freie österreichische Kochkunst*, A. Hartleben's Verlag, Vienna
 & Leipzig, ca. 1900
Dorn, Anna *Neues Universal oder Grosses Wiener Kochbuch*, Vienna 1827
Duch, Karl *Kalte Gerichte*, Hippolyt Verlag, Vienna/St. Pölten 1956
 Gut gekocht, gut gelaunt, Hippolyt Verlag, Vienna/St. Pölten 1960
Duch, Karl and Witzelsberger, Richard *Die Wiener Mehlspeise in der Gaststätte*,
 Vienna 1939
Gartler, Ignaz & Hickmann, Barbara *Wienerisches bewährtes Kochbuch in sechs
 Absätzen*, 30th edition, Gerold Vienna 1812
Hess, Olga & Alfred *Wiener Küche*, 28th edition, Franz Deuticke, Vienna
 1949
Hagger, Conrad *Neues Saltzburgisches Koch-Buch für hockfürstliche und andere
 Höfe*, druckts & verlegts Johann Jacob Lotter, Augsburg 1718
Grosse Küche, Jahrbuch für Österreich 1989, Orac 1988
Heinrich, Elisabeth *Die gute alpenländische Küche*, 7th edition, Verlag the
 Salzburger Druckerei, 1976
Kernmayer, Hans Gustl *Steirisches Kochbuch* (unter Mitarbeit der Meister
 der steirischen Küche Frieda & Victor Juza) Almathea, Vienna 1972
 So kochte meine Mutter, Mary Hahn, Berlin 1976
Kofranek, Albert *Gute Wiener Küche*, Verlag A. Göschl, Vienna 1950
Kronen-Zeitung Kochbuch, Verlag Dichand & Falk, Vienna (no date) (neu
 bearbeitet und auf den letzten Stand gebracht)
Die gute Küche, Kochbuch der illustrierten Kronenzeitung, Vienna 1950
Lang, George *The Cuisine of Hungary*, Penguin, London 1985
Leitich, Anna Tizia *Das süsse Wien*, E. Hunna Verlag, Vienna 1964
Das kleine Linzer-Kochbuch, zusammengetragen von mehreren geschickten &
 berühmten Köchinnen, neueste Auflage gedruckt bey Johann Huemer, Linz
 1841
Maier-Bruck, Franz *Das grosse Sacher-Kochbuch*, Schiller Verlagsgesellschaft,
 Munich 1975
Vom Essen auf dem Lande, Kremayer-Scherian, Vienna 1981
Der *Marianka*, Mundköchin des Hans-Jörgel von Gumpoldskirchen, durch
 vieljährige persönliche Ausübung und praktische Erfrahrungen erprobtes
 Kochbuch oder die Kunst sowohl vornehme Tafeln delikat, zierlich und
 elegant zu bereiten als auch die österreichische Hausmannskost wie sie seyn
 soll für mittlere Haushaltungen in theuern Zeiten billig und schmackhaft
 herzustellen. Jakob Dirnböck, Vienna 1846
Mayer, Eduard *Wiener Sußspeisen*, Trauner Verlag, Linz 1968
Miklau, Lia *Kärntner Kochbüchl*, 2nd edition, Johannes Heyn, Klagenfurt
 1967
Neuber, Wolf *Die k. & k. Wiener Küche*, Fritz Molden, Vienna 1975
 Die k. & k. Böhmische und Ungarische Küche, Fritz Molden, Vienna 1978

Neudecker, Maria Anna, gebornen Ertl, *Die Baierische Köchin in Böhmen*, Salzburg 1819 in der Mayer'schen Buchhandlung

Neuwirth-Pabst, *Die gute österreichische Küche:Salzburger Kochbuch*, 12th edition, Verlag Eduard Höllrigl, Salzburg

Niederösterreich-Kochbuch, 3rd edition, Verlag Niederösterreichiches Pressehaus, 1983

Nützliches, *Hausbuch für Frauen & Mädchen* ... verlegt bey Joseph Gerold, k. & k. Hofbuchdruck auf dem Dominikanerplatz, Wien 1797

Allerneuestes *Osterreichisches* Kochbuch für herrschaftliche & andere Tafeln, herausgegeben von einem erfahrenem fürstlichem Koch, Grätz 1792 bey Christian Friedrich Tröschler

Perwanger, Hanna *Südtiroler Leibgerichte*, 2nd edition, Heimeran, Munich 1968

Deutsche Kochschule in *Prag*, Sammlung von erprobten Speisevorschriften Verlag der Deutschen Kochschule in Prag 1907, 8th edition

Prato, Katharina (Edle von Scheiger), *Die Süddeutsche Küche*, 34th edition, Styria Graz 1903

Rokitansky, Marie von *Die österreichische Küche*, 6th edition, Vienna 1910

Rösch, Rudolf *So kocht man in Wien*, Ernst Reinhardt Verlag, Munich 1939

Rudisch, Maria Anna *Mein eigenes geprüftes Kochbuch*, 2nd edition, Vienna 1789

St. Hilaire, Josephine *Illustriertes Pester Kochbuch*, Verlag Hoffmann & Molnar, Budapest ca. mid-late 19th century

Schönthan, Gaby von *Die Konditorei Zauner*, Wilhelm Goldmann Verlag, Munich 1982

Seleskowitz, Louise *Wiener Kochbuch*, 18th edition, Druck Gebrüder Stiepel, Reichenberg, Wien 1917

Skrach, Hans *Die Wiener Konditorei*, Verlag für Jugend & Volk, Vienna edition 1949

Stradal, Otto *So kocht nur eine Wienerin*, recipes by Franz Ruhm, Forum Verlag, Vienna

Treichlinger, V. M. *Alt Österreich bittet zu Tisch*, Sanssouci Verlag, Zurich 1962

Türck, Frau Josefine *Jubiläums-Kochbuch*, 2nd edition, H. Hierhammer & G. Geitner, Vienna 1909

Uiberacker, E. J. *Wildpret*, H. Kapri & Co. Vienna 1947

Waldbott, Marietheres *Burgenländisches Kochbuch*, Roetzer, Eisenstadt 1976

Kochbuch seinem hochedelgebohrnen Fräulein Henriette Barronne von Poton gewidmet von Anna *Wimmer*, ca. late 19th century.

Witzelsberger, Richard *Das grosse Mehlspeisbuch*, Verlag für Jugend und Volk, Vienna 1950.

Das österreichische Mehlspeisen Kochbuch, Kremayer & Scherian, Vienna 1979

Zenker, F. G. *Theoretisch-praktische Anleitung zur Kochkunst*, gedruckt Anton Strauß, Vienna 1817

Ziegenbein, Hans & Eckel, Julius *Die gute Wiener Mehlspeise*, Leitner & Co. Wels, 1953 (first published 1932)

INDEX

The index of German titles with English equivalents in brackets appears in the left column, and the English titles with German equivalents on the right. In cases where no English equivalents are given the recipes appear only in the German index.

SOUPS AND THEIR GARNISHES

FISH

GAME AND POULTRY

OTHER MAIN COURSE DISHES

CHEESE AND EGG DISHES

DUMPLINGS AND PASTA DISHES

VEGETABLES AND VEGETABLE DISHES

SALADS

SAUCES, RELISHES AND ACCOMPANIMENTS

PUDDINGS, HOT AND COLD, WITH THEIR SAUCES

CAKES, PASTRIES AND BISCUITS

CAKES AND PASTRIES WITH YEAST

GATEAUX AND ICINGS